Candles in the Dark

A New Spirit for a Plural World

The aspirations fueling progress should be consistent with what the heart and spirit have taught humanity about its origins, its essence and, most importantly, its purpose:

Equality before the law and in the political process, as well as equal opportunity in the market place are important but not enough to describe what people look for to satisfy their sense of obligation and belonging. Human beings are not disembodied pursuers of maximum utility or of some other abstract principle. *Nitin Desai*

The key to "Confucian learning" is learning for the sake of the self, not as an isolated individuality, but as a center of relationships. On the one hand, each person's subjectivity and dignity ought to be respected and on the other, sociality, communication, and reciprocity should be developed. *Tu Wei Ming*

Love for its own sake, as an attachment that requires no other justification, is surely the most universal and powerful source of meaning. Attachment implies a relationship to that particular, irreplaceable individual whom we love. If we try to reinterpret such attachments in terms of generalizable, theoretically marketable goods—for instance as a need to nurture and be nurtured —we miss their essential quality. *Peter Marris*

Humans are usually not conscious of, nor perceptive of, Love and disregard Her regularly. On the phenomenal plane, assuming Love to be embodied in what appears as a young and beautiful person, the players on (life's) stage fail to recognize Love's incarnation, which, in a time honored No play, is that of an old white-haired and wizened woman. Her temporal appearance reflects the actuality of Her ceaseless struggle in the world. She suffers many pains gladly as She travels the world around, knowing no rest, respite, and interruption in her work of bringing blessings and resolving problems. *Noriko Hashimoto*

To restore a grand and noble sense of "love" to modern societies as a whole, material progress must be balanced by attention to humanity's moral and spiritual condition. This equilibrium requires considerable humility. It also demands respect for ways of knowing other than by empiricism and instrumental rationality over which humankind considers itself master.

CANDLES IN THE DARK

A NEW SPIRIT FOR A PLURAL WORLD

Edited by Barbara Sundberg Baudot

Foreword by Vaclav Havel

New Hampshire Institute of Politics at
Saint Anselm College
Manchester, NH

in association with

University of Washington Press
Seattle and London

University of Washington Press
PO Box 50096
Seattle, Washington 98145-5096

Editor:
Barbara Sundberg Baudot

Design:
Imprim' Offset
Tresnay, France

Cover Art and Drawings:
Philippe Dumas

Library of Congress Control Number: 2002111248
ISBN 0-295-98292-6

The paper used in this publication is acid-free and recycled from 10 percent post-
consumer and at least 50 percent pre-consumer waste. It meets the minimum
requirements of American National Standard for Information Sciences—
Permanence of Paper for Printed Library Materials, ANSI Z39.48-1984.

Dedication

This book is dedicated to
Rangaswami Krishnamurti and John Kenneth Galbraith,
for their devotion to building a humane world community

In Memoriam

Henning Friis, mentor, and friend

TABLE OF CONTENTS

ACKNOWLEDGMENTS

I am overwhelmingly and most gratefully indebted to many organizations and individuals including those at the summit of global public policy making as well as many working in their offices, homes, colleges and universities in the shadow of high politics. Although my acknowledgments cannot be exhaustive, I will mention those who were most directly involved in the realization of this work.

The initial impetus for this book came from a United Nations Seminar on Ethical and Spiritual Dimensions of Social Development organized by the United Nations Secretariat and hosted by the government of Slovenia as part of the prelude to the Copenhagen Summit on Social Development, that took place in March, 1995. The ideas developed in the mountain town of Bled, Slovenia are reflected in the following core message of the Summit:

> We (Heads of State or Governments) (...) are committed to a political, economic and spiritual vision for social development that is based on human dignity, human rights, equality, respect, democracy, mutual responsibility, and cooperation, and full respect for the various religious and ethical values and cultural backgrounds of people.

Subsequently, a number of us, having met around the discussion table in Bled, formed an organization called the Triglav Circle, devoted to fostering this message. I set about putting this book together with the help of some Circle members and many others committed to these ideals.

Most recently, this work has attracted the support of the newly established New Hampshire Institute of Politics at Saint Anselm College. Their grant to help realize this publication is greatly appreciated.

In writing and editing texts that propose sweeping changes in public policy thinking, it is extraordinarily fortuitous to have the support of those political leaders whose vision and writings you highly esteem. I am deeply grateful to Vaclav Havel for his profound Foreword. And, I am particularly indebted to Kofi Annan for his willingness to write his powerful Message for this book.

This book would not have been possible without the efforts put into the research and writing of each essay. Thus, my greatest debt must be paid to the contributors to this book. Their passion for the subject, patience, wealth of knowledge, and willing cooperation made its final realization possible. Among the contributors, I wish to especially recognize Ruud Lubbers, who in the earliest stages of the work, conveyed the request to Czech Republic President Vaclav Havel to compose the book's Foreword; to Peter Marris for his advice on the overall organization of this book; and to my husband Jacques Baudot for his total support and substantial editorial help. Richard Falk and John Fortin, O.S.B. should be acknowledged for their special assistance in the initial stages of this project.

The steady and strong encouragement from John Kenneth Galbraith has also been a great source of inspiration. To him, whose work I have long studied and admired, I am greatly obliged.

Other eminent thinkers and scholars helping greatly in this work include my friend and former director in the United Nations, Rangaswami Krishnamurti, who has been an anchor and principal adviser throughout the project. I am particularly thankful for his unwavering faith in the necessity for this book that pushed me during those bleaker moments when the work seemed interminable and the skeptics and critics overwhelming. I would also like to express my great appreciation to Saad Nagi for his generous help in finalizing this work.

No book should be without an artist's touch. The cover design and text sketches of Philippe Dumas have enlivened the text. In his own work as a French artist and illustrator, he has pursued in many directions the message of this book. I am profoundly grateful to him for his willingness to grace this book with his art.

My superb students JoEllen Saeli, Paul Nolette, and my daughter Amelie Baudot greatly facilitated the tasks of copy-editing, organizing, assembling, and harmonizing references. It is not only their dedication, but their spirit of enthusiasm and genuine interest in the ideas that made this project a special kind of adventure. I heartily thank Patrick McCaffrey, who generously volunteered his computer skills in assembling the various drafts of the manuscript. I am also very grateful to Laurie Toupin for her editorial assistance.

Among other friends who have been very helpful at various stages of this work and deserve particular recognition include Allison Phinney, not only for his essay, but for his abiding faith in the good of the work, and Audrey Beardsley for her constant support.

Most importantly, I could not have completed anything without the enormous help of the other members of my family. The careful reading by my mother, Ruth Sundberg, of each contribution to correct the details of grammar was essential. Her passing before the completion of this book was a sad loss. My daughter Laura Baudot's contribution to the editing work and also my daughter Elise Queguiner's keen eye in correcting the text deserve the highest appreciation. Their career experience has served the project well, especially in the final stages of completing the manuscript.

Finally, I am exceedingly grateful to the staff of Imprim'offset in Tresnay, France, in particular, to Monique Raphaël and to Pierre Michel, who, with great skill, patience, and warmth helped design this book and prepared it for printing.

Birna Arnbjörnsdóttir, Professor of Linguistics and English literature, University of Iceland, Reykjavik, Iceland.

Barbara Sundberg Baudot, Professor of Politics, Saint Anselm College, Manchester, New Hampshire; Founder and Coordinator of the Triglav Circle; formerly an economist at the United Nations.

Jacques Baudot, Coordinator, United Nations International Forum for Social Development; former Controller of the United Nations, Coordinator of the World Summit for Social Development [1995].

Nitin Desai, Under Secretary General for Economic and Social Affairs, United Nations.

Richard Falk, Professor Emeritus of International Law and Practice, Princeton University, Princeton, New Jersey; Member of the United Nations Commission on Palestine; Author of numerous books on international law and politics.

Vigdis Finnbogadóttir, Chair of the UNESCO Commission on Ethics, and UNESCO Ambassador for Languages; former President of Iceland.

Father John Fortin O.S.B., Professor of Philosophy, Saint Anselm College, Manchester, New Hampshire; Director of the Institute for the Study of the Work of Saint Anselm.

Robert Gamer, Professor of Political Science, University of Missouri, Kansas City; Author of many books on development.

Noriko Hashimoto, Professor of Philosophy and Aesthetics, Aoyama Gakuin University, Tokyo; Secretary General of the Centre International pour Etude Comparée de Philosophie et d'Esthetique, Tokyo, Japan.

Tomonobu Imamichi, Professor Emeritus of Philosophy, Tokyo University; Honorary President of the International Institute of Philosophy; and Director General of the Centre International pour Etude Comparée de Philosophie et d'Esthetique, Tokyo, Japan.

Vyacheslav Ivanov, Professor of Language and Linguistics, University of California, Los Angeles; Professor and Director of Institute of World Culture, University of Moscow; Member of the Russian Academy of Sciences; Member of the Russian Writers Association.

Dr. Ruud Lubbers, United Nations High Commissioner for Refugees; former Prime Minister of the Netherlands [1982–1994]; Professor of Globalization Studies, Tilburg University, Netherlands and at the John F. Kennedy School of Government, Harvard University.

Princeton Lyman, Ph.D., Director of Globalization Program, Aspen Institute; former Ambassador of the United States and Assistant Secretary of State for International Organization Affairs, Washington, D.C.

Peter Marris, Lecturer in Sociology, Yale University; Development Sociologist, Institute of Community Studies, London; Professor Emeritus, Urban Studies, University of California, Los Angeles; Author of *Politics of Uncertainty*.

Thomas Odhiambo, Professor of Biology, President Emeritus of the African Academy of Science, founder of ICIPE; Managing Trustee, The Research and Development Forum for Science led Development in Africa (RANDFORUM), Nairobi, Kenya.

Allison W. Phinney, poet, author, editor, and religious scholar, Boston, Massachusetts.

Giandomenico Picco, Former Assistant Secretary General for Political Affairs in the United Nations, Representative of the Secretary General for the Dialogue of Civilizations, New York, New York.

Roy Smith, Kenneth Langone Professor of Entrepreneurship and Finance, NYU Stern School of Business, New York.

Tu Weiming, Professor of Chinese History and Philosophy and of Confucian Studies, Harvard University, Director of the Harvard-Yenching Institute, Cambridge, Massachusetts.

Muhammad Suhyel Umar, Director, Iqbal Academy, Lahore, Pakistan.

Ingo Walter, Director of the Salomon Center, and Charles Simon Professor of Applied Financial Economics, New York University, Stern School of Business, and at the INSEAD, Fontainebleau and author of many books on international business including *Street Smarts*.

Message from the Secretary General of the United Nations

We live in an age shaped by globalization. This hallmark of our age brings many benefits, but it leaves many excluded from them. The great challenge facing us at the start of this millennium is to ensure that globalization becomes a force that benefits all people, not a windfall that rewards only the privileged few. No shift in the way we think or act can be more critical than this: we must put people at the center of everything we do.

No calling is more noble, and no responsibility greater, than that of enabling men, women and children, in cities and villages around the world, to make their lives better. We must apply the values that are shared by all peoples, and that are of particular importance to our age: freedom; equity and solidarity; tolerance; non-violence; respect for nature; and shared responsibility. Only in this way can we make globalization inclusive, allowing everyone to share its opportunities. It is my hope that this publication will serve as a source of inspiration to our efforts.

Kofi A. Annan

FOREWORD

Many wise words are spoken and written about the state of the world and of humanity in the dawn of this new age. It seems that millennial visions are no less prevalent in our times than they were a thousand years ago. What we see, at first glance, is their heterogeneity and incongruity. Few of them take a complex, holistic approach to the world and its problems. Few offer a universal cure for its ills. Although some of them purport to do this, they are, in fact, unable to offer even a moderately coherent view of the state of contemporary civilization and of the place of human beings—free individuals and co-creators of a unique history that cannot be repeated.

According to some thinkers, history is already finished—all its enigmas revealed. They say nothing can overturn the victory of traditional liberal values. Others see an imminent clash of civilizations, of mutually irreconcilable cultural and religious groups, at the root of current local conflicts in different parts of the world. These visions predict that major non-Western groups—while taking advantage of the so-called Western modernization—will, in fact, never accept it and will even fight against it in the interest of maintaining their own cultural and religious identities, frequently using their opponent's weapons.

As the 20th century fades into history, we cannot avoid experiencing, often painfully, sorrow for the loss of many traditional values, unquestioned or taken for granted until now. In this dawning period, vividly familiar images of an integrated humanity, rooted in the safe structures of family, religious communities, and traditional societal forms appear before our eyes. However, these images cease to be a life-giving inspiration or a guide to follow.

The new age, the Euro-American age, has developed a coherent value system for human coexistence which is recognized as a foundation of coexistence among nations. It embraces the idea of human rights and freedoms, based on respect for the individual human being and his or her dignity, as well as democracy and all its commonly recognized characteristics. How long will this age endure?

This value system is being challenged today from many directions. There is a yearning for a rebirth of authentic authority and authentic local traditions. There is justified skepticism and disappointment with the inadequate functioning of the present systems of government, which suffers from an absence of authority of a positive nature.

Together with these indications of crisis we observe an ever more perceptible absence of a transcendental aspiration to which everything on earth strives. This absence is leading to a gradual collapse of the foundations of human values. A person devoid of respect and regard for a transcendent authority is not a freer person: freedom can be neither experienced nor realized without exercising this responsibility. But, if today this human responsibility is inadequately exercised, it is not the failing of democracy, it is, on the contrary, democracy's challenge.

In contrast, dictatorship does not open any space for the expression of this human responsibility and consequently cannot create a space which can give rise to the authentic authority that is so badly needed. For that reason, every one of us who perceives the dawn of the millennium and the Euro-American modern age as a challenge should not hasten to prepare a funeral for democracy and freedom by accepting an ostensibly terminal diagnosis dignified and craftily justified by cold intellectual luminaries.

Globalization and the obvious shrinking of our planet shift the discussion of elementary values that can and should be shared by everyone to a new plane. Artificial contrasts are often made between East and West, simplified as the contrast between the authoritarian systems (or dictatorships), allegedly anchored in the religious systems of the East, and the allegedly foreign democracy and foreign canon of human rights, imposed by a self-important West.

If we turn to the fathers of Eastern thought, Confucius among others, we find profound passages defining real authority. Its norms have nothing in common with the norms of dictators or other men of brute force. Authority, whether that of the father of a family or the leader of a state, is, for Confucius, a metaphysically anchored gift, which does not draw its force from the strength of its instruments of power but from its heightened responsibility.

Although, the two value systems of the East and the West are sometimes contrasted, they often share the same experience. They stray from their own deepest spiritual roots. If both were able to return to these roots, not only would they be better in themselves, but they would more easily understand each other. The assumed multiculturalism of a global civilization should not be an eclectic conglomerate which fails to embody the heart and soul of different peoples and cultures. Each people must seek inward solace from their own spiritual and cultural sources and, at the same time, search for the common spiritual roots of all cultures and religions.

This global civilization demands not only that we must live next to each other, willingly or unwillingly, but that we must live together. If we realize that love for our neighbor is the universal commandment for all our cultures, even though these cultures are sometimes in conflict and often only pretend to tolerate each other, perhaps we will be able to transcend the present experience of democracy as a mere battleground of individual interests. Our global civilization is already beginning to allow for such a qualitative shift. A newly awakened consciousness of the Heaven that stretches above us, and the uniqueness of the earth we live on is, perhaps, prompting a sense of the togetherness of all humanity, marked by a common respect for and gratitude to that power which transcends all of us.

At the beginning of the new millennium, I cannot deny my perspective as a European, a citizen of the "Old Continent," in many ways a weary and tired continent. Its fate, shared by all European peoples, calls for a quiet discussion of its roots, ambitions, and goals. We will never widen or deepen Europe without widening and deepening ourselves.

The authors of this anthology, having gathered around a "candle in the darkness" to formulate their thoughts on an ethically and spiritually enriched political renaissance in the 21st century, have experienced a need for quietude, contemplation and reflective assessment—that Biblical "singing of old and new treasures."

Let us all, likewise, use our time in history as a valuable gift, a time of spirit. Let us carefully examine the eternal human problems from the point of view of experience, in particular from our own experience. Let us search for the universal dimension in scientific knowledge, even though it be concealed by specialization, commercialization, and the frequently superfluous newspeak of "scientific" communication. Let us search for the causes of the present-day debasement of spiritual and moral values, often even enforced at the state level. Let us listen to the cries of an embattled world at the beginning of the millennium. Let us recall the visible and hidden paths by which we have arrived at our present condition.

Now we are free from many controlling ideologies, but, quite often, we are also deprived of faith in elementary goodness and the transcendent meaning of life. Let us try, as so many generations before us, to light the radiant spark of hope within ourselves. Let us search for the reason for meaningful life on this planet, for a compassionate hope "against all hopelessness," an understandable and visible reason, like a candle lit in the darkness. Let us not cast off our responsibility, equipped as we are with free will, the capacity for knowledge and love, and the gift of hearing and speech.

Vaclav Havel

CANDLES IN THE DARK

A NEW SPIRIT FOR A PLURAL WORLD

INTRODUCTION

Barbara Sundberg Baudot

In Utopia, citizens live in blissful peace and harmony with one another, free from deprivations, physical dangers, and conflicts that in the real world fill ordinary lives with unhappiness and insecurity. Such, for example, is the perfection of the pastoral life of the Houyhnhnms of Jonathan Swift's *Gulliver's Travels,* or the just ordering of life in Thomas More's *Utopia.* Karl Marx with his eschatological vision of a classless, harmonious society, and Plato with his transcendent vision of *The Republic* convey other blueprints for just and virtuous societies. These utopian designs do not necessarily have strong appeal, even to the people who conceive them. They may be too perfect, too comprehensive, and they are often lifeless. The value of such paradigms, however, does not lie in descriptions of perfect societies, but in the controversial interest they generate by their criticisms of the societies of their times. They reveal social inequities, exploitation, political repression, private vices and other evils that would have no place in an ideal world.

Conceived perhaps in a humanist's dream of a kinder, more gentle world, and often fed by nostalgia for an imagined past, utopian thinking challenges contemporary societies with ideas intended to awaken thought to brighter horizons. No society should overlook this kind of conceptualizing of its future, so long as it questions prevailing assumptions about necessities of life and/or critically explores and inspires desirable, practical changes. The sense of a better, realizable state of the world not only gives substance to critical engagement but also encourages interest in meaningful change through political action.

The central theme of this book is the need to rediscover and articulate ethical and spiritual values in the ethos of modernity and in the emerging global economy and society. Some critics might consider this an utopian undertaking. In the sense of critically exploring and offering inspiration for desirable and practical changes in the prevalent conception of development and progress, it is certainly at least *eutopian*, or "seeking the good place" in the meaning of Thomas More. However, unlike utopianism, it does not prescribe a single path to social progress, nor does it design the contours of a perfect society. Rather, it explores different ideas and approaches to enriching the contemporary political discourse. Each contribution to this book offers a candle shedding a particular light on the dark images of the modern world.

Three assumptions underlie, explicitly or implicitly, the various contributions to this book. The first is that moral and spiritual inclinations and aspirations are inherent in human nature. Heeded, they give meaning and orientation to human thoughts and actions; they render possible distinctions between good and bad, right and wrong, and between truth and error; and they determine the quality of human relations and civilizations. Being in touch with reality requires that we recognize the centrality of the moral and spiritual dimensions of life in society.

The second assumption holds that individuals, independently or collectively, have the capacity to foster or impede the realization of moral and spiritual values in society. Institutions providing forms of social intercourse—families, schools, churches, the media, private businesses, national and international public agencies—are instruments that have ability to concretize and promote values and thus influence ways people construe ethical behavior and qualities of the spirit. Individuals, especially those with the privileges and responsibilities of power, have significant roles to play in protecting and advancing moral and transcendent values.

The third assumption is that societies must use their freedom of thought and their capacities to acquire knowledge for purposes of giving greater importance to the moral and spiritual dimensions of life. Prevalent political discourses on the most egregious problems in international relations, political economy, and social well-being ignore a host of unexplored, often forgotten but vitally important interests, beliefs and values, setting aside the critical questions of meaning and purpose in human life.

These assumptions justifying the appeal for an enriched perspective on globalization, development, and progress have been reflected in the discourse of the United Nations. They defy a narrow materialistic understanding of the "faith in the dignity and worth of the human person" affirmed in the Charter written by "We the peoples of the United Nations." They obviate a purely individualistic interpretation of the Universal Declaration of Human Rights, which states in Article 29 that: "everyone has duties to the community in which alone the free and full development of his personality is possible." The world conferences convened at the end of the 20th century by the United Nations proclaimed unambiguously the necessity of a different path to social progress. The 1992 Rio Conference on Environment and Development declared "unsustainable" the "current patterns of production and consumption." The Social Summit, held in Copenhagen in 1995, called on societies to "respond more effectively to the material and spiritual needs of individuals, their families, and the communities in which they live." Most recently, the United Nations Millennium Declaration stated that freedom, equality, solidarity, tolerance, respect, respect for nature, and shared responsibility were values "essential to international relations in the twenty-first century."

These pronouncements challenge the ideology shaping the global culture that sees human lives best organized by institutions that promote and facilitate competitive individualism, acquisitiveness and materialism. According to this ideology, ever-increasing levels of economic activity, income, and consumption constitute the indicators of successful development and social achievements that are essential for a healthy economy. Given the increasingly global span of their implementation, these ideas have generated immense fortunes, drawn people from all over the planet into megalithic enterprises, and affected millions of lives by attempting to transform traditional societies into modern market economies.

This ideology is problematic. Many people in the North and many millions more in the South are deprived of the opportunities this global economic culture has stimulated. The grim facts of their existence and living conditions challenge global leaders to reconsider the wisdom of this perception of progress with its strongly material vision of human worth and purpose. Social critics are troubled by the growing ubiquity of market-type societies allowing money and the logic of profit to rule most spheres of public and private life. They perceive a thickening atmosphere of moral entropy particularly in developed parts of the world and, apart from times of crisis, they observe a rising tide of commodity fetishism that chills generosity, sympathy, and solidarity in social relations.

A renowned literary critic of the 20th century, Ortega y Gasset, characterized this impoverishment of the modern global culture as a form of simplistic reductionism that has eradicated purpose and poetry from human life:

> For us the real is the perceptible, what our eyes and ears pour into us. We have been brought up by a spiteful age, which has beaten the universe into a sheet and made it a surface, a mere appearance. When we look for reality we search for appearances. But the Greeks took reality to be the opposite: the real is the essential, the profound and latent: not the external appearance but the living source of appearance.[1]

Gasset reminds modern society how far its thinking has strayed from a practical sense of the immaterial dimensions of human life as well as from any notion that reality might conceivably be determined by unseen forces that animate, inspire and give depth and meaning to life in its largest sense. Since the industrial revolution, objective material perceptions of life have dominated, and the values, expectations and demands of modern life have absorbed the mental energies of humanity and rendered the notion of any deeper meaning obsolete or irrelevant. One way to envision enriching the public discourse would be to follow a path such as one earlier enunciated by the classic Greek philosophers and seek the essential in human relations, in the organization of society, in economics, and in politics.

Correspondingly, Vaclav Havel perceives in the modern society a conflict between an "impersonal, anonymous, irresponsible, and uncontrollable juggernaut of power (the power of 'mega machinery') and the elemental and original interests of the human being as a concrete individual." On this theme he has written:

> I'm persuaded that this conflict—and the increasingly hypertrophic impersonal power itself—is directly related to the spiritual condition of modern civilization. This condition is characterized by loss: the loss of metaphysical certainties, of an experience of the transcendental, of any super-personal moral authority, and of any kind of higher horizon. It is strange but ultimately quite logical: as soon as man began considering himself the source of the highest meaning in the world and the measure of everything, the world began to lose its human dimension, and man began to lose control of it.[2]

With a vision that embraces many belief systems and levels of perception, Havel has admonished societies to rediscover their spiritual roots. Linking theism and spirituality, he has invited people to live as if all human activity was being recorded in the infinite Consciousness that governs the universe. Blending the spiritual with the intellectual, he has called for renewed interest in moral philosophy and a place for this type of thinking in the shaping of the modern society. A mental horizon that transcends material objectivity is essential to his sense of the spirit. For Havel the very nature of being human is having the capacity for this depth of thinking.

In general, many contemporary critics of modern politics see the need for a shift towards non-material concerns and for enriched conceptions of "quality of life" to promote sustainable economic and social progress. They emphasize that everyone needs an economic base. But attainment of adequate levels of food, clothing, shelter, health care and education should be considered a step in the direction of the higher goal of progress in the art of living. In economic terms, the marginal utility of an extra unit of economic growth is negative when the opportunity cost of "having" is an elevating experience of "being."

The realization of "being" implies recognition of the centrality of the moral and spiritual dimensions of life. It suggests giving some attention to intuition, imagination, historical sense, and the visions of the prophet, the poet, and the artist. In different words quoted from Isaiah Berlin, it implies proclaiming the value "of the sudden illumination of genius, of the immemorial wisdom of tradition or of the common people—beings untouched by sophistication or too much logic—simple rustic sages or the inspired bards of a nation."[3]

For significant historical and political reasons, however, translating such intellectual and moral preoccupations into practical recommendations for changes in modern political and economic life is a difficult endeavor. While the Western political and intellectual world drifted successively through the movements of humanism, the Enlightenment, and the reign of science and technology, transcendent thinking—second nature to the Stoic citizen philosophers of Greece and Rome, to the Scholastics and to the Eastern sages—became increasingly unnatural and unrealistic. It faded almost altogether from the Western ethos under further blows of empiricism, pragmatic materialism, and scientific rationalism. Over the past three centuries, Western thinkers—irrationalists, idealists, romanticists, and/or transcendentalists—who stubbornly defended the non-material dimensions of human life and society have been ignored or, at best, considered irrelevant.

Equally consistently, democratic regimes, sober in tone, although not always secular in language, and vigorous defenders of individual autonomy and property rights, have relegated the essential moral and spiritual concerns to the private and religious spheres. In the business world, it has long been inappropriate to evoke non-material values. "Business ethics" is currently *a la mode*, but generally because it is supposed to make good economic sense. Most importantly, when societies esteem empirical facts and laws of natural science as the sole credible sources of knowledge, it is difficult to imagine individuals, let alone institutions, giving credence to intuitions and inspirations from their "spiritual" roots.

Despite these obstacles, the contributors to this book, including poets, scholars in a variety of disciplines, and leaders in international business, diplomacy and public policy have accepted the challenge. Around the central theme they provide a panoply of ideas and analyses. Some deal more specifically with moral principles and ethical rules of behavior, others with spirituality. But what are the meanings attached to moral principles, ethical behavior and spirituality in this collection?

"Morals," "ethics," and "spirit" are verbal signifiers for vast subjective domains of human inquiry that evoke multiple meanings and elicit a rich variety of ideas, theories, and beliefs. The design of the book reflects not only the diverse understandings and usages of the concepts of "moral," "ethical," and "spiritual" with their varied interpretations gained from the cultural, historical, and existential perceptions of the contributors, but also the strong common threads that bind these essays. The following sections explore these concepts as relevant to the contents of this book.

The Ethical and Moral Dimension

Although ethics is derived from the Greek *ethos* and moral from the Roman *mores,* both words have been given almost the same meaning in general usage, evoking custom or common practice and generally associated with virtue, goodness, justice and integrity. Thus, in common parlance, they are often employed interchangeably. In philosophy, however, they represent two different branches of normative analysis. Morality involves individual and collective values and beliefs about what constitutes the good and the bad. Ethics is the process of choosing and doing what is right or wrong on the basis of these moral values.

Theoretical reflection on the foundations and the legitimacy of moral values varies over time and civilizations. Dominant for long periods in the past, and still very much present in many cultures, is the view that morality is rooted in religion. Moral values are equated with, or derived from, divine law revealed in texts such as the Ten Commandments, the Sermon on the Mount, the Koran or the Vedas. Emphasizing practical wisdom and prudence, Aristotle, and more than a thousand years later, Thomas Aquinas, in his recasting

9

of Aristotle's philosophy, regarded human virtue and personal character as the major determinants of moral statecraft. Happiness derives from human flourishing—an activity of the soul in accord with rationality and virtue. Excellence involves the unfolding of the full range of human characteristics in harmony with the broader values of moral virtue and wisdom. In the Kantian tradition, moral philosophy must establish the necessary *a priori* principles to which moral reasoning must conform and by which moral reasoning must be motivated. Kant's categorical imperative rests on the assumption that *a priori* transcendent and universal norms exist and can be apprehended by rational reflection. "Nature" is an umbrella term for different theories attributed to enlightened empirical schools variously founding moral values on inherent human sentiments of sympathy, benevolence, or self-love.

Utilitarianism is the most generalized source of ethics in modern Western society and in the forefront of the current globalization process. In its origins, this philosophy had much in common with the foundation of morals provided by the Enlightenment. For John Stuart Mill, if not for Jeremy Bentham, the pursuit of happiness was equivalent to the pursuit of virtue, and reason underpinned the appreciation of pleasure and pain. Utilitarianism, however, did not draw a line between empirical and philosophical investigations. Great cataclysms such as the 18th century earthquake in Lisbon—equivalent in impact to the terrorist attacks on the United States of the 11th of September 2001—had shown that lives and societies could not be controlled by reason. They were fragile and precarious and needed to be protected. Thus for the Utilitarian, evaluations of pleasurable or painful outcomes of actions and practices rather than motivating principles became the proper domain of ethics. This was emphasized because the inherent problem of the utilitarian doctrine—how individual pursuit of self-interest can lead to collective harmony without coercion—often proved to be insurmountable.

For many reasons, including skepticism and cynicism generated by two world wars and the generalization of a secularized view of human life as a mere chance accident in evolution, utilitarianism has progressively become identified with the search for material advancement, pleasure and self-gratification, giving strong emphasis to individual autonomy, individual freedom from any constraints, and individual rights. It is this modern version that appears most influential in shaping the current version of the emerging global culture.

From the premises of this modern interpretation are derived distinctions between the public and the private spheres, the self and the general interest, the personal and the political prescriptions. Within this logic, private moral principles govern interpersonal relationships, while other sets of rules, including those generated by the diplomatic culture, or through notions of national interest or profit, control the functioning of public institutions. Because it is assumed that private interest is easy to comprehend and define, "the general interest" at the national, international, and global levels tends to be construed as a mere addition of individual interests. This has led to difficulties in the political management of conflicts of interests between groups. These difficulties may be social or geopolitical as in the case of the division between countries of the North and countries of the South. They may affect the theoretical and practical acceptability of notions such as the common good and the general interest of the whole of humankind, present and future. Typically the most powerful groups and nations impose their views, often convincing others that "the interest of X is also the interest of all."

While coming from different moral philosophical traditions and expressing different views on the intrinsic qualities and sustainability of this modern utilitarian doctrine, the contributors to various essays in this volume share the conviction that human beings are capable of conceiving and living the noblest and most altruistic moral virtues. They imply that cynicism in human affairs is a temptation rather than a demonstration of realism. They note that, notwithstanding very significant differences in philosophies, traditions, cultures—including languages giving different meanings to apparently similar concepts—history and observation show certain fundamental moral values to be timeless and universal. These values and virtues reflect what Jesus, Mohammed, Buddha, African philosophical and religious traditions, Confucius, as well as Hammurabi, Socrates or Kant saw as defining humanity: Do not lie.

Do not cheat. Do not steal. Do not murder. Do not do unto others what you would not like others to do to you. Treat all fellow human beings with respect for their dignity. They also note that it is from this "moral core" that values proclaimed in international declarations—notably equality, justice, peace, tolerance, solidarity, respect for fundamental freedom and rights—derive their legitimacy and their appeal.

Specifically several essays give attention to ideas for a better integration of ethics and global politics. They intend to demonstrate the practicality of bridging the gap between public and private morality. Princeton Lyman analyzes the tension between personal morality informed by the transcendent "still small voice" and the political morality pursued in foreign policy. Jacques Baudot argues that the power of the United Nations is above all of a moral nature premised on virtue and universal principles and indicates some conditions for the effective realization of this power. Giandomenico Picco argues for the decisive role of virtue, wisdom, and *a priori* moral principles in the diplomat's conduct of negotiations and mediation. Robert Gamer stresses the need to take seriously the centrality of values that reflect natural human sentiments and needs in development discourse and practice. Vigdis Finnbogadóttir and Birna Arnsbjörnsdóttir argue for the preservation of language diversity on values that reflect enlightened self-interest and natural human sentiments. Ingo Walter and Roy Smith argue the need to broaden the ethical dimension of international financial transactions and dealings based on utilitarian principles and enlightened self-interest. Nitin Desai suggests drawing on many ethical traditions in the quest for a global ethic that allows for diversity and ordered pluralism.

The Spiritual Dimension

The other contention of this book is that it is vital to emphasize the relevance of the spiritual dimensions of human life as well as the importance spirit holds for progress in the art of living. "Spirit" and "spiritual" are complex terms as evidenced by the many pages of definitions and usages offered in the *Oxford English Dictionary*. "Spirit" derives from the early French word *esperit* meaning breath, or air. Early English usages derive from passages in the Vulgate wherein the term *spiritus* evokes the Greek *pneuma*. For at least six hundred years, these usages have merged to render notions of the life force, the vital principle of being—the breath of life.

"Spirit" has also conveyed the notions of "being" or "intelligence" as independent of anything physical or material. This meaning is recognized in both religious and intellectual contexts. From time immemorial, religious sources and philosophical inspiration have variously construed "Spirit" as the active essence or essential power of Deity, including the Deity's creative animating or inspiring influence. It has also connoted the foundation for higher moral qualities based on the distinction between the religious or spiritual and the material and temporal.

Since the 16th century, "spirit" has been identified as an emanation from the intellect or highest faculty of the mind, and the word "spiritual" evokes the resulting quest for elevated and refined thoughts and feelings. "Spirit" with or without a capital *S*, now also refers to aesthetic qualities mixed with noble moral attributes including beauty, charm, liveliness, mettle, vigor and courage.

The efforts in this book to invoke a spiritual dimension in human affairs captures in a variety of ways and contexts these diverse but complimentary understandings of the word "spirit." In every case they transcend questions of religious affiliations, religious institutions, and theological concepts and controversies. Although religion is treated in several essays reflecting a particular conception of "spirit" or the "spirit of humanity," none of these papers debate the existence of God, or seek to answer questions about people's moral responsibility to God. Nor do these essays delve into questions of dogma, rituals and forms of worship, however important these may be to those who share a particular faith.

In other words, the spiritual dimension of life, while universal, takes its various forms and modes of expression from different religious or intellectual sources and standpoints. These perspectives derive variously from philosophical thinking, intuition, scientific inquiry, empiricism or religious faith. They reveal three contemporary schools of thought on the locus and essence of the human spirit. The identification of these schools facilitates appreciation of the complementarities in the usages of the terms as well as the breadth of possibilities for enriching the political discourse. It underscores that faith in a transcendent power beyond the capacity of human faculties to comprehend is not a prerequisite for spirituality. To consider otherwise would be to exclude the secular humanist from the task of enriching the dialogue on the spiritual dimensions of life and society and lessen support for the enrichment of modernity along this path. Moreover, as the historical usage of the term has demonstrated, that view is blatantly wrong.

The first or scientific school conceives the human spirit as an intrinsic part of the material and temporal world. The universe is a composite of organic and inorganic matter and humankind is the most advanced earthly product of a continuous process of evolution. The nature of the universe and humankind will ultimately be explained by sciences, which are already making great advances in knowledge of the operations of the mind. As described by E.O. Wilson, in his recent book, *Concilience*, "There is no apparent reason why they (the brain sciences) cannot in time provide a material account of the emotions and ratiocination that comprise spiritual thought."[4]

The French biologist Jean Paul Changeux has suggested, in his recently published dialogue with Paul Ricoeur, that it has long been scientifically established that the brain is the situs of human thinking and today scientists are on the threshold of great discoveries concerning movement, memory, and language, even the soul.[5] Perchance spirit will be found in the ether of the brain and is the source of humankind's neurologically stimulated instinct for seeking the good and the ideal. Building the human capacity to express this part of human corporeality is the way to wholeness in the person and in society. Furthermore, Wilson affirmed that: "True character (…) is the internalization of the moral principles of a society, augmented by those tenets personally chosen by the individual, strong enough to endure through trials of solitude and adversity. [It] is the enduring source of virtue."[6] From this perspective, character attributes and moral values express the spiritual dimension of the individual.

The second, or transcendent school, identifies spirit with a universal and infinite consciousness, as the fount of life and intelligence. Intuition, reason, and revelation communicate this consciousness, which imparts the appearance of animation to matter and breathes meaning into perceptions of physical objects and the impulses of ideas on the senses. With many variations, this metaphysical outlook is shared by Platonicians, Stoics, Gnostics, Transcendentalists, and by many adherents to non-Western religions. For Plato, the soul exists outside the body and is prior to it. For Stoics, matter and spirit are coterminous: matter being inert and without any determining qualities. This same idea is conveyed in Eastern philosophy. Wang Wei, an aesthetician, poet, and painter in the Chinese Middle Age articulated such an idea in the following way: "For the painting of a mountain, it is not necessary to let us identify what mountain is painted here, but it is absolutely necessary to let us feel the spirit of the mountain."[7]

It is important to note that some significant theories of modern physics essentially deny the existence of matter as humans conceive it and suggest scientific credibility to this metaphysical perspective of life and spirit. Albert Einstein's conceptions of the real external world and the religious experience of the profound scientific mind are instructive. On the first he has written: "physics treats directly only of sense experiences and of the 'understanding' of their connection. But even the concept of 'the real external world' of everyday thinking rests exclusively on everyday thinking."[8] On religion he has remarked: "The scientist is possessed by the sense of universal causation. (...) His religious feeling takes the form of rapturous amazement at the harmony of natural law, which reveals an intelligence of such superiority that compared with it, all the systematic thinking and acting of human beings is an utterly insignificant reflection."[9]

The third school of thought is dualism. It divides the universe and humankind between the opposite poles of materiality and

15

metaphysics. Both are real and have a separate existence. Life experience swings back and forth between these two realities: the material and the spiritual. The soul or spirit is immortal. The body is mortal. But soul and body, the spiritual and the material realms, need each other. Through faith and ritual, human beings attempt to approach the superior Consciousness that guides and protects the mortal creature. It is the soul that longs to reestablish its ties to nature and the cosmos. It is also the soul that expresses love, care, appreciation for beauty, and imparts these qualities to human relationships. In accordance with this standpoint, institutions, economic and political arrangements, and human endeavors derive their virtue or malevolence from the inclinations of the spirit or the independent human will that vie in shaping their contours and objectives.

Contributors to the different essays in this book would recognize their inclinations in one of these three schools of thought, albeit *pari passu* and with all the nuances called for by such a difficult subject. Scientificism, monism, and dualism indeed represent contrasted philosophies on the source and nature of spirit and a sincere dialogue between their proponents contributes to the advancement of knowledge.

This collection suggests that whether one believes the spirit is grounded in the epigenetic material of the human brain or in the transcendent ether of an unseen Universal Intelligence, some would call God, this dimension of life is essential to the humanity and harmony of modern society. Furthermore all seem to agree on certain of its attributes. Wisdom, appreciation of beauty, nobility and dignity, humility and courage are among the virtues offering glimpses of spirit. Respect for human dignity and for those aspects of the human condition that are not quantifiable is necessary for the building of a viable and sustainable world community.

Several approaches to the spiritual enrichment of the contemporary discourse on matters relevant to public policy are considered in this book including the political, the philosophical, the religious, the aesthetic, and the literary. Richard Falk reviews the impact of secularism on society and suggests the need for reconceiving a place for the sacred in public affairs and for giving thought to ways of integrating spirituality and global politics. Barbara Sundberg Baudot examines how different perspectives on the spiritual dimension of life in society influence the notion and path of human progress.

A number of papers explore specific religious and philosophical traditions and how these can contribute to the contemporary discourse on progress and well-being in a globalized world. Tomonobu Imamichi contrasts the Western empirical and descriptive concept of truth to the Japanese metaphysical conception that embodies perfection, goodness, and beauty, suggesting that a combination of both conceptions would further the international search for meaning in the modern global society. Tu Weiming applies Confucian teachings to deepening moral sensitivity in the global society by stressing the full realization of the individual by way of loving and respectful relationships to all the basic dimensions of life ranging from the family to the universe. Traditional African philosophy and religious beliefs evoked by Thomas Odhiambo demonstrate the relevance and practical import for society of notions of continuity of life, nature, and destiny that should figure in development projects. Suhyel Umar contrasts Promethean humanity with spiritually grounded humanity and considers the consequences of each ethos for the future of humankind. John Fortin examines St Benedict's rules for monastic life as a source of inspiration for living more meaningfully in modern society.

Literary and aesthetic approaches to articulating the spiritual dimension of life suggest other considerations for the public discourse. Vyacheslav Ivanov merges philosophical and semiotic approaches in his consideration of the modern transformation of the noosphere, the intelligence sphere enveloping earth's biosphere, linking its possible shrinking to the disappearance of cultures, languages and traditional symbols in human communication. Allison Phinney explores the implications of a poet's reading of voices of spirit in modern society. Noriko Hashimoto follows paths of art in the Japanese tradition toward a sense of oneness with Nature, suggesting that development and human progress must include this dimension for the well being of humanity. Taken together all these papers offer a rich variety of ways to understand and appreciate the spiritual elements of life and reflect in one way or another all three schools of thought on the concept of spirit.

Organization of the Book

This book divides into four parts. Part I addresses the need to rediscover and articulate ethical and spiritual values in the context of a political renaissance. In so doing it critiques the dominant approach to human progress and development and outlines alternatives. Part II explores the contemporary relevance of ethical and spiritual traditions derived from philosophy and religion. Part III delves into art, literature, and language in search of ideas for enriching the contemporary discourse. Part IV considers ways to apply spiritual and moral values in international diplomacy, development, finance, and intergovernmental organizations. Each of these parts is preceded by a summary introduction.

Endnotes

1 - Jose Ortega y Gasset, "Meditations on Quixote" as quoted in *Theory of the Novel: A Historical Approach*, ed. Michael McKeon (Baltimore: Johns Hopkins University Press, 2000), 276.

2 - Vaclav Havel, *Disturbing the Peace* (New York: Vintage Books, 1991),10-11.

3 - Isaiah Berlin, ed., *The Age of the Enlightenment: Basic Writings of Locke et al* (New York: A Meridian Book, 1984), 271.

4 - E.O. Wilson, *Concilience* (New York: Alfred A. Knopf, 1998), 246.

5 - Paul Ricoeur et Jean Paul Changeux, *Ce qui nous fait penser: la nature et la règle* (Paris: Editions Odile Payot, 1998).

6 - Wilson, *Concilience*, 246.

7 - Tomonobu Imamichi and Noriko Hashimoto, *The Modalities and Essence of Beauty: Historic and Systematic Thoughts in the Aesthetics* (Tokyo: Universe of Air Press, 1987), 44-45.

8 - Albert Einstein, *Ideas and Opinions* (New York: Bonanza Books, 1954), 290.

9 - Ibid., 40.

PART I

THE NEED FOR A
POLITICAL RENAISSANCE

Countries and peoples of the world are increasingly interlinked by various technologies of communications and transportation, but this growing proximity is neither a source of security nor a generator of harmonious international relations. The process of globalization, while materially enriching the few, is destabilizing the life of millions more. There is, in the spirit of the time, not only fear and insecurity, but also a sense of loss of control, of moral decay, and of a spiritual vacuum. While its potential for global material advance is not to be discounted, globalization's contribution to the non-material dimensions of human life is problematic. Lacking is the moral and spiritual inspiration that gives meaning and orientation to life, offers criteria for distinguishing the worthwhile and the worthless, the truthful and the erroneous, the good and the bad, and determines the quality of human relations and civilizations.

The contributors to this part recognize the inevitability and ultimate virtue of an open world. But on the global scene, they observe a high level of violence, growing inequalities of all types and the threatening emergence of a dual world. They see nation-states weakened by transnational forces and democracies suffering from inequitable concentrations of wealth and power. They note that the Western political ethos, now shaping the process of globalization, applies market principles in domains of life and social relations where they do not belong. The current process of economic globalization is not only physically unsustainable because of the predatory attitudes that it generates, but is also morally wrong because it ignores the attachments and the social identities that are essential to human well-being. But, at the same time, the contributors bear witness to an enormous creativity and energy, the slowly emerging sentiment of the equal worth of every human being, and the conviction that the building of a world community based on harmonious and compassionate relations between all its members is an achievable ideal cherished in the spirit of humankind. It is this creativity, conviction, and faith that will fuel a morally and spiritually enriched political renaissance imperative for the survival and flourishing of civilization in the integrity of its natural environment.

> The central issue of our time is to address the problem of exclusion, alienation, and anonymity within each society and in the interactions between them. This will require us to reexamine the paradigms that guide economic, social, and political policy at the national and global level, and recognize that these policies must be driven by an ethical consensus. The starting point must be to recognize that the basic principles that define political, social, and economic structures cannot be value-free.
>
> *Nitin Desai*

The global ethic foretold by Nitin Desai draws on all traditions and leaves room for diversity in its interpretation and application. The process of formulating universally applicable ethical principles is as important as the end result. It requires cultural dialogues open to both similarities and differences and executed with the kind of empathy and understanding that cannot be secured by law, but only by a meeting of hearts and minds. It requires the involvement of diplomats, religious leaders, academics, community leaders, writers, artists, lawyers, doctors, and ordinary citizens. It must be conceived not as a hierarchically superior order, but as universal principles that reflect the responsibilities entailed in being truly human, overriding parochial loyalties to nation, neighborhood, or family. This global ethic should have a degree of fuzziness that allows for varying interpretations of common principles. Although somewhat untidy, such an outcome will have the strength that resides in the heart rather than the head. And finally, Desai points out that a global ethic would amount to little if it is not accompanied by measures to bring democracy closer to people and to make markets more mindful of equity.

> Secularism and modernity are closely associated, and to be contrasted with medievalism, which above all stresses the fusing of political and religious institutions and authority on the basis of faith in shared transcendent truth. To the extent that modernity is, itself, now being partially superseded by a series of developments associated with "globalization," the status and nature, and above all, the monolithic character of secularism is also being drawn into question from a variety of different angles.
>
> *Richard Falk*

The revisited and reconstructed secularism envisaged by Richard Falk would, in the same vein as Nitin Desai's pluralism, seek both an ethos of tolerance and areas of agreed universality. It would imagine a future community that celebrates diversity while affirming the solidarity of the human species. It would facilitate the revival of support in civil society for a new variant of the compassionate state that takes account of the profound changes being wrought by globalization. But for Falk, a reconstructed secularism involving the extension of human rights based on an ethos of solidarity would also imply collaboration between religion and politics, and possibly a reversal of the Western tradition of separation between church and state inherited from the neat dualisms of Greek thought. Falk observes that, in many diverse settings, individuals and groups are rediscovering their core spirituality with or without the support of institutional religion. This rediscovery might pave the way for the reemergence of a centered spirituality, for post-modernity recreating a space for spiritual and normative creativity, and for the reaffirmation of belief in the mystery of life and the sacred character of the world. For Falk, the most crucial struggle in the early 21st century will be the encounter between this vision of life and human destiny and the overbearing forces of the capitalist market ethos.

> In considering the "Four Freedoms," we ask: What did they mean during the war? What do they mean now? What will they mean in the future? Essential to the understanding of these freedoms are the values that underlie them—truth, dignity, and spirituality. These are the principles according to which these freedoms can be most fully enjoyed and perpetuated, and without which they would lose much of their meaning and sustainability.
>
> *Ruud Lubbers*

A new balance between the religious and the secular is also very much at the center of Ruud Lubbers reflections on the "Four Freedoms," articulated by Franklin Roosevelt. He perceives that the building of a path towards a world community that expresses ideals of truth and dignity requires public institutions to establish strong relationships with religion. He believes there is a continuum between moral philosophy, spirituality and religion. Lubbers argues that the real satisfaction of human needs and aspirations requires general moderation, frugality, and generosity, and that responsibility for the earth, its beauty and bounty, is a fundamental value to be nurtured. "Living in truth" means the search for fundamental values that give direction to life. "Living in dignity" means to be a free and responsible person integrated in a community. The building and maintenance of a civilized society require conscious and steady efforts on the part of individuals and deliberate and purposeful policies conducted by democratic and efficient public institutions—a critically important observation shared by other contributors to the first part of this book. History shows that a general *laissez-faire* attitude is not conducive to progress. Furthermore, Lubbers expresses the conviction that spirituality is both contemplative and fully immersed in action. It is about non-violence, and yet the courage, in times of darkness, to defend humanity, with patience and conviction in words and deeds.

> The meaning we make of our lives is embedded in the history of our relationships, and the histories of the communities of which we are part. Our sense of it, at any particular moment, depends on how we use those histories to confront the present and the future. It is a subtle, intricate structure of organization, never finished nor wholly consistent, constantly adapting and assimilating. It is both unique to each individual, and responsive to events that affect its crucial relationships.
>
> *Peter Marris*

For Peter Marris, translating values into meaningful practice, and therefore making progress towards a political renaissance depends on a social and psychological understanding of the way we construct meaning in our lives. The ability to sustain a meaningful sense of life, to feel purposeful and confident in interpreting the world around us, is, of itself, an essential aspect of well-being. Therefore, from Marris's perspective, the ethical and spiritual values society adopts arise out of that struggle to construct, adapt, and protect meaning in human life. It is an effort to inscribe moral principles and norms into concrete social and personal history. Like all his colleagues in this book, Peter Marris believes in the universality and the timelessness of a number of fundamental values, including compassion, generosity and solidarity. Marris notes that the meaning people make of their lives is embedded in the history of their relationships and the histories of the communities of which they are part. He also notes that even when people have to make moral choices in isolation, they have in mind, not just their consciences, but how an imagined community will affirm their integrity. "Love," for its own sake, as an attachment that requires no other justification, is, for Marris, the most universal and powerful source of meaning. Changing the balance between human needs and market needs is the condition for a morally and spiritually enriched renaissance.

CHAPTER 1

GLOBAL ETHICS IN A PLURAL WORLD

Nitin Desai[1]

Nationalism, democracy, and the market economy are the three ideas that have dominated the political and economic history of our times. They form the basis for a social philosophy that holds the nation-state to be the most appropriate expression of political sovereignty. They require this sovereignty to be exercised through representative democracy, the rule of law, free speech, the protection of individual rights and perhaps, secularism in mundane matters. This school of thought argues for a market economy with modest public interventions as the most workable form of economic organization.

It is a philosophy that has been challenged many times in the past, most notably by imperialism with respect to nationalism, by fascism with respect to democracy, and by communism with respect the market economy.

Imperialism and fascism were no longer influential as ideologies after the Second World War and, after the collapse of communism in Europe in the late eighties, there was a sense that we had come to a defining moment—the phrase used was "the end of history."[2] From this point on, it was argued, the world could be put on autopilot, ideological differences were at an end, and it was just a question of the gradual extension of a market economy and liberal democracy to the rest of the world.

Since then, there has been a reaction to this ideology, a growing recognition that it has not delivered even its own objectives and that it has not given people the freedom or the equality that it promises. We see the persistence of poverty, homelessness, and marginalization; the phenomenon of growing unemployment; the spread of deviant criminal behavior including drug abuse and trafficking; the horrors of ethnic violence; and the obscenity of ethnic cleansing. These factors show the limitations of an ideology which many thought was going to lead to a convergence of the world system to some Kantian ideal.

A Loss of Faith

The disenchantment with the direction of development of our societies and the emerging world order relates to what are seen as departures of the actual from the ideal for all three elements: nationalism, democracy, and the market economy.

Take first the principle of nationalism. The nation-state was and still is seen by many as the basis for self-government. Its origins lie in what could be described as wars of identity and the struggle for self-determination. But what is the defining characteristic of the "self" in the terms "self-government" and "self-determination" ?

Language, race, religion, tribal bonds, historical antecedents, and ecological boundaries have all worked to give some groups a sense of togetherness and common purpose, as well as a sense of difference *vis-à-vis* others. Nations were sometimes constituted from such groups with a long history of cohabitation and interaction in a given territory. In other instances, this sentiment emerged as a group came through the traumas of wars and revolutions. It is this sense of an "imagined community" that confers legitimacy on the rulers and rules of governance. The link with democracy comes from the necessary belief in the equality of all citizens, for if this is denied, there is not one but several nations within a given territory.

Today, many of these "imagined communities" are in disarray. Many states are far from this sense of common purpose of a united community. Some even reject the notion of equality for all who reside within their borders. Old identities are being rediscovered and new ones being forged so that the "self" that seeks political expression in "self-determination" is less accommodating and more parochial than what the present political geography of the world would allow. At the same time, while these fragmentary identities find political expression, the sovereign states themselves are losing their autonomy because economic, ecological, cultural, and even criminal structures and processes are increasingly transnational. The nation-state, the principal expression of political identity at present, is under threat from fragmentation and globalization.

The democratic ideal is that of a community governed by decisions arrived at by all citizens after an informed public debate. Politics is not a profession but an obligation on all citizens. There exists no special class of persons who are political leaders. Leadership, to the extent required, is provided by citizens who are political amateurs and have other callings. The working democracies of today depart substantially from this ideal. Politics has become a profession. The distance between leaders and citizens has widened, and public opinion is formed from superficial information supplied by an often manipulated media industry.

If ever there was an ideal democracy, one can conceive of what we have today as the result of a linked set of changes in the:

- Source of effective authority from citizens' assemblies to elected representatives to party bureaucracies;
- Modalities of communication between leadership and citizenry from public meetings to parliamentary debate to media outreach;
- Content of communication from substantive debates to slogans and sound-bites to spin-doctoring;
- Quality of political leadership from statesmanship to factional politicking to manipulative public relations;
- Ends of political activity from the good of the community to the good of the group to the good of the leadership.

Our sense of identity requires that we think of ourselves as part of this or that community, actual or imagined. A sense of community derives from shared values about economic, social, and political relations. In the past they were derived, perhaps, from a shared religion and communities were organized around temples, mosques, and churches. In our more secular times, we see ourselves as part of the community, which inhabits the city or the settlement in which we live. In these communities, institutions such as local authorities, cooperatives, and trade unions give people a sense of direct influence on the instrumentalities of the state and the market and provide a modality for consensus building and cooperation at the local level. Yet, we are witnessing a breakdown of communities and establishments and a loss of institutional effectiveness. The net result of this debasement of democracy is, at the very least, a mistrust of politicians and politics, low voter turnout, and the growth in influence of wealthy, well-organized special interest groups who often challenge the fundamentals of the liberal ideal. Thus we face a potential loss of legitimacy for the government in the eyes of the people whose sovereignty is the constitutional basis for democracy.

The economic counterpart of the democratic ideal is supposed to be a market economy based on perfect competition, freedom of choice, and fairness of outcomes. The departures of the actual from the ideal are even more marked in the operations of the market economy—the concentration of wealth and market-power, barriers to entry and other departures from equal opportunity, an unacceptable inequality of outcomes and the unequal distribution of the burdens of market instability. Even the strongest believers in the virtues of the free market would recognize that in some cases the underlying conditions for the efficient and equitable operation of markets do not hold, for instance, when there are externalities or when the goods exchanged are public goods. But even here the fundamentalist would seek procedures that simulate a relationship that mimics the market. There are also differences in opinion among those who are less fanatical but who accept the value of a free market economy, about the nature and extent of justifiable restraint on the free exchange of goods and services and the values and objectives that define justifiability.

The problem is not simply one of market failure but whether civic virtue and solidarity is possible in a capitalist world. In the nineteenth century, there was a vigorous debate in the United States as to whether or not industrialization and wage labor were consistent with maintaining the virtuous and independent citizenry that a self-governing republic required. Some thinkers, for example, Thomas Jefferson, believed that political liberty was safe only when no one was economically beholden to another.[3] Today, when confronted by vast corporate bureaucracies and a small plutocracy of corporate leaders, who are often transnational and for the most part only accountable to shareholders, the loss of agency can and does lead to a certain lethargy in the exercise of civic rights and responsibilities.

The market organizes relations between persons in terms of the equality of worth of the goods and services exchanged, implying that such a cost-benefit calculus should underlie all relations of this nature, or at least those that involve transactions in goods and services that, on account of their scarcity, have a potential market value. A contrary view would argue for altruism and solidarity, for loyalty and responsibility and for custom and tradition in relations between persons, not just in familial relations but also in social and political relations and in the exchange of goods and services. It would demand that space should be created for unrequited transfers of goods and services and value-based bounds on the outcome of market-based relations.[4]

The problem is, therefore, that the system of nation-states, organized as market-based democracies, is being undermined by globalization and fragmentation, the debasement of democracy, the inequities of the market, the erosion of solidarity and the decay of local institutions. There is a pervasive sense of a loss of control and a sense of moral decay that is alienating individuals and vulnerable groups from the social and political structures of which they are a part and marginalizing countries from the international system. What we have are groups and persons excluded from:

- Development processes—which manifests itself as poverty;
- The economy—which shows up as unemployment;
- The mainstream of political, social, and cultural processes which shows up as marginalization, discrimination, and rootlessness;
- Security networks—which shows up as vulnerability.

The central issue of our time is to address this problem of exclusion, alienation, and anonymity within each society and in the interactions between them. This will require us to reexamine the paradigms that guide economic, social, and political policy at the national and global level and recognize that these policies must be driven by an ethical consensus.[5] The need for the latter is perhaps greatest at the level at which the instrumentalities of power are the weakest. Hence we focus next on the need for a global ethic.

The Need For a Global Ethic

The starting point must be to recognize that the basic principles that define political, social, and economic structures cannot be value-free. There is a great deal of talk today about life in the global village. As Kofi Annan, the Secretary-General of the United Nations has said: "If that village is to be a truly desirable place for all of us on this planet, it must be embedded in and guided by broadly shared values and principles."[6]

The conception of an individual in the ideology of liberal democracy and free-market economies is that of a person who is isolated and unencumbered and who has rights and entitlements. This ideology demands that political and economic processes be capable of reconciling conflicts between the rights of individuals and offer procedural justice. The paradigm for interpersonal relations, at least between strangers, is the legally binding contract. But, in fact, individuals accept constraints on their rights and entitlements not simply out of respect for another person's rights and entitlements but out of a sense of obligation to history, family, neighborhood, nation, religion, ethnic group, and even to humanity as a whole. In politics, not only do people need procedural arrangements for reconciling conflicts of rights but also an active citizenship which encompasses commitment to civic virtue and willingness to accept obligations as a member of a neighborhood, a city, a country, the world. In economics, they accept the pursuit of self-interest, but the "icy water of egotistical calculation" is warmed by a sense of solidarity and social responsibility.[7]

Equality before the law and in the political process, as well as equal opportunity in the market place are important but not enough to describe what people look for to satisfy their sense of obligation and belonging. Human beings are not disembodied pursuers of maximum utility or of some other abstract principle. Historical antecedents, cultural traditions, religious beliefs, and unconscious psyche, also shape their behavior. They see themselves not as isolated and unencumbered individuals but as members of a family, clan, community, nation and hopefully, of the human race—with the obligations that arise from such memberships. Nor can we ignore this on the ground that these attachments are matters of sentiment and not of principles. This may be relevant in a philosophical analysis of the coherence and justifiability of ethical beliefs. But if our interest is more in the motivations that influence choice, then we need to recognize that each of these identities finds expression in the aims that persons pursue in social, political, and economic relations.

Values matter, but values differ. This diversity would perhaps be the case even in a community that is homogenous in terms of its religious beliefs, history, methods of upbringing, and education. But today, the jurisdictions relevant to social discourse are more diverse in all of these respects, and range in geographical terms, from the global to the local. Multiculturalism is the norm at the national and most certainly, at the global level. Our problem is to reconcile diverse cultural loyalties and the need for a sense of community with that which is good and valuable in the liberal ideal, the sense of tolerance and respect for others. Parochialism, fundamentalism, and communalism, which are so frequently sources of violence and stress, are the enemies not just of a liberal order that is neutral between ethical alternatives, but also of a plurilateral, global ethic.[8]

If a global community did not exist, we would not need a global ethic. The world is a community, in part, because all who are in it share in risks, such as those that arise from weapons of mass destruction, environmental stress, the globalization of crime, and the interdependence of economic prospects. In the words of Jurgen Habermas, the world today is "an involuntary community founded on the sharing of risks.''[9] However, interdependence is not the only reason why we need a global ethic. There is also a sense in which the equal moral worth of every individual is central to the idea of democracy and therefore requires us to agree upon the moral consequences of this sense of a universal human community.

But does a global ethic have to be a universalizing ethic? The European Enlightenment believed in the notion that human nature has certain universal characteristics and that humans have shared ends, which are enough to bring them together in social institutions informed by a universal morality. It is a belief that underlies the *Universal Declaration of Human Rights*, which is the product of a global process that involved participants from many cultural traditions, and related efforts to articulate a shared vision of human dignity that should define relations between and amongst individuals and the State.

Universalizing claims can also arise from some notion of the ends of history or, in a more recent instance, from an empirical judgment that we have reached the end of history. Western imperialism was based to a certain extent on such a notion with its cry of "manifest destiny," and even Engels justified territorial conquests in Europe on the basis of "the right of civilization as against barbarism, of progress as against stability."[10] A global ethic that draws largely on just one cultural tradition will never attract the willing allegiance across cultures, without which it loses its very purpose. It must draw on all ethical traditions and leave room for diversity in its interpretation and application.

The ethical impulses that drive individual behavior are seldom monolithic. Most of us are confronted by moral dilemmas that we resolve in one way at one time and in another way at some other time. We do not expect to follow the same moral standard in every context in which we are required to judge the acceptability of acts that are basically similar. Actions that we would consider selfish in the context of a family may well be acceptable in a larger context of the economy. Behavior that would be criticized as inconsiderate of others in a neighborhood may be tolerated in a wider geographical context. Whether an act is considered cruel depends, regrettably, on whether the victim is a friend or a foe.

The real hope for a global ethic rests precisely on this incoherence in the moral character of individuals. In the words of Sir Stuart Hampshire:

> We are citizens who have a feeling for justice in public affairs, only because we have faction-ridden souls, ambivalent desires and the experience of contrary impulses and we are persons who are normally on dispute with ourselves.[11]

The threat comes from fundamentalists of different persuasions who want a single set of rules to apply to all persons, at all times, in all contexts, an attitude captured well in the French term for such persons—*integriste*.[12] Fundamentalism involves a type of ethical imperialism where a group seeks to apply its beliefs beyond the group, without the willing acceptance of these beliefs by others. It often involves the misapplication of norms relevant for one sphere, say religious practices, to another, such as community relations. Above all, fundamentalists seek to apply rules rigidly, without the tempering effect of compassion that allows one to respect and tolerate differences and even forgive lapses, as the less doctrinaire often do, at least for those who have a claim on their affections. But we must also recognize that fundamentalism thrives when there is a moral vacuum. As Michael Sandel says: "Fundamentalists rush in where liberals fear to tread."[13]

A problem of a different character arises from the close links that exist between religion and morality in most cultures. Monotheistic religions are virtually required to believe in the equality, at least of all believers, before the one God. Some of the proselytizing monotheistic religions require the believer to convert others to the faith. Thus their treatment of non-believers and their incapacity to accommodate gods other than their "One" leads to intolerance, not just of differing concepts of divinity, but also of moral codes, cultural norms, and social practices.

Some would argue that ethical norms are not comparable across cultures and that there is no universal basis for defining the

right and the good. Such relativism is a good corrective to the fierce
rigor of fundamentalism. However, it does not provide a basis for
devising acceptable procedures for the functioning of multi-cultural
jurisdictions that, on account of interdependence, sentiment or mere
historical accident, require a common framework of norms and core
principles.

What could these core principles be? At the very least one
can accept a thin consensus that, in any dispute, particularly a moral
dispute, all sides should be heard. John Rawls developed a political
conception of justice based on fairness and described a procedure
that would allow persons with differing comprehensive moral conceptions to agree on the basic structure for social cooperation.[14] But
if we stop here, and bracket all ethical concerns other than fairness
and procedural justice, we may be aiming too low. A stronger consensus may be possible if we recognize that some virtues like
respect for life, charity, love, and truthfulness find a place in a wide
variety of ethical belief systems.

If people who are in a position to choose always make similar choices, for life instead of death, freedom instead of slavery,
good health instead of illness, knowledge instead of ignorance, then,
as Brian Barry suggests, such a revealed preference could provide a
set of core principles that would allow us to judge at least some elements of every society and provide the principal elements of a global ethic.[15] Judging by the outcome of recent global processes, the
elements for such a shared ethic could be those that every society
must have: [16]

- An economy that provides the material means and public services
  required for human dignity;
- A sense of responsibility for the welfare of others, particularly
  future generations;
- Commitment to equality of status and of opportunity;
- Respect for diversity; the right of others to be different;
- Political processes that are inclusive and participatory;
- Commitment to non-violence—an acceptance that differences can
  be resolved in peace.

These broad principles provide but a beginning; the challenge is to devise a process that can draw out the implications of this commonality for a global ethic.

The Dialogue of Cultures

Any moral code that might apply across societies and cultures must be based on freely given consent, therefore on consensus.[17] How we get to a formulation of a set of ethical principles applicable across societies and cultures is as important as the end result itself. Samuel Fleischacker, in his contribution to the UNESCO Universal Ethics Project, urges us to recognize that "moral norms tend to be inextricable from cultural ones."[18] He argues for a cultural dialogue, open to both similarities and differences across traditions, which allows each to be acknowledged, understood, even delighted in, and rejects legislative or philosophical approaches that do not permit the "slow building of respect that a global ethic needs."[19] We need more than just respect for the rights of others to be different. We need empathy and understanding. These cannot be secured by law but only by a meeting of hearts and minds. That meeting should be the real purpose of the cultural dialogue.

The dialogue can take place only if there is an underlying sense of urgency, built perhaps on the sense of shared risks and the need to find a *modus vivendi* for living together. If it is to be constructive, it cannot be simply a confrontation of opposites. It would need an attitude well captured in John Rawls' precepts of reasonable discussion put forward in his description of a process to identify an "overlapping consensus" among persons with differing moral doctrines:

> First, the political discussion aims to reach reasonable agreement, and hence so far as possible it should be conducted to serve that aim. Second, when we are reasonable we are prepared to find substantive and even intractable disagreements on basic questions. Third, when we are reasonable, we are ready to enter discussion crediting others with a certain good faith.[20]

37

The dialogue concerning the need to develop a global ethic cannot be simply a diplomatic process designed to negotiate treaties and covenants between sovereign governments. Diplomatic dialogue is important as long as the monopoly of authority and legitimacy stays where it is. But governments cannot be separated from the culture or, more correctly to use the plural, the cultures that support them. Religious leaders, teachers, academics and intellectuals, community leaders, authors and artists, lawyers, doctors, and a host of ordinary citizens shape the ethical premises that guide these cultures. They are the ones who have to be reached in the cultural dialogue for they will determine the possibility of a consensus far more than the formal participants in a diplomatic process.

A dialogue between cultures must recognize that we think of ourselves not just as unencumbered individuals but also as members of a variety of religious groups and social communities and as inheritors of diverse cultural traditions. The dialogue has to be structured to give expression to all of these identities, not just through individuals but also as collectivities. The dialogue should not be separated from normal contacts between communities, cultures, and religions. What we need, however, is an ecumenical spirit, a willingness to talk and to listen where and when moral questions arise in these contacts.

Another necessary ingredient for successful dialogue is "the habit of argument within solidarity."[21] This means the acceptance of responsibility for the well being of one's fellow members in a community so that solidarity is seen not as charity but as empowerment, as a necessary condition for the survival and development of the community, and as an ingredient in the cement that binds it together.

But is there a sentiment that binds together all humans, some form of loyalty that goes beyond local and national allegiances? In a sense, the great global religions created supranational consciousness. A Muslim, a Christian, or a Buddhist shares common beliefs and even a certain sense of community with fellow believers in other countries and cultures. In our more agnostic times, a sense of community can emerge as education, travel, and communication break down barriers of strangeness, and the practical requirements of economic, ecological, and political interdependence bring peoples and nations together in contracts, covenants, and treaties.

In the world of diplomacy and commerce, relationships and commitments are moving beyond the bilateral structures of colonialism to a broader multilateralism and deeper forms of regional integration. Global and regional networks of activist groups, professional and trade associations are establishing webs of influence over diplomatic and commercial processes. The United Nations and a host of other multilateral organizations provide the platform for negotiation and dialogue that increasingly engages what could be described as an international civil society.[22]

Two features of these multilateral processes are of particular importance for the emergence of a global ethic. The first is that the diplomatic process is driven not just by the balance of power but also by the search for rule-based international regimes for regulating relations between states, even in situations of conflict. Agreements have been concluded for managing international commerce and for coping with specific environmental problems and shared resources beyond national jurisdiction. These compacts are based not just on the recognition of interdependence and mutual benefit, but also on what could be described as ethical principles involving an agreement on what constitutes right and good behavior. This ethical dimension is even more explicit in the agreements that deal with human rights, humanitarian and refugee relief, development assistance, and certain aspects of disarmament. The point here is not that these agreements are adequate but that they do seek to set a standard of acceptable behavior, which, regrettably, is not always observed.

The second feature is the growing involvement of civil society in the multilateral process. Local and national activists have come together in global networks to promote human rights, women's advancement, equal opportunity for the disabled, the protection of the elderly, the eradication of poverty, worker's rights, the protection of the environment, development support and debt relief for the materially impoverished countries, and other such causes. They are driven by ethical impulses that cut across the boundaries of nations and cultures. Precisely because such activist groups are outside the formal structures of national governance and the system of states, their emergence as international collectivities provides a basis for moving beyond the balance of power to a norm-based world order. By conveying to the powerless the sense that they are not alone, these groups counter the helplessness engendered by the vast bureaucracies of power. As in the case of the global religions, they generate a feeling of fellowship and create a community of concern that cuts across other, more parochial loyalties. This educative, socializing function of the political process is as important as its substantive purpose and is crucial for the emergence of a civic identity.[23]

In a fragmentary way, a global civic identity is emerging, and Richard Falk, for instance, has spoken of a new global citizenship "premised upon global or species solidarity."[24] It is this sense of global citizenship that can confer legitimacy and moral authority on the institutions of global governance. There is, however, a danger that a gulf may emerge between global activists and transnational players who are a part of this global civic community and others in their societies and cultures who remain tied to more parochial identities. Diplomats, corporate leaders, globetrotting academics, and international activists may think of themselves as global citizens. But in the political processes that matter at the local or even national level, they are a minority. It is impractical to imagine that a global ethic or a cosmopolitan identity can replace more parochial loyalties based on history, cultural traditions, and religious beliefs. A way has to be found to link the global with the parochial and allow them to coexist.

An Ordered Pluralism

Those of us who are not fierce fundamentalists have multiple loyalties and, corresponding to this, multi-faceted identities. In some contexts, say survival in a famine, we may place the interests of our family above the interests of the community while in certain others, like isolating a family member with a communicable disease, the reverse may be the case. Similarly when voting for budgets and taxes, we may place the interests of the community above those of the country but not so if the defense of national territory is at issue. There is no hierarchy here with one level of loyalty always superior to another. In this sense, a global ethic has to be thought of not as being hierarchically superior but, more modestly, as something that applies when we consider our responsibilities as human beings to be more important than our loyalties to a nation or neighborhood or family. The central problem of a global ethic is to secure an agreement on how and when these different loyalties should be determined.

The process of arriving at the content of a global ethic has to include within it the rules that would allow the latitude of interpretation and application that can accommodate the diversity of ethical concerns that is the reality of the world today. Mireille Delmas-Marty argues for an ordered pluralism that seeks initially to harmonize moral codes rather than unify them. This approach recognizes what the European Court of Human Rights acknowledges as the national margin of appreciation, a margin that may vary with the strength of the consensus on each principle, and that is founded on a process whose legitimacy is derived as much from a consensus building in civil society as from the law making power of sovereign states.[25]

The central element of an "ordered pluralism" must be an agreement on what is relevant where. This may not be as definite as setting an agenda for a negotiating process and the areas that are agreed to be of common ethical concern may expand or change over time. Today, we would accept our obligation to act as part of a human community at the expense, if necessary, of other loyalties: to stop genocide; prohibit slavery; assist innocent victims of war, strife, and disaster; or protect children. Tomorrow, we may be willing to extend our sense of obligation to other areas like eradicating poverty or protecting freedom of belief.

The expansion of this area of common concern depends not so much on a shared theology but on the evolution of each person's conscience, which may be shaped as much by literature, art, and the mass media, as by philosophical debate. A cultural dialogue that accepts the legitimacy of all ethical traditions and then tries to find common ground, not through disputation but through empathy and understanding, stands a better chance of arriving at a core that would command widespread allegiance rather than a more formal diplomatic process. The time for diplomacy and formal agreements comes later when a developing consensus needs to be crystallized in a more coherent form and be given the legitimacy of legislative approval.

We must also accept that a global ethic will have a degree of fuzziness, which allows varying interpretations of a common principle. Take free speech for instance—one must accept that each culture will define it in a manner that is consistent with its norms of appropriate social behavior. If such a margin of interpretation is not allowed, then an agreement can only be realized when norms of acceptable behavior are more uniform across cultures. Allowing for a margin allows for evolution, and over time, the margins may become narrower. The actual outcome of an ordered pluralism based on a cultural dialogue may well be untidy, but it would have the strength of an ethic that resides in the heart rather than the head.

An ordered pluralism is a way of defining the ethics of tolerance. It specifies limits to tolerance in the form of some inviolable norms that we all accept as a necessary consequence of our humanity. It circumscribes a space for tolerance in some areas where an agreement is fuzzy and leaves a margin for interpretation. It seeks a better understanding of differences in other areas where a consensus does not exist. An ordered pluralism is a middle path between sectarian fundamentalism that seeks to overwhelm all other ethical traditions and a relativism that is content to let all ethical traditions function independently of one another.

Growing interdependence and our sense of common humanity require that we develop an ethic strong enough to provide a basis for global cooperation on many issues. This paper has focused on the cultural dialogue and ordered pluralism required to implement such an ethic. This approach may also be relevant within nations that have a multiplicity of cultures and ethical traditions. Beyond this, social cohesion at the national level requires that citizenship must be seen as a source of obligations to others and as a basis for individual rights. Citizenship must also be exercised, not just through the constitutional structures of governance, but also through a civil society organized in interest groups, community associations, municipal institutions, and advocacy bodies. A global ethic would amount to little if it is not accompanied by measures to bring democracy closer to people and make markets more mindful of equity. These programmatic dimensions, however, are beyond the scope of this paper.

Democracy began with a cry for liberty, equality, and fraternity. We have achieved much with respect to the first and at least recognized a commitment to the second of these goals. But the third has been overwhelmed by individualism. The principal task of a global ethic is to correct this neglect and assert the obligations of solidarity.

Endnotes

1 - The views expressed in this are those of the author and do not necessarily reflect those of the United Nations. They draw on various statements made by him at preparatory meetings for the World Summit on Social Development, held at Copenhagen, 1992. His principal debt is to the Coordinator of this Copenhagen Summit, Jacques Baudot, and to the organizing spirit of the Triglav Circle, Barbara Baudot, for their insistence on recognizing the ethical dimension of social development.

2 - Francis Fukuyama, *The End of History and the Last Man* (New York: The Free Press, 1992). In fairness to Fukuyama, one must note his later work which recognizes the perils of individualism. See Francis Fukuyama, *Trust, The Social Virtues and the Creation of Prosperity* (New York: The Free Press, 1995).

3 - Michael J. Sandel, *Democracy and its Discontents* (Cambridge, MA: Harvard University Press, 1996), 177.

4 - Minimum wage legislation, labor rights, social welfare provisions, and development assistance are all examples of value-based bounds or unrequited transfers.

5 - This programmatic dimension is not developed in this paper.

6 - United Nations, *Partnerships for a Global Community: Annual Report on the Work of the Organisation, 1998*, by Kofi A. Annan (1998), 6.

7 - Karl Marx argued that the logic of cost-benefit calculation would inform all social relations in a capitalist economy

8 - The call for a global ethic has come recently from the Commission on Global Governance in their report, *Our Global Neighbourhood* (Oxford: Oxford University Press, 1995). Also UNESCO, *Our Creative Diversity*, by the World Commission on Culture and Diversity, 1996.

9 - Jurgen Habermas, *La paix perpetuelle, le bicentenaire d'une idee kantienne* (1996) quoted in, Mireille Delmas-Marty, "Three Challenges to a Common Law for Humanity," in *Archive of Participant Contributions of the Universal Ethics Project* (Paris: UNESCO, 1998), 86.

10 - Quoted in Brian Barry, "Against Cultural Relativism" in *Archive of Participant Contributions of the Universal Ethics Project* (Paris: UNESCO, 1998), 65.

11 - Sir Stuart Hampshire, "Address to Second Meeting of the UNESCO Universal Ethics Project," in *Archive of Participant Contributions of the Universal Ethics Project* (Paris: UNESCO, 1998), 128.

12 - This usage of the French word "integriste" as a better substitute for fundamentalist is suggested in Sir Ralf Dahrendorf, "Towards the Twenty-First Century" in *The Oxford History of the Twentieth Century*, eds. Michael Howard and Wm. Roger Louis (Oxford: Oxford University Press, 1998).

13 - Sandel, 322.

14 - John Rawls, *A Theory of Justice* (Cambridge, MA: Harvard University Press, 1971); John Rawls, *Political Liberalism* (New York: Columbia University Press, 1993).

15 - Brian Barry, "Against Cultural Relativism," in *Archive of Participant Contributions of the Universal Ethics Project* (Paris, UNESCO, May 1998, (mimeo), 69.

16 - The global processes that have dealt with ethical issues include all of the processes that deal with Human Rights and the cycle of UN Conferences held in the nineties, notably the Conference on Environment and Development held at Rio de Janeiro in 1992, the World Conference on Human Rights held at Vienna in 1993, the Conference on Population and Development, held at Cairo in 1994, the World Summit on Social Development, held at Copenhagen in 1995, and the Fourth World Conference on Women held at Beijing in 1995.

17 - The Latin "con-sensus" means "feeling with." This is presumably obscured for people who misspell it with a c which suggests – if anything – some sort of counting procedure see Brian Barry, "Against Cultural Relativism," 56.

18 - Samuel Fleischaker, "From Cultural Diversity to Universal Ethics: Three Models," in *Archive of Participant Contributions of the Universal Ethics Project* (Paris: UNESCO, 1998), 102. According to Fleischaker the term "culture" was coined in the late 18th and early 19th century by the followers of Herder to "find a secular replacement for [the] network of daily practices that religions had once underwritten."

19 - Ibid 109, 110.

20 - John Rawls, "The Domain of the Political and Overlapping Consensus," in *New York University Law Review* (1989): 233-55, reprinted in John Rawls, "The Domain of the Political and Overlapping Consensus," in *Contemporary Political Philosophy,* eds. Robert E Goodin and Philip Pettit (Oxford: Blackwell Publishers, 1997), 275-276.

21 - Sir Stuart Hampshire, "Address to Second Meeting" 128.

22 - The reference here is to the growing involvement of non-governmental organizations in the diplomatic processes of the United Nations. The number who have consultative status with the Economic and Social Council has gone up from 41 in 1948 to 1,521 in 1998. They constitute a civil society in the sense that they are free associations, not under the tutelage of governments or international bureaucracies, and have a significant influence on policy. There are also many instances of norms set by non-governmental organizations to coordinate and regulate the behavior of members. On the characterization of civil society see Charles Taylor, "Invoking Civil Society," *Philosophical Arguments* (1995): 204-224. Reprinted in Charles Taylor, "Invoking Civil Society," in *Contemporary Political Philosophy,* eds. Robert E Goodin and Philip Pettit (Oxford: Blackwell Publishers, 1997), 303-335.

23 - Tocqueville in his *Democracy in America* draws attention to the educative role of town meetings and municipal institutions.

24 - Richard Falk, "The Making of Global Citizenship" in *Global Visions: Beyond the New World Order,* eds. Jeremy Brecher, John Brown Child, and Jill Cutler, (Boston: South End Press, 1993), quoted in Michael J. Sandel, *Democracy and its Discontents* (Cambridge MA: Harvard University Press, 1996), 341.

25 - Mireille Delmas-Marty, "Three Challenges to a Common Law for Humanity," in *Archive of Participant Contributions of the Universal Ethics Project* (Paris: UNESCO, 1998), 86.

45

CHAPTER 2

SECULARISM, GLOBALIZATION, AND THE ROLE OF THE STATE: A PLEA FOR RENEWAL

Richard Falk

> How to hold secure one's own moral and spiritual self, one's personal, reflective destiny—amidst the crushing institutional forces of the state, but also of the marketplace and, yes, the church in its decidedly secular aspect.
>
> *Robert Coles*[1]

> That a delicate shuttle should have woven together the heavens, industry, texts, souls and moral law—this remains uncanny, unthinkable, unseemly.
>
> *Bruno Latour*[2]

Points of Departure

Secularism is difficult to disentangle from kindred ideas of "the Western Enlightenment heritage," "modernity," "rationalism" and "The Age of Reason." There is about these widely used terms a shared sense of worldliness, of scientific method, of suspicion about claims of transcendence, and a refusal to be bound by tradition. Instead, there exists a belief in progress, in technological innovation, in Western superiority and destiny. Secularism is also tied historically and ideologically to the fate of the sovereign state as the primary organizing unit of world order. Thus, at a moment when these keystone terms are all subject to doubt and controversy, the challenge of situating "secularism" in relation to religion, and otherwise, is indeed formidable.

The secular character of the state was an invention of Western Europe that took hold of the Western political imagination in the 17th century, and emerged powerfully in response to specific historical factors. Secularism as an intellectual, and later ideological, current was, of course, a broader phenomenon than the ideological identity of the state. Its main tenets were rooted in the desirability of grounding knowledge and the governance of society on the non-religious foundations of scientific rationality to the extent possible. As such, secularism and modernity are closely associated, and to be contrasted with medievalism, which above all stresses the fusing of political and religious institutions and authority on the basis of faith in shared transcendent truth. To the extent that modernity is itself now being partially superseded by a series of developments associated with "globalization," the status and nature, and above all, the monolithic character of secularism is also being drawn into question from a variety of different angles.[3] The same sense of rupture can be expressed futuristically as well, often by deploying the terminology of postmodernism.[4]

Secularism as the foundation for the orientation of the modern European state was intimately associated with the struggle to limit the impact of religion on the public order, but perhaps even more so to confine ecclesiastical influence to civil society. Religious warfare in Europe, culminating in the Thirty Years War, produced a broad political consensus that the role of religion was a matter to be decided within the confines of territorial sovereignty. Religiously motivated intervention became unacceptable. A further intertwined, yet distinct, development involved internal relations between state and society with respect to the proper role of religion. Particularly important was the emergent view that the state should become neutral with respect to the religious orientation of its population, and that the ruler is obliged to uphold the freedom of conscience and belief of all citizens by adhering to an ethos of toleration.[5] In a genuine sense, the international movement to protect the religious liberty of individuals marked, in effect, the origins of international human rights, and although often not implemented in practice, at least provided a benchmark for assessing the behavior of states.

This secularist outcome was far from being a foregone conclusion. There was an established widespread assumption that the stability of a state and the loyalty and obedience of the people within a given set of territorial limits was crucially dependent on a sense of identity and solidarity arising from adherence to a common religion. Further, it was widely believed that religious disunity in civil society would breed struggles by opposed tendencies to control the state, and was almost certain to produce either oppression by the dominant religion or periodic civil war between rival religions seeking control over the state. This belief in the benefits of religious unity provided the rationale that underlay the maxim *cuius regio eius religio*. Only after much turmoil was this ethos of religiously homogeneous states successfully challenged by the internal application of the secularist alternative ushering in an era of religious tolerance.[6]

Some account must also be taken of the degree to which nationalism and patriotism moved into the vacuum created by this secularist rejection of religious identity for the state, thereby paving the way for modern forms of mass warfare and interventionism.[7] Closely related to the secularist stance is the degree to which such states were particularly susceptible to "realist" world pictures of a fragmented humanity in which the outer limits of community were co-terminus with territorial boundaries.[8] The medieval world of the West was much more sensitive to the non-territorial claims of Christendom, and the identity flowing therefrom. With the recent rediscoveries of civilization-wide identity, especially given the diminishing importance of states, there is once more a widespread feeling of community larger than state and nation, and linked to civilization and world religion, but still not inclusive of all humanity.[9]

Nations relied on the idea of sovereignty to justify the concentration of power internally, and then later in relation to external actors. The concept of sovereignty reinforced the view that the leaders of the state were accountable, if at all, only to their own citizenry when they acted internationally and that war was discretionary for the sovereign state, subject only to the restraints of prudence and rationality.[10] It is only in this century that a slow and inconsistent process of external accountability emerged, recently evident in the Hague Tribunal on War Crimes of the Former Yugoslavia, the establishment of the International Criminal Court, and the prosecution of the former Chilean dictator, Auguste Pinochet. The indictment of Slobodan Milosevic in March 1999, while a sitting head of state, was an additional move in the direction of international accountability, but somewhat tainted by being issued in the midst of the NATO air campaign against Yugoslavia over its actions in Kosovo.[11]

A major concern in this paper is to explore the impact of secularism upon political life, especially as it bears upon the changing and varied role of the state facing a range of contemporary challenges in differing civilizational circumstances. In essence, the nature of secularism, as it evolved in Europe, altered with a changing societal setting and, it has also adapted to very disparate circumstances in the course of a series of borrowings by non-European countries during this century. There is, then, an interplay between trying to identify several varieties of secularism through time and across space, with the complementary inquiry into whether the secular state is resilient enough to cope with the denationalizing challenges of globalization. And, if so, how this will affect our understanding of its character.[12] In effect, does secularism have a future in an increasingly globalized world? And even more crucially, does the global resurgence of religion challenge the prevalence of secularism during the modern era?

There is another aspect to this inquiry into the displacement of secularism. The emergence of international human rights, in the course of the last several decades, has imposed on governments a set of requirements to uphold religious freedom in accordance with notions of tolerance. In a sense, the traditional stress on secularism seems superfluous in relation to the old agenda of protecting religious pluralism or ensuring that the state was autonomous in relation to internal and external ecclesiastic authorities and theological claims. At the same time, the virtues of "secularism" are very much being vigorously upheld in a number of countries currently confronting one or another form of religious nationalism. But, the focus of concern seems significantly different than the earlier European experience.

It is less a matter of protecting the freedom of religion than it is of fearing the socially and politically oppressive impacts of a religious state using its coercive powers against those accused of violating religious orthodoxy, in some way, decreeing punishment. Notoriously, such a tendency was dramatized by Ayatollah Khomeini's fatwa against Salmon Rushdie for the alleged apostasy of his novel, *The Satanic Verses*.[13] In this respect, the typical adversary of such a non-Western religious state is not secularism, as such, but Westernization, its decadence, and its responsibility for the destruction of indigenous traditions and identities, including those associated with religion, or more specifically, with "the true religion." Iran, in the first decade or so of its revolutionary existence typified this pattern, but has now retreated somewhat. It now cautiously accepts the view that for an Islamic state to persist and flourish it must respect the diversity of beliefs among its citizenry and it would not jeopardize its Islamic identity by embracing modern science and technology, despite their Western origins.[14]

These themes inform the inquiry of this paper: first of all, the original adoption of secularism by the modern state in the West as it progressed internally from absolutism to constitutionalism, and its mixed legacy; second, a brief consideration of the dogmatically anti-religious secularism of the Marxist/Leninist tradition; third, the extensions of secularism to three non-Western countries, mainly located outside the orbit of the Judeo-Christian tradition; fourth, the pressures on the secular state arising from migration and capital flows that are characteristic of the current phase of globalization; fifth, a short meditation on the uncertain future of the secular state as traditionally conceived; and, finally, a plea for a reconstructed secularism that could also give rise, either to a new kind of "compassionate state," or could facilitate "a world of regions." Either eventuality would certainly encourage the respiritualization of political life, and reconnect the civic virtues of a regionalized and globalized citizenry with religious devotion and practice, nurturing the recovery of the sacred in the setting of religious and political pluralism. This respiritualization seems to be the most likely, and hopeful next phase in world order.

The Initial West European Embrace of Secularism

It is difficult to separate the rise of the modern state in Europe from the adoption of a secular outlook by political leaders. As Ernst Cassirer and others have convincingly argued, the statist embrace of secularism should not be confused with an anti-religious climate of fundamental ideas or popular opinions.[15] The story of the rise of the secular state is complicated, confusing, variable, and somewhat contradictory, although the dominant trend was evident. The Peace of Westphalia, concluded in 1648, brought the religious wars to an end. It is generally treated as the starting point of the modern state system. The state there endorsed the principle of sovereignty vis-à-vis religion, and pledged not to make war or engage in intervention against other states so as to impose a particular religion.

Secularism, in its central sense of worldliness and denial of transcendence, underlay this move in specifying the character of the state. The secularizing motivation was also associated, at the time, with several other related ideas: repudiating a destructive path of warfare associated with "holy wars;" consolidating the authority of the centralized state in relation to Rome, especially for Catholic countries; and, minimizing the clerical or ecclesiastical role in the dynamics of government. But there were other tendencies abroad at the time that did link secularism to a repudiation of tradition and superstition, which were seen as elements of the medieval foreground inimical to the rise of commerce, and later of industry.

On this path of repudiation, in relation to the past, "the modern mind" of empirical science and rationality emerged. Again as Cassirer clearly shows, the concern was not with a rejection of beliefs associated with a religious mentality, which was exhibited even by those seminal scientific minds that shaped the emergence of the modern. The main impulse of secularism was to remove religion from the social domain of public activity where its influence was hopelessly intertwined with outmoded and constraining traditions associated with magic, taboos, rituals, inhibitions, superstitions, and the like.[16] Indeed, the major intellectual efforts to move toward modernity were careful to insist upon their acceptance of religious truth, even while the animating mood was to set forth new bases for thought and action that rested on reason rather than revelation or faith.

The situation varied from country to country in Europe, and from time to time within countries, making generalizations misleading. In France, the Enlightenment thinking of the 18th century adopted a definite anti-clerical outlook that was combined with the view that, from a rational perspective, religion, as such, was little more than an assemblage of superstitions. The French Revolution, and its Napoleonic aftermath, initiated a crucial modern trend involving a transfer of political identity from religion to nation. As religion was privatized, the public morality of the state was premised on nationalism, giving birth to a new creature, the "nation-state." This new creature was half descriptive, half myth. It represented for some a reality, for others an aspiration, and for still others a project to be supported or resisted.[17] The notion of "nation" remains, to this day, deeply ambiguous—partaking both of the juridical power of the state to confer nationality, and of the primordial sense of nationality arising from shared ethnic memories as confirmed by a common religion, history, language, customs, dress. Many contemporary tragedies arise from these two meanings of nations coming into violent contention, especially when the primordial sense of nationality is awakened to challenge its submergence beneath the juridical claims of nationality.[18]

In the laudable effort to ensure an end to religious warfare and persecution, secularism, as a posture toward reality, incorporated several other features that have disturbing implications for the future. The first tendency was to associate a secularized public order with an amoral and instrumental rationality that was devoid of spiritual, and even ethical content. The modern state, from an early stage, invited into its midst a kind of technocratic sensibility that was purely manipulative in character, and without moral scruple.

This technocratic personality is illustrated by such prototypic figures in recent times as Albert Speer and Robert McNamara, men who served their respective states unconditionally on the basis of an extreme reliance on decontextualized reason, enabling the commission of massive crimes with a clear conscience.[19]

An intensified variation of this kind of rationalist outlook came to assert a dominant influence on the way the state conceived of the world. It moved from the outlook of Machiavelli, who entreated the prince to be unscrupulous in upholding the well-being of the city, to Hobbes, who incorporated the Newtonian view of force-fields to portray the interplay of a world of sovereign states. Hobbes, who had translated the great classical work of Thucydides, believed that in relations among states power alone mattered. Hobbes portrayed the international setting as altogether lacking a societal character, making it incapable of providing a legal framework or even a code of comity and civility. In these respects, his views contrast with those of Immanuel Kant, who depicted an evolutionary view of international relations as gradually assuming the shape of a humane and commercially guided world civil society.[20]

Of course, secularism as a posture did not necessitate such outcomes. Other possibilities were present, but within the historical circumstances of trying to free society more generally from the shackles of medievalism, the secular outlook tended to get merged with certain epistemological and geopolitical tendencies. Among the paths not taken was the possibility of a more skeptical view of the role of logic and reason, an alternative depicted by Montaigne as opposed to the prevailing approach deriving from Descartes.[21]

The secular state clearly proved itself capable of inhabiting a religious society, as the case of the United States exemplified in many ways. As well observed in the early 19th century by Alexis de Tocqueville, "religion in America takes no direct part in the government of society, but nevertheless it must be regarded as the foremost of the political institutions of that country."[22] Secularism has served well by separating church and state, allowing religious pluralism to flourish at the level of civil society, and yet keeping alive the relevance of religious ideals to political undertakings.

The Marxist/Leninist Challenge to Liberal Secularism

There is one strong variant of secularism that moved from the same Western historical background to adopt an aggressively anti-religious outlook, and that is, of course, the ideology and practice associated with Marxism/Leninism. From Marx's famous strictures against religion as "the opiate of the people," with anti-revolutionary effects, to the ultra-empirical embrace of atheism, the position of Communist thought has illustrated a radically anti-religious potentiality, present in the secularist demand that the state refrain from imposing any particular religion within its borders or beyond.

This kind of "secular fundamentalism" often led to the "return of the repressed" even in surprising new guises, and suggests the futility of seeking to stamp out religious belief. The strength of religious commitments led Communist authorities to back off somewhat from the initial Soviet impulse to destroy the religious dimension of society. Indeed, some Marxist writing came to the point of acknowledging that religious faith can generate welcome commitments to achieve social justice. Movements in certain economically poor countries, especially in Latin America, adopted forms of "liberation theology" that resembled some features of Marxism.[23] Further, the veneration of Lenin, in the Soviet Union, definitely assumed a "religious" character, with chapels set aside and statues of the departed leader illuminated by soft light, or even by candles. The latest episode, confirming the vitality of religiosity, is the rise and repression of the Falun Gong "spiritual movement" in China.[24]

Non-Western Adaptations of Secularism

Along with the acceptance of the statist model for political community, many non-Western states have self-consciously emphasized their secularist identity, whereas others have not. Secularism, as such, functions more explicitly in these countries as a principle of order—sometimes contested—than it does currently in the West. There, it is part of the cultural debate, but rarely articulated as directly relevant to controversies about public policy. Secularism for non-Western countries is deliberately borrowed from the West; it is

55

not indigenous to such countries, and thus is not nearly as deeply rooted in the cultural life and historical memory of such societies.

The borrowing of secularist orientations by non-Western societies must be seen in a very different light than their adaptation to societies where Christianity prevailed. In such settings, the motivations were different, either to repudiate religion in favor of modernity or to provide minority religions with the assurances that they would not be persecuted under the aegis of state power. Secularism was not, in such countries, trying to affirm the values of a particular religion while making sure that different doctrinal interpretations of its beliefs did not induce violence and strife. Such a role for secularism might have been adopted in certain Islamic countries where the Sunni/Shi'ia split is prominent, but it does not seem to have been an important factor. Instead, the secular state was deemed to be anti-religious and pro-modern, with the assumption being that the two projects were mutually exclusive. Thus to encourage a modern state, as in Turkey or Iran, it was seen as necessary by its leaders to cast doubt on religious devoutness, even in the private domain—putting religion on the defensive socially, as well as politically.

Also, for many non-Western countries, the path to modernity was based on a cultural heritage that did not rest on the neat dualisms bestowed on the West by Greek thought. Such heritages emphasized the unity of opposites, and the artificiality of separating religion and politics. Of course, it is adapted for specific ends, varying with context.

"Secularism," currently functions in Turkey mainly as a code word for containing Islamic "secular" influence. This includes disallowing religiously oriented political parties to compete on a level playing field for access to state power and public sector finance. There are dangers in such a course, including driving the Islamic political movement in more extremist and violent directions.

The ideology of the Iranian revolution was directed against the secular Western ideas of modernism brought to the country by the Shah. Secularism was, thus, as identified with the "foreign," "decadent," and "modern," as it was with a liberal political order that limited religious influence. Khomeini was a powerful symbol for an Iranian recovery of tradition and independence, as well as for the return of religion to a dominating role in the public sphere.

The current leader has more moderate leanings and espouses the secular virtues of moderation, support for science and technology, and a commitment to normal diplomatic relations with non-Islamic states. Nonetheless, Iran still retains the structure and many of the practices of a theocratic state that rejects, as immoral, the idea that religion should be confined to civil private domains, or that the state should not be, itself, Islamic in character.

In India, secularism has less to do with avoiding a religious orientation within the state than it does with ensuring social peace in a highly pluralistic, and volatile, society. Hinduism does not have a clerical tradition in the Western sense, and there is no history of religious rule in India, partly, no doubt, because the caste system deliberately separates power and wealth from religious guidance in a pervasive manner.

The religious tension in India was resolved by Nehru's modernization of the state, modeled on the West. Yet, Nehru's India was morally sensitive, in a manner that was quite alien to Western styles of statecraft. Nehru's secularism, which was pronounced in certain respects, did not preclude a strong sense of normative identity for India as non-aligned, as anti-nuclear, and as in solidarity with the Third World.

The Relevance of Globalization

Against such an inconclusive background, and given the transformation of the world by the process of globalization, it is necessary to recontextualize the consideration of "secularism." Should secularism be viewed primarily on its own in relation to the claim that worldliness is sufficient as a comprehensive posture toward reality? Or, does secularism depend, for contemporary relevance, upon freeing itself from a close identification with the sovereign state and its role, and associating identity and order more closely with the wider settings of region, civilization, and world?

Globalization is an elusive, background reality that can be interpreted from many different angles, with important implications for the state and its role.[25] The wider trends toward religious resurgence, micro-nationalism, and ethnic moves for self-determination seem linked overall to the declining capacity of the state to function as a "nation-state," that is, to provide a continuing basis for loyalty and patriotism.[26] Appadurai puts this issue of state decline in arresting language by observing that the state system: "appears poorly equipped to deal with the interlinked diasporas of people and images that mark the here and now. Nation-states, as units in a complex interactive system, are not very likely to be the arbiters of the relationship between globality and modernity."[27]

The relevance of secularism to this changing context of governance is difficult to assess, especially in light of cultural diversity. For many non-Western settings, there is a single dominant religion that is taken for granted as the basis of public morality, the idea of either/or dualism is culturally alien and unacceptable, and the compatibility of science and religion is not, and in many cases never was, an issue. Of course, such non-Western societies have other serious issues bearing on minority rights, religious extremism, and an educational system ill-equipped to provide scientific training.

To a significant extent, secularism as a mediating orientation embodied in the modern state was a Western adaptation to a series of specific problems. These issues derived from the combined impact of the deep cleavage between Catholics and Protestants, the classical Greek dualistic approach to problem-solving, and the convergent pressure to liberate science from religious dogma (a dynamic dramatized through the ages by Galileo's encounter with the Roman Church). Secularism incorporates an attitude toward reason and knowledge that introduces a dogmatism of its own, based on the supposed access of reason and empirical observation to reality and truth. As Toulmin and others have shown, this Cartesian strain in modern Western thought is partially a compensation for the loss of religious certitude arising from "the death of God."[28] Today, with civilizational diversity extending, in many countries, well beyond Christianity, and with Protestant/Catholic bellicosity, a matter of rather remote historical memory, it is questionable whether secularism remains the most socially acceptable way to reconcile religious and worldly concerns.

Thus, in a globalizing world the relevance of secularism seems limited. Many of its goals can be more directly and effectively pursued by way of international human rights, and their specific application to problems of religious liberty, including the freedom of citizens to reject a religious identity for themselves. There are special concerns about the way in which a religious state handles a range of worldly matters, but whether the secular logic of strict separation is a useful approach seems very much in doubt. This doubt is reinforced by the tendency of the state to diminish its social activist role, given the ideological impact of neo-liberal globalization. Over the last two hundred years, capitalist states have exhibited a range of possible adjustments, beginning with the cruelty of early comprador capitalism based purely on market forces, as portrayed by Charles Dickens and Émile Zola, to the compassionate engagement of Scandinavian social democracy. The neo-liberal state, with its bias toward privatization, its repudiation of welfare policies, its vulnerability to international competition, its emphasis on fiscal discipline, and its downsizing of expenditures on non-defense public goods, is definitely pushing toward a mean-spirited recreation of "the cruel state."[29]

With the defining role of the state increasingly related to the facilitation of efficient market participation, issues of human well-being are pushed into the background, although due to the realities of electoral accountability, such concerns still remain on the political agenda. In this context, secularism, as such, does not seem to address, directly enough, the causes of human suffering or contemporary forms of alienation, and the means of cure; nor does the state seem capable, in the present setting, to recreate itself as "the compassionate state."

Finally, the normative potential of the state has been seriously eroded by the neo-liberal climate of opinion that has dominated governmental policy since the end of the Cold War. It seems doubtful that the secular state can again become the agency for compassion toward the weak and marginalized under these circumstances. For a variety of reasons, the extent such a possibility exists is likely to depend on wider frameworks of political identification and governance, the most promising of which is the European Union. From this perspective, the most hopeful secular future seems based on the image of "the compassionate region" or some kind of "global social contract" that is committed to the implementation of the full range of human rights. These would include economic and social rights, that engender a new climate of postmodern religiosity that is ecologically sensitive and culturally inclusive, and embrace also those who are most marginal and disadvantaged. In the background there remains the struggle to preserve the advantages associated with markets and technological innovation, while recentering political life on the well-being of the human person in his/her individual and collective endeavors.

Is There a Future for the Western Secular State?

Such an inquiry is distinct from the question "is there a future for the state?" The underlying question here is whether secularism has outlived its usefulness in the West, especially given some special problems posed by intensifying globalization, and its fraternal twin, fragmentation. With the decline of the state as a creative social actor, the state can no longer provide as satisfying a basis for political identity as when it was relatively more homogeneous and autonomous. Transnational ethnic, religious, ideological identities are of growing importance, and territorial affiliation seems generally less important. Other models of the state are challenging the secular state, especially the unexpectedly popular ethnic or religious state.

The question focuses also on the relevance of the secular dimension in which the cultural heterogeneity of the territorial space has increased greatly and where intra-Christian tensions have mostly abated. There appears to be even greater need for the state to ensure an ethos of toleration that is operative on a behavioral level, but the priority is now inter-civilizational rather than intra-civilizational. If the secular state is to revive its role under these altered circumstances of economic and cultural globalization, then it needs to turn its emphasis towards inter-civilizational relations, starting with dialogue aimed at grasping differences and uniformities, seeking pathways to comprehension, compromise, diversity, and areas of agreed universality.

Of course, civilizations themselves are in internal tension, with many diverse and even contradictory tendencies, suggesting the relevance of intra-civilizational reflection and self-criticism as well. Such a course of action is especially relevant in the West, which has so often projected its power to control, exploit, and even exterminate other civilizations during its history. It has been fortified in these ventures by both crusading religious and crusading secular attitudes, especially the conviction that Western beliefs and practices have universal validity.[30]

If secularism is to have a vital role to play in the future, then it needs to shift its focus in these directions, taking account of the new setting that is undermining the autonomy of the state as territorially and nationalistically conceived. It seems evident that such a reformulated secularism, which would be based on a blend of civilizational and species identity would require a religious, as well as an ethical/human rights foundation. Thus, a reformulated secularism for the 21st century might begin to disavow the traditional separations of religion and politics, and instead explore the possibilities for their creative reunion, while being mindful of the need to protect political and social space for religious diversity.

Toward a Reconstructed Secularism

There is, finally, the possibility of "rethinking secularism" in the specific setting of given Western states. Here, at least, the heritage is relatively clear, and its contributions remain of great importance in the historical course of Western development. It is also true that secularism became unnecessarily fused with technocratic rationalism and political realism at the level of the state, and that these features can be and are being "deconstructed" by various forms of critical thought. On such a basis, one can conceive of a reconstructed secularism as facilitating the revival of support, in civil society for a new variant of the compassionate state. This variant must not be merely a rerun of social democracy or even "the Third Way" of Tony Blair or Anthony Giddens, but a genuinely new orientation of the state toward human well-being, which takes account of the profound changes being wrought by globalization. As such, the undertaking of this reconstructed secularism would involve the extension of human rights based on an ethos of solidarity that implies some collaboration between religion and politics, church and state, including, possibly, a reversal of the tradition of separation.

At present, in many diverse settings, individuals and groups are rediscovering their core spirituality within or without the settings provided by institutional religion. Partly this rediscovery is prompted by the deterritorializing pressures of globalization, giving more and more people a stark choice between being rootless nomads traveling the planet on behalf of global corporations and citizen pilgrims intent on a cosmopolitan journey to a better future. This better future can be associated with "humane governance" for the planet, a process calling into question the heritage of political violence and cultural exploitation and imagining a future community that celebrates diversity, while affirming the solidarity of the human species.[31]

To the extent such a political reality takes shape, secularism as we have known it will seem anachronistic, and the religious underpinnings of governance will seem so natural as to be taken for granted. Such spiritualizing anticipations may appear utopian at this moment, but history has strange ways of surprising us, not always unhappily! The fact of inhabiting this space and time between a discouraging acknowledgment of hyper-modernist global capitalism and the hopeful reemergence of a centered spirituality gives a mysterious and precarious tone to any sensitive assessment of future human prospects.[32]

The foundations for such a future are the main modes of thought and action that entail "a recovery of the sacred." In a profound philosophical sense, such a process is an overdue corrective to Nietzsche's electrifying pronouncement over a century ago that modernity had killed God. In this sense, the most intriguing challenge of post-modernity, here conceived as a space for spiritual and normative creativity, is to resurrect "spirituality." This does not necessarily mean to resurrect "spirituality" as a theistic claim of divinity, but at the very least, the reaffirmation of belief in the mystery of life and the sacred character of the created world, which will only be sustained to the extent that it evokes awe as well as understanding.

It is the exemplification of this way of conceiving of the postmodern moment that makes the citizen pilgrim such a potentially inspirational and transformative political actor. For it is this bearing of witness to the meaning of life and human destiny as essentially a spiritual endeavor, that provides us with the needed radical alternative to the global mentality fostered by the overbearing ethos of the capitalist market. Such an encounter is the most crucial site of struggle in the early 21st century. Whether secularism, as we have understood it, survives this struggle in a mutated form, or is superseded altogether, is among the great unanswerable questions as we await the unfolding of this new millennium.

Endnotes

1 - Robert Coles, *The Secular Mind* (Princeton, NJ: Princeton University Press, 1999), 166.

2 - Bruno Latour, *We Have Never Been Modern* (Cambridge, MA: Harvard University Press, 1993), 5.

3 - Significantly, at this time there are various uses of the terminology of "the new medievalism" to describe world order, reflecting the rise of overlapping authority sources displacing the clarity of "a world of states." For an influential formulation see Hedley Bull, *The Anarchical Society: A Study of Order in World Politics* (New York: Columbia University Press, 1977); also, Andrew Linklater, *The Transformation of Political Community* (Columbia, SC: University of South Carolina Press, 1997); the use of "medievalism" as a metaphor for an emergent world order has not been extended to the revival of the religious state, but it could be, if qualified.

4 - There are many post modernisms, but in particular is the split between deconstructive postmodernism that consists of radical criticism of modernist pretensions of knowledge and ethics and reconstructive (or restructive) postmodernism that seeks to nurture an emergent respiritualization of culture and society. For an excellent exploration along these latter lines see David Ray Griffin, ed., *Spirituality and Society: Postmodern Visions* (Albany, NY: State University of New York Press, 1988); Charlene Spretnak, *The Resurgence of the Real: Body, Nature, and Place in a Hypermodern World* (Reading, MA: Addison-Wesley, 1997); see also Chellis Glendinning, *My Name is Chellis and I'm in Recovery from Western Civilization* (Boston, MA: Shambhala, 1994); David Ray Griffin and Richard Falk, eds., *Postmodern Politics for a Planet in Crisis* (Albany, NY: State University of New York Press, 1993).

5 - For an account of this point stressing the influence of John Locke's *Letter Concerning Toleration* see W. Cole Durham, Jr., "Perspectives on Religious Liberty: A Comparative Framework," in Johan D. van der Vyver and John Witte, Jr., eds., *Religious Human Rights in Global Perspective* (The Hague: Kluwer, 1996), 1-44, esp. 7-12.

6 - See Natan Lerner, "Religious Human Rights Under the United Nations," in van der Vyver and Witte, Jr., note 3, 79-134, at 83-6. Note here that the secularizing moves have two dimensions: first, and earlier, the agreed prohibition upon religious wars between sovereign states; and secondly, and largely via domestic initiatives, the neutralization of state and ruler via the religious orientation of citizen and subject.

7 - Arjun Appadurai, *Modernity at Large: Cultural Dimensions of Globalization* (Minneapolis, MN: University of Minnesota Press, 1996), 27-47, 178-99.

8 - A wide ranging commentary along these lines is to be found in the latest book of Hans Küng, *A Global Ethic for Global Politics and Economics* (New York: Oxford University Press, 1998), esp. 1-28.

9 - See Samuel P. Huntington, *The Clash of Civilization and the Remaking of the Global Order* (New York: Simon & Schuster, 1996).

10 - See Raymond Aron, *Peace and War: A Theory of International Relations* (Garden City, NY: Doubleday, 1966). Such a statist view was always challenged, although marginally, by a normative counter-tradition associated with the just war doctrine, and more recently, by the efforts of international law to prohibit all non-defensive uses of force in international relations.

11 - It is also tainted by the evident unwillingness to arrest the main indictments of Serb leaders flowing out of "ethnic cleansing" of Moslems in the Bosnian War. See Philip Shenon, "War Crimes Suspects Seen as Living Openly in Bosnia," *New York Times*, 13 December 1999, A14.

12 - For one account of globalization in relation to the state see Falk, *Predatory Globalization: A Critique* (Cambridge, UK: Polity, 1999).

13 - For a valuable exploration and critique (from within an Islamic frame of reference) see Mehdi Mozaffari, *Fatwa: Violence and Discourtesy* (Aarhus, Denmark: Aarhus University Press, 1998).

14 - Such is the viewpoint propounded in lectures by the outstanding Iranian scholar and thinker, A. Soroush, Princeton University, November 1998.

15 - See Cassirer, *The Philosophy of the Enlightenment* (Princeton, NJ: Princeton University Press, 1951), esp. 134-96, 234-74.

16 - Cassirer, 161.

17 - For minority peoples, the nation-state project was, and remains, deeply threatening. It was generally experienced as a fusion between the dominant nationality and state power, with negative effects for others.

18 - Even if not activated, national minorities may suffer passively, enduring subordination and humiliation.

19 - For illuminating discussion of the general problematique, with explicit reference to McNamara see John Ralston Saul, *Voltaire's Bastards: The Dictatorship of Reason in the West* (New York: Free Press, 1992), 23-25.

20 - See the important modification of Hobbesian realism by identifying the rudimentary, yet significant, societal dimensions of international life despite its anarchical structures, in H. Bull, *The Anarchical Society*, note 1.

21 - For an expansion of this argument on behalf of a different possible modernism deriving from Montaigne see Stephen Toulmin, *Cosmopolis: The Hidden Agenda of Modernity* (New York: Free Press, 1990). There is an irony present in the triumph of the Cartesian view of modernity. Descartes, as a religious sensibility, tried above all to remove doubt from the workings of reason. As such, he transferred the quality of certainty from the religious domain of faith to the secular domains of science and politics, providing the foundations for secular fundamentalism and political absolutism.

22 - *Democracy in America* (London: Oxford University Press, H. Reeve tr. of 1835 edition, 1946), 235; see also 238-239, 304.

23 - See Huston Smith, *Beyond the Post-Modern Mind* (Wheatley, IL: Quest Books, 1989), 191-2.

24 - According to newspaper accounts, more than 35,000 members of Falun Gong were "detained" by Chinese authorities in the period between July 22—the day the group was banned—and October 30, 1999. See John Pomfret, "China Is Reported to Detain 35,000," *The Washington Post*, 30 November 1999, A22, A24.

25 - For one line of interpretation that focuses on the changing role of the state see Falk, *Predatory Globalization* (Cambridge, UK: Polity, 1999).

26 - See Appadurai, 6-9.

27 - Ibid., 19.

28 - See *Cosmopolis*, note 15.

29 - See George Soros, *The Crisis of Global Capitalism* (New York: Public Affairs, 1998); John Gray, *False Dawn: The Delusions of Global Capitalism* (New York: New Press, 1999).

30 - For an illuminating presentation of anti-imperial counter-hegemonic thinking by leading Enlightenment figures see excellent article by Sankar Muthu, "Enlightenment Anti-Imperialism," *Social Research* 66, no. 4.

31 - This perspective is set forth in Richard Falk, *On Humane Governance: Toward a New Global Politics* (University Park, PA: Penn State University Press, 1995).

32 - For a suggestive exploration of these emancipatory potentialities see Joel Kovel, *History and Spirit: An Inquiry into the Philosophy of Liberation* (Boston, MA: Beacon Press, 1991), esp. 197-237.

CHAPTER 3

RETHINKING THE "FOUR FREEDOMS" FOR THE GLOBAL COMMUNITY

Ruud Lubbers

Not long after I stepped down as a Prime Minister of the Netherlands, having served from 1982 until 1994, I was honored with the *Four Freedoms Award*. A few years later, I was asked to contribute to this book on ideas for an ethical and spiritual renaissance.[1] In the intervening years, I served as a part-time professor of economics lecturing on globalization and its effects on society. From the perspective of this proverbial ivory tower, I reflected on interdependence in today's globalizing world, rendered increasingly borderless by the powers of science and technology and a prevailing ideology of "free market democracy." This world is indeed different from the one that preoccupied President Roosevelt. Nevertheless, knowledge of history is essential for reflection on today's and tomorrow's socioeconomic aspirations and values.

The "Four Freedoms"

In expressing gratitude for the *Four Freedoms Award* in 1995, I recalled that President Roosevelt had mobilized resistance to National Socialism and called for this tyranny to be driven back. National Socialism used *Gleichschaltung* and dehumanization as instruments to create a new order, one that led to dehumanization and oppression. President Roosevelt set against this process a moral order, encompassing, as he so concisely put it, the "Four Freedoms": freedom of speech and expression; freedom to worship God; freedom from want; and freedom from fear.[2] These are the four pillars on which our civilization continues to rest, four assignments to keep our spirits and hearts alive.

Roosevelt articulated the "Four Freedoms" in anticipation of the *Universal Declaration of Human Rights* adopted in 1948 by the United Nations. This Declaration has since become the fundamental code of the world community. Thus, while time and events have altered the social and physical contexts of human life, repeatedly challenging these basic rights, history shows that these four fundamental freedoms remain, in the eyes of humanity, steadfast objectives for all peoples to enjoy. For these reasons, rethinking their importance is vital.

In considering the "Four Freedoms," we ask: What did they mean during the war? What do they mean now? What will they mean in the future? Essential to the understanding of these freedoms are the values that underlie them—truth, dignity, and spirituality. These are the principles according to which these freedoms can be most fully enjoyed and perpetuated, and without which they would lose much of their meaning and sustainability. These questions and concepts are examined below.

The "Four Freedoms" in World War II

Every Dutch family has its own story to tell, its own experience with war and occupation. I think back with gratitude to my parents to whom Roosevelt's "Four Freedoms" meant so much in those bleak war years. These were years dominated by fear, especially for my mother, who knew no "freedom from fear" during this time. The reign of terror began in May 1940, with the bombing of Rotterdam and the great fire; to be followed soon after by an abiding dread of the occupying forces. My father, thirty-nine at the time, managed a metalworking company. When he refused to work for the German occupying forces, he was arrested and locked up in a police cell. My mother, although terrified, mustered up courage and went to the authorities. She wanted her husband released. Why was he detained? Just because he said "No," when asked to work for the German war machine? My father was being denied precisely that freedom of speech and expression to which Roosevelt referred. The police told my mother, "He is not sympathetic to the Germans." It was as simple as that. I am still grateful to my father for standing by his principles at this crucial time. He was subsequently released, but later taken hostage, together with many others including prominent figures and ordinary citizens. This detainment ushered in a fresh period of anxiety for my mother.

Freedom from fear was something she did not have for years. On 15 August 1942, five of my father's fellow hostages were executed. The next morning he wrote to my mother : "The blow has fallen and personal danger has been averted on this occasion, thanks to our joint prayers." After a description of what happened, he continued: "We have personally managed to survive this very sad business. You know that I had resigned myself to my lot. I did not experience any fear at all, only concern for you all. It is as well that you, too, should always be prepared for the worst. All we can do is hope and pray. After all, nothing can happen to us unless God permits it, and then we must resign ourselves to His will." What my father expressed at the time was the "freedom to worship God," to which Roosevelt had referred.

Finally, we come to the fourth freedom: freedom from want. Food was universally scarce and many died of starvation in the western region of the Netherlands during the winter of 1944. As a small boy my main memory, however, is of the first spring Sunday, in April 1945, shortly after noon. We heard the sound of approaching aircraft, but this time they did not inspire fear. On the contrary, chattering excitedly, we ran upstairs and on to the flat roof to see the planes heading for our church tower, turning and then dropping their food parcels above the Kralingen Woods. This event marked the end of what has come to be known as the Hunger Winter. That was how my parents, to whom I owe so much, experienced Roosevelt's "Four Freedoms" in a very real sense, back in those dark years.

The "Four Freedoms" Fifty Years Later

As I stood to receive my "Four Freedoms" award, I was moved by the knowledge that I was now part of the tradition that is to keep these values alive. How important it has been to grow up and breathe in the free world in contrast with life under the oppressive darkness of Soviet communism and under other forms of coercion including colonialism and apartheid, which have largely been overcome in these intervening 50 years. The end of these forms of oppression can be explained in many ways. The faith and mental resistance of the brave among the oppressed peoples, however, has been an important factor.

Today, the "Four Freedoms" that Roosevelt evoked face new challenges. Referring to freedom from fear, Roosevelt pointed to one nation's fear of another nation's acts of aggression. Today, people are still calling for this type of freedom, but there are many more things to be afraid of, making such freedom all the more difficult to achieve. Since the end of the Cold War, which dominated international politics and imagination for more than a generation after the Second World War, older members of society appear to be more insecure than ever before. They fear the growth of crime in their streets that are no longer safe; they bar their doors for fear of intruders. Many of the young, on the other hand, harbor great anxiety as they anticipate unemployment. And everyone, to some extent, worries about the deterioration of the environment and the difficulties of preserving the natural world entrusted to humanity by the Creator.

Once again there are calls for freedom of speech and expression. While billions more people enjoy the liberty to express their ideas and opinions this privilege is neither absolute nor without its challenges. Only alertness will ensure that this right is not eroded by repressive regimes, or by individuals in public or private sectors in positions to oppress others. Freedom of speech can be experienced only in a climate of spiritual tolerance and respect for differing beliefs.

But, even more is required than alertness. To defend one's beliefs, a person must first be able to evolve them. To do this, there must be access to quality information. Today, information is available in vast quantities, but its very abundance is confusing. The media, especially through the Internet, brings the world to each person's doorstep 24 hours a day. Many individuals, publications, businesses, and governments are involved in this information revolution. Many are involved in good faith. But some use these communication methods for mere sensationalism and personal gain. In some countries, the tabloid press and hate radio are growing like noxious weeds in the garden of freedom of expression. These poisonous plants are a mockery of free speech and expression. Next to them, television, in efforts to attract large audiences and widespread attention for its commercials, has specialized in abundant violence. This stimulates primitive instincts and leads to the inverse of the expression of human dignity and spirit. Society is challenged again to be on guard, even in the absence of totalitarian or oppressive regimes, and to give real and good meaning to the this Freedom.

The freedom to worship God in one's own way is something no one can do without. It sounds so simple. But the privilege to worship Him or not is a fundamental necessity of life. Thus, there is a moral obligation to oppose any regime that smothers this right. This freedom is defined in Article 18 in the *Universal Declaration of Human Rights* as follows:

> Everyone has the right to freedom of thought, conscience and religion; this right includes freedom to change his religion or belief, and freedom, either alone or in a community with others and in public or in private, to manifest his religion or belief in teaching, practice, worship and observance.

Moreover, the International *Covenant on Civil and Political Right* provides in Article 20 (2) that:

> Any advocacy of national, racial or religious hatred that constitutes incitement to discrimination, hostility or violence shall be prohibited by law.[3]

This Covenant has yet to be ratified by a large number of countries and the implementation of its provisions remains a mobilizing project for persons and institutions of good will.

Presently, this freedom raises several complex issues. For many people, the everyday pressures and burdens of modern life are more than they can bear. The "spirit of the age" seems to focus only on material values, on living "horizontally" that is, living only in the present, synchronized with other people and things. Furthermore, people are confused by the many forms of fundamentalism and sectarianism they encounter. Most dangerous for freedom of religion is the rising tide of fundamentalism, which threatens to exercise oppression in open societies in the name of the "Almighty." The freedom to escape these trends is of immense importance.

Many people are also concerned that if sectarianism takes full hold, the overwhelming intensity of the here and now may sweep away respect for religion and spiritual belief. They question anxiously whether the pressures of satisfying the demands of modern everyday life in this material age will rip them away from the moorings of the vertical dimension of their lives—that dimension which anchors their present and future "being" in their historical, cultural, linguistic, and spiritual roots.

Freedom from want means the abolition of poverty and abject need, and the restoration of healthy, peaceful lives for the inhabitants of the world. After the Second World War, this freedom was largely translated into better opportunities for the underprivileged. Efforts to improve their lot have not been without success, although billions of people still live below the poverty line according to the standards of developed countries. Today, people find themselves wrestling with "new times." Roosevelt spoke of inhabitants of every nation. Increasingly, the "inhabitants of nations" confront a single world economy. This gives increased significance to rereading Roosevelt's conception of "freedom from want." In Roosevelt's words:

> Freedom from want—which, translated into world terms, means economic understandings which will secure to every nation a healthy peacetime life for its inhabitants—everywhere in the world.[4]

His message still warns the world that such economic understandings must form the basis of economic growth otherwise it will not bring about freedom from want.

Clearly, the "Four Freedoms" that Roosevelt addressed continue to be very much alive. Roosevelt took a stand against totalitarian regimes, and at the same time, he made plain that peace must be given meaning. To cherish peace is to experience a sense of responsibility. Everyday people relive the challenge of preserving values in a changing world. Year in, year out, generation after generation, people must keep the moral order alive to ensure that the whole story of "Life" will be written.

Because the world is becoming increasingly borderless for communications, economic life, technology, and the free market way of life, there are impressive results to behold in terms of the "Four Freedoms," including the general recognition of human dignity and the universal recognition of certain human rights. At the same time, an increasing number of people fear growing exclusion and poverty. Others are concerned about preserving a viable planet for future generations. Finally, societies are becoming increasingly convinced of the need to protect cultural and biological diversities.

The "Four Freedoms" in the Future[5]

The potential for the so-called world society to allow individual freedom for all its citizens, to protect pluralism, and promote developments in the fields of science and technology, as well as to conserve a healthy economy is enormous, but the risks are not small. Traditionally, most societies and governments were equipped to safeguard the quality of life through values. But, in the era of globalization with its weakening of nation-states, its virtual lack of any acceptable and recognized global authority, and its increasing prioritization of the material aspects of life as monetization and consumerism spreads, the challenges are enormous and growing.[6]

The global village, made possible by technological advances and dramatically increased economic and financial transactions on a world scale, has yet to be constructed in social, cultural, and political terms. A global market is not necessarily nor automatically a global society. Such a society requires shared values as well as cultural pluralism, common policies, and a democratic process for decision-making. Essential to the construction of a global society will be universal communication and understanding. All civilizations have a contribution to make in the search for shared values. Positive ideas for the policies, norms, and institutions of a peaceful world community will emerge only from dialogue between different cultures.[7]

Freedom of speech and expression is no longer the privilege of a few individuals or nations. It has become an element of the global common good. Increasingly, as technology generates power and gives widespread dissemination to words and images, freedom of speech is to be immersed in a spirit of tolerance for the voice of others and responsibility for the consequences of what one says, writes, or shows, as well as, respect for the truth. Moreover, each human being, in a position to influence others, should feel the obligation to identify freedom of expression with the search for the planetary common good.

Freedom of expression is defeated when the world of the media is beyond any control by democratic institutions responsible for the pursuit of the general interest. It is imperative to maintain public controls of the media through democratically established and operated institutions. Self-regulation is not sufficient in situations where individuals and companies primary objectives are to gain profit and power. To this end, balance between local, national, and international media sources must be considered. Such a balance includes respect for diversity. Moreover, information cannot be treated as an ordinary commodity, globally any more than nationally, since it is a service to humankind. Because of its potential influence on young minds, it is to be treated with a sense of the highest ethics and responsibility.

All the great religions offer moral and metaphysical insights to guide human beings in their daily life and to provide answers to fundamental questions that will never cease to torment humanity. Expressing an inescapable facet of the human condition, religions are both natural and indispensable. In their absence, individuals and societies turn to substitute gods, that is to human and material idols from which they hope to obtain power, identity, and well-being.

It is becoming increasingly vital to enrich the value of freedom to worship God beyond mere tolerance, or liberty for individuals to worship the God of their choice. If the world beyond tomorrow has a chance to become a world community instead of a battlefield and an environmental wasteland, religions have a critical role to play. It is through a religious and philosophical quest that a sense of common humanity, transcending differences and conflicts among cultures and nations, will emerge. In the past, much thought was devoted to the notion of human nature and to the construction of human rights and to the tolerance and respect owed to other persons or races. Today, it is also an expression of gratitude for one's spiritual heritage. The meaning of this common human and humane nature is to be followed again along the path that the great prophets have marked.

Religion is both a private and public matter. In the same way that it is desirable to reconsider the respective responsibilities of the public and private domains, it is constructive to stimulate thinking again about the balance between the religious and the secular. It is difficult to imagine the path to a world community, reflecting norms and ideals, without national governments and regional and international organizations establishing strong relationships with religions.

To continue to preserve the integrity of the freedom to worship God, a respectful dialogue is now needed between various religions and forms of belief. People of different spiritual persuasions are asked to exercise tolerance and respect for one another, to listen to one another; and indeed, where possible, to pursue shared ecumenical ideals.

Freedom from want remains an objective and mobilizing vision in many parts of the world. It begins with "das Projekt Hoffnung," the principle of hope. Article 25 (1) of the *Universal Declaration of Human Rights* states that:

> Everyone has the right to a standard of living adequate for the health and well-being of himself and his family, including food, clothing, housing and medical care and necessary social services, and the right to social security in the event of unemployment, sickness, disability, widowhood, old age and other lack of livelihood in circumstances beyond his control.

Everyone would be well inspired to note that this right to adequate well-being was in direct correlation with Roosevelt's ideas, proclaimed by the democratic victorious powers as early as 1948. But only people with control over their destiny, and power over their living conditions can experience this freedom. Contrary to what was thought at the beginning of the decolonization process, the benefits of technological progress and economic growth do not automatically trickle down to materially impoverished individuals, groups, and regions. Both in the mature economies and in the less developed countries, exclusion is widespread. The globalization of economic and financial transactions may be generating more inequalities and exclusion. There will be no possibility for sustainable development on the planet without deliberate and forceful global actions to fight exclusion and eradicate the various forms of deprivation that still plague large groups of humanity.

Deprivation, misery, the suffering of the mother who cannot feed her children or give them a proper education, the despair of all those who have no hope and no future, the plight of the marginalized who feel useless and rejected are scars upon the modern world. They evoke a moral outrage and offer evidence of the malfunction of the dominant economic and political system.

A market economy can be neither humane nor efficient without public institutions insuring the overall welfare of people through purposeful distributive and redistributive policies. The provision of basic income and services to all citizens is a critical element of the common good. In the future, one must think in these terms at the world level. Freedom from want is both a universal aspiration and a right.

Betterment of the human condition, evident in a higher quality of living for humanity as a whole, is impossible in a modern culture that is excessively materialist. The dominant culture would seem to have confused an efficient market economy with an oppressive market society. Economic preoccupations and objectives have invaded the modern psyche to a point that threatens virtual domination. It seems hardly possible to realistically provide for all people when there is more interest in gaining and acquiring than in sharing, and when material and profit considerations invade practically every sphere of life and domain of society. Sustained freedom from want will be achieved not only through economic development and redistributive measures, but also through the adoption of more equitable and less acquisitive behavior by the affluent and powerful. The satisfaction of human needs and aspirations require shared moderation, frugality, and generosity.

Freedom from fear will not be easily achieved in tomorrow's world. From diseases to terrorism, and from environmental degradation to urban insecurity, there are, unfortunately, many reasons for people in the global society to be apprehensive. There can be no real security if laws and law enforcement are not buttressed by shared values and norms of behavior. In this vast domain for political scientists and philosophers, two values are decisive in the struggle to gain freedom from fear: solidarity and responsibility.

The need to experience solidarity is an intrinsic part of human nature. As such, solidarity is a source of trust, comfort and security. When it extends beyond immediate, familiar groups it requires imagination, empathy, and recognition of our common humanity. As emphasized by the Copenhagen Seminars for Social Progress, solidarity requires the understanding that self-realization and happiness are inseparable from the welfare of others or the harmony of society. We must add solidarity among generations to solidarity with the other, including the different and the weak. This is a value easily overlooked in an economic culture focused on short-term economic gains.[8]

Tangible evidence of the terrible damage inflicted on mother earth has prompted the realization that the welfare and simple survival of humanity demand a less predatory attitude. Responsibility for the earth, its bounty, and its beauty is a fundamental value to be nurtured to free humankind from fear and despair. Everyone has a role to play in protecting the environment and ensuring, to the extent possible, that scientific research and technological advances be put to the service of humanity. In the years to come, mature economies will continue to have a special duty to invest resources in halting the destruction of the planet. This means that efforts to develop environment-friendly techniques have to be relentless and readily transferred to areas where they are most needed.

Removing fear also implies the responsibility to provide employment opportunities to a maximum number of people. Not all labor saving techniques need be systematically introduced. Governments have other responsibilities than to facilitate a smooth interplay of market forces, particularly when such interplay is obviously not favorable to the general well-being of its people. Public authorities are far from powerless when they are determined to give concrete meaning to the objective of full employment and to the right for an adequate standard of living.

Values that Sustain the "Four Freedoms"

There can be no harmonious future unless the global village is transformed into a society that sustains the "Four Freedoms." Market plus democracy does not translate automatically into such a society which, by definition, is founded on values, among which truth and dignity are foremost. These fundamental values are essential prerequisites for restoring and protecting the moral integrity of the person and for the full appreciation and expression of human freedoms.

Truth is the principle that leads to human fulfillment. People who do not "walk in their integrity" may be free from ethical constraints and can choose what they want in the market place, but they will never be whole. Such people will never enjoy the kind of freedom that builds sustainable societies that will remain free from fear and want and which can long fully enjoy the fruits of free exchange of ideas and religious liberty.

Living in truth also means that people are searching for meaning in life and for markers that give direction to their life. In their communities and organizations they can experience meaning. There, initiatives and actions can have noticeable results. There, conflicting interests have to be weighed. There, values have to be applied.[9]

Dignity is about the inherent nobility, decency, sublime humility, and courageous spirit of human beings, endowing them with the potential not only to act responsibly as free individuals, but also to connect harmoniously and caringly with others. Living in dignity means that the human being should be seen as a fundamentally free, equal, and responsible person. For this dignity to fully develop, individuals need communities and organizations in which to feel at home, to feel secure, to show and practice concern for their neighbors and for the natural environment. Responding responsibly to the needs of others, the individual flourishes. In this sense, dignity is an integral part of the social aspect of life and the key to positive freedom.

In many forms of day-to-day activities in the different sectors of society, both dignity and truth can be experienced. There, following the tradition of civil society as a strategy of liberation, fossils of the old order can be circumvented, outsmarted, and overcome. Together, they promote a climate of responsibility, the ultimate bulwark for positive freedom against all forms of oppression.

But, a civilized society cannot simply be introduced from above nor does it just happen. It requires conscious efforts on the part of many to build it. It is strongly influenced by the general cultural climate. This climate—in the sense of prevailing values, beliefs, institutions, and rituals—may be such that the importance of truth and dignity remains unnoticed or that they are recognized. Many factors promote or suppress this receptiveness: good or bad examples in the community, children's upbringing, the economic environment, the school, the family, the media. The ways human responsibility and essential values shape decisions within different sectors of society have strong implications for actually realizing civility and perpetuating freedom.

For me, the foundation of moral philosophy, and therefore the essence or substance of these values of truth and dignity, are in the spiritual realm. At this level, while others rely on secular humanism, I see a continuum between morality, spirituality and religion. And to live one's spirituality means having roots, living with traditions and history and directing one's life toward a meaningful and satisfying future. For this there is a need for something higher than oneself. For many this means the God who created them—in the palm of whose hand they live, or He who stands at the end of time and beckons humanity to follow the Way.

Spirituality is about a way of life that nurtures the human spirit, enabling the person to find harmony and to refuel his/her mental batteries in society even when it is dominated by materialism and utilitarianism. It is also about the dialogue with reality; it is about the mystery to have been created and to be entrusted with creation. Spirituality is practiced by individuals, and also by societies celebrating spiritual values—societies that acknowledge and value those citizens who concentrate on activity and those whose lives are devoted to contemplation. Finally, spirituality is about mutual respect among religions, secular convictions, and peoples around the globe—it means cherishing diversity. Spirituality is about practicing non-violence while having the courage, in times of darkness, to defend humanity with patience and conviction in words and deeds. Spirituality is about an individual's awareness of being a part of humanity and Nature and at the same time entrusted with a mission in the fulfillment of history.

Conclusion

The revival and progressive worldwide implementation of the "Four Freedoms" would amount to the construction of a fine human community and effective world society. Never has humanity had so many means at its disposal for this construction. Critical to this endeavor is sufficient trust to bind individuals, communities, and nations. Trust implies freedom to give and receive tolerance and respect. It also implies the availability of the material means to enable each person to enjoy a fulfilling life experience. Above all, trust implies the absence of fear.

Also critical to the building of societies shaped by the "Four Freedoms" is the recognition that deliberate efforts and purposeful policies are needed. A market economy cannot be humane or efficient without public institutions insuring the overall welfare of the people through purposeful distributive and redistributive policies.

All social conquests of humanity, be they the abolition of slavery, the prohibition of various forms of exploitation, or the promotion of workers' rights, have been made against the mainstream.[10] There is scant evidence in human history to support the view that a laissez-faire attitude and philosophy brings more equality and more fraternity. It is a great illusion of the dominant political philosophy of the 1990's to pretend that the spontaneous interplay of market and other forces alone can solve the problems of humanity and bring about real social progress. It ought to be obvious to all that efficient democratic public institutions are indispensable to the functioning of societies and to the protection of the freedoms that define the common humanity.

The history of humankind is the history of candles in the night overcoming the horror and vacuity of the darkness. It is in this illumination that truth and dignity give full radiance to the meaning of human freedom and thereby insure its perpetuity. Given the interdependence of mankind and the present state of science, technology, and economy, there is vital need to cherish truth and dignity as the principles underlying all freedoms enjoyed in a civilized society.

Endnotes

1 - The author would like to thank Patricia Morales for her valuable comments in the preparation of this paper.

2 - *The Four Freedoms*, Address by President Franklin D. Roosevelt to the United States Congress, 6 January 1941, Congressional Record, 1941, Vol.87.

3 - This Covenant was adopted by the General Assembly of the United Nations in New York on 16 December 1966. It entered into force on 23 March 1976. See UN General Assembly resolution 2200(XXI), GAOR, Supplement No16.52, UN Doc.A/6316 (1967).

4 - Roosevelt, *Four Freedoms*.

5 - Ideas for a global society were debated in particular by the Copenhagen Seminars for Social Progress organized by the Danish Ministry of Foreign Affairs in the aftermath of the United Nations World Summit for Social Development held in Copenhagen in March 1995. See *Building a World Community, Globalization and the Common Good,* edited by Jacques Baudot (Copenhagen: Royal Danish Ministry of Foreign Affairs, in association with the Seattle, WA: University of Washington Press, 2001)

6 - Ideas for consideration of the "Four Freedoms" in the future are explicitly offered in the reports of the Copenhagen Seminars 1996, 1997, written by Jacques Baudot. The Copenhagen Seminars were convened by the Danish Minister for Development Cooperation to pursue the issues of poverty, unemployment, and social alienation addressed by the World Social Summit, held in Copenhagen in March, 1995.

7 - The necessity for numerous forms of partnerships in a globalized world was examined by an International Symposium organized by the Government of Switzerland on the occasion of the five-years review of the implementation of the recommendations of the World Summit for Social Development. I had the privilege of chairing this symposium. See *Final Report and Summary of Proceedings, International Symposium, Partnerships for Social Development in a Globalizing World* (Geneva 2000).

8 - On the question of solidarity, see *Building a World Community,* 95-98.

9 - See *Dignity and Truth, Civil Society and European Cooperation,* Research Institute for the Christian Democratic Party, The Hague, Netherlands, August 1996.

10 - On the notion of humane economy and on the need for public policies, see *Building a World Community,* 55-75.

CHAPTER 4

WHAT CAN BE WRONG WITH GROWTH?

Peter Marris

The nations of the world have never before been so alike: alike not only in the sweat shirts and jeans we all wear, our taste for sodas and martial arts movies, hamburgers and soccer, but in the guiding philosophies of our governing institutions. Banks, corporations, governments, even hospitals, universities and art galleries, increasingly share a common set of assumptions, and speak a common language. It is a consensus so pervasive and so universally acknowledged, that it has come to be taken for granted. Yet for all its persuasiveness, this consensus represents a conception of human progress that is neither satisfying nor sustainable. In this essay, I want first to articulate the premises of this consensus, and explain its appeal; and then to explore other ways of thinking about purpose and the human meaning of development, which expose the potential destructiveness of its single-minded economic prescriptions.[1]

The Ideology of Economic Growth

The consensus rests on four assumptions, all of which can be derived from the political economy of Adam Smith. Growth in capacity makes all things possible and growth depends upon allocating resources more efficiently, so that they become more productive. Efficiency, in turn, depends upon competition for resources;

and competition implies open markets. These four assumptions imply, in turn, constraints on the role of government, both as an allocator and controller of resources.

Governments secure the institutions which enable markets to function: they provide law, peacekeeping, basic infrastructure, and the protection of the currency, trade and essential natural resources. More controversially, governments may also intervene to compensate for instability, monopolistic tendencies, and inequities in distribution, through taxation and regulation. But government intervention, because it inevitably inhibits the open competition of the market, always risks stultifying the most efficient allocation of resources, and therefore the rate of growth. For the same reason, the provision of services by the government is likely to be inefficient, since governments can escape the "discipline" of the market. In the long term, growth is poor peoples' best friend, even when it increases inequalities, as the historical record shows.

This is not a materialistic philosophy. It argues simply that whatever your ambition, whether it be for a cow, a car, an education, to create a work of art or achieve spiritual enlightenment, growth will, by increasing the capacity of society, increase your chances of achieving it. Economic growth is concerned with all manner of services, with mastery of time and space, as much as with the production of consumer goods: it promises greater and greater freedom to be and do whatever your heart desires. Who can quarrel with that? Because it is a purely instrumental philosophy, its appeal is universal.

Like all ideologies, it idealizes and, in part, misrepresents the economic relationships it seeks to justify. The leaders who use its arguments to advocate free trade agreements also defend subsidies, tariffs, price controls, manipulation of the market by tax incentives, the giving away of public resources, and even monopolies when the political need arises. The practice of any ideal is compromised by expediency.

But the ideology also misrepresents, more fundamentally, what motivates the economy. Corporations do not seek growth, or the most efficient allocation of resources, for their own sake, but to maximize shareholder value over the long term—increasingly, in the United States, in the short term. If laying off workers and cutting back on production is the more profitable strategy, a business will follow it; if suppressing an improved technology will protect investment in an existing one, innovation may be sacrificed to profit. Famines, notoriously, are caused as much, or more, by the manipulation of supply in times of scarcity, as by drought itself. The wealth of modern nations is as much a by-product of their economic relations as the beauty of flowers is a by-product of their reproductive strategies.

But despite the hypocrisy of some of its advocates, and its idealization of markets, the ideology of economic growth remains a powerful legitimator of government policies and corporate behavior. In its name, the International Monetary Fund and the World Bank have imposed, upon struggling nations, drastic cuts in subsidies and public services, the privatization of government monopolies, and the abolition of tariffs, all designed to restore the primacy of the market. Its arguments justify the ambitions of the North Atlantic Free Trade Agreement and the World Trade Organization. The economic policies of almost every nation subscribe to it. So the ideology deserves to be taken seriously on its own terms: this is what the governing élites of the world believe in, and this is how they justify their practices to the people they govern, employ, and serve.

The consensus has two powerful arguments in its favor. Apart from Cuba, all the nations which have attempted to achieve economic growth and end poverty by means other than a market economy have abandoned the experiment, for the very reasons the argument of the consensus proposes—that such planned economies ultimately stultify growth and allocate resources very inefficiently. Secondly, a sixth of the world's population is desperately poor, and as many more can barely manage, so any objection to the most efficient strategies of growth seems either misguided or callous. For advocates of the poor in the wealthiest nations to decry sweat shops and child labor, for instance, can be represented as both presumptuous and self-serving, since it deprives poorer nations of their greatest market asset, exploitable cheap labor. Paul Krugman, the distinguished, politically liberal economist, makes this argument constantly in his New York Times editorials, as does Jeffrey Sachs, the former Harvard development economist.

Yet it still seems profoundly wrong that children should be exploited for their cheap labor; that in the twenty-first century we eagerly reproduce some of the worst abuses of the nineteenth century factory system; and casually destroy the traditional livelihoods of communities, redistributing their resources to international companies. The dominant ideology of progress seems at once rationally inevitable and morally repugnant.

International conferences on the issues of poverty and inequality in the global economy, as at the United Nations "Social Summit" on development in Copenhagen in 1995, or in Geneva in 2000, rarely take hold of this dilemma. The speeches are compassionate and self-reproaching, social and spiritual values are reasserted, goals are set. Meanwhile, in other more private but more influential meetings, the same governments are pursuing the liberalization of world trade. To connect these two political discourses would subvert both of them, exposing the hypocrisy of good intentions and the ruthlessness of profit maximization. But a coherent, morally satisfying and realistic conception of human development can only evolve by connecting them. Good intentions are worthless, without the resources to realize them; but the ways in which resources are generated are not as neutral in the values they promote as the ideology of the international economic consensus pretends. Let me try, then, to suggest how we might begin to disentangle the contradictions at the heart of the development agenda.

In the first place, economic development tends to be seen, by default, as an end in itself. Just because it does not prescribe the ends to which increased wealth should be applied—consumer goods or education, churches or football stadiums—it becomes itself the one good upon which everyone can agree. So, for instance, a dedicated advocate for better health care for pregnant and nursing mothers finds that the most powerful argument she can make to governments is the contribution healthier mothers and healthier children make to economic development. In the calculation of value, it is no longer what economic development can contribute to their health and well-being that counts, but the potential return on that human capital. This inversion of means and ends is inevitable, so long as there is a powerfully convergent consensus about the means, but only a weak, indeterminate consensus about the ends. The result is not an open-ended expansion of human freedom to choose, but the subjection of everyone to a particular, capitalistic logic of accumu-lation—which may, or may not, in practice promote an overall increase in well-being.

So we cannot, after all, avoid thinking about the purposes of development, as if these would resolve themselves, as the six or eight billion of us pocket our share of the wealth and bring our desires to market. The momentum of global capitalism may take us in a direction none of us, ultimately, will want to go. And so, too, we cannot avoid thinking about how to constrain development to pro-mote well-being. But what does well-being mean?

The Importance of Meaning

The director of a United Nations relief agency visits a refugee camp, and happens to notice a child bleeding from the head. He urges the father to take the child to a doctor, but the father replies, "Let him die, our lives here are so miserable, his life is not worth living." What accounts for his despair? It is not lack of the basic necessities of life, or at least the hope of them, which the United Nations agency is there to provide; nor lack of hope that his son can be treated. It is, more profoundly, loss of faith in the possi-bility of a future for his family that can give their lives any mean-ing. The sense that our lives are meaningful is more fundamentally important to us than survival itself. We will risk death or submit to martyrdom to protect it. The tragedy of refugee camps is to be bereft of everything that gives life purpose. They represent, in the most extreme form, the grief provoked by loss of meaning. And the resist-ance to global capitalism springs, above all, from the fear that it robs our lives of meaning, even as it provides at least many of us with more to eat and more to own. Unless economic development is responsive to that need, it will itself be overwhelmed by the pas-sionate resentment it provokes.

I do not mean simply that we resist change, because the disruption of familiar habits can be stressful. Most people are resourceful and adaptable enough to cope with changes, even when they are unwelcome, so long as they can make sense of them. Coping strategies only fail when people lose their sense of agency—of being someone who matters, in a world of relationships where they can act meaningfully. That sense of agency grows out of both an inward and outward looking organization of experience, which together constitute a workable combination of purpose and strategy. The vitality of this structure of meaning is as fundamental to human well-being as is the vitality of the human biological structure.

What, then, are the conditions that enable us to sustain meaning? And what happens when circumstances undermine it? A meaning is an organization of experience, which enables us to identify those events that matter to us, relate them to previous experience, and determine how we should respond to them. It involves classifying events, acknowledging our feelings about them and recognizing our purposes. Meanings constantly evolve, reiteratively, as events provoke emotions, which influence purposes, which in turn influence the events that follow, and how we feel about them. They are nested, more immediate interpretations contained within larger frameworks of our understanding, though they are not necessarily fully integrated or compatible with each other. The same person may contradict, in one set of relationships or mode of thought, beliefs, which he or she holds to in another. The viability of the meanings we live by depends in part, therefore, on avoiding situations that expose these contradictions.

We would not be able to survive for any length of time without these meanings. Unless experience can be perceived as patterns, which recognizably repeat, we cannot learn or predict anything. We can only deal with the unintelligible by submitting it to strategies of investigation, which are themselves familiar. Correspondingly, unless we know who we are and what we want, even the familiar becomes a meaningless jumble of experience, to whose organization we have lost the key.

Meanings are organized as social institutions as well as personal understandings, for example, science, religion, ideology, law, art and most fundamentally in the structure of a language. The ethical and spiritual values we adopt arise out of that struggle to construct, adapt, and protect meaning. The loss of a language, as Vigdis Finnbogadóttir and Birna Arnbjörnsdóttir argue in this book, represents a loss of meaning that no act of translation can truly redeem. These institutionalized meanings, too, have a life of their own, evolving as they are reiterated. As much as our personal understandings, which incorporate them, they create the predictability of human interaction.

We depend on this structure of meanings to survive, since without it we would be bewildered and unable to act. The more it is threatened, the more intransigent our defense of it is likely to become. The less experience confirms it, the more self-destructive may be the strategies by which we continue to validate it. And the harsher the circumstances in which our understanding of ourselves and our world evolved, the more unyieldingly defiant, untrusting, unloving and self loathing that understanding is likely to be. Under what conditions, then, can we create for ourselves a structure of meanings that is robust and resilient, able to acknowledge experience and adapt to it, giving us confidence in our sense of who we are, and effective as an instrument of, and guide to our purposes and emotions? Although the terms of this question do not define moral or spiritual awareness, they do, I believe, describe the conditions from which such awareness will naturally arise.

Attachment and Meaning

The attachment of a child to its parents is the first and most crucial relationship through which people learn to organize meaning. Through this interaction between parent and child, each learns a set of strategies by which to manage the relationship. Even within the first few months, an infant's strategies begin to be informed by learning. Long before a boy or girl can express meaning in words, each has already established a powerful organization of emotions, desires, and patterns of experience centered upon the two essential tasks of childhood: to secure the attention of attachment figures and to learn to use growing abilities. A young child has to figure out, above all, how to get what he or she needs from attachment figures—including the need not to be interfered with when trying to learn some new skill, without ever being abandoned to the consequences of failure.

Since this attachment relationship is the source of virtually all security, comfort and nourishment in early life, the management of attachment is the starting point for understanding every other kind of relationship. How a child learns to handle it will form that child's basic assumptions about order, control, trust, self-protection and self worth. Since his or her coping strategies will evolve out of these assumptions, each new experience is likely both to confirm and modify them. From this a sense of identity will gradually mature—a sense of who one is in the world, and what kind of world it is, grounded in the experiences of childhood. It is made up of an intricate set of assumptions about the social groups to which one belongs, the rights and obligations entailed thereby, and how conflicts between incompatible loyalties are to be resolved.

The social identities one later assumes provide both material and emotional support. They admit one to communities of mutual help, from which one may gain respect, collective pride, and a sense of being part of a more enduring, powerful human presence than a single life can accomplish. A kin group, a gang, a profession, a political movement, a nation or religion is typical of such communities and they convey, as well as rights and obligations, a history. Such identities can be burdensome, involving obligations, the tedium of ritual reaffirmations, and the cant of self-serving historical myths.

We cannot live without these identities, and we can only sometimes choose which ones to live with. They provide the crucial framework of reciprocity within which each of us can create a sufficiently stable and predictable set of relationships to cope with the world around us and achieve our purposes. They define what others expect from us, what their behavior should mean, how we should respond, what we can reasonably hope for, and why it all makes sense as a meaningful way of living. Even when we have to make moral choices in isolation, we have in mind, not just our conscience, but an imagined community that will affirm our integrity, drawn from our experience of those who have loved and respected us.

The meaning we make of our lives, therefore, is embedded in the history of our relationships, and the histories of the communities of which we are part. Our sense of it, at any particular moment, depends on how we use those histories to confront the present and the future. It is a subtle, intricate structure of organization, never finished nor wholly consistent, constantly adapting and assimilating. It is both unique to each individual, and responsive to events that affect its crucial relationships. Under the stress of unemployment, migration, cultural innovation, social conflict, both the internal and external organization of meaning is likely to be threatened. How it resists these threats will depend in part on its internal structure, and in part on the structure of external pressures. It may become more rigid and defensive, or enrich itself by creative assimilation. But it is not infinitely adaptable, and its disintegration is the worst misfortune that can befall us, since it robs us of any reason to live.

Attachment and the Ideology of Development

Now compare this account of human wellbeing with the account implied by the prevailing ideology of economic development. In its references to poverty, the economic ideology is concerned primarily with our biological well-being—with food, water, shelter, and health-care. Insofar as it addresses our psychological needs, it is concerned mostly with education, such as the learning of instrumental skills to enhance our ability to meet such needs, and with freedom, as the precondition of effective markets. These needs are certainly crucial, but they have in common a characteristic that they do not share with the conditions for our mental well-being. That is they can all be met by interchangeable units of consumption. One nourishing meal is equivalent to another; one competent teacher as effective as another; any properly trained doctor can treat a common illness.

This interchangeability is central to the logic of markets. Prices are determined by quantifying supply and demand. This would be impossible unless the good in question is reproducible. Confronted with less tangible, psychological needs, the ideology can only try to reduce them to the equivalent of a good—as units of utility or happiness, and therefore once again, something which can be quantified and interchanged. But the sense of meaning, of identity and worth is not like that. It matures in unique relationships, which are not interchangeable or readily transferable. Children attach themselves to their own, unique parents, not to a generic source of parenting skills. The people we love are unique individuals. If we lose them, we grieve for them; we do not turn to a substitute. Grief itself, especially when we are bereft of someone very close to us, is a long, painful, at times despairing search to recover faith in the meaning of life. Hence, the conditions that support the well-being of our mental organization are fundamentally different from those that can support our biological organization. Because the logic of global capitalism takes no account of this, it undermines the relationships on which our mental well-being depends.

Ideally, children should grow up in a family where their crucial attachments are secure—stable and intact throughout the length of their childhood. And that family should be supported by a network of relationships of which it is part, through which mutual help and mutual respect are exchanged, and shared values affirmed—a kinship group, the congregation of a church, a trade union, a circle of friends. Most people anywhere in the world would, hopefully, recognize and endorse this basic prescription for a nurturing society. Not that every family or community is benign. But unloving parenting, or the punitiveness of insecure communities, are not arguments against attachment and belonging. They show, rather, how deeply both individuals and societies can be damaged when attachment is perverted or denied.

Sustaining attachment implies the need to support and maintain crucial specific, unique, nurturing and mutually affirming relationships over long periods of time. It is in such relationships that we characteristically speak of love, and the love of someone or something. Love for its own sake, as an attachment that requires no other justification, is surely the most universal and powerful source of meaning. Attachment implies a relationship to that particular, irreplaceable individual whom we love. If we try to reinterpret such attachments in terms of generalizable, theoretically marketable goods—for instance as a need to nurture and be nurtured—we miss their essential quality. Erotic attachment becomes prostitution; mothering and fathering become childcare. Not that childcare is undesirable, but it has a different meaning. So it is impossible, and misguided to try to subsume these relationships under some cost benefit analysis of supply and demand.

By contrast, the ideology of competitive capitalism promotes an ideal of minimal commitment. In an uncertain world of constantly evolving markets and products, the goal of the successful firm is to accept the fewest possible long term obligations, especially to its workers, and to shrink the size of its core organization to the smallest possible constant. In this way, it maximizes its chances of survival, nimble enough to switch products, relocate its production, dismiss workers in one place to exploit the potential of a cheaper labor force elsewhere, shuffle its management and open new markets. But this freedom of maneuver would be ineffective, without the power to constrain others to respond as desired when a strategy is chosen. The firm needs assurances that should it decide to locate here or there, a compliant government will be ready and eager to provide the tax incentives and planning clearances it desires, help to recruit the workers, suppress disruptive militancy, and provide the necessary education. But the firm will seek to avoid any reciprocal commitment that might constrain its future action. Powerful firms insulate themselves from the fluctuation of the market by subcontracting production. At the same time, they rid themselves of any social responsibility for the conditions their subcontractors impose. Again and again, in the hope of gaining jobs and economic growth, cities and nations grant concessions and undertake policies, only to see the firms they sought to attract go elsewhere, or abandon them after a few years.

Apologists may argue that competitive capitalism, by ending poverty, will, in the long run create the basis of universal security. But such an argument fundamentally misunderstands the nature of security. To meet everyone's material needs while destroying the basis of their psychological needs is a prescription for universal despair. Even in countries with high per-capita incomes and low rates of unemployment, the inability to sustain stable, long-term relationships impoverishes the meaning of life. And the malaise of insecurity can only intensify, as the logic of global economic competition plays itself out. When trillions of dollars wash around the world each day, and an economic crisis in Thailand can destabilize the economy of Brazil; when corporations striving for competitive advantage are richer than most nations, the potential for social disruption is amplified to a scale we can barely grasp.

As vital relationships are threatened, people will look for a sense of meaning and security in communities, which seem invulnerable to the insecurities of everyday life. Such communities are necessarily detached from the realities of experience. The sense of identity and worth they offer is an idealized abstraction that nothing can impugn. They demand absolute and unquestioning adherence. The harder it becomes to make sense of life, the more people will be drawn to such mythological, other worldly ideologies which seem to offer an escape from all the bewildering uncertainties of their present circumstances. So, for instance, the orphaned Afghan refugees of decades of civil war grasp at the redemptive meaning of a messianic, puritan Islam, which holds out the promise of a glorious martyrdom. But that other worldliness also renders them impotent, except to justify acts of wholesale repudiation and destruction. Both fundamentalist religion and idealized ethnicity can readily be manipulated into violent conflict when the frustrations of everyday life become unbearable. The whole enterprise of economic growth risks foundering under the rage, frustration, apathy and despair it provokes. The "galoshes of fortune," as Barbara Baudot writes, become the "shoe that pinches."

We almost certainly understand more about attachment than we do about growth, since we have lived in families and social groups for thousands of years, while the economic theory that both justifies and explains the processes of industrial capitalism is a creation of the last two centuries. But because our knowledge of attachment is largely personal and intuitive, while economic knowledge is assertively theorized and intellectually prestigious, societies have tended to assume that the prescriptions of economics are unassailable. There are no Nobel prizes for psychological understanding. The assumption prevails that we can work social relationships around economic changes, one way or another. But this assumption is false and dangerous. Unchecked, the logic of competitive economic growth puts an intolerable strain on relationships that are fundamental to human well-being.

Reconciling Attachment and Growth

Arguments for policies of economic growth, therefore, have to be qualified by a broader framework of analysis that gives equal attention to social consequences. However persuasive, in terms of economic theory, the arguments for, say, free trade areas, abolishing tariff restrictions, cutting subsidies or public services, that in itself does not make them right, in terms of what they would contribute to human well-being. It does not necessarily make them wrong, either, but the outcome is unknowable until their social implications are examined with as much careful analysis as their economic advantages. And this is rarely even attempted. The result is a sense of inevitability about changes that leave some bereft and everyone profoundly uneasy.

Only by confronting the incompatibilities between the conditions that sustain attachments, and the conditions that allocate resources most productively, can nations begin to think how to reconcile them. Farming on small scattered plots may preclude the growing of higher yielding seeds or valuable cash crops, but it supports a way of life embedded in a network of social reciprocity, which land consolidation destroys. Abolishing tariffs may give people access to better quality goods at lower prices, but it may destroy the communities that depended on protectionism. Whenever resources are reallocated, the relationships in which they had been embedded wither, and the repercussions of that loss may spread throughout society. Once this is acknowledged, other strategies of growth begin to emerge—cooperatives through which very small-scale farmers can market crops; microlending; new technologies adapted to the conditions of an emerging market.

But is any deeper reconciliation possible between two such fundamentally different conceptions of what constitutes well-being? Do we have to trade off social stability for growth, and growth for stability? Just to recognize that we have such a choice is some progress, especially if we acknowledge that those who benefit from the growth and those who suffer from the social disruption are often not the same. But beyond that, cooperation and social reciprocity may have more economic advantages than the logic of competitive capitalism implies.

In the face of uncertainty, the winning strategy for dominant actors maximizes their own freedom of action and minimizes their commitments, while binding others to be available, if needed, to meet their demands, constraining their adaptability. And as everyone tries to maneuver in this way, in the best way possible, an ever more crushing burden of uncertainty is passed down from stronger to weaker, until it rests most heavily on those with the fewest resources. But the effect of this is to create a world in which all relationships are increasingly unpredictable, as everyone is forced to play the same game. If employers seek to minimize commitment to their employees, the employees will in turn have no loyalty to them. If corporations refuse to accept obligations to the nations that court them, those nations have little incentive to honor commitments they have been forced to make. Thus, if no one is making any commitment to the fifth of the world's population living in desperate poverty, that fifth has little to lose by turning against the rest of us.

The logic of competitive control eventually undermines the predictability of all relationships, maximizing uncertainty. But the greater the uncertainties, the higher the economic cost of investment, because the risks of failure from all manner of social causes increases. Long term planning is inhibited, otherwise promising opportunities are rejected. Banks become more cautious, insurance costs are higher. So, perversely, unconstrained competition over the distribution of resources ends by creating fewer resources to distribute.

There is, therefore, a powerful argument that reciprocity and commitment are, after all, in the interests of the powerful as well as the weak. Though they inhibit freedom of action in the immediate future, they make the longer-term future more predictable, extending the range of both investment and research. The ethically consistent corporate leadership, which Roy Smith and Ingo Walter advocate in this book, is an aspect of this. The single-minded, unconditional advocacy of competitive markets would lead ultimately to such disintegrated societies that no markets could flourish.

There are signs that some corporate and financial leaders are beginning to realize this—partly because a parallel ecological argument makes cooperation essential. The World Bank has recently begun to acknowledge the limitations of market-based reforms. Some corporations are beginning to concede more responsibility for the social consequences of their competitive strategies. But farsighted and enlightened self-interest is unlikely to prevail in the everyday struggles of a global market economy, unless there is sustained pressure on both government and corporations to make economic relationships socially and environmentally responsible.

As the people of the richest nations can use their buying power to influence corporate behavior, they can use their power as workers to demand that the companies they work for treat those companies' employees in poorer countries, where workers' organizations may be weaker and more vulnerable, with equal respect. As workers, as consumers, as citizens, people have the power, if they choose to mobilize it, to create a more even balance between the economic agenda of business and financial capital and the social and cultural agenda which economic development itself can never satisfy.

The growing crowds of protesters in Seattle, Quebec, Genoa, and Washington D.C. may seem incoherent or naïve, but they understand that there is something fundamentally wrong with an economic logic that takes no account of the qualities of human relationships on which our well-being depends. Every culture evolves an understanding of the qualities of relationships within a family, a work place, a community or in the relationship between communities that foster mutual respect, a sense of self-worth, of being loved and of purposeful activity. People everywhere understand what it means to belong, to have a sustaining social identity. We know how to nurture all this, and we know how readily it can be destroyed. This understanding is the premise of a spiritually satisfying life. It affects every aspect of economic policy, from international tariff agreements to the location of a particular plant or the exploitation of a coastal fishery, from the governance of the World Bank to the treatment of workers. Development is a complex social, environmental and economic negotiation, in which the economic arguments are neither the most fundamental, nor the most securely grounded in experience. Recognizing that may slow the rate of growth, but only in this way can we hope to make it meaningful.

Endnotes

1 - I am grateful to Peter Mattick for his comments and suggestions on this essay.

PART II

PERSPECTIVES FROM RELIGIOUS
AND PHILOSOPHICAL TRADITIONS

The emerging global civilization leaves unanswered fundamental questions of sense, value, and direction of human life that are central to all generations and all cultures. What would human reality be if devoid of any spiritual or moral dimension? Can the finiteness of mundane existence satisfy the heart? As Allison Phinney suggests in Part III of this book, to aver that there is no spiritual or metaphysical dimension is tantamount to saying that life breathes without air. These dimensions of existence embrace the vast realm of wisdom, ideas, and meaning accessible through religion, philosophy, art, and meditation.

The essays in this part develop three core messages on essential gifts of the spiritual and moral dimensions to modern life. First, in the vein of the reflection of Peter Marris, is the importance that ought to be attached to the central question of the meaning of human life. Recovering the validity of this question, in the private as in the social domains, is a fundamental aspect of the search for a postmodern global humanism. The second is the recognition that it is vitally important to revisit the traditional and sometimes forgotten sources of wisdom. One can accept change and modernity, welcome technological and scientific innovations, and yet look to the past as a rich well of inspiration for the future. And third, there is considerable agreement in ideas, coming from very different intellectual horizons and experiences, on the necessity to feed the emerging world community with the values of love, generosity, respect for the other, and community spirit applied to the local as well as the global settings.

> The spirituality of the Rule of Saint Benedict offers to the world a direction for approaching some of the issues that confront contemporary society; a direction that is humanistic, balanced, and sound. The Rule speaks to all traditions because it is based on what is fundamental to all as human beings—creatures in search of destiny and purpose—"the knowledge of who they are," so that they might know how they should live.
>
> *John Fortin, O.S.B.*

Voices from great religions have traditionally offered solutions to problems of meaning, identity and purpose. John Fortin invites us to share the Christian spiritual message given by Benedict of Nursia when he established in the 6th century the rules that are still followed in monasteries throughout the world. In contrast to the leanings of the modern culture of comfort, the teaching of St Benedict is that real need should be distinguished from want, that a simple, austere life is necessary to avoid the distractions that attend both luxury and destitution, and that it is in the generous helping of others that one can experience true Goodness. Daily life should be ordered and balanced, giving priority to the transcendent values of truth, goodness, and beauty—ideas also developed by Professor Imamichi. The "garden," that is the world, is a trust to humankind. As to the modern notion of individual rights, Benedict believes that the fulfillment of human life is in the union, with joy and love, of Creator and creature. This union can be sought and experienced in all places and all aspects of daily life. Fortin contends that the realization of this spiritual dimension of life can provide a firm ground for the prudence and wisdom necessary to the building of a global civilization.

> From a Confucian perspective, the persuasive power of the Enlightenment project will be greatly enhanced if it incorporates self, community, nature, and Heaven (or a generalized idea of the spirit) into a holistic vision. The intellectual horizon of the global ethic, informed by the Enlightenment, should be extended and the moral sensitivity of those determined to see the universal application of Enlightenment ideas should be deepened.
>
> *Tu Weiming*

Confucian humanism offers a holistic understanding of the human condition. For Confucius, spirituality is grounded in humanity, through individual bodies, families, communities, and the natural world. Human beings are Heaven's partners, entrusted with the sacred mission to actualize the inner virtue of all elements of the universe. Not unlike the prescriptions of St. Benedict evoked by John Fortin, Tu Weiming points out that Confucian paths to human flourishing, through spiritual development, include the ordinary and humble facets of life. And the idea of reciprocity, as an active response to the hearts and minds of those in need, is central to this humanism. One major contribution that Confucian humanism can make to the elaboration of a global ethic is the observation that the

Enlightenment mentality needs fundamental restructuring. Rooted in the values of primacy of reason, equality, liberty, and community spirit, the Western Enlightenment was originally meant to be culturally ecumenical. Tu submits that the message of the Enlightenment will have, again, universal value when enriched and reoriented through a dialogue of civilizations, seen as a continuing joint venture.

> Modern thinkers should consider what, in the African tradition, is essential to the development of humane governance and the protection of the environment from the excesses of rationality, material progress, and acquisitive individualism. In other words, there is perhaps as much to be learned today from the African experience as there was in ancient times of the philosophical and metaphysical nature and meaning of life, those dimensions threatened with burial in the materialism of the spirit of the time.
>
> *Thomas Odhiambo*

The cultural and religious traditions of Africa include the belief in God as an omnipotent, omniscient and invisible omnipresence, at the same time, the Creator, Protector and Governor of all Creation. The figurative descriptions and the many concrete objects revered in the African culture are generally metaphorical representations but not incarnations of God. Human nature, created by God, has material and immaterial elements, but the spirit and/or soul are the vital essences of the person and the sources of well-being. For Thomas Odhiambo, the repositioning of Africa in history is vital for the world. He argues that this African culture is at the origins of the Western civilization through Egypt and the Greeks. This inheritance, while it may have been forgotten, is still alive and has a lot to offer to the advancing global culture. He notes that the currently dominant vision of progress and development is tragically marked by the absence of sages, philosophers, theologians, and other thinkers whose vocation is to fathom the mysteries of life, destiny and existential continuity. He considers that humanity has to distance itself from the occidental focus on the individual as the center of ethics. For Odhiambo, the creation of a global community requires deep contemplation, prayer, and retreat from the clamor of wealth and power that crushes the human spirit.

> We, in all probability, do not have a superior system of thought
> that provides sufficient grounds for disregarding our traditional
> systems. If this humble recognition is registered and fresh "infu-
> sions" are incorporated in the emerging social discourse, we
> may take it as a sign that the wheel has come full circle and the
> "native" has decided to come back home.
>
> *Muhammad Suheyl Umar*

Muhammad Suheyl Umar argues that, at some point, Western
thought took a sharp turn from the collective heritage of humanity
and claimed the autonomy of reason, unguided by revelation and cut
off from the Intellect that was regarded as its transcendent root. Its
philosophy came to an impasse. Excessive individualism followed.
Politics and social sciences separated themselves from higher cognitive and spiritual pursuits. Self-interest ignored virtue and a
divorce occurred between the ideal and the real. Umar asserts that
the dominant Western culture needs to be rectified and reoriented by
"infusions" from its own past and from other great traditions and
religions. He recalled that St. Augustine said that "to be human
means to be more than human." This "more" evokes the spiritual
dimension of life and the cosmic order of which "reality" is part.
Umar also notes that all great religions contain the three facets of the
human psyche and determinants of human attitudes that are knowledge, love, and fear. For him, the human self should be regarded as
the point of intersection where the Divine touches the human realm
and where the human microcosm is placed in a hierarchical relationship with other levels of being.

> My research method, which begins by concentrating on philo-
> logical comparisons and then progresses to metaphysical con-
> siderations, seems at first to be meaningless in the context of
> examining the big issues arising from the realities of globaliza-
> tion. But language is the fundamental element of logic without
> which no system of thought is possible, and metaphysics is the
> definitive meditation without which no ethical rule and practice
> can be understood.
>
> *Tomonobu Imamichi*

The world has not simply entered the 21st century but has entered a
new age. The situation is chaotic and dangerous. There is a critical

need for a mutual understanding of cultures and for exploring the dimensions of a new world culture. Philosophy can make a significant contribution to this endeavor. This is the approach taken by Tomonubu Imamichi. A vital task for philosophy is a rigorous comparative analysis of the Eastern and Western cultures. A prerequisite for such analysis is a full knowledge of the original language of the moral concepts used by the two cultures. Such a philosophical dialogue can begin with the concept of truth, focusing on the meanings of the Greek *aletheia* and the Japanese *makoto*. *Aletheia* infers descriptive correctness. Imbedded in the concept of *makoto* is the secret of beauty, and the axiological unity of the values of truth, beauty, and goodness. The global community could benefit from an understanding of truth as a meaningful balance between the two concepts. Expanding his reflection, he notes that, in the 20th century, there has been a radical opposition between metaphysics and science conceived as logical positivism. If we take a laissez-faire attitude, the word "philosophy" might disappear, to be replaced by two separate disciplines, metaphysics and logic. Imamichi views the task of the 21st century as the reconciliation of these two poles of philosophy, with a reintegration of ethics in politics as "social ethics." His contribution to this task is the elaboration of a theory called *Eco-Ethica*.

.

CHAPTER 5

BENEDICTINE SPIRITUALITY: A BASIS FOR REEVALUATING MODERN DEVELOPMENT TRENDS

John R. Fortin, O.S.B.

Introduction

One of the classic texts of Western thought is the famous *Consolation of Philosophy* by the sixth century Roman philosopher and theologian, Anicius Manlius Severinus Boethius [480-524 A.D.]. He composed this text in his prison cell where he awaited execution for promoting the rights of the Senate and for allegedly conspiring with Justin, Emperor of the East, against the Emperor of the West, Theodoric.

As the text opens, Boethius laments his predicament and sings doleful songs with the Muses of poetry, his life worth nothing after years of intense study in the liberal arts and of generous service to the state. This "wake" is interrupted by the appearance of the personification of philosophy who tries to lift his mind and his spirits from mourning over his sad condition to the heights of philosophical speculation. Having dismissed the poetic Muses, Lady Philosophy begins to apply her medicine and soon comes to realize what the prisoner's basic problem is: he has some sense of whence he has come but he has no understanding of where he is going.

"How then, she went on, is it possible that you can know the origin of all things and still be ignorant of their purpose?"[1] A few more questions posed to the prisoner then yields the stark conclusion: "Now, I know another cause of your sickness, and the most important: you have forgotten what you are."[2]

Like Boethius in his age, contemporary humans rattle their "prison cages," cry out against the injustice they see, but still find themselves unable to escape or reconcile the contradictions that confront them everyday. In the West, the situation is tantamount to an individual and societal schizophrenia. People see a health care system that has the technology and the skill to battle disease better than ever before in human history yet its high costs result in an inequitable distribution that leaves many without its benefits. They find enormous wealth and opportunity in a growing economy, and yet are confronted with the reality that one-quarter of the nation's children are born into poverty. They desire peace and stability in their lives, happiness and success for their offspring, and the comforts of growing old surrounded by loved ones. They tremble at the spiraling divorce rate, the violence surrounding them, the abuse and exploitation of young and old alike. All these issues make Boethius' questions ever new, ever pertinent. Where then have we come from? Where are we going? Who are we who are on this journey? And to whom should we turn to help us seek answers to these troubling issues and concerns?

Many expressions of the problems of contemporary society can be traced to this central issue. In an article entitled "Are We Living in a Moral Stone Age?" Christina Sommers, an ethicist and professor at Clark University raises this issue in an piece about the moral sense in America:

> We hear a lot today about how Johnny can't read, how he can't write, and the trouble he is having finding France on a map. It is also true that Johnny is having difficulty distinguishing right from wrong.[3]

In the essay, Sommers continues to argue that the problem for Johnny lies in a "cognitive moral confusion." This confusion has arisen because of society's failure as a whole to appreciate and pass down a positive moral environment, a moral environment that honors and practices such moral basics as civility, honesty, consideration of others, and self-discipline. If a society speaks of these virtues but acts otherwise, moral confusion arises and the result is a relativism and subjectivism that recognizes no outside authority of value and truth. What is the source of this confusion? Sommers traces the malaise of the present moral environment to societal and cultural shifts that began in the 1960s when civil (and indeed one could add religious) authority began to be challenged, especially in light of the Vietnam War and the Civil Rights Movement. There are different ways of interpreting this cultural shift away from a high regard for authority to a critical, even skeptical attitude toward it. One way is to consider it as a challenge to the Western Enlightenment principles that served as a foundation for the American experiment in a democratic republic some 200 years ago. The exaltation of reason by such *lumières* as Locke, Voltaire, Hume, Rousseau, and Kant led to the view that all human problems could be solved by reason appropriately applied, yielding such results as peace, progress, and the spread of civilization. For the reasonable person, the proper form of civil government was a form of democracy. The proper structure of society was egalitarian. True knowledge issued from the scientist's laboratory. Religion was a respectful bow of the head proffered to a deity, perhaps undefined, but nonetheless acknowledged to be a Higher Power.

Western Enlightenment principles are an undeniable force on the formation of democratic republicanism in many nations of the globe. Even further, a global civilization appears to be emerging from the interconnectedness of economic, social, and information forces—forces which themselves were nurtured in the womb of human reason and empiricism. Some of these forces are global capitalism, scientific and technological progress, and the supremacy of the rights of the individual. While all these developments are positive and inevitable evidence of scientific progress, there is a sense that something is either missing from or perhaps even wrong with the way these principles are practiced in contemporary society. The two world wars, the cold war, the "logic" of a once touted policy of mutually assured nuclear destruction and other examples from modern history can be marshaled to question the power of human reason alone to order all things rightly. It is this critique that forces itself forward in contemporary criticism about modern society and culture, a criticism that often finds expression in concern for the moral climate of the times and in concern, most of all, for the children and what they will inherit. Sommers is one of those voices; so too is John Updike who decries the blatant consumerism and materialism that infects the country: "America teaches its children that every passion can be translated into an occasion to buy."

The central issue then lies beneath the principles of the Western Enlightenment. These define, one way of looking at human life, its values, its goals, its ultimate meaning and purpose in the same way that one must examine one's moral judgments and principles in the light of one's overall moral theory. To evaluate and critique the principles of the Western Enlightenment requires that one first establish some truths about human nature itself, which serve as the basis for subsequent discussion. Many voices including those of all the great religions have offered solutions to these problems of identity and purpose; many have raised their voices in the debate and dialogue. Christianity, for example, has argued on the basis of the divinely revealed Scriptures and its 2,000-year tradition that humankind was created by a loving God, redeemed by Jesus Christ, and sanctified by the power of the Holy Spirit. This is the tradition Boethius followed. Humans, he teaches in his *Consolation*, are ordained for glorious and eternally joyful union with the Godhead without loss of personal identity. As Saint Augustine says in his *Confessions*: "Our souls are made for God, and we will not rest until we rest in God."

Within this same tradition lies Benedictine monasticism, begun in the sixth century by Benedict of Nursia [born the same year as Boethius, 480 AD]. Benedict was the founder of Monte Cassino and the author of a Rule for monasteries that is still observed today in hundreds of communities of men and women throughout the world. The spirituality of the Rule of Saint Benedict offers to the world a direction for approaching some of the issues that confront contemporary society—a direction that is humanistic, balanced, and sound. The Rule speaks to all traditions because it is based on what is fundamental to all as human beings—creatures in search of destiny and purpose—"the knowledge of who they are," so that they might know how they should live.

The purpose of this essay is to discuss the Rule as a basis from which to re-examine and re-assess values and human purpose in the post-modern liberal democratic society. It will do so by considering the teachings of the Rule of Saint Benedict in the light of three contemporary issues: the culture of comfort, technological progress, and individual rights.

Culture of Comfort and the Call to Stewardship

While the life of a sixth century monastery might not pass for "comfortable" in contemporary society, Benedict's understanding of what comfort is and how it is to be used offers ideas for reflection. One is simplicity of lifestyle. Benedict would agree with Aristotle that some basic means of well-being are necessary for a good life, that is, a life of virtue. Yet those basic means are not meant to separate one person from another, one society from another, for it is precisely in the generous helping of others that one can experience the goodness of God. Stewardship of the goods of the world, then, is for the good of all, especially for those with special needs. This is Benedict's response to the predominant desire to secure material comfort in our modern culture.

The Rule prods the reader to reflect on and to distinguish real need from real want. Even a cursory reading of the Rule will convince the reader that Benedict's monastery, though austere and Spartan, was not meant to be uncomfortable. The over-arching purpose of cenobitic life is the communal and individual search for God through public prayer, spiritual reading, and service to one another in the community. Thus, it is necessary that the monks be able to live in such a way that they avoid the distractions that attend both luxury and destitution. Hence, for example, Benedict directed that monks be clothed in attire that fit and that be of such material as to afford proper protection and covering in any season or climate (55.1-8).[4] Benedict's monks were to receive proper nourishment to sustain them in their work, which could include heavy farm labor, and in the rigors of the monastic schedule, even to the point of adding to the regular fare should circumstances warrant it (39.1-6).

While there were days for fasting, Benedict understood this to mean not less food, but that the main meal would be taken later in the day. Yet even this was to be mitigated if the monks were required to do strenuous manual labor under the hot sun (41.2). In these and other instances, Benedict is so ordering the monastic life that the monks may attend to their prayers and their other duties in peace and contentment. Balance in daily life, giving priority to the transcendent values of truth, goodness, and beauty, while, at the same time practicing good stewardship over the goods of the earth and an altruistically motivated regard for the well-being of others, would be the secular translation of this monastic example.

While each individual must in the long run make prudent determinations about what is truly needed for a happy and genuine human existence, Benedict would raise a further issue: if one person or group takes possession of something, to whom is it then being denied? Is the criterion of purchasing power (I can afford it, therefore I can, should, ought to have it) or any other kind of power (military, economic, social) sufficient to make the claim of possession without regard for the bona fide needs of others?

In addressing this question, Benedict would think and speak in terms of good stewardship, recalling the words of Jesus who praised the wise steward who distributed rations of grain in due season (Luke 12:42 of the New Testament of the Bible). The abbot and all the monks are required to practice wise stewardship over the goods and property of the monastery because in reality none of it is theirs. Monks see themselves as guests in the house of God (31.19; 53.22; 64.5), that is, the monastery, and as such are called upon to use with great care all the goods of the monastery, which are provided so that they may continue their search for God in peace and harmony. Thus, the tools and goods of the monastery are to be treated as the sacred vessels of the altar (31.10): they are to be distributed by wise overseers, kept clean and in good working order, returned to the storeroom, and accounted for when the work is done (32 passim). On the world scale, today, what one labels "environmental concerns" were for the monks the management and care of God's creation by worthy stewards.

Another application of the teaching on stewardship is generosity. It is only when one comes to realize that everything a person possesses of transcendent nature, including life itself, is a gift that cannot in any real sense be earned or merited, that one can come to understand and reflect in one's daily life, the gracious spirit of the gift-giver. The instructions that Benedict gives regarding guests, the sick, the elderly, and the young are clear statements of generosity of goods. If any person's physical comfort has priority in Benedict's monastery, it is that of the guest or the sick. These categories of people are to receive the best that can be offered, the others making due with what remains. Benedict makes it abundantly clear that guests are to be received as Christ and are to receive the most cordial treatment in the monastery (53.1). While the guests are expected to be aware that they are being received into a distinctly monastic setting, Benedict takes pains to arrange that they enjoy what comforts the monastery, however materially impoverished, can provide and that they are accorded every sign of hospitality. The same concern for physical comfort and well-being is legislated for the sick brothers in the monastery (36 passim). Benedict rules that they are to be cared for in a separate facility by specially trained attendants who are "God-fearing, attentive, and concerned." He allows the sick to eat red meat and take baths—both of which in Benedict's time were considered to be physically stimulating and thus conducive to the restoration of health—and he admonishes the brothers to bear patiently the demands and orneriness of the sick.

In sum, Benedict would argue that simplicity of lifestyle enables one to focus attention on what is really valuable, to give oneself over, as in the parable of Jesus, to the pearl of great price, the true treasure to which one should make his/her heart's devotion. The passing nature of this world moves Benedict to remind his monks to keep death daily before their eyes (4.47) as a reminder that possessions do not make for salvation in the hereafter or even for happiness in this life. Thus, in the practice of liberality, a person or a society can be freed from the grasp of dependency on purely material possessions as the source or cause of happiness.

Technological Progress and the Abbey Artisans

At first glance, it may not appear that the Rule of Saint Benedict would have anything relevant to say about the issue of technological progress. The slow, rural, agrarian life of a sixth century monastic community would seem to have little in common with today's high-tech culture, where "rapid change" is a phrase that hardly appears able to express the rate of development and advancement. Yet, Benedict never eschewed technological progress. History attests, for example, that monks contributed to the advancement and development of the arts of farming, husbandry, and forestry. Indeed, whatever eased the monks' labor so that they could pursue the spiritual life more directly would be welcome.

Technology was aligned with the practice of art. Benedict would admonish his monks and contemporary society to be artists in all aspects of life. All that is done ought to be crafted with care and concern first of all for the well-being and the good of the one crafting, because the work is meant to bring the person into the work of the Creator. If, indeed, the work that humans perform is to reflect the beauty of creation, then it needs to be practiced as an art or a craft. Benedict would find matter for reflection in a poem composed by fellow countryman Michelangelo Buonarroti in 1532. Dedicated to his good friend Tommaso Cavalieri, the poem employs a favorite image of Michelangelo's, who often uses fire to symbolize love:

> The smith when forging iron uses fire
> to match the beauty shaped within his mind;
> and fire alone will help the artist find
> a way so to transmute base metal higher
> to turn it gold.[5]

The architecture of monastic buildings is the embodiment of the marriage of art and technology with an eye to the spirit. Following Benedict's logic, the cloister should contain all that is really necessary: shops for the practice of the crafts, wells, mills, and gardens. While all this again shows the practicality of Benedict's thought, it did not preclude his followers from constructing beautiful monasteries and to become especially adept at the use of the arch. Here technology is used not only to create what is beautiful to the eye, but also to lift the mind to God, for the arch serves not only as an architectural and structural device, it is also a symbol of the heavens. Let us assume that technology and its progress are expressions of work or attempts to redefine work to allow more time for leisure and for enjoying the culture of comfort. If so, what Benedict has to say about work in general and about skilled labor in particular may be pertinent to the discussion as an example of an attitude and approach that could give direction and purpose to the use of technology today.

In chapter 48 of his Rule, Benedict discusses daily manual labor. Above all, work is never pursued for its own sake. He will not have his monks so absorbed by work that they are unable to appreciate and benefit from the purpose of the monastic life. All work is what needs to be done to permit the monks opportunity for private prayer and spiritual reading, common prayer in praise of God, common meals, and fellowship. In his discussions of work, whether in general or in specific regard to the artisans, Benedict is, in the final analysis, invoking an intensely spiritual attitude.

Benedict's practical view of work can be seen in the language he uses to present it: work is that which needs to be done to sustain the existence of the monastic community (48.3,11,14). No one is to be preoccupied with work; no one is to shirk from it. Work is one aspect of life; it is necessary to provide the stuff for living. In this regard, Benedict is eminently practical when he tells the monks to carry out the tasks they are assigned because that work is simply what must be done. At the same time though, and underlying this practicality, is the view that work is part of a whole that is encompassed by a profound and all-pervasive spirituality. Work as manual labor is ordered to meet the spiritual ends of the monastic life. Furthermore, it is to be noted that Benedict never looks upon work as something for which his monks should be rewarded. Indeed, Benedict is clear that monastery-produced goods are to be sold at a

JOHN R. FORTIN, O.S.B.

reasonable price and not for the sake of profit (57.4-9). Here again work is subordinated to another purpose, since disregard for profit is to govern the sale of the works produced, so humility should govern the work of the artisan.

Humility is the guiding principle of the artisans. When Benedict speaks of the skilled laborers, the tradesmen, the craftsmen of his abbey, he is likewise practical and sagacious (57 passim). Benedict recognizes the need for skilled workmen, artifices, in the monastery (carpenters, masons, etc), but he wants them to practice their skills within the context of the monastic life with great humility. Thus, not only are they to work only under orders from the abbot (at other times, it is implied, doing what needs to be done in other areas, e.g., at harvest time), they are also to practice their crafts humbly (57.1). Indeed, Benedict further enjoins the artisan that he must not become proud and go so far as to consider himself a benefit to the community. If he does, he is to be removed from his trade until he returns to humility and receives the abbot's blessing to continue his craft. Benedict devotes a great deal of time to the notion of humility. Again in its simplest incarnation, humility is the recognition that one is a guest in God's house, a servant who is seeking to be faithful to the master's wishes.[6]

All the monks were to take part in the work of the monastery, which at Benedict's time was primarily agricultural—the system of copying and illuminating manuscripts came later in Benedictine history—in addition to the daily work of maintaining the abbey property and buildings, preparing and serving meals, caring for the guests, the sick, and so forth. The work period, usually about six hours on the weekdays and Saturday, does not dominate the day. It does not drive the lives of the monks. That does not mean that some work would not be arduous and toilsome, for indeed as Genesis 3:19 teaches, man will earn his bread by the sweat of his brow.

The highest work to which mankind is called is to continue to cultivate the "garden," as referenced in the Bible.[7] Although he never directly refers to the Genesis passages cited here, it could be argued that Benedict is drawing his inspiration from them. Benedict teaches contemporary society that its work must be understood and practiced as a cultivation of the garden, a theme prominent in many world religions. "The garden" is a metaphor for the world. The world is a trust to humankind. To be fully human requires that each generation strives to make better that which will be passed on to their heirs, not as sometimes appears to be the unsustainable case: the living generation spends the inheritance of those who will follow.

Individual Rights and Living in the Presence of God

In the Prologue to his Rule, Benedict issues an invitation to the reader:

> Listen, my child, to the master's instructions, and attend to them with the ear of your heart. This is advice from a father who loves you; welcome it, and faithfully put it into practice. The labor of obedience will bring you back to him from whom you had drifted through the sloth of disobedience. This message of mine is for you, then, if you are ready to give up your own will, once and for all, and armed with the strong and noble weapons of obedience to do battle for the true King, Christ the Lord.

This is a very personal invitation; it is addressed to "you," who are reading this text or listening to it. In Benedict's view, the individual is always regarded as a child of God who seeks to be united with God, to be able to enjoy in some true measure in the here and now the peace and serenity of God's kingdom. Benedict's Rule is a program, a "little rule for beginners" as he calls it (73.8), to bring the individual back to the joy and love that is the goal of every human heart. It is in the union of the Creator and the creature that the ultimate fulfillment of human life will be found; the individual becoming truly what he/she was made to be.

For Benedict, every human being is destined to this fulfillment but cannot experience it without seeking it. For the monks, fulfillment could be sought in very different places: in the oratory when at prayer, whether in common or in private; in the work places; in the guesthouse; in the infirmary. It is experienced at different times of the day: in the darkness of the early hours of the morning; at dawn; at the time for common meals; at the end of the day, when the last common prayer is recited and it is time to retire.

Awareness of a spiritual dimension of life that can only be accounted for by reference to some kind of transcendent reality, of a higher power, is for Benedict the surest means of living in the truth. Contemporary society wavers as it tries to process and assimilate contradictory claims about the world. Realization of the spiritual dimension of life provides one with a solid basis upon which to judge the multifarious opinions and interpretations of reality that are proposed. Lacking such a firm ground, one will struggle even harder to achieve his/her destined fulfillment, than would another one who has some insight into that larger dimension of life which the transcendent proffers man. Benedict has ordered the life of the monks so that they are continually reminded that they are living in the presence of God—their chief solace and support; awareness of this truth enables the monks to contextualize and situate the difficulties, problems, and struggles they encounter on life's way. An awareness of this spiritual reality and its implications can help contemporary society in its understanding of the dignity of each individual person and how that person's potential can be fulfilled.

From the sixth century, then, Benedict can be seen to address the contemporary concern of Sommers, Updike, and so many others about the moral education and the future of the world's children. Perhaps it is this that partly underlies Benedict's great concern for the care of the children sent for education to the monastery. Their natural optimism needs to be nurtured and strengthened by examples of virtuous and generous lives so that when they come to face the difficulties and hardships of life, they will not be discouraged and turned inward to mere self-gratification and pure self-interest. Rather they will continue to say in their wisdom and prudence that it is a great world, a wonderful world.

Conclusion

Philosophy told Boethius that, while he knew where he had come from, he did not know where he was going. Once that problem is resolved in Book III of *The Consolation*, it is Boethius who rises to the occasion and seizes the control of the conversation from Philosophy. He directs it to the issues that were appropriate to the fulfilling of his newly found, or perhaps more correctly stated, rediscovered understanding of the meaning, purpose, and goal of his and of all life. What Boethius came to understand in the lonely, unjust isolation of a death-row prison cell after a life of public service and philosophical inquiry was similar to what his contemporary Benedict came to understand in his monastic cell at Monte Cassino after a life of prayer and humble service to his brethren. The ideas found in the Rule of St. Benedict of Nursia offer but a small sample of Benedict's overall teaching and doctrine on the search for understanding and discernment, a search that also marks Boethius' *The Consolation.*

Benedict wrote his Rule for those who held the same Christian faith as he did, indeed the same Christian faith Boethius held, but that does not preclude the application of his teachings and principles to the world at large. Indeed, the Rule he composed makes a serious contribution to the re-examination of the moral, spiritual, and ethical values of modern time and their relation to the principles of the Western Enlightenment. Eminent scholars, such as Jean Leclerq and Adalbert de Vogüé, have made learned contributions to studies of Benedictine monasticism and monastic culture in general. The popular works of such writers as Thomas Merton, Kathleen Norris, Esther De Waal, Joan Chittister, and others have sought to bring Benedict's holistic spirituality of realized eschatology into the daily lives of women and men today, who are surrounded and almost suffocated by the pressures of contemporary culture.

The principles of the Western Enlightenment have lent themselves to such contemporary expression as capitalism and material comfort, technological and scientific progress, and the exaltation of individual rights. If they are to be useful to the task of preparing for a global civilization, then they must be further refined in the context of the agenda set forth by Boethius: Where have we come from? Where are we going? Who are we? Here is where the wisdom of Saint Benedict can be most helpful and enlightening.

Afterword

John Milton brought his epic poem *Paradise Lost* to a conclusion by describing the departure of Adam and Eve from the Garden of Eden. They had lost what was theirs from the beginning:

119

the innocent joy, the knowledge of all things, the natural and easy friendship with one another and with God. They had admitted their sin and repented. Now armed only with the glimpse into the future revealed to them by the Archangel Michael, they leave the garden of delights with his words echoing in their ears:

> This having learned, thou hast attained the sum
> Of wisdom; hope no higher, though all the stars
> Thou knewest by name, and all the ethereal powers,
> All secrets of the deep, all Nature's works,
> Or works of God in heaven, air, earth, or sea,
> And all the riches of this world enjoy'dst,
> And all the rule, one empire. Only add
> Deeds to thy knowledge answerable; add faith;
> Add virtue, patience, temperance; add love,
> By name to come called Charity, the soul
> Of all the rest: then wilt thou not be loth
> To leave this Paradise, but shalt possess
> A Paradise within thee, happier far.[8]

It is this "Paradise within thee" that humans have been searching for since Adam and Eve were driven from Eden. The Western Enlightenment principles are part of that search, but not all of it, for they are not sufficient to regain Paradise. They require the spirituality, ethics, and the morality demonstrated by people like Boethius and Benedict to make them work for the good of all.

The final words of *Paradise Lost* read:

> They, looking back, all the eastern side beheld
> Of Paradise, so late their happy seat,
> Waved over by that flaming brand, the gate
> With dreadful faces thronged and fiery arms:
> Some natural tears they dropped, but wiped them soon;
> The world was all before them, where to choose
> Their place of rest, and Providence their guide;
> They, hand in hand, with wandering steps and slow,
> Through Eden took their solitary way.[9]

The authors of the Western Enlightenment likewise saw "the world was all before them, where to choose their place of rest." Their principles need to be examined in a larger, spiritual and moral context if they are to help humankind find the peace and progress they claim to contain. The Rule of Saint Benedict offers a sound, profoundly spiritual, and universally applicable basis for such a project.

In sum, the monastery for Benedict is the world writ small, for within its walls and beyond, in its fields and forests, lies all that creation has to offer. Perhaps he would try to persuade the world today that contemporary society needs to recover its sense of values and virtues and thus perhaps come to see the world as a monastery writ large.

Endnotes

1 - Boethius, *The Consolation of Philosophy*, trans. Richard Green (New York: MacMillan Publishing Co., 1962), 19.

2 - Ibid.

3 - Christina Sommers, "Are We Living in a Moral Stone Age?" in *Imprimis* 27, no. 3 (March, 1998). In an essay entitled "Teaching the Virtues," she argues that at the undergraduate level ethics should be taught by studying the philosophy of virtue while students in elementary and secondary schools should be taught the stories and biographies of great men and women. *Vice and Virtue in Everyday Life*, 4th edition, ed. Christina Sommers and Fred Sommers (Orlando: Harcourt Brace, 1997), 677-687.

4 - All references to the Rule of St. Benedict will be according to the chapter and verse divisions used in *RB 1980*, ed. Timothy Fry, O.S.B. (Collegeville, MN: The Liturgical Press, 1981). For a recent commentary with a complete bibliography, see Terrance Kardong, *Benedict's Rule: A Translation and Commentary* (Collegeville, MN: The Liturgical Press, 1996).

5 - George Bull, *Michelangelo: Life, Letters, Poetry* (Oxford: Oxford University Press, 1987), 142.

6 - While Benedict devotes chapter 7 to a thorough and lengthy examination of the virtue of humility, the term itself *humilitas* and its cognates occur dozens of times in the Rule.

7 - Genesis 1.28-30 NAB *(New American Bible)*.

8 - John Milton, *Paradise Lost*, annotated by Edward Le Comte (New York: Mentor, 1981), 341.

9 - Ibid, 343.

CHAPTER 6

CONFUCIAN HUMANISM AND THE WESTERN ENLIGHTENMENT

Tu Weiming

In an essay entitled, "Crisis and Creativity: A Confucian Response to the Second Axial-Age Civilization,"[1] I asked how Confucianism could enrich the spiritual resources of the Western Enlightenment without abandoning its comprehensive humanist vision, its sensitivity to nature, and its dialogical response to Heaven.[2] In offering a Confucian perspective on the "core values" of the global community, I would like to examine that question as a point of departure.

I must first give an account of how this question was formed. I am keenly aware that the majority of Chinese thinkers struggling to appreciate the significance of the Western Enlightenment mentality for China's modernization have already dismissed their Confucian heritage as the outmoded feudal past, largely irrelevant to modern China's intellectual self-definition and future aspirations. They have assumed that the concerted effort, since the late 19th century, to transcend the Confucian habits of the heart, was motivated by a strong desire to allow China to take part in the modernizing process informed by the Western Enlightenment mentality. For them, the contemporary Confucian revival is an indication of cultural conservatism, if not political regression. The suggestion that Confucian humanism can actually contribute to the enrichment of the Enlightenment project may be considered to reflect wishful thinking at best and, at worst, pernicious cultural chauvinism.

However, modern perceptions of the human condition informed by ecological insights clearly show that the mentality of the "age of reason," narrowly focused on progress as characterized by the desire to conquer nature, is not only incompatible with sustainable growth but, in the long run, detrimental to human survival. The basic anthropocentric assumptions embedded in progressivism are antithetical to the cosmic story in which the viability of the human species is framed. If Western Enlightenment values, such as reason and liberty, are to continue to inspire the human community, they must be liberated from an outmoded anthropocentrism and recontextualized in a new humanism. This requires humanity's engagement in a sort of mental archaeology to understand how the anthropocentric mentality actually evolved in the 18th century.

It is interesting to note that the perceived secular ethics of Confucian China attracted a great deal of interest among the Enlightenment thinkers such as Voltaire, Quesnay, and Diderot.[3] While the humanism that emerged in 18th century Europe was both anti-spiritualist and anti-naturalist, opinions ranged widely concerning religious matters. This spiritless and denatured belief that human rationality alone can provide the transcendental justification of ethics may be taken as a defining characteristic of Western Enlightenment thinking.

It is naive to believe that there was indeed an age of reason as envisioned by Kant. The preference given to instrumental rationality at the expense of other forms of rationality, in the subsequent developments of the Enlightenment mentality, is only part of a very complex story. The dynamic of the modern West, as seen by those from the outside who were overwhelmed by its creative and destructive power, was not merely instrumental rationality but the Faustian drive to explore, know, master and conquer. This combination of detached analytical ability and intense passion, fueled by social Darwinism narrowly applied to inter-civilizational competitiveness, led to the development of international rules of play which defined the fittest exclusively in terms of wealth and power.

Colonialism and imperialism certainly poisoned the well of the Western Enlightenment mentality as a source of inspiration and direction for the emerging global community. Yet, the vitality of Enlightenment thinking is predicated on two observations. First, virtually all the spheres of interest in modern societies are bound up with it including science and technology, market economy, democratic polity, mass communication, multi-national corporations, and research universities. Second, the values underlying these spheres of interest—notably liberty, equality, human rights, private property, privacy, and due process of law are also rooted in its precepts. It is highly unlikely then, that societies can develop an alternative ethic without considering these principles. Nevertheless, the mindset underlying the Enlightenment has generated so many unintended negative consequences that a fundamental restructuring of its basic value orientation is necessary.

It is vital to put the Enlightenment mentality in a comparative civilization perspective so that its historical particularities can be thoroughly studied as forms of local knowledge that cannot be generalized beyond specific territorial boundaries. What is truly universal about both the spheres of interest and the core values of the Enlightenment mentality can only be determined by encounters with different cultural universes. The assumption that the modern West is so complex and richly endowed with symbolic resources that it can reconfigure itself as a standard of inspiration for humanity, without reference to complex non-Western civilizations, is theoretically indefensible and practically unworkable.

Indeed, to gain a full appreciation of the historical rootedness of the Enlightenment, one must investigate anew the spiritual traditions in the West at that critical juncture of transformation. The continuous significance of the Western Enlightenment for the future depends on its relevance to the aspirations as well as the concrete manifestations of non-Western spiritual traditions throughout the world.

The Confucian reflection on, and its critique of the Enlightenment mentality exemplifies this larger vision that involves the dialogue of civilizations as a continuing intellectual joint venture. There is historical significance in the Enlightenment thinkers' preoccupation with China. The very fact that the shapers of the values of the Enlightenment took Confucian China as the primary reference society indicates that in its original conception the Enlightenment was meant to be ecumenical. Leibnitz's philosophical reflection on natural theology is illustrative of this point.

Hegel's philosophy of history in the 19th century signaled a critical turning point that relegated Confucianism, together with other non-Western spiritual traditions, to the back rooms of the museum of Spirit. The common practice in cultural China of defining the Confucian ethic as "feudal" is predicated on the thesis of historical inevitability implicit in the Hegelian vision. The irony is that the whole Enlightenment mentality, as captured by the Kantian question: "What is Enlightenment?," was actually an affirmation that cultural traditions outside the West, notably in Confucian China, got right without the benefit of revelatory religion. What happened in the 19th century when the dynamics of the modern West engulfed the world in a restless march toward material progress was distinctly not a straightforward working out of the Western Enlightenment.

On the contrary, the Enlightenment was thoroughly undermined by the "unbound Prometheus"—to borrow David Landes' suggestive term—the unmitigated quest for complete liberation. While the demands for liberation from all constraints of authority and dogma characterized the Enlightenment in the West, the rest of the world experienced conquest, hegemony, and enslavement at the hands of the West.

Hegel, Marx, and Weber shared the belief that, despite all its shortcomings, the modern West informed by Enlightenment thinking was instrumental in making the world a more humane place for human flourishing. Hegel's idea of the unfolding of the Spirit, Marx's notion of historical inevitability, and Weber's "iron cage" of modernity—essentially a European predicament—are thought to be general statements about the human condition. Confucian East Asia, Islamic Middle East, Hindu India, and Buddhist Southeast Asia were on the receiving end of this process. Eventually, modernization as homogenization would make cultural diversity insignificant. It was inconceivable that Confucianism or, for that matter, any other non-Western spiritual tradition could exert any shaping influence on the modernizing process. The shift from traditional to modern ideology was irreversible and inevitable.

In the global context, what some of the most brilliant minds in the modern West assumed to be self-evident turned out to be sheer fantasy. In the rest of the world and, arguably, in Western Europe and North America as well, the anticipated complete transition from traditional to modern society never occurred. As a norm, elements of traditional societies in the modern West continue to exist and, indeed cultural forces, generated by distinct traditions, continue to shape the modernizing process. Thus, the 18th century thinkers' self-understanding, gained through recognizing the relevance of "radical otherness"—such as Confucian China—is more applicable to the current situation in the global community than the 19th century thinkers' disregard for any possible alternative to their own Western mindset. For this reason, the openness of the 18th century as contrasted with the exclusivity of the 19th century may provide a better guide for the dialogue of civilizations now in the early years of the 21st century.

In light of the controversial hypothesis of the "coming clash of civilizations,"[4] there is an increasingly compelling need to explore a global ethic and to open civilizational dialogues. The dichotomy of "the West and the rest" is too simplistic and restrictive a perspective from which to account for and deal with the complexity of the emerging global situation.

Among those subjects for which an inter-civilizational dialogue would be particularly critical is the issue of community. Of the Enlightenment values advocated by the French Revolution, fraternity or the functional equivalent of community, has received scant attention from modern political theorists. Since Locke's treatises on government, mainstream Western societies have been preoccupied with the relationship between the individual and the state. While this has of course not been the full picture of modern political thought, it is undeniable that communities, especially the family, have been largely ignored in this Western political discourse.

Hegel's fascination with the "civil society" situated some-where outside the family concept and below the state was mainly prompted by the dynamics of bourgeois society, a distinct urban phenomenon threatening to traditional communities. This was a prophetic gaze into the future rather than a critical analysis of the value of community. The transition from *gemeinschaft* (a natural community) to *gesellschaft* (an organized society for a distinct pur-pose) was thought to have been such a rupture that Weber referred to "universal brotherhood" as an outmoded medieval myth unreal-izable in the disenchanted modern secular world. In sociological terms, the Kantian vision of the kingdom of ends is merely a philo-sophical utopia.

The upsurge of North American interest in community in recent decades may have been stimulated by a sense of crisis, the fear that social disintegration is a serious threat to the United States and Canada. But the local conditions in these republics, precipitated by ethnic and linguistic conflicts, are general throughout the highly industrialized First World. The advent of the "global village" sym-bolizes difference, differentiation, and outright discrimination as well as integration. The conflict between globalizing trends, includ-ing trade, finance, information, migration, disease, and localism rooted in ethnicity, language, land, class, age, and religious faith makes the task of exploring global ethics painfully difficult.

On the surface, the Enlightenment's basic value-orientation seems the only hope for such a task. Understandably, those modern adherents of the Enlightenment tenaciously argue for rationality, lib-erty, equality, human rights, individual dignity, and due process of law as the core values of modernity. Liberal-minded Western thinkers' common practice of offering a minimalist argument for global ethics is predicated on the belief that only a thin description of the Enlightenment—the "human rights" discourse is a case in point—can overcome relativism. Yet, critiques of the Enlightenment from ecologists, feminists, and religious pluralists strongly suggest that a minimalist argument for global ethics based on such a super-ficial description of the Enlightenment is insufficient. Without dis-cussing why consensus formation at this elementary level is problematic, I suggest that a fundamental reconfiguration of the Enlightenment is a necessary precondition for exploring the possibility of a global ethic. Any attempt, no matter how comprehensive, within the bounds of the Enlightenment is unlikely to transcend its structural limitations imposed by anthropocentric rationality, aggressiveness toward nature and inattention to spiritual matters. A comparative cultural approach informed by an ethical-religious sensitivity to the civilizational dialogues is a more viable alternative.

I suggest that Confucian humanism is strategically positioned to reconfigure the Enlightenment by broadening its anthropological vision and deepening its ethical foundation. Admittedly, such an enterprise is complex and requires interdisciplinary and trans-professional collaboration. Let us first examine the claims of the Confucian humanist vision.

Confucian humanism is both anthropological and cosmological and, indeed, Confucian life-orientation is "anthropocosmic."[5] Confucians fully acknowledge that humans are "embedded" in this world and even celebrate their earthly destiny. While other world religions, such as Christianity and Buddhism, envision a spiritual sanctuary outside the mundane human existence, Confucians, by focusing on the life here and now, inadvertently undermine or deliberately reject such notions as the Kingdom of God yet to come and Pure land as the "other shore." Embeddedness means not only passively accepting one's "conditionalities"—such as race, gender, and age—as inseparable dimensions of life, but actively realizing oneself through these human parameters. Humanity's "earthly" nature means that biological, physiological, bodily, familial, and communal conditions define each individual.

As earthly beings, our spirituality is grounded in humanity. Humans do not become "spiritual" by departing from or transcending their earthly nature. Instead, their bodies, families, and communities provide the proper home for their spirituality. Earthly embeddedness then makes each person who he or she is. Human beings are fated to be "human" not as the result of an arbitrary decree beyond their rational comprehension, but as the consequence of a promise, a covenant: Heaven engenders but the human completes. As co-creators of the cosmic process, human beings are spiritual by nature. They are Heaven's partners and, individually and collectively, they are entrusted with a sacred mission to transform the earth, body, family, and community into the emanations of Heaven's inner virtue, *de*. While Heaven is omnipresent and may be omniscient, it is definitely not omnipotent. Its creativity can be enlarged and ought to be continued and appreciated by human participation.

This Confucian anthropocosmic idea is, in principle, compatible with the Enlightenment concept of human rationality. Yet, the Enlightenment concept could be extended to include the Confucian metaphysical vision, which incorporates the story of the cosmos into an inclusive humanism, rather than an exclusive anthropocentrism. This reconfigured Enlightenment would be liberated from its anthropocentrism and regain a profound sense of awe toward the spirit and a deep sense of respect for nature. The Confucian life-orientation informed by the anthropocosmic vision is reverential toward Heaven and Earth. In Herbert Fingarette's characterization, it is a world-view that reveres "the secular as sacred."[6] The form of life imagined and practiced in Confucian "inclusive humanism" is of this world because it takes the earth, the body, the family, and the community as constituent parts of a path of human flourishing.

The path to human fulfillment is a spiritual exercise that cherishes the process of learning to be human as the "Holy Rite." In such a "Holy Rite," the earth is sanctified, the body is divine, the family is beatific, and the community is sacred. Humans are blessed as earthly creatures. To have bodies, families, and communities is to have a richly textured life. Such a life is spiritually significant. Since each thing is a specific configuration of vital energy *qi*, all matter—sun, moon, star, animal, tree, or rock—is alive and spiritual. This idea of shared spirituality or continuity of beings as an underlying motif enables each one to experience consanguinity with all other modalities of being.

Recognizing that human beings are an integral part of the cosmos prompts them to establish an ever-expanding network of intimate relationships. The full realization of their nature is none other than the transformation of what they are into all-embracing expressions of themselves as the co-creators of the cosmic process. There is no reason for each person to transcend ethnicity, gender, age, land, class, age, and faith to become what he or she ought to be. An individual's earthly, bodily, familial, and communal realities are not necessarily constraints or limitations. Instead, these parameters are efficacious instruments for self-realization. Confucians cultivate the art of learning to be human in ordinary daily existence—of living the secular as sacred.

The introduction of the Confucian theory and practice of self-cultivation into the Enlightenment is vital. The Socratic vision that an unexamined life is not worth living ought to have been a spiritual source for the Enlightenment. Unfortunately, the Faustian drive for wealth and power has so fundamentally undermined self-knowledge as wisdom for human fulfillment that the trajectory of the Western development model has constructed the already mentioned "iron cage" of Weber's description.

In the Confucian perception of self-cultivation, the earth, body, family and community as proper arenas for human flourishing ought to be respected and cherished as real treasures. Since the ultimate meaning of life is realizable in ordinary human existence, the "life world" here and now is intrinsically valuable. Ordinary activities in the life world should not be viewed merely as a means to an end. Human beings and the surrounding environment are not there to be used or exploited. As an interconnected community, people can, through communication, create a meaningful life together and avoid the danger of reducing those they encounter—animals, plants, and things as well as humans—to merely a collection of objects.

The ethic of responsibility demands that all people bear full responsibility for what they have done to themselves, their fellow human beings, and the world around them. This notion that people are co-creators and, therefore, duty-bound to preserve the order of things in the universe can serve as a corrective to the Enlightenment's implicit aggressiveness against nature.

A corollary of this stature as co-creator of the cosmic process is the power of destruction. As a result of the Enlightenment's aggressive anthropocentrism, people have seriously polluted the land, water, and air; substantially depleted the supply of unrenewable energy; eliminated numerous species; destroyed many indigenous traditions; and reduced thousands of human communities to utter destitution. In short, by embarking on a restless march toward material progress, human beings have blatantly demonstrated their self-destructive power. The Confucian quest for harmony between the human species and nature and for mutuality between the human heart-and-mind and Heaven, as an articulation of inclusive humanism, offers an alternative—a path of healing.

If the Enlightenment is to serve as a guide for human flourishing, it must broaden its humanistic vision to regain its spiritual vitality. At a minimum, humanity must transcend the parochial dichotomy of "the West and the rest." In ethical terms, the emerging global community must be the proper reference for international relations. Arguments for national self-interest as a dominant ideology, no matter how persuasive, must yield to the realization that as co-creators and co-inhabitants of this blue earth, we must all think globally.

The Confucian idea of reciprocity is a defining characteristic of this global thinking. Embodied in the golden rule stated in the negative: "Do not do unto others what you would not want others to do unto you,"[7] this principle of reciprocity has been widely acknowledged as a core value in the global ethic since the Parliament of World Religions at Chicago in 1993. To empathize with others in their own terms is to respect difference; moreover, it is to authenticate and empower humanity. Reciprocity is not a passive acceptance of limitations but an active response to the hearts and minds of those in need. The golden rule must, therefore, be supplemented by a positive charge, the principle of humanity: "In order to establish ourselves, we must help others to establish themselves; in order to enlarge ourselves, we must help others to enlarge themselves."[8]

This inclusive sense of human-relatedness is predicated on the observation that in most cases social intercourse is mutually beneficial and that, even in apparently zero-sum games, communication, negotiation, and consensus formation are often necessary and desirable. Confucian humanism has rich symbolic resources for enabling Enlightenment anthropocentrism to become a truly ecumenical global ethic. It is a form of practical idealism worth exploring.

The exploration of the relevance of Confucian humanism to the modern West remains, at this juncture, problematical. Nevertheless, Confucianism's role in the development of a communal critical self-consciousness in East Asia, with particular reference to Cultural China, is a matter of great urgency and requires a shift of mindset among East Asian cultural and political leaders.

An example of such a change and shift would be a comparison to India as a reference society for Cultural China. If Confucian intellectuals in the Sinic world would take India seriously as a spiritual challenge to their own cultural choice, they would be greatly motivated to retrieve their own indigenous spiritual traditions, notably Mahayana Buddhism and religious Daoism. Informed by a much broader vision of human flourishing, the world order defined exclusively in Western terms of wealth and power would appear inadequate. A possible consequence of this restructuring of the scientistific, materialistic, and utilitarian Chinese mindset would shift the notion from Tibet as a political threat to national unity, to Tibet as a spiritual resource. This could lead to China's incorporation of the many cultural and inter-religious perspectives of China's minorities—numbering more than 60 million and occupying more than two thirds of China proper—into a culturally sophisticated development strategy, enriching the conceptual apparatuses and symbolic resources in China's spiritual self-definition. Such a self-definition is heuristically valuable for the globalization of a reconfigured Enlightenment mentality. This local knowledge—how an imported Enlightenment anthropocentrism, through critical self-examination and dialogue of civilizations, transformed itself into an inclusive humanism—may turn out to be globally significant.

The Islamic-Confucian dialogue, initiated in the United States and Malaysia in 1995, signaled the feasibility of a Confucian ecumenism in encountering other axial-age civilizations.[9] The circulation of terms such as "Confucian Christian," "Confucian Buddhist," and "Confucian Muslim" in inter-religious dialogues suggests that the adjective "Confucian" defines a specific world view that appeals to Christians, Buddhists and Muslims. The Confucian life-orientation has been wrongly characterized as an "adjustment to the world."[10]

Yet, the crisis of the world demands that human beings be politically concerned, socially engaged, and culturally sensitive. The Confucian Christian, Buddhist, or Muslim, in response to the spirit of the times, takes the improvement of the world from within, rather than personal salvation on the other shore, as the primary concern.

As Confucian thinkers begin to reflect on the human condition as it has been shaped by the modern West, they find the need for the cultivation of an ecumenical humanist spirit compelling. Self, community, nature and Heaven, the four dimensions of the Confucian humanist project, will have to be integrated into a holistic vision of human flourishing. The key to "Confucian learning" is learning for the sake of the self, not as an isolated individuality, but as a center of relationships. On the one hand, each person's subjectivity and dignity ought to be respected and, on the other, sociality, communication, and reciprocity should be developed. Learning to be human entails a broadening and deepening process.

Horizontally, people learn to interact with an ever-widening circle of human-relatedness. From the family to the global community, all the social space in between is relevant to personal growth. People learn to be children, students, friends, colleagues, spouses, parents, teachers, clients, and patrons through continuous interaction with community variously understood. To learn to be fully human each being needs to transcend selfishness, nepotism, parochialism, ethnocentrism, and anthropocentrism. Indeed, the fruitful interaction between self and community is predicated on an ontological insight that the true nature of being human is both anthropological and cosmological. The cosmic story, including the evolution of the human species, is intimately connected with self-knowledge.

Vertically, people must try to articulate a harmonious relationship between human beings and nature and aspire to fulfill the covenant as a co-creator of the universe. The highest human aspiration in the Confucian tradition is the mutuality of the human heart-and-mind and the Way of Heaven. The notion that "man is the measure of all things" fails to account for the human capacity to perceive the world from a transcendent perspective. The full measure of humanity responds to the spiritual realm and resonates with nature. It is dynamic, transformative, and open to new possibilities.

From a Confucian perspective, the persuasive power of the Enlightenment project will be greatly enhanced if it incorporates self, community, nature, and Heaven—or a generalized idea of the spirit—into a holistic vision. The intellectual horizon of the global ethic, informed by the Enlightenment, should be extended and the moral sensitivity of those determined to see the universal application of Enlightenment ideas should be deepened. The core values that are thought to be essential for the global community may, as a result, assume a different constellation. Today the global village is only a virtual reality, if not merely an imagined possibility and the sense of priority in formulating the global ethic is a matter of intense debate. But even a small step toward the right direction is a worthwhile spiritual joint venture.

Endnotes

1 - See Tu Weiming, "Crisis and Creativity: A Confucian Response to the Second Axial Age," in Steven Chase, ed., *Doors of Understanding: Conversations in Global Spirituality in Honor of Ewert Cousins* (Quincy, Il:Franciscan Press, 1997).

2 - Hereafter just referred to as Enlightenment.

3 - Under the sponsorship of the Committee on Studies of the American Academy of Arts and Sciences, I organized a series of three informal discussions under the general topic of a Confucian reflection on and critique of the Enlightenment in the spring of 1997.

4 - Samuel Huntington's idea, first appearing in the *Foreign Affairs,* 72, no. 3 (Summer 1993), is predicated on the highly problematical dichotomy of "the West and the rest." See Samuel Huntington, *The Clash of Civilizations and the Remaking of World Order* (New York: Simon and Schuster, 1966).

5 - Tu Weiming, *Centrality and Commonality: An Essay on Confucian Religiousness* (Albany: New York State University Press, 1989), Epilogue.

6 - Herbert Fingarette, *Confucius – the Secular as Sacred* (New York: Harper and Row, 1972).

7 - *Analects*, XII:2, XV:24.

8 - *Analects*,VI:28.

9 - An international symposium organized by the University of Malaya, Kuala Lumpur, 13-15 March 1995.

10 - Max Weber, *The Religion of China: Confucianism and Taoism,* trans. Hans H. Gerth (Glencoe, IL: Free Press, 1951), 235.

CHAPTER 7

ESSENCE AND CONTINUITY OF LIFE IN THE AFRICAN SOCIETY

Thomas Odhiambo

What is the purpose and meaning of human life? This, the mother of all questions, has baffled philosophers and theologians in all societies throughout the ages. Likewise, the question that naturally follows: What is the destiny of a human being within that purpose? These fundamental yet troubling questions are as relevant and perplexing today as they were during the Pharaonic times of Africa, beginning more than 5,000 years ago. Answers provided by sages, philosophers, theologians, and thinkers whose prime concerns are the mysteries of life, destiny, and existential continuity are still vital to society. Social institutions are built and shaped accordingly.

In contrast to the dominant contemporary world-view expressing the depersonalizing, materialistic dogma formulated by mega-giants of market societies, almost all major religions, including indigenous African religions, emphasize the evolution of human beings to a higher level of righteousness, compassion, peace, and divine insight. Righteousness and divine insight are highly personal spiritual values. Compassion and peace encompass "others"—the family, the community, the society, the international community, the

137

aliens, and the outcasts. The preservation of these values depends on the work of those devoted to the personal spirit within, through contemplation, retreat, prayer, study, and meditation.

A tragedy at the dawn of the third millennium is that humanity, having invented unparalleled information technologies offering leisure for thoughtful discourse and unhurried contemplative study, is unable to benefit thereby. This is so because human beings are frenetically occupied with political power and the elevation of their "physical selfhood" to a new market utopia. All humanity is called upon to notch up the economic ratchet-wheel to the level of the modern industrialized societies of the West, regardless of their values and living conditions. There is overwhelming interest in information and knowledge, without concern for insight. Such powerful materialistic forces that consider less technically developed societies on a lower rung of cultural, scientific, and religious accomplishment are leading to the homogenization of human experience on a wholly Western neo-liberal model that emphasizes the spread of consumerism and aggressive individualism. Sadly, inherent in this vision is the absence of sages, philosophers, theologians, and other intuitive thinkers whose prime vocation has been fathoming the mysteries of life, destiny, and existential continuity.

There is need now for Africans, and for that matter every one on this earth, to give pause to these forces, to ponder again the vital questions of life's meaning. There is also need to reposition Africa on the main highway of the development of the human spirit—not as an anthropological study, nor as an apologia—but rather as a dynamically insightful plant in the grove of human experience. This essay will consider Africa's early contribution to the evolution of human knowledge, thereafter describing contemporary African visions of the nature of God, the human spirit, and life. I will raise questions on notions of the continuity of life, nature, and human destiny, and their relevance to family and society. The traditional African world-view is highly relevant to the contemporary social and economic development process. In view of the troubling trends mentioned above, this traditional African world-view is highly relevant to the contemporary social and economic development process.

Africa's Place in the Evolution of Human Knowledge

The roots of Western religious thought may be traced to Africa, whose influence extends to Greece and underlies classic philosophy and religion. But, for the past five centuries, African history and culture have been shrouded in guilt and shame, as Maya Angelou has eloquently stated the case:

> [Transported to distant lands in the western hemisphere,] African slaves themselves, separated from their tribesmen and languages, forced by the lash to speak another tongue (...), were unable to convey the stories of their own people, their deeds, rituals, religions, and beliefs. Within a few generations, details of the kingdoms of Ghana and Mali and of the Songhai Empire became hazy in their minds. The Mende concepts of beauty and Ashanti idea of justice all but faded with the old family names and intricate tribal laws. The slaves too soon began to believe what their masters believed: Africa was a continent of savages. Save for the rare scholar and the observant traveler, the African at home (on the continent) was seen as a caricature of nature: so it followed that Africans abroad (blacks everywhere) were better only because of their encounters with whites. Even in religious matters the African was called a mere fetishist, trusting in sticks and bones. Most failed to see the correlation between the African and his gris-gris (religious amulets) and the Moslem with his beads or the Catholic with his rosary.[1]

Unfortunately, the Western Enlightenment occurred at a time when mercantilist Europe became technologically capable of overseas expansion. Without scruple, adventurers and fortune seekers began what became an unfettered conquest of Africa among other neighboring lands. Scholars provided the apologia for slavery and colonialism, sanctifying the brutalization of African lands, resources, and peoples in the drive for power, wealth, and progress. For example, David Hume wrote in his famous footnote to an essay, "On National Character:"

> I am apt to suspect the Negroes to be naturally inferior to the whites. There scarcely ever was a civilized nation of that complexion, nor ever any individual eminent in action or speculation, no ingenious manufacturer amongst them, no arts, no sciences.[2]

139

Other luminaries, including Immanuel Kant and Hegel, repeated such formulations of philosophical prejudice. The latter positioned Africa outside History, as the absolute, non-historical beginning of the movement of Spirit.[3]

Maya Angelou appropriately inquires:

> How, then, to explain that these people, supposedly without a culture, could so influence the cultures of their captors and even of distant strangers with whom they have had no contact? [4]

Myths about Africa emanating from prejudice, deliberate ignorance, and guilt's need for self-justification cannot bury the reality of the gifts that the peoples of Africa made to embryonic Western civilization; gifts that were transmitted through Egypt to the Greeks. There is growing archeological evidence and scholarly support for the proposition that the brilliant civilization of Pharaonic Egypt was rooted in black Africa. While the intellectual contribution of Egypt to Greek thought had never been denied, the theory that the intellectual and philosophical roots of the great Egyptian civilization may have originated in black Africa has not been widely acknowledged, notably in Western countries.

In 300 B.C., an Egyptian priest began to compile a history of Egypt for the reigning monarch Ptolemy. Manetho's chronology supports the legend that by 3100 B.C., King Menes of the Upper Nile was able to conquer the delta part of the lower Nile and establish ancient Egypt's first dynasty. Further, according to legend, he ruled 60 years before being carried off by a hippopotamus. By 3,000 B.C., Africans of this region had also apparently invented systems of hieroglyphic writings. There is considerable archeological evidence that these early Egyptians may be descendants of an advanced black people who inhabited the wilderness of the Sahara desert for some 4,000 years. During this time, beginning in 8,000 B.C., they evolved a highly organized way of life that included the invention of the first known calendar presumably for predicting the rains. A shift in climate caused these highly developed people to migrate eastward into the Sudan and the upper Nile Valley regions, as well as towards the horn of Africa.[5]

Along the same vein, Henry Olela argues that the modern African world-view, as well as that of the Greeks and Romans, came from ancient Africans (Egyptians, Nubians). Olela, assuming Hellenic culture originated in Crete, inquired about the origins of this island's people. He found various sources suggesting that they may have been descendants of a family branch of western Ethiopians, whose origins are traced to the Sahel in 2,500 B.C.. He also cites other researchers who aver that the Minoan civilization had none other than an African foundation. Archaeological evidence in Egypt also supports the proposition that the Egyptians were descendants of a number of African nations. So intimately intertwined are the histories of Egypt, Kush (established by the Nubians of Sudan and the Upper Nile), and Axum (a civilization in the horn of Africa) that they are inseparable in the Egyptian foundations of universal philosophical thought. Some of these peoples who had tremendous impact on the Egyptians are thought to be descendants of the Gallas, Somolians, and the Masais of the area that is now Kenya.[6]

In 1987, Martin Bernal's extensive study emphasizing the African roots of classic civilization was published. This work quoted Herodotus and Plato, as well as other sources on which he built his Black Athena theory.[7] Bernal describes the interest of the Greek historian, Herodotus [450 B.C.], in how Egyptian and Phoenician colonies influenced Greek civilization—the former through the introduction of writing to the Hellenes, and the latter by their transference of the Egyptian religious mysteries, including the art of divination. The names of many Greek gods were adapted from Egyptian formulations. Herodotus claimed that the names of all gods had been known in Egypt from the beginning of time. Early inhabitants of Greece offered sacrifices while praying, but their gods were neither named nor titled.

The Greeks started to use the Egyptian god-names only after the Pelasgians received the approval to do so from their most ancient, and only, oracle at Dodona. Also according to Bernal, Plato spent time in Egypt around 390 B.C., and in his *Phaidros*, Plato has Socrates declare that the Egyptian god of wisdom, Theuth-Thoth, is the inventor of arithmetic, geometry, and writing. In his *Philebos* and *Epinomis*, Plato furnished further descriptions of Thoth as the creator of writing, language, and all the sciences. A few years later, having borrowed material from the library of Alexandra, Aristotle stated in his *Metaphysica* his belief that Egypt was the cradle of mathematics because of the work of the Egyptian caste of priests who had the leisure to engage in such theoretical pursuits. Thus, geometry was not invented, as Herodotus had believed, simply to measure land after principle landmarks had been washed away by the periodic floods of the Nile.[8]

The association between Egypt's old religion and the extraordinary rise of mathematics and science in ancient Egypt is an intriguing one. The philosophy of the old Egyptian religion was not concerned with the ephemeral and material world of "becoming" with its cycles of growth and decay. Instead, the religion emphasized the immortal realm of being, as exemplified in numbers, geometry, and astronomy. This approach to life also influenced Greek metaphysical thought. Many scholars believe that Egyptian ideas strongly influenced the writings of Plato and Aristotle on these subjects. Plato may have adopted the Egyptian view of the immortality of the soul as well as its view on creation and its doctrine of the Good. There is a strong basis for speculating that Aristotle adopted the Egyptian notion of the "unmoved mover," the creative process developed from disorder to order. This process was performed through mind and word—or pure intelligence, as Olela recants it. Aristotle may also have learned from Egypt the doctrine of the soul discussed in the *Book of the Dead*.[9]

Not unlike their ancient forefathers, contemporary Africans, past and present are extremely religious. Most individual and group activities, of whatever nature—political, economic, social, or military—are heavily influenced by considerations essentially of a mystical and religious character. Their knowledge of God is expressed in proverbs, short statements, songs, prayers, myths, stories, and religious ceremonies. While there are no sacred writings in traditional societies, many Europeans traveling in Africa from the seventeenth century onwards found a similar monotheistic and, in many ways, metaphysical thread of thought regarding God and the human spirit across the continent. This discovery may be confirmed by comparing a number of reports and studies. For example, the philosophical, esoteric, and metaphysical aspects of Western African thought were reported by the French scholar Maurice Delafosse [1879-1926] in a series of monographs on indigenous religions and cultures of Africa that teased out the ritualistic and institutionalized facets from their philosophical frameworks on life and thought. Delafosse's work is part of an extensive project on African religions, carried on by William Leo Hansberry.[10] Recently, John S. Mbiti has carried out a wide-ranging study of African traditional religions. His work spans the continent and covers some 300 African people's beliefs.[11] He has also amassed an impressive bibliography of studies on individual traditional religions.

The Nature of the Supreme Being

Although the cultural, geographical, and environmental characteristics of each nation color concepts of God, there are sufficiently significant elements of commonality of belief that enable one to speak of an African concept of God. It can be stated with reasonable confidence that all African cultures tend to believe that God, whatever title or name is used, transcends perception by human faculties. While God has been associated with concrete thought forms, i.e. single objects or supernatural forces in the visible universe such as the sun, the moon, the high mountain, forest, or thunder, and lightning, none of these figurative descriptions are incarnations of God, nor are they worshiped as gods. They are generally metaphorical representations to promote understanding of God and to enable people to draw closer to Him/Her. As a Dutch scholar, who visited the Kingdom of Benin in West Africa, wrote in an eye-witness account of 1705: "Because God is invisible, they—the citizens of Benin—say that it would be foolish to make any corporeal representations of Him, for they insist that it is impossible to make an image of what one has never seen."[12]

Generally, the physical or metaphorical descriptions of God are associated with the invisible nature of God and reflect certain attributes that people correlate with the invisible God and are natural touchstones to further understanding of God.

For example: [13]

- The Luo of Nyanza, in Kenya, living astride the Equator on the shores of Lake Victoria, regard the sun, or Nyasaye, as an expression of an aspect of the Supreme Being, who is the author of life and death and the creator of all things.

- The Wachagga, who live on the slopes of Mt. Kilimanjaro, just south of the Equator, in Tanzania, know the Supreme Being as Ruwa, and associate him with the sun and the sky. They see God as the omnipotent creator of all things, who changes not.

- The Barotse, who live in the Upper Zambezi valley of Zambia in Central-Southern Africa, know the Supreme Being as Nambe, who created the universe and is the great cause of everything. He is omnipotent and nothing can be done against his will. The Barotse personified God through the sun and sky, which are the more conspicuous abodes for their God.

From these and numerous other accounts, the following characteristics would seem to capture, in very broad terms, commonalities in the African conception of God. God possesses the eternal, intrinsic attributes of omnipotence, omniscience, and invisible omnipresence. God is the first cause and creator of the universe, that which is visible to the physical senses, and, that which is invisible (the visible universe is of lesser importance than the invisible one). God is the Great Protector and Governor of all Creation. Many concrete examples throughout Africa express these attributes: [14]

- On omnipotence—there is a saying among the Yoruba of Nigeria that duties and challenges are easy to meet when God performs them, difficult to do without such help.

- On omnipresence—the Bamum from Cameroon call God "Nnui" which means "He who is everywhere." The Shilluk in the Sudan and the Langi of Uganda liken God to the wind and air to convey this attribute.[15]

- On omniscience—for the Zulu of South Africa and the Banyawanda of Rwanda, God is known as "The Wise one" and to the Akan of Ghana, as "He who knows and sees all."

Human Nature

The relationship between God and humankind is as that of Parent and child. God is the Father, the Parent, or the Mother of humanity. What then is the nature of the human being? Having a divine origin, how can human beings be considered mere flesh and bones? Generally, the human spirit and/or soul is assumed to be immaterial and divine. Each person is a complex of material and immaterial elements, the immaterial being the vital essence of the person reflected in his/her health and well-being. There are different versions of this view.

According to the religious culture of the Mandingos,[16] who live throughout the dry savanna areas of West Africa, from Niger to Senegal, the total human being is comprised of three entities: the visible, physical mortal body, by far the least significant entity; and two distinct, invisible, non-corporeal entities—*Dia* and *Nia*— housed in the mortal body.

Mandingos consider the first non-corporeal entity, the *Dia*, a vital force or energy, which has no will or intelligence or personality of its own. It enters the physical body at the time of conception and imparts to the body the vitality that energizes it throughout its mortal existence. The *Dia* is believed to be a portion of a universal and eternal form of impersonal energy that permeates the whole of nature, including inanimate as well as animate things. This universal and eternal life force springs ultimately from the Supreme Being.

The *Nia*, on the other hand, provides the will and the intelligence that directs the operations of the *Dia* as it resides in the physical body. The *Nia* has its own personality and, like the *Dia*, is believed to exist long before it enters the physical body during the uterine development of the forming infant. It is responsible for controlling and harmonizing the various materials, which contribute to the development of the fetus. The *Nia* exists beyond the death of the physical body. During that existence, this disembodied form preserves the same moral temperament and intellectual powers that characterized it during its sojourn in the terrestrial world, as well as retaining its knowledge and interest in the physical environment and human personalities with whom it had meaningfully interacted. The *Nia* is even able, for a time, to reestablish contact with these persons. It is clear that striving toward spiritual perfection—the perfection of the *Nia*—is a principal purpose of human life.

Likewise, the Akan people of Ghana consider a human being to be constituted of three elements: the *okra, sunsum*, and *honam (nipadua)*. The *okra* is the innermost self, or life force of the person expressed as a spark of the Supreme Being (*Onyame*) in the person as the child of God. It is also translated as the English equivalent of Soul. The *sunsum* seems to be equivalent to the spirit of humanity, and with close analysis is not essentially separate from the *okra*. The *honam* refers to the physical body. The Akan thinkers believe that there is clear interaction among these three parts. In cases of obvious bodily illness there are often times where modern Western medicine can have no effect but where traditional medicine has proven extremely effective. In such cases the bodily illness is considered to objectify a troubled spirit—bringing it in line with the Superior Being will bring about the healing. From the point of view of Akan metaphysics the human person and the world in general cannot be reduced to physics or an assemblage of flesh and bones. The human person is a complex being that cannot be explained or satisfied in terms of a purely physical mindset concerning the universe.[17]

An essentially similar description of human nature and life purpose is exemplified in the religious belief system of the peoples of southern Nigeria, recorded by the English anthropologist, Arnaury Talbot [1926].[18] However, in this belief system, the human personality comprises five separate but associated entities, of which only the first is visible. These are:

• The physical body, considered the least important entity of the total human being, because it is only the material, corporeal framework through which other entities operate while resident in the earthly environment.

• The ethereal body, or the "feeling self," believed to be the inner frame of the physical form. Though invisible, the "feeling self" consists of a material substance and, like the physical body, is subject to death on earth. It serves as the vehicle for the vital force animating the physical body during the period of earthly life.

- The mental body, or the thinking self, considered immortal, acts as the vehicle for human consciousness.

- The spiritual body, or the minor ego, believed to be immortal, originates from the Superior Being, and is not necessarily confined to the physical body to which it is attached.

- The transcendental self, or the over-soul or the major ego is thought to be the spark of divinity found as a kind of individualized fragment of the Supreme Being himself. It is not, and never becomes, an integral part of the mortal to whom it belongs but always remains with God, of whom it is a veritable and inseparable part. In its spiritually pure and perfect state, the divine spark continually transmits a stream of consciousness to the four other entities on earth, to whom it belongs, in this way potentially enabling the latter to advance toward spiritual perfection.

The growth toward spiritual perfection is slow. The major ego keeps surveillance over the thoughts and actions of its earthly embodiment, offering to the latter rewards or punishment according to perceived good or evil. Punishment includes sickness, poverty, or other misfortunes; rewards include property, honor, and children. The major ego never prescribes a particular life style; consequently, each individual is the architect of his/her own destiny. Reincarnation is a part of the process of spiritual perfection. Following death, the soul is repeatedly sent back to earth, to be reborn in human form to a particular station determined by its previous existence on earth.

Continuity of Life

The concept of continuity is partially related to the notion of spirits, which like people, are creations of God and serve different purposes. Spirits are relevant not only for immortality but also to earth life's meaning and to ethics.[19]

Among the southern Luo of Kenya, Tanzania, and Uganda, as well as among the Nilotic peoples in the Sudan and Ethiopia—the

147

Shilluk, Dinka, Mao, Kunama—the Supreme Being (*Juok* or *Jok*) with his supernatural power is associated with destiny. Humans and other creatures, as well as inorganic objects contain differing levels of supernatural power. But only humans and animals possess spirits and souls in addition to their shadows and physical bodies that decompose upon death. The spiritual attributes, the soul and spirits, continue to exist after physical death. Humans are regarded above animals because they possess more spiritual power. Nevertheless, since animals and plants provide the resource base for human existence, they also possess some spiritual power of their own. Certain religion-ritual relationships have been established to manage this co-existence in an ethical manner.[20]

In the tradition of the Luo, life is perpetual. After death, the person is said to be sent back to where he/she originated, that is to the spiritual world, where all needs are met. In that spiritual world, some of the residents are older than others. The oldest of them all is *Juok*, who possesses the highest order of wisdom and is the source of supernatural power. This is the basis of the cardinal belief among the Luo peoples that age is a barometer of the accumulation of insight and wisdom.[21]

The temporal and hierarchical spiritual continuity of life has profound impact on the ethics and moral values of the Luo. Immorality influences the spiritual welfare of the entire family or village or clan, not simply that of the concerned individual (*Chara*). Thus, souls of humans are members of a spiritual republic, dwelling for a while in the flesh. The invocation rites that an individual and the public perform, such as funeral ceremonies and sacrifices to lineage or clan, are necessary so that the community at large might be afforded insight into its condition as a spiritual entity.[22] In this context, moral strength is deeply rooted in the soul, not simply the brain.

Before concluding this discussion on African traditional beliefs, it is important to make the following observations. From the 17th century onwards, many foreigners' observations on African religion have revealed serious misunderstandings, if not deliberate determinations to denigrate traditional thought. Notably, Charles de Brosses [1760] found fetishism to be the original foundation of all religion, particularly in the traditions of Africa. August Comte, who adopted De Brosses's theory, promulgated it with additional flourishes. He added that fetishism was the indisputable foundation of the African religious belief system and that Africa's notion of one Supreme God was introduced by Jewish and Christian travelers.[23] Although these detractors and others have taken part in a long history of disavowals of any central place for the African thought system, their disclaimers have so far failed to extinguish the Africans' basic belief in their own religious conceptual frameworks.

Four of the most common misconceptions concern ancestor worship; superstition; animism, zoolatry or paganism; and fetishism. While departed relatives are believed to live on as spirits revealing interest in their surviving families, acts of proper respect towards the departed do not mean that the departed are worshiped. It means that their wisdom and goodness should not be forgotten. Acts of remembrance and communication through prayer is only a small part of traditional religion. Most beliefs are based on deep reflection and long experience and, therefore, have little in common with mere superstition. Nevertheless, superstition penetrates every religion to some degree, but this does not mean religion should be equated with superstition. While African religions acknowledge the existence of spirits, some of which are believed to inhabit physical objects, this is only a small part of religion. And, this part should be understood in the framework of the belief that God is Supreme over all spirits and humankind, all of whom are part of God's creation. Such beliefs are not the equivalency of animism or zoolatry anymore than these beliefs are part of Christianity or Islam. African religion is not constructed on magic. While Africans wear religious charms, they are no more fetishists that the Christian who wears a St. Christoper's medal or a Muslim carrying his beads.[24]

Nature and Human Destiny

In sharp contrast to the religious tradition underpinning the African world-view, is the prevailing Western world-view driving the powerful forces of globalization, enshrining aggressive individualism. Some early Western Enlightenment thinkers denigrated what was African in their apologia for colonialism and slavery. Modern thinkers should consider what, in the African tradition, is essential to the development of humane governance and the protection of the environment from the excesses of rationality, material progress, and acquisitive individualism. In other words, there is perhaps as much to be learned today from the African experience as there was in ancient times of the philosophical and metaphysical nature and meaning of life, those dimensions threatened with burial in the materialism of the spirit of the time.

It is clear that ethics in Western thought is focused on the ideal of the individual, while neglecting the larger human community and the wider biological and physical domains. Generally, this globally prevailing thought regards humans as distinct from the rest of nature, and not as a component of a systematic totality. This conception has led to environmental degradation on a broad scale. Current concerns about the environment revolve largely around two principal questions: First, should ethics be restricted to human beings or should non-human but sentient beings should also be subjects and agents of ethics? Second, should any other material objects in nature such as hills, rocks, and rivers possess any moral value?[25]

Indeed, in Christian doctrine, nature is usually interpreted as a bundle of resources to serve humans. This view is consistent with that articulated by Aristotle in his hierarchical justification for the ecological dominance of humans. He asserted that plants exist for the sake of animals, while animals exist for the sake of man. Such anthropocentric, utilitarian, and hierarchical ecological insights attained the status of divine wisdom by the time of Thomas Aquinas. And, since the dawn of the modern scientific movement in the early fifteenth century, elements of nature have largely been regarded as objects for analysis and experimentation or for commercial transactions. This approach recognizes no limits to industrial exploitation, which by now has exceeded all previous limitations on the accumulation of riches and property by single individuals, corporations, or nations, since the beginning of the industrial revolution in the seventeenth century. Yet, wholesale exploitation of nature's abundance and the disruption of its intricate web of associations and relationships may well bring the entire biosphere to a grinding halt, just as intensive and unsustainable exploitation of the Fertile Crescent, the valley between the twin rivers Euphrates and Tigris, led to the sudden end of ancient Mesopotamia.

The conventional human-centered, utilitarian view of nature has not been questioned sufficiently and thus the pace of nature's destruction has proceeded unchecked. There is no doubt that a shift from excessive individualism to a more compassionate universalism would provide a humane solution. Universalism approximates nature's idea of the good. It would, to a degree, oblige humanity to move away from the occidental focus on the human individual objective as the center of ethics.

But is it feasible that such a shift could be accomplished in the lifetime of the youngest in the present span of living generations, or even in the course of the next few future generations? The shift is only remotely possible, provided a monumental change can be made in several theaters of human endeavor. It should not be forgotten that there is guidance to be found in African traditional religion.

Conclusion

It is clear from this brief overview of African belief systems that there is a shared cardinal belief in the Supreme Being that has been translated into a complex relational system between God and the human person. This system penetrates the whole of the education of the person with an ethic of service to the "other" and respect for nature. For example, the Luo—among other indigenous peoples of the continent—have regarded the education of a person to be a life-long experience or the sum total of experiences that mold attitudes and govern the conduct of both the child and the adult.[26] The emphasis on the role played by the personal growth of each individual does not lead to a lessened regard for the collective. Rather, collective good hinges upon each member of the community seeing his or her actions as contributing to the well-being of the community.

Thus, for the Luo there exists a continuum between individual and collective action. This embraces education for personal growth and stresses social norms and moral ethics. Respect for age and human endeavors are guided according to values that promote unity. The elders share a common responsibility for the youth. In turn, children must respect not only their parents, but also everyone who undertakes responsibility for them, including members of the lineage, clan, and tribe. With this method of education, young people accomplish many things. This method strengthens kinship ties throughout the particular ethnic group; provides an education for family life; instructs children about the clan's religion; and teaches the normative rules of social conduct. It is interesting to note that a prison system was unheard of among the Luo peoples. Professional education operates on a different level, being confined to selected people, sometimes within a single clan, whose skills and knowledge are transmitted by a strict code of apprenticeship from one generation to the next. These professions, including blacksmithing, medical practice, or theology, again have the well-being of the other in focus. Possessive individualism is a behavior, which was, and still is abhorred in traditional African society.

From the perspective of this African world-view, global measures of human progress should be more inclusive. They must extend beyond gross national product, expenditure on the armed forces, and other similar comparative national statistics. And, a modified ranking should take into consideration other perceptions of progress—not necessarily quantifiable—in the field of social and community relationships. These include the practice of personal moral values: love for one's family, neighbors, and strangers; attention to community goals; compassion for the economically poor, the orphans and the widows, and the use of incentives and social sanctions against offenders of social and community norms—rather than imprisonment and execution. These factors are also essential signs of human progress.

The foundation for this wider and more humane vision of progress would be firmly built if based on a continuous search for divine insight, central belief in a supernatural order, and a deep sense of humility and tolerance for others' views. In international relations, this includes an integral belief in peace, an evolution beyond the need for the political and military domination of other nations, and the progressive adoption of a thought system that recognizes no chosen people or superior race. Such a repositioning of Africa in the grove of human experience and attention to the role it can play in renewing the human spirit are matters that require deep contemplation, prayer, and study in retreat from the clamor for wealth, power, and prestige that crush the modern human spirit.

Human progress should be the focus of the third millennium. Inclusion is a contextual value in the mainstream of the process for the achievement of social and community harmony in the works today. By being more inclusive of all the varied facets of human life in the physical universe and, in so doing, embracing spiritual continuity as the essence of living, the African world-view makes a fundamental contribution to dominant thoughts and attitudes in a rapidly globalizing world. The question is whether the African has the confidence to affirm this contribution. The reverse question is whether the dominant forces are ready and willing to recognize and place in the mainstream, market-led, technology-oriented ethic of the emerging global village, African attitudes and contributions.

The South African poet, H. I. E. Dhlomo, became physically ill and fell into despair because of deprivations visited upon him and his black people by foreign imperial power and racist greed. Should we not, like him, "struggle to invoke his ancestral spirits whose presence he feels" in the Valley of a Thousand Hills in his native Natal Province of South Africa, the most beautiful panorama in his entire country?

> Our world, our thoughts, our all is in the Self.
> God is as great as the individual soul!
> Our bigness makes life big; our smallness, cringed
> Not God or man or Devil or the world,
> But Self chastises or enthrones the soul. [27]

Thus, our research leads us back to the very beginning, as T. S. Eliot tells us so succinctly:

> We shall not cease from exploration
> And the end of all our exploring
> Will be to arrive where we started
> And know the place for the first time. [28]

THOMAS ODHIAMBO

Endnotes

1 - Maya Angelou, *Even the Stars Look Lonesome* (New York: Bantam Books, 1997), 15-16.

2 - Cited in E. Chukwudi Eze, "Modern Western Philosophy and African Colonialism," in *African Philosophy*, ed. E. Chukwudi Eze (Oxford: Blackwell Publishers, 1998), 214.

3 - Ibid.

4 - Angelou, 16.

5 - Similar accounts are offered in the following sources: John Lanphear and Toyin Falola, "Aspects of Early African History" in *Africa 3rd*, ed. Phyllis M. Martin and Patrick O'Meara (Indianapolis: Indiana University Press, 1995), 73-75. Vivian Davies and Renee Friedman, *Egypt* (London: British Museum Press, 1998), 16-28.

6 - Henry Olela, "The African Foundations of Greek Philosophy," in *African Philosophy*, ed. E. Chukwudi Eze (Oxford: Blackwell Publishers, 1998), 43-49. Olela cites Willis N. Huggins and John G. Jackson, *Introduction to African Civilization* (New York: Negro Universities Press, 1969), 77. Leonard Cottrel, *The Penguin Book of Lost Worlds* (London: Penguin, 1966), 24.

7 - Martin Bernal, *The Fabrication of Ancient Greece 1785-1985* in vol. 1 of *Black Athena, The Afroasiatic Roots of Classical Civilization*, (New Brunswick: Rutgers University Press, 1987), 98-99, 106-109.

8 - Ibid., 49-52.

9 - Henry Olela, "The African Foundations of Greek Philosophy," 48-49.

10 - William Hansberry, "Indigenous African Religions" in *Africa from the Point of View of American Negro Scholars*, ed. J.A. Davis (Paris: Presence Africaine, 1958), 89.

11 - John S. Mbiti, *African Religions and Philosophy* (Oxford: Heinemann Press, 1969), 81.

12 - William Hansberry quotes David Von Nyendael in: William Hansberry, "Indigenous African Religions," 85.

13 - For examples see: Ibid., 89-90.

14 - E.W. Smith, *Doctrine of God* (London: Lutterworth Press, 1944), 55.

15 - John S. Mbiti, *African Religions and Philosophy* (Oxford: Heinemann Press, 1969), 31.

16 - Maurice Delafosse, "Souffle vital et esprit dynamique chez les populations indigenes du Soudan occidental," *Compte-rendus des seances de l'Institut Francais d'Anthropologie*, Supplement No. 5 (1912): and "Croyances et Pratique Religieuses, Les Noirs de l'Afrique," Chapter IX (1922). Cited in William Hansberry's essay in: William Hansberry, "Indigenous African Religions," 90-96.

154

17 - Kwame Gyeke, "The Relation of Okra (Soul) and Honam (Body): An Akan
Conception," in *African Philosophy*, ed. E. Chukwudi Eze (Oxford: Blackwell
Publishers, 1998), 59-65.

18 - P.A. Talbot, *The Peoples of Southern Nigeria* (London: Oxford University,
1926), 93-96. As cited in: William Hansberry, "Indigenous African Religions."

19 - See for example: John S. M Mbiti, *Introduction to African Religions, 2nd
Edition* (England: Clay Ltd., St Ives, 1975), 70-82.

20 - A.B.C. Ocholla-Ayayo, *Traditional Ideology and Ethics among the Southern
Luo* (Uppsala: Scandinavian Institute of African Studies, 1976), 101-200.

21 - Ibid., 172-174.

22 - Ibid., 55-56.

23 - See for example: C. DeBros, "Du culte des dieux fiches," 1760, quoted by:
William Hansberry, "Indigenous African Religions," 97-98. Also: J.L. Wilson,
Western Africa: Its History, Condition, and Prospects (New York: Harper and
Bros., 1858), 220.

24 - Mbiti, 17-20.

25 - H.O. Oruka and C. Juma, "Ecophilosophical and Parental Earth Ethics" in
Philosophy, Humanity, and Ecology, vol.1 of *Philosophy of Nature and
Environmental Ethics*, ed. H.O. Oruka (Nairobi: Acts Press and The African
Academy of Sciences, 1994), 115.

26 - Ocholla-Ayayo, 58-60.

27 - Ezekiel Mphahlele, *The African Image* (London: Faber and Faber, 1962),
183-185, briefly reviews and quotes from Dholomo's 1,000-line poem, "The
Valley of a Thousand Hills," (Durban, South Africa: Knox Printing Co.,
1941).

28 - T. S. Eliot, "Little Gidding" in *Four Quartets* (London: Faber and Faber,
1943).

CHAPTER 8

RETURN OF THE "NATIVE"

Muhammad Suheyl Umar

Somewhere, during the course of its historical development, Western thought took a sharp turn in another direction. It branched off as a tangent from the collective heritage of all humanity and claimed the autonomy of reason. It chose to follow that reason alone, unguided by revelation and cut off from the Intellect that was regarded as its transcendent root.[1] Political and social realms quickly followed suit. Autonomous statecraft and excessive individualism in the social order were the elements that shaped a dominant paradigm that did not prove successful.[2] A few centuries of unbridled activity led Western philosophy to an impasse.[3] Commenting upon the situation, Huston Smith remarked:

> The deepest reason for the crisis in philosophy is its realization that autonomous reason—reason without infusions that both power and vector it—is helpless. By itself, reason can deliver nothing apodictic. Working, as it necessarily must, with variables, variables are all it can come up with. The Enlightenment's 'natural light of reason' turns out to have been a myth. Reason is not itself a light. It is more than a conductor, for it does more than transmit. It seems to resemble an adapter who makes useful translations but on condition that it is powered by a generator.[4]

The nature and direction of these "infusions" is still being debated.[5]

A similar awareness could be discerned in the arena of politics, humanities, and social sciences. The impasse, though with different implications, was reached by the parallel paradigm of autonomous politics and social sciences that had refused to accept any "infusion" from a higher domain. This time the need for a revision of the paradigm was felt in the United Nations itself. The awareness materialized in the convening of the World Summit for Social Development, in Copenhagen in March 1995. Issues of poverty, unemployment, alienation, and social disintegration largely dominated the agenda. In order to enrich the controlling discourse and to make it less technocratic and materialistic, the secretariat of the Summit decided to convene a seminar to clarify and highlight the ethical and spiritual dimension of the issues before the Social Summit.[6]

The views expressed by most of the participants about the present human predicament converged. The opinions about the nature and origin of the "infusions" that could rectify or change it for the better were, however, divergent. It was similar to the case of philosophy mentioned at the beginning. Some of the participants tried to find an alternative from within the dominant paradigm. Others suggested the possibility of a search for these "infusions" in a different direction whether in different cultures, other civilizations, religious doctrines, or sapiential traditions.

The issues discussed were just as important for the contemporary world as they were for the past. This point needs a little elucidation, since we are often unaware that contemporary arguments continue in the same lines as earlier theological debates. Take, for example, the issue of free will and predestination, a central bone of contention among the schools of Kalam. This debate, which has also been important in Christian civilization, lives on in modern secular society, though it is no longer posed in terms of God. For example, many contemporary scholars—biologists, psychologists, sociologists, philosophers, and political scientists—are actively involved in the discussion of nature versus nurture. The basic question is simple: Does nature determine human development, or can people change themselves substantively by means of training and education? Free will and predestination, like nature and nurture, is merely a convenient way to refer to one of the most basic puzzles of human existence.

Professor F. J. Aguilar, one of the participants and a leading authority on organizational analysis, presented his analysis of successful business organizations, saying that one of the fundamental elements of corporate success and business excellence was adoption of ethical limits and rules of behavior. Participants questioned whether these rules and limits were adopted because the time was opportune or if the motive for the choice was supplied by some other set of principles. Here was the age-old debate of sincerity and its opposite: Is honesty, or, for that matter, any other positive attitude, good because it produces tangible results or is it a virtue in itself, with transcendent roots and repercussions beyond the immediate realm of human experience.

Gustave Thibon wrote:

> Cut off from self-interest, virtue loses the weight by which it is incarnated; nothing binds it any longer to the earth. But self-interest, in its turn, separated from virtue, loses the power of flight which is its deliverance; there is no longer anything to raise it to heaven. This is the divorce between the ideal and the real: on the one hand a verbal and inoperative morality, on the other an anarchic swarming of unbalanced egoisms which devour one another, with, as an inevitable result, the degradation of individuals and the dissolution of societies. [7]

Or, when the role and duties of governments, *vis-à-vis* the people are debated, the core problem is that which, in older parlance, was called "spiritual authority and temporal power," though we no longer refer to it in the older context. Similarly, issues discussed in the context of "religious pluralism" are, in fact, the questions once referred to as the transcendent unity of religions, in the Islamic civilization and "salvation outside the Church," in the Christian context.

Closely allied is the issue of tolerance and intolerance described by the terms "discrimination," "oppression," "violence," etc. This, once again, is another way to put the timeworn question that related these attitudes to their metaphysical roots. From the metaphysical point of view it can be asserted categorically that only the Supreme Principle, the Ultimate Real or what, in the climate of monotheism, is usually referred to as the Godhead, the Divine Essence or the Divine Ground has no opposite, for it transcends all duality. The very act of creation or the cosmogonic process implies, of necessity, duality and opposition. In the Divine Order where the domain of relativity commences, one can observe duality, multiplicity and also the roots of opposition. This order embraces, not only the Supreme Essence or the One, but also Its Energies, Hypostases—or what in Islam is called the Divine Names and Qualities.

To live in the world of manifestation is, therefore, to live in a world of opposites that can be transcended only in the reality which is the *coincidentia oppositorum,* and which, on their own level, are often in opposition and usually intolerant of each other. That is why tolerance and intolerance are not only moral issues but have a cosmic dimension. This point is emphasized by traditional doctrines in the Orient, where human and moral laws have not become divorced from each other. This was also true in the traditional West until modern times, when the link between human morality and cosmic laws became severed.

Another example of "old wine in new bottles" discussed at the Seminar, was the Agenda document concerning "self-interest and common good," which remarked upon "transcending the God of Fear." The issue that was at the core of the discussion was the perennial question of the ternary aspects of the human psyche, which pertain to knowledge, love, and fear. The question was not to make a choice between alternatives of fear and knowledge or love. It was in fact, a matter of emphasis. All three aspects exist side by side and, from Hinduism to Islam, every great religion and tradition contains the three perspectives.

These perspectives determine inner human attitudes. "Fear of the Lord is the beginning of Wisdom," say the Psalms.[8] Moreover, one can only transcend something that one possesses. In this regard we recall an anecdote about a Zen master visiting the West. The master was giving a lecture at one of the Western universities when somebody from the audience stood up and said, "Is it not the teaching of Zen to burn up the scrolls and throw away the Buddha images?" The master, replying calmly, said, "Yes, but you can burn only something that you have and throw away something you possess."

One of the most remarkable and striking features of the debates in the Seminar was that the basic assumptions of the dominant discourse and the prevalent world-view were brought into question.[9] The participants probed, in their diverse ways, and from the perspective of different disciplines, the viability and even the authenticity and soundness of the underpinnings of the contemporary mind-set. Discussions about "human dignity," "human rights," the "human predicament," eventually led participants to ask the inevitable question: "What is Man?" The other inevitable question, which dovetails the earlier one, lurked in the wings: "What is the cosmos?" The answers were neither easy nor unanimous.

"To be human means to be more than human," St. Augustine stated. What does this "more" indicate? The supra-individual dimensions of human personality as well as the cosmic order are linked up with the concept of reality itself: reality as a multistory building or as a mansion that has no upper story. This in turn is connected to the microcosmic reality of the human self, of which we have two models. One regards the human self as the point of intersection where the Divine touches the human realm, and this view situates the human microcosm in a hierarchical relationship with other levels of being. This model and its governing concept of reality are the shared heritage of all the known spiritual, metaphysical and religious traditions of humankind. Lord Northbourne summarizes the two approaches to the question, "What is Man?" in a simple and straightforward manner:

> Are you in fact a being created by God in His own image, appointed by him as his representative on earth and accordingly given dominion over it, and equipped for the fulfillment of that function with a relative freedom of choice in thought and action which reflects the total absence of constraint attributable to God alone, but at the same time makes you liable to err? Are you essentially that, and only accidentally anything else?

Or, alternatively, are you essentially a specimen of the most advanced product so far known of a continuous and progressive evolution, starting from the more or less fortuitous stringing together of a protein molecule in some warm primeval mud, that mud itself being a rare and more or less fortuitous product of the evolution of the galaxies from a starting point about which the physicists have not yet quite made up their minds?[10]

In other words, the two models suggest that man could either be a Viceroy, Vicegerent or Pontiff or else a cunning animal with no destiny beyond the grave.[11] Regarding the former model, S. H. Nasr says:

The concept of man as the pontiff, bridge between Heaven and earth, which is the traditional view of the anthropos, lies at the antipode of the modern conception of man which envisages him as the Promethean earthly creature who has rebelled against Heaven and tried to misappropriate the role of the Divinity for himself. Pontifical man, who, in the sense used here, is none other than the traditional man, lives in full awareness of the Origin which contains his own perfection and whose primordial purity and wholeness he seeks to emulate, recapture, and transmit (...). He is aware that precisely because he is human there is both grandeur and danger connected with all that he does and thinks. His actions have an effect upon his own being beyond the limited spatio-temporal conditions in which such actions take place. He knows that somehow the bark which is to take him to the shore beyond after that fleeting journey that comprised his earthly life is constructed by what he does and how he lives while he is in the human state.[12]

A tremendous difference separates the perspective represented by the foregoing texts and the contemporary paradigm of progress and social development that Tage Lindbom has aptly described as "the kingdom of man." Given that the prevalent paradigm is losing its viability and there is a growing mistrust about its future, we are hardly in a position at this juncture to reject any alternative out of hand. "Infusions" from other domains hitherto considered alien to social development may be carefully examined and we can ask ourselves individually, as well as collectively, as in the case of the Bled Seminar, which of the alternatives has a greater ring of truth. In this respect the Seminar, and hopefully the Summit itself, may prove to be the spearhead of a broader process of revising the future with the help of the past.

The message of change that this overall intellectual exercise gives to the actors and the world at large is not to underestimate the magnitude of the challenge presented by these unfamiliar "infusions" and systematic claims of past philosophies and sapiential doctrines. For what they say to current thought and the contemporary mind-set is in effect: "Either accept this overall standpoint or do better by finding or inventing a superior system of thought." The Bled Seminar suggested that we, in all probability, do not have a superior system of thought that provides sufficient grounds for disregarding the traditional system. If the message is registered and fresh "infusions" are incorporated in the emerging discourse, we may take it as a sign that the wheel has come full circle and the "native" has decided to come back home.

Endnotes

1 - See Martin Lings, "Intellect and Reason" in *Ancient Beliefs and Modern Superstitions*, rpt. (Lahore: Suhail Academy, 1988), 57-68; F. Schuon, *Gnosis Divine Wisdom* (London: J. Murray, 1978), 93-99; S. H. Nasr, *Knowledge and the Sacred* (Edinburgh: Edinburgh University Press, 1981), 1-64; Huston Smith, *Forgotten Truth* (San Francisco: Harper, 1992), 60-95. Also see his *Beyond the Post-Modern Mind* (Wheaton: Theosophical Publishing House, 1989).

2 - See René Guenon, "Individualism" in *Crisis of the Modern World* (Lahore: Suhail Academy, 1981), 51-65. Also see "Social Chaos" in the same document.

3 - For a few representative writings that indicate this situation, see "Scientism, Pragmatism and the Fate of Philosophy" in *Inquiry*, 29, 278; Hilary Putnam, "After Empiricism" in *Behaviorism* 16, no.1 (Spring 1988); Alasdair MacIntrye, "Philosophy; Past Conflict and Future Direction," *Proceedings and Addresses of the American Philosophical Association*, Supplement to 16/1, (September 1987); also see *Proceedings of the American Philosophical Association* 59 (1986), and Kenneth Baynes et al., *Philosophy: End or Transformation?* (Cambridge: MIT Press, 1987).

4 - Huston Smith, "Crisis of Modern Philosophy," in *Beyond the Post-Modern Mind* (Wheaton: Theosophical Publishing House, 1990), 142.

5 - Huston Smith has pointed towards the possibility of accepting these "infusions" from *Philosophia Perennis* or *Religio-Perennis,* the sapiential doctrines of mankind. See his "Two Traditions and Philosophy" in *Religion of the Heart: Essays Presented to Frithjof Schuon on his 80th Birthday* (Washington, D.C.: Foundation for Traditional Studies, 1991), 278-296. In this regard also see F. Schuon, "Tracing the Notion of Philosophy," *Sufism Veil and Quintessence* (Lahore: Suhail Academy, 1985), 115-128; *Logic and Transcendence,* trans. Peter N. Townsend (New York: Harper and Row, 1975).

6 - The Seminar was held in Bled, Slovenia, 28-30 October 1994.

7 - "Gustave Thibon, *Retour au Réel; Nouveau Diagnostics* (Lyon: II Lardanchet, 1943), 161.

8 - Ps. 111:10 KJV (King James Version).

9 - "Basic assumptions" are used here in a broader sense than regulating concepts. For a description and telling critique of the assumptions of the contemporary world, see Tage Lindbom, *Tares and the Good Grain* (Lahore: Suhail Academy, 1988). On another level these assumptions are challenged by S. H. Nasr's *Knowledge and the Sacred.*

10 - Lord Northbourne, *Looking Back on Progress* (Lahore, Suhail Academy, 1983), 47.

11 - On the traditional conception of man, see G. Eaton, *King of the Castle* (Islamic Texts Society, 1993); "Man" in *Islamic Spirituality* 1, ed. S. H. Nasr, (New York: Crossroad, 1987), 358-377; Kathleen Raine, *What is Man?* (England: Golgonoza Press, 1980); S. H. Nasr, "Who is Man?", *The Sword of Ghosts,* ed. Needleman (London, England: Penguin, n.d.): 203-217; S. H. Nasr (ed.) *The Essential Writings of Frithjof Schuon* (New York: Amity House, 1986), 385-403. Of special importance in this regard is René Guenon's *Man and his Becoming According to the Vedanta* (Delhi: 1990), which presents the concept of man in Hindu terminology, which, nevertheless, is shared by the other traditions as well.

12 - S. H. Nasr, *Knowledge and the Sacred,* 161-162.

CHAPTER 9

UNITY BETWEEN THE VALUES OF TRUTH, GOODNESS, AND BEAUTY

Tomonobu Imamichi

Prologue

We are now facing a new age. This does not mean that we are simply entering the 21st century. The world is confronted with new challenges: the ethos of globalization penetrating every region through technological innovation; the common request for world peace under the conditions of a multicultural encounter; and the necessity for a relative harmonization of many religions without losing the integrity of each.

Confronted with such intellectual challenges we must seek a concrete path toward an order of mutual collaboration involving the whole of humanity. The presupposition and the condition for this kind of collaboration is the recognition of the necessity for cultural understanding. In turn, this recognition presumes that none of us desires cultural monopoly, but that we are willing to explore the dimensions of a new world culture as the result of our mutual understanding.

In this endeavor, philosophy can make a significant contribution to advancing mutual cultural understanding. One task of philosophy is to carry out a methodologically rigorous comparative study of the philosophies of the Orient and the Occident, whose cultures have been in the forefront of world history.

To outline the nature of this comparative work within the limited scale of a brief chapter in this book, I will only evoke the East Asian and Greek philosophies. The prerequisite for scientific research of this nature is complete knowledge of the original language in which the moral values of each culture were couched. Because of this rigid rule of research I could not include Hinduism, one of the very important moral guides in the East, or Judaism as the equivalent in the West.

In the context of comparative philosophical research, one of the most important tasks is to reflect on widely used concepts whose meaning may seem self-evident. My method, which begins by concentrating on philological comparisons and then progresses to metaphysical considerations, seems at first to be meaningless in the context of examining the big issues arising from the realities of globalization. But language is the fundamental element of logic without which no system of thought is possible, and metaphysics is the definitive meditation without which no ethical rule and practice can be understood.

The comparative analysis in this paper seeks to determine the theoretical possibility for a cultural dialogue between East and West on the key concept of "truth," by comparing the essence of the Greek word *aletheia* and the Japanese word *makoto*. "Truth" is an ideal focus for this comparative analysis because it is so often used unconsciously, as if its meaning were fully understandable. In every culture, there is some notion of "truth." In every culture, "truth" is a fundamental word whose concept is familiar to almost every individual. I also chose it because its Greek and Japanese expressions can be used to illustrate the paradoxical relation of "compatibility in opposition" and "incompatibility in equality." This complicated relation is the appropriate premise for building cultural understanding. The semantic contrast between the Japanese and the Greek word for "truth" is a significant starting point for the axiological meditation that follows.

Rather than launch into a confusing description of "truth" using Oriental terms, as if I were defining the idea to Eastern scholars seeking to understand "truth," I have taken a comparative philosophical approach and begin with Greek terminology and texts dealing with this concept. The choice of Greek is based on the assumption that Greek philosophy is the foundation of contemporary Western philosophy. A parallel clarification of the concept will then be made in the Japanese language of philosophy, which constitutes one of the cultural foundations of the Eastern world. Such a comparison is a valid basis for promoting the value of Oriental philosophy in the global society. I also suggest some areas for philosophical collaboration between Eastern and Western scholars for the benefit of humankind.

"Truth" in Greek Philosophy

In the Greek language, "truth" is expressed by the word *aletheia* whose etymological meaning rests on two seemingly opposite but complementary theories. According to one theory, *aletheia* refers to "the discovered." According to the other, it refers to the coming out of the "forgotten secret." The first meaning emphasizes the human endeavor to seek out reality; it highlights the active seeking of "truth" through, for example, human research. It underscores the "hidden reality," the "something" in existence waiting to be discovered. The other theory stresses the self-movement, or revelation of the secret to the human mind, the dynamic aspect of the hidden reality, and the enlightened situation of the human mind. It insists on the passive character of the search for "truth."

These seemingly opposite theories have in fact the same origin. *Letheia* derives from *lethe*, that is to say "oblivion." The "a" signifies something negative in the sense of "to take away," or "to go away from." Thus, one may say that "truth" is the knowledge of reality enlightened by human research or by some universal conscious power. In either case, it is "the taking away of the unknown." Since this study is a comparison of philosophical traditions, it will not deal with religious "truth," as implied by the second theory. "Truth" will be considered as that set of ideas to be discovered through human activity.

To access "truth," philosophers must think, which is to say that they must use their principal mental instrument. What is this instrument? According to Plato, Socrates says in his *Politeai*, that the most important instrument of a philosopher is the *logos*.[1] What then is the *logos*? This word is not unequivocal. Its meaning includes both subjective and objective components. The subjective refers to the nature of an object as it is known in the mind, as a distinct thing from itself. In other words, it relates to properties or specific conditions of the mind, as distinguished from general or universal experience, for example, practical reason or pure reason. The objective means "to intend upon" or "deal with things external to the mind," or, in other words, pertains to that which can be known, can be found by thinking, for example the cause of some occurrence. Sometimes, *logos* can signify axiological or value-driven motivations for doing something. "Reason" works as a noun in that instance, but also can work as a verb meaning "to argue, to discuss something," in the transitive sense, or "to think," as an intransitive verb.

English speaking people are capable of distinguishing the proper meaning of "reason" from this range of possibilities, depending on the context in which the concept is used. *Logos* is similar to the word "reason" in English. It is one of the most important words in Greek. The terms "word," "concept," "principle," "cause," and "sentence" are all representations of the word *logos*. The choice of meaning depends on the particular context in which it is used. In order to understand *aletheia,* meaning "truth," the human being must choose the "word" according to the "concept" revealed in the logic of a specific argument. Thus "principle" and "cause" may be clarified in the final "sentence" revealing "truth."

It can then be stated that "truth" in Greek philosophy infers self-movement of the *logos* in the human mind. In other words, it is the self-refinement of the *logos,* which points in the direction of perfect integration of all the meanings of *logos*. Following the same logic, "truth" can be said to be a categorical description of the object sought in research, which is carried out by and through the *logos*. "Truth" is the descriptive perfection and the objective description: *Veritas est identitas intellectu ad rem.*[2]

To illustrate these points, the example will be used of a "child carried away by the slow current of the river on whose bank I stand." To give a fully objective description of this situation, in other words to know the "truth" about this event, one must gather all the empirical information on the details of the observed occurrence. According to *aletheia*, "truth" is the objective description of this scenario, namely, the result of the integration of the categorical facts of what, when, where, and how the act occurred. To tell the "truth" about this example, one must say: "On August 15, in the River Sumida, a child, approximately five years old, is being carried by a slow current in the direction of the mouth of the river and there is no ship or other person in the river at this moment."

One may add other information concerning the weather, the temperature of the water, the speed of the current, the depth of the river, the exact place where the observer is standing and so on. Although it is not wrong to do so, adding such information is not relevant to the immediate observation, or to the "truth." If one were to use information to complete the "truth" as *aletheia,* one must add, after a few minutes, the completely different fact that the child had disappeared, supposedly drowned. Thus, one cannot complete the description of the event with historical or contextual information. This is the paradox of the Greek theory of *aletheia* as "truth." According to this way of thinking, one cannot actually attain the full "truth." The closer one tries to come to the "truth," the farther the "truth" moves away.

For this reason, people limit the concept of the "truth" to natural phenomena, which can be repeatedly observed in the laboratory. Thus, natural science is accepted as "the correct way" to the "truth." But, if one thinks very precisely, one must say that the phenomena tested according to scientific method are nothing other than selected phenomena in a technical construct of abstract space. The experiment can always be correct within this abstraction, but the more abstract it gets, the farther away it gets from reality. Therefore, research according to the natural science methodology cannot escape this paradox.

The remaining route towards attainment of "truth" as *aletheia* is through logic. Although one can discuss logical problems in very sophisticated ways, this discussion accomplishes nothing other than to polish up the instrument itself. It does not alter the basic facts underlying the process. With logic alone, one simply cannot attempt anything involving history or nature, because in having only logic, one has only the instrument without the objects for this instrument. One can search for the "truth" with logic, using metaphysics. But most logicians deny metaphysics through their logic. This seems, indeed, to be a fundamental paradox of logic itself. Historical development, as it culminated in the 20th century, allows for the conclusion that "truth," as *aletheia,* is valid only in logic as "description."

Koto, Object or Situation

As described above, *logos*, one of the most important words in Greek, is the principal concept used to explain "truth" as *aletheia*. The word *koto* is the equivalent of *logos* in Japanese. *Koto*, which signifies word, object, situation, fact, thing, and so forth is the basic element in a group of related concepts in which each is distinguished by an added suffix or prefix. This group of concepts—called the *koto*-group—expresses a structural function illuminating relationships between world, logic, theory, deed, art, and the "truth."

Although the simple term *koto* is to Japanese philosophy what *logos* is to Greek philosophy, normally this concept appears with the suffix *ba*. In earlier times, the suffix *ha* was used to signify "peripheral part."

An important concept in the *koto* group is a *koto-wari*. *Wari* means "analysis." Thus, *koto-wari* means the conceptual analysis of an object. By extension, it means theory or logic. The three terms *koto*, *koto-wari,* and *kotoba* have the following relationship: *koto* > *koto-wari* > *kotoba*.

The explanation of this scheme is as follows: if we wish to know something objectively, we must analyze the object, or *koto*, from the perspective of a certain field of inquiry—the *koto-wari*, for example, history, biology or some other scientific discipline. By doing so, we select only specific aspects of the object derived from a certain scientific discipline, thereby rejecting the other facets that might have been derived from other disciplines.

A *koto-wari* theory is always constructed in light of a particular dimension of the object discovered by research in a specific limited scientific field. Indeed, *koto-wari* assumes breaking the "something" into smaller parts, revealing the many dimensions of that "something." Therefore, the *koto-wari* theory must refer to less than the whole of the "something," also called the "object." This is to say, a *koto-wari* theory refers to *koto* in terms of the "object's" breadth and content. *Koto-wari* theory derived according to the rules of a particular scientific discipline must be expressed in words. The "word" is, therefore, very important for theory, but as its building block, the word has only a fraction of the theory's breadth and content. Put differently, the *koto-wari* is the theory expressed in many words, and each word, according to Japanese logic, is a *kotoba*, which means a tiny part of *koto*—the something or object.

In summary, we can express a theory by the use of words. We can describe the dimension of something by a theory. But we cannot completely express the allness of something—or object—a theory; a theory is only one part of something. Because a theory must be expressed by many words, which are only tiny parts of *koto*, it is clear that individual words, alone, can never capture the full meaning of the object, or something.

"Truth" in the Japanese language

Normally, and especially in the field of science, many Japanese use the word *shinri* to signify "truth." But, *shinri* is derived from the Chinese language, meaning "true principle" or "true theory." This word has been completely assimilated in the Japanese language, because both the Chinese characters *shin* and *ri* have been used in Buddhist temples in Japan since the 6th century. This is long before the Japanese intellectual world decided to use these characters to translate the English word "truth," in the second half of the 19th century. Nevertheless, *shinri* is not an original Japanese word, so no linguistic relationship exists between *shinri* and *koto* as the object of knowing. As already stated above, the most fundamental and important Japanese word, which is the equivalent of the Greek *logos,* is *koto,* both by itself and as combined with other words in the *koto* group.

Which Japanese word is closest to the translation of the English word "truth" in the *koto* word group? The word is *makoto.*[3] *Makoto* is used today both in daily conversation and in philosophical books. *Makoto* is often used as the name for a male. *Shinri* is rarely used as a name. *Makoto* is one of the most important concepts that stem from two Japanese root words.

The prefix *ma* is basic to understanding the concept *makoto*. *Ma* denotes "beautiful or perfect."[4] In speaking about a circle, if one wishes to speak of the center of the circle, one would use the word *naka*, meaning the center point. If one wishes to indicate the exact point of the center, one would use the expression *ma-naka*. If, when speaking of the "mind," one does not intend to speak about *kokoro*—or normal mind, but wishes to talk about the purely beautiful self-sacrificing mind, one would say *ma-gokoro*, which comes from *ma-kokoro*, meaning beautiful mind. In speaking about cleanliness, but not just ordinary clean and transparent as *sumi*, but the perfectly clean, transparent, and clear, the term *ma-sumi,* meaning perfectly clean is used. In all of these examples the prefix *ma* signifies perfection. Consistently, *ma-koto* intends "truth" as the "perfect thing or perfect condition."

"Truth" a State of Perfection

What does this idea mean? Human beings always stand somewhere at a distance from the "truth." "Truth" is never clearly recognized, nor realized, in the beginning. Neither in Eastern nor Western philosophy is "truth" conceived as the starting point of mental activity. It is, according to both philosophical traditions, the final point of this activity. Remember, that as stated above, "truth" or *aletheia* is realized only at the end of the logical accumulation of the analytical description.

Eastern "truth," expressed as *makoto*, resembles the Western concept—"truth" can only emerge at the end of mental activity. If the "truth" can only be attained at the end of a thinking process, then at the beginning of the mental activity the thinkers must be at some distance from "truth." Moreover, it follows that if the "truth" is, as in the Japanese language, *makoto*—the perfect and beautiful situation—and if the thinkers are far from the "truth" at the beginning of the mental activity, then the thinkers must be in an imperfect and ugly situation in the beginning.

It appears, in both the West and the East, that before arriving at the "truth," human beings are quite imperfect. As such, they cannot have arrived at the "truth." Otherwise they would be in some state of perfection. If we each reflect seriously about our own particular situation, we must find many imperfect aspects in ourselves. And, if we reflect seriously on our environment, we must find many defects that require effort to be corrected in order to bring about "truth" as *makoto*, or, in other words, the beautiful and perfect thing. This means that we are living in the imperfect state. To use the Buddhist expression, "we are situated in a wounded world, in a broken condition."

Return now to the example of the child who is drowning in the river. One can be sure that this circumstance is not a perfect and beautiful predicament. It is, in fact, an imperfect, ugly, and wounded predicament. Thus, one may ask, what is the relevance or significance of the correct description of this imperfect and ugly situation? It is the epistemological confirmation of the objective state of the wounded reality. Although we could get a correct description of the wounded situation, the real situation remains wounded.

The perfect and beautiful condition to be achieved in this moment and in this given situation, is not to perfect the correct description by entering into details of the drowning. It is to make an effort to save this child by entering the water, if possible, or to make an emergency call for help to perfect and beautify this ugly picture, or broken *koto*.

Therefore, the only epistemological emendation of the subjective defect by obtaining descriptive knowledge, translates into the objective sacrificing of the life of a child. The truly perfect and beautiful predicament, for which the given broken and ugly condition must be emended and integrated, is saving this child, through sacrificing subjective curiosity for the correct description of the details in the broken and ugly situation. In this sense, there is a metaphysical unity of "truth," beauty, and goodness. There is the possibility for a union between epistemology, aesthetics, and ethics in the value of *makoto* as "truth."

Naturally, before entering the river to save a child, we must have additional descriptive knowledge. For example, one must determine that the drowning, floating object is in fact a child, and not a rucksack, which is neither ethically nor aesthetically the object to be saved. Also to be determined is whether or not one can cope with the swift current, etc. So, there must be harmony of judgment and description. "Truth" as *makoto* depends more on judgment than on description. Most important, is that the core of the judgment makes moral sense, whereby in the dynamic hierarchy of this situation the value of the human life is precisely determined and prioritized.

The "truth" as *makoto* is, therefore, at least in the Japanese language, always in an ambiguous balance between descriptive correctness and goodness. In this balance lies the secret of beauty, because the desired harmony requires the splendid breadth of spirit that is the symbol of cosmic beauty.

Axiological Trinity

To explain the harmonious unity of integrated "truth," that is "truth" on a higher philosophical level than the correct descriptive proposition, I begin again with the explanation of the Japanese concept *makoto*, with its philological reflection. We will return to the concrete example of the child in the river. This approach conveys a Buddhist view of the world, particularly to the extent that the given situation is conceived as a wounded one.

We should not think that this systematic axiological unity of the values of "truth," beauty, and goodness, derived from the logic of *makoto*, is merely an insignificant Asiatic local philosophy. There are many minor philosophical concepts that are highly interesting on the level of information, but are not universally significant because of their specific grounding in the ethos of a particular culture, its local language, and habits. Such philosophical ideas should not, however, be overlooked. As a minimum, they enrich knowledge in a peripheral field. Also to be found, however, in local philosophical traditions are important universal ideas necessary for progress in human philosophy, even if these ideas are sometimes closely associated with local linguistic concepts. The concept of *makoto*, as "truth" in Japanese, conveys a Buddhist world-view, which belongs precisely to that category of local philosophical ideas that have universal significance. Why?

Through its long splendid history, at least from the origins of the word "philosophy" employed by Socrates in the 4th century BC until today, Western philosophy has developed into universal philosophy. In this dominant philosophical tradition, there is the concept of the "Absolute," namely God, who expresses axiological unity, or specifically, the integrated unity of the "truth" with goodness and beauty. The highest being must, therefore, have the highest axiological unity. As far as the formal definition is concerned, the *makoto* and the absolute "truth" are the same, except for the notion of the Absolute as a living person, which is inherent in some Christian thought.

In this Western tradition, only the "Absolute" is perfect. Other beings are created by this "Absolute," thereby making them less than absolute. They are not, however, separated from the Absolute. They are in a subordinate position. In this sense, all beings other than God are neither perfectly self-sufficient nor self-governed. They are imperfect. Similarly, the fundamental assumption of the Buddhist view of the world is that the condition of human life is always a wounded one. This view conforms with the view of the world in the Western tradition, namely that every created thing or situation is imperfect.

The wound must be cured to enable the human condition to approach perfection as nearly as possible. In the human context, however, the perfect cure is essentially impossible, because by nature human beings are imperfect, feeble, and integral parts of a wounded existence. They can, nevertheless, approach a relatively better situation, if they attempt to ameliorate a given wounded object or condition. It requires giving primacy to practical participation in the tiny daily and private phenomenal wounds. In the Asiatic world, in general, there seems to be many private symptomatic therapies, speaking allegorically.

In this case, subjective intention—such as self-sacrifice, self-contention, discreet joy and efforts to moderate one's faults—is superior to the universal, public, theoretical, and objective methodology for social reconstruction, which presupposes the correct description of the given imperfect situation, according to the Western tradition of "truth" as *aletheia*. Here, the curing of the wound appears to imply use of quantitative methods, which in itself introduces the idea of correctness and the notion of success in terms of scientific achievement. Then, a tragic gap is introduced between scientific correctness and metaphysical depth in terms of "truth." By contrast, the subjective intention provides the axiological unification of "truth," goodness, and beauty, but suffers from the absence of a correct quantification and an objective description of the situation.

The Task of Philosophy in the 21ˢᵗ Century

The East, which has tended toward a transcendent unification of values, and the West, which has moved in the direction of analytical quantification have taken irreconcilable roads in the field of philosophy. The division between East and West has moved from the geographical to the mental dimension. This means that East and West are not geographical categories in this globalized sense. East and West are typological categories that characterize this schism. In the 20th century, there has been radical opposition between metaphysics and science, conceived as logical positivism. In most cultures these two conceptions conflict. Each one despises the other and rejects efforts toward mutual understanding. The question arises: should philosophy become two disciplines? If we take a *laissez-faire* attitude, then in the 21st century, the word "philosophy" might disappear. In its place there will be two disciplines—metaphysics and logic. To our regret, in many universities throughout the world, chairs of philosophy are being converted to chairs of anthropology, religious studies, sometimes metaphysics, and sometimes logic.

From its beginning, both in the West and East, logic and metaphysics have been the *alpha* and *omega* of philosophy and the two most important disciplines in this field. Logic is the starting point, the basic science of thinking, and metaphysics is the final point, conceived as the integrated knowledge of transcendence—be it in Socrates, Plato, or Aristotle in the Western world, or in Confucius and Kukai in the Eastern world. The task of the 21st century is to create the way for the integration of the philosophical *alpha* and *omega*.

Logic and metaphysics have been proud of their acknowledged standing as the fundamental principles of philosophy. But, today they are being pressed to merge under the heading of "ethics." In considering metaphysics, Levinas[5] and Jankelevich[6] propose, each for different reasons, that metaphysics should be made subordinate to ethics. Previously Moore,[7] recently Hare,[8] and now Raphael,[9] proposed, also for different reasons, that logic be the way to access ethical problems. Thus, ethics and political philosophy would become the shared tasks of the logicians and metaphysicians.[10] According to the classical tradition, both in the East and the West, ethics was integrated or absorbed in politics as "social ethics." Aristotle's *Ethics* meant individual ethics and his politics meant social ethics, as the ethics of the *polis*. In Confucianism, private ethics constituted the necessary first half of politics, understood as social ethics. In this sense, the works of Paul Ricoeur and Jean Ladriere[11] are remarkable in their attempt to unify the two tendencies. Since 1970, my theoretical proposal, *Eco-Ethica,* has aimed at the same orientation.[12]

Perhaps, as the first step in linking the two concepts, I would like to recommend to logicians and metaphysicians the concept of "meta-technica," which refers to philosophical reflection of the technological dimension as the new environment of human life. For no matter what one's frame of reference or definition of "truth," we all must learn to live with and come to terms with advances in technology and science. The collaboration of logicians and metaphysicians would serve to harmonize the philosophical and scientific concepts.

And with this merging of Eastern and Western concepts, the integration of metaphysics and logic, come solutions. The two theories complement each other as can be seen in the illustration of the child in the river where facts are necessary to heal the wounded situation. But before solutions must come acceptance and understanding, an acceptance of each concept's importance in human thought, as well as an understanding of the differences in terminology, usage, and theory. Perhaps, through this process, a larger and more complete "truth" will emerge.

Endnotes

1 - Plato, *Politeia,* 582 d9 (translated from the Greek meaning *"logos"*).

2 - "Truth" is the unity of intellect with reality.

3 - In explaining the word *"makoto,"* I would like to mention three books I have written: *Betrachtengen Uber das Eine* (Tokyo: Faculty of Letters University of Tokyo, 1968); *Doitsu-sei no Jiko-sosei (Self-formation of the Identity),* (Tokyo: Tokyo University Press, 1971); *Studia Comparata de Aesthetica* (Collected papers written in English, French and German) *Journal of the Faculty of Letters of the University of Tokyo,* vol. 1 (Tokyo, 1976), esp. "Die Krise der Wahrheine und das Problem der Objektivitat," 15-27. My English article on this problem, "The Character of Japanese Thought," is found in *Contemporary Philosophy: a New Survey,* ed. G. Floistad, in vol.7 of *Asian Philosophy,* (Dordrecht, 1993), 269-281.

4 - There are three different words *ma* in Japanese. We can identify the semantic differences among them through intonation and context. Naturally there are also differences in their pronunciation. It is, however, almost impossible to distinguish them with phonetic signs, because their pronunciation is different in each dialect spoken in Japan. The three different terms *Ma* are: a) the prefix which we have explained above, b) the dynamic between or among – concerning time-space and which is used to express spiritual elasticity especially in the aesthetic domain, c) a devil that is not of Japanese origin, but which came from China. These three words have entirely different origins and different meanings. And they are almost always written in Chinese characters. In that case, the prefix *ma* denotes *shin,* which means "true" in Chinese.

5 - E. Levinas. In his dialogue with Nemo, Levinas has clearly declared that in place of metaphysics, ethics must be treated as the first philosophy. According to his conviction this idea follows genuine platonic tradition, because the Good as the highest ideas is *epekeina tes ousias*. Cf. *Totalité et Infini*.

6 - Vladimir Jankelevich, *La Philosophie Première* (Paris: Presse Universitaire de France, 1954) is one of the earliest books in which not the metaphysics but the ethics is mentioned as the first philosophy. This is, in my opinion, along the French tradition: Decartes wished to build ethics as the ultimate discipline.

7 - G.E. Moore, *Principia Ethica* (Cambridge: Cambridge University Press, 1903) was one of the most important ethical books in the Anglo Saxon philosophy in the 20th century. Ch. L. Stevenson, *Ethics and Language* (New Haven: Yale University Press, 1944) was also an exceptional book of ethics in the analytic philosophy.

8 - R.M. Hare, *The Language of Morals* (Oxford: Clarendon Press, 1952) was one of the earliest books of ethics in the logical group after the Second World War. Hare's regards to the perceptive character of moral proposition is perhaps the point of passage from the content of categorical imperative to the linguistic analysis of imperative proposition.

9 - D.D. Raphael, *Moral Philosophy* (Oxford: Oxford University Press, 1980). We could find after this book many positive points of ethical thought after 1980 in the realm of analytic philosophy.

10 - See for instance, Ch. Larmore, *The Morals of Modernity* (Cambridge: Cambridge University Press, 1996).

11 - Paul Ricoeur, *Du Texte a l'Action* (Paris: Éditions du Seuil, 1986); Paul Ricoeur, *Soi-Même Comme un Autre,* (Paris: Éditions du Seuil, 1990); Paul Ricoeur, *Philosophie de la Volonté* (Paris: Aubier, 1950 and 1960); Jean Ladrière, *L'Éthique dans l'Univers de la Rationalité* (Louven: La Collection "catalyses" Artel-Fides, 1997).

12 - There are 19 volumes of the Acts of the International Symposium of Eco-Ethica edited by myself. Since 1983 these acts have been issued annually in the Revue International de Philosophie Moderne by my institute, the Centre International pour L'Étude Comparee de Philosophie et d'Esthétique, established in Tokyo in 1975. *Eco* means the dimension of human acts and action, which includes not only our society on earth as the global situation, not only our environments, not only intersideral cosmic space, not only nano space within our body, but also our cultural sphere. *Eco-ethica* is ethics for the complicated world of our time.

PART III

INSIGHTS FROM ART, LANGUAGE, AND LITERATURE

Thoughts are the molecules of a society. The emotions they articulate, the attitudes they project, and the desires they embody define the spirit of the time. Thus, it is necessary to reflect on the significance of intellectual and spiritual resources as the essential elements of social change. First, moral and spiritual inclinations and aspirations are inherent in human nature, giving meaning and orientation to human thoughts and actions. Second, individuals, independently or collectively, have the capacity to foster or impede the realization of moral and spiritual values in society. And among them writers and artists have a vital role in building harmonious and vibrant societies. As eloquently stated by George Bernard Shaw in his play *Back to Methuselah*: "Without art, the crudeness of reality would make the world unbearable."

In his discussion of the Russian intelligentsia, Isaiah Berlin drew attention to this important role of the writer and artist in society. These thinkers held that if one spoke in one instance as an artist and in another as a politician with a different set of values and biases, one spoke falsely, because humankind is an integral soul, not a storehouse of values and ideas that can be selected according to the occasion. Attitudes to life and to art should be identical, and these are ultimately moral attitudes. Writers, poets, and artists are in the first place, human beings and they are directly and continually responsible for all their expressions, whether in novels, poems or paintings, or in private letters, in public speeches or in conversation.

> Introducing the notion of the noosphere to a wider audience, a lay audience, if you like, would promote the sense that preserving human culture should be conducted with the same urgency as preserving the diversity of the biosphere. The noosphere provides a concrete term and a place for the intangibles of human thought. And the noosphere, because it is built around the capacity for self-conscious thought, provides the key to its own survival, a greater awareness of that which it contains.
>
> *Vyacheslav Ivanov*

In the early 20th century, the French Jesuit Teilhard de Chardin and the Russian member of the intelligentsia Vladimir Vernadsky met at the Sorbonne in Paris, where Vernadsky was lecturing. Building on Vernadsky's conception of the biosphere, de Chardin conceived the "noosphere," the thinking layer superimposed on the biosphere. The noosphere is the sphere of mind, conscious invention, and the heartfelt union of souls, for the development of which the most crucial element is the human capacity for self-reflective thought, expressed in art, literature, and music and a myriad of other ways. It encapsulates the moral, intellectual, aesthetic and spiritual dimensions of society. In his paper on this crucial sphere of human life, Vyacheslav Ivanov, probes the very elements of human thought and their inventions reflected in, for example, the different modes of intercommunication in human society. The greater the number and complexity of modes of expression of ideas and communications, the more substantial is this sphere, the very foundation of the moral, spiritual and intellectual life of the world and essential to the survival of the biosphere.

Modern society and globalization have threatened this sphere of life, argues Ivanov. We are concerned today about the protection of the biosphere from the assaults of pollutants. We should be even more concerned about the assault on the sphere of thought, on the nature and richness of ideas, creative imagination, and modes of human communication, which is shrinking as society loses languages and leaves creative imaginings to electronic devices.

> Although economic progress contributes to a comfortable existence and sense of security, it does not usually nurture such nonmaterial resources, as for example, the search for harmony, wisdom and beauty, which is essential to coping well with life's personal hardships(...). Without linkages between information, knowledge and wisdom, or between technological change and the flourishing of the individual in nonmaterial ways, modernization might just mean seeing the world abstractly, objectively, and generally quantifiably. Science and economy tend to become their own ends, offering humanity the prospect of life anchored in spiritually dormant societies where the shoe pinches inordinately.
>
> *Barbara Sundberg Baudot*

From a different perspective Barbara Sundberg Baudot addresses issues of the meaning and content of progress that are at the same time relevant to preserving and promoting the development of the noosphere. Her point of departure is a brief exchange between Soren

Kierkegaard and Hans Christian Andersen that seems to oppose progress as the individual's journey towards spiritual fulfillment and progress as the material development of society driven by technological change. As the argument develops, Adam Smith and Karl Marx are shown to underscore what Ivanov implied, that technological progress and economic growth for their own sakes combined with neglect of the moral and intellectual expansion of the individual will reduce society to a meaningless sphere of barter and exchange. Baudot then invites thinkers, as different as Albert Einstein and Ralph Waldo Emerson, to help demonstrate the relevance of non-empirical and non-scientific ways of gaining knowledge and show how these sources can enrich and lend meaning to the development discourse. Development, thus, must be carefully crafted and shepherded by ideas generated from philosophy, art, and literature as well as science. In every stage of technological and economic progress, the intellectual and spiritual condition of humankind must be carefully guarded and nourished. The pitfalls are clear but avoidable.

> The master must be one with the Spirit of Nature and represent It in his/her work of art; the person who appreciates the art thereby learns about the Spirit of Nature. Travelling this path of art, human beings are purified and perfected. They concentrate on nature to be one with Spirit or of the Cosmos, not only through creation but also through the appreciation of works of art and thereby have possibilities to experience a cathartic ecstasy that lifts them from the pains and grief of the real world.
>
> *Noriko Hashimoto*

Modernity tends to compartmentalize in different spheres economics, politics, the aesthetic and the spiritual. Intellectuals have little interest in economics and sometimes even disparage the relevance of art. For example, Allan Bloom in his response to Francis Fukuyama's "The End of History" reports that Alexandre Kojeve, considered by many to be the most authoritative interpreter of Hegel, saw in traditional art forms of Japan—the tea ceremony, flower arrangement and the No Play—nothing more than pure snobbism of form and a graceful empty activity

Noriko Hashimoto's essay poetically and profoundly refutes this contention of empty formalism, showing how much is really at

185

stake. She plumbs the depth of these ceremonies, probing into the deep moral and spiritual essence of these ancient arts and demonstrating how the practitioner and the observer move toward Nature and into the presence of Spirit in their performance. The practices of these arts are as sacred to those who understand them as are the most profound religious ceremonies to the faithful. To those decision-makers striving to design effective public policies for building more humane societies and protecting the environment, Noriko's work is inspiring. Unfortunately, education today emphasizes the practical sciences to the neglect of these arts. The intellectual loss is incalculable to those seeking meaning in life and society.

> In their private lives poets may be no more moral, courageous or perceptive in regard to family and friends than any other humans, but wittingly or unwittingly poets create a record of the consciousness of being alive. Theirs is often an isolated passionate struggle to find the words to share "what it was like" with unknown others—to find words for scarcely expressible joys and sorrows, for the nuances of yearning, the cosmos that is human consciousness.
>
> *Allison W. Phinney*

Similarly, the traditionally narrow focus of most leaders seeking primarily outward economic and social improvements offers little hope of elevating and enriching human thoughts increasingly dispirited by pervasive materialism. In this context, Allison Phinney introduces the poets. These sculptors of verbal forms have been left aside in the work of social engineering. The transformation of society according to the prescriptions of scientific modernity has so weakened idealism as to engender a new necessity for looking pragmatically not only to the poets, but also the filmmakers, dramatists, artists, musicians and composers, philosophers, and theologians. If humanity is to be fulfilled rather than enslaved by continuous acquiescence in finitude, we must heed the poets' visions. They draw attention to society's greatest issues: the human spirit denigrated, starved, unfulfilled, or destroyed. As Phinney emphasizes, poets do not live a daily lives of heroic choices any more than anyone else, and in point of fact, the hardest battles are often fought not with visible opponents but with the inertia, apathy, and dullness that constrict, or deconstruct, life and spirit.

CHAPTER 10

TOWARDS NOOSPHERE

Vyacheslav Ivanov

In the 1920s, Teilhard de Chardin [1881-1955] and Vladimir Vernadsky [1863-1945] developed the concept "noosphere." It emerged in an exchange of ideas between these two great minds, while the latter was lecturing at the Sorbonne, after fleeing the Russian communist regime.[1] Building upon Vernadsky's notion of biosphere as a living envelope of the Earth, Teilhard de Chardin, together with his friend, Le Roy, a philosopher of Bergsonian orientation and a mathematician, fell upon the idea of a noosphere.[2] "Noosphere" is a neologism formed from the Greek *noos* (meaning mind, intelligence, understanding, thought) and designates a thinking layer superimposed on the biosphere, a new film or membrane on the earth's surface.[3] Chardin described the "noosphere" as "*une sphere de la reflection, d'invention consciente, de l'union sentie des ames*" (a sphere of thought, of the conscious invention, of the heart-felt union of souls).[4] Chardin thus describes how the noosphere came to be:

> As a result of some 'hominizing' cerebral mutation, which appears among the anthropoids towards the end of the Tertiary period, psychic reflection–not simply 'knowing' but 'knowing that one knows'–bursts upon the world and opens up an entirely new domain for evolution. With man (apparently no more than a new zoological 'family') it is a *second species of life* that begins, bringing with it its new cycle of possible patterns of arrangement and its own special planetary envelope (the noosphere).[5]

As this passage from de Chardin indicates, the most crucial element in the development of the noosphere is the human capacity for self-reflective thought.

In December of 1958, the British biologist, Julian Huxley, another friend of Chardin's, verging on a similar discovery remarked: [6]

> In 1925, Teilhard coined the term noosphere to denote the sphere of mind, as opposed to, or rather superposed on, the biosphere or sphere of life, and acting as a transforming agency promoting hominisation (or as I would put it, progressive psychosocial evolution). He may perhaps be criticized for not defining the term more explicitly. By noosphere did he intend simply the total pattern of thinking organisms (i.e., human beings) and their activity, including the patterns of their interrelationships: or did he intend the special environment of man, the systems of organized thought and its products in which men move and have their being, as fish swim and reproduce in rivers and the sea? Perhaps it might have been better to restrict noosphere to the first-named sense, and to use something like noosystem for the second. But certainly noosphere is a valuable and thought-provoking word.[7]

Orthodox Father, Pavel Florensky [1882-1937], another Russian scholar and thinker personally linked to Vernadsky, also developed his thoughts on the biosphere incorporating the noosphere in an original way. In a letter to Vernadsky written in 1929, Florensky wrote:

> There exists in, or perhaps on, the biosphere what may be called pneumatosphere, that is a special part of a substance that has been drawn into the cycle of culture, or more exactly, the cycle of spirit. Undoubtedly, this cycle is not the same as the general life cycle. But there is a large amount of data, admittedly not yet sufficiently worked out, which points to a special kind of stability shown by material formations created by spirit, for example, objects of art.[8]

Suggesting a special term "pneumatosphere" from the Greek *pneuma*, meaning soul or spirit, as opposed to the material body in Pauline religious philosophy, Florensky stresses how the symbolic function of an object transforms the object materially. This refers to the process of transformation of the material aspect of a symbol or a sign in the semiotic sense, as it is influenced by the symbolized aspect. Florensky was particularly interested, for example, in the material differences between Orthodox icons and other objects of a similar kind.[9] He considered how, because transformed by a system of meanings, colors in icons differ from the same colors in another type of artistic painting. The development of semiotics has made it possible to study this particular part of the noosphere.

Introducing yet another noospheric type analogy to the biosphere in Vernadsky's sense, Yurii Lotman [1922-1993], a Russian semiotician, found that all the signs and different semiotic systems of culture might be considered to constitute a "semiosphere."[10]

Before his death, Vernadsky succeeded in publishing a brief summary of his views on the relationship between the biosphere and the noosphere. He considered the noosphere to be a higher stage in the evolution of the biosphere.[11] The general views of noosphere in Vernadsky's theory, as well as the semiosphere of Lotman, were based on the rational notion of evolution towards the highest type of reasoning, while Chardin, and partly also Florensky, interpreted a similar idea in a Christian way. But, for Vernadsky, as well as for Chardin, the crucial fact of biological evolution consisted in the increasing complexity of the nervous tissue.[12] Vernadsky called this crucial fact, Dana's principle after the American geologist and biologist, James Dwight Dana [1813-1895]. Dana established the existence of a non-interrupted cephalization that continued in different branches of the living world.[13]

From many interesting remarks on the evolution of the brain found in Chardin's work, it follows that, for him, increasing cephalization was the core and the main path of the human physical evolution. Chardin studied this phenomenon from the perspectives of both paleontologist and thinker. According to Chardin, although the physical aspect of the brain is not expected to continue its evolutionary change, still the movement does not stop.[14] Chardin was thinking mainly about the social interaction of many human individuals creating mind with all minds joined together.[15] Besides socialization, Chardin saw the continuation of this movement in humankind's increasing awareness of itself and the universe:

> We newcomers of the twentieth century are coinciding in time and place with a happening which is as massive as the initial formation, vitalizing, and humanizing of the earth, and is developing at a tempo which keeps pace with our own experiences. This happening is the awakening of the sense of man, by which I mean that terrestrial thought is becoming conscious that it constitutes an organic whole, endowed with the power of growth, and both capable and responsible for some future.[16]

In his vision of the ultimate earth, Chardin pays particular attention to the organization of research and to the discovery of human beings as the main object of exploration. In this connection, one may recall the predictions of Claude Levi-Strauss on the future of the humanities in the 21st century. For similar reasons, Vernadsky approached the study of noosphere through his works on the history of science.[17]

Just as the increasing cephalization leads to the growing complexity of the nervous tissues, in the history of culture, or of the noosphere, one may observe, the growing complexity of the whole network of cultural sign systems in their intersection with each other, as well as inside each of them. The particular role of different sign systems and symbols of language, art, mythology, religion, philosophy, and science in this movement can be appreciated in so far as each of them promotes the growth of information. The tendency seems to be remarkably consistent if relatively large time intervals are examined. Once again the parallel to Dana's principle in biological evolution is striking. The time line in the human biological evolution as well as in the history of "noosphere/pneumatosphere/semiosphere" is defined by the growth of information just as the time direction in the physical world is measured according to the second law of thermodynamics. Both the works of Chardin and Vernadsky suggest the general tendency towards growth in amounts of information. One may consider a probable proof of Chardin's ideas to be found in technological progress achieved in the years since his death. The movement he foresaw might be reflected in the rapid successes of computer engineering and other branches of artificial intelligence.

Since the development of mathematical "information theory," enabling information to become finely measurable, it has become possible to consider study of the noosphere based on principles of exact science. To discover the order in which different sign systems might develop in the course of human history and prehistory, one may try to combine data of biological sciences, including molecular biology and embryology, and those of linguistics and other semiotic disciplines. Because linguistic abilities are directly connected to the shape of the structure of the speech zones of the dominant, largely the left, hemisphere of the brain, it seems that the co-evolution of brain and language is a meeting-point in the biological and sociocultural development of the noosphere.

191

If the achievements of human knowledge were made possible by the co-evolution of brain and language, the main part of these achievements should be attributed to the dominant hemisphere of the brain; the hemisphere responsible for speech, logical thinking, counting and other operations with discrete signs and objects.[18] According to Sir John Eccles, brain specialist and 1963 Nobel prize winner, self-consciousness is connected to particular zones of the left hemisphere. It has been proposed that some of its functions developed recently. This sociobiological trend is continued through modern engineering, since computers can help develop or, to a certain degree, substitute for some of the special fields of activity of the left hemisphere of the brain.[19] Similarly, the development of all the capacities of the brain should also be achieved in greater degree. But, there are great problems and possibilities relating to this challenge and to the evolution of the noosphere. Some of these are described in what follows.

Modern studies of endangered languages suggest that no more than 600 languages out of 6,000 that exist in the world may survive in the next generation. This possible catastrophe of the near future might be even more serious than the one studied by the specialists in ecology. Humankind is rapidly losing the degree of linguistic diversity that it has possessed for the past thousand years. Most of the American Indian languages that are still spoken in USA will be dead by the next generation. No matter how persistent national feelings are in Ireland, the Irish language is spoken by no more than thirty thousand people and is doomed to extinction, though poets still compose in it. The number of young children who willingly get their school education in their native tongue determines a language's survival. Global capitalism practically excludes this possibility for a vast majority of languages that are still spoken.

There are a few possible ways to reduce the number of disappearing languages that, at the same time, do not prohibit the integration of their speakers into the modern world. More active integration of native speakers into modern economic, technological, and informational networks may aid survival of their language as has been demonstrated, for instance, in Greenland where there are optimistic predictions for the future of the local Eskimo language. The recent establishment of an Eskimo-speaking self-ruling area in Canada may be a step in a similar direction, provided it will not be too isolated from the rest of the country (see chapter 16).

At the same time, the disappearance of the majority of existing languages may be at least partly off set by the formation of newly independent languages, off shoots from the more widely used languages. For instance, former Chinese dialects such as Cantonese may acquire a more independent status. Also possible, may be a transformation of different forms of creolized and pidgin languages into new languages such as Neo-Melanesian, a state language based on the former Pidgin English.

Other possible solutions to the disappearance of languages are the wider use of different translation techniques—including automatic translation and multilingual school education.[20] Both ways have some interesting historical precedence.[21] In the interest of protecting and developing the noosphere, not words and sentences alone, but the meanings they convey are important. Thus, the elaboration of a translation technique is related to the understanding of the main concepts of civilization and from this point of view is relevant for the noosphere in which all the concepts expressed in different languages are an integral part.

For humanity and the evolution of the noosphere, not only linguistic diversity but also, the coexistence of different semiotic systems, beginning with the earliest periods of history, is very important. Mankind is losing the wealth of mythological images and ritualistic systems that characterized the Third World in the beginning of the 20th century. The fate of archaic mythologies is partly connected to that of the native languages that were used to encode their symbols. A certain concept may be expressed not only through words of different languages, but also by means of several different sign systems. The following brief outline of some aspects of the evolution of the noosphere will reveal that language is not the sole player in the gradual formation of human culture.

Gestural sign systems are of particular interest. In modern societies these systems replace natural phonemic language in the case of sensory loss such as deafness, as well as in some exceptional social situations.[22] But the extraordinary importance of this type of semiotic system was still observed among American Indians in the 19th century, not only for communication—particularly between tribes speaking different phonemic languages—but also for the archaic intellectual processes.

The great American anthropologist Cushing [1857-1900], who was introduced into the mysteries of the Zuni tribe, performed an experiment that Levi-Bruhl called possible only for a genius. He achieved the formation of manual concepts connected to gestures.[23] In our century, the experiment was repeated by the great Russian filmmaker and aesthetician Sergei Eisenstein who was fascinated with Cushing's discovery. Studies in primate communication made it possible to suppose that gestures were more important than sounds for the intellectual operations of early hominids; even though they coexisted with a small number of sound signals, which had not yet developed into a phonemic language.[24] The common origin of the latter and of gestural communication may be reflected in the relation between the modern systems of gestures and the left (dominant) hemisphere of the brain.[25]

If the earliest human societies could use both gestural signs and phonemic language to express the ideas of the primitive culture, then another major step was achieved with the creation of visual art.[26] Hands are widely represented as symbols in the earliest visual signs of the Paleolithic art. According to new discoveries in Southern France, Paleolithic art begins no later than 30,000 years ago—approximately 10,000 years after Homo sapiens had appeared in Europe. These visual representations of hands seem to be connected with gestural communication, which is a function of the left hemisphere of the brain. However, judging by our knowledge of modern man, visual art and musical creativity belong to functions of the non-dominant hemisphere of the brain.

The earliest representations of the universe having ritualistic and mythological meanings are those of Paleolithic art. Later development of the archaic religious traditions was based on the use of oral language combined with singing, musical performance and other artistic forms. There must have been some selective pressure, in the Darwinian sense, for musical abilities to become genetically transmitted since they are localized in the areas of the non-dominant hemisphere that are symmetrically positioned in respect to the speech zones of the dominant one. A possible, partial explanation for this symmetry is the role of singing accompanied by music in memorizing long texts, such as epic poems, in illiterate modern societies. It seems that, for several thousand years, cultural memory was mostly connected to singing and music.

Let us suppose that early performances of this kind were really based on the synthetic combination of different arts. Then we may suppose that the modern ideas of *Gesamtkunst* (total or synthetic art) as put forward by Wagner and his followers, such as Skriabin in his unfinished "Mysterium," may be attempts to return to the original sources of human creativity, which combined the right and left sides of the brain. The right side of the brain is responsible for visual and musical expression, while language, oral and written, falls under the province of the left hemisphere. Natural language, a combination of the products of the left and right side of the brain, is vitally important to express different notions and images. In this sense, sign systems of literature and science, products of the left-hemisphere may be called secondary as suggested by the Moscow-Tartu semiotic school, the natural language remaining the main primary system of signs. Today, however, harmony between the left and right sides of the brain has been overshadowed by the current high status of the left side of the brain, which is party explained by the substitution of oral memory by writing.

A further important step in the development of the noosphere was a partial substitution of this kind of oral memory for a written one. As supposed by Schmandt-Besserat, the first precursors of writing appeared after the Neolithic revolution in connection with the necessities of a society in its formative stages.[27] The early hieroglyphic sign systems based on pictorial or pictographic representation slowly moved towards a logographic link to the phonemic language.[28] A further major step in the evolution of the noosphere and the noosystem was a shift from logographic representation of words to the alphabetic principle. In the development of a normal child in a modern society one may see an ontogenetic analogue to this phylogenetic part of evolution. After a certain degree of knowledge is achieved based on learning holistic, predominantly right-hemispheric, images, the acquisition of literacy makes it possible to perform successive, largely left-hemispheric, operations not only on letters but also on natural numbers and other sequences of discrete symbols. This achievement paves the way to understand notions of orders and sets and to open the way for rational and legal reasoning.

Diachronic historical research on a similar change from logographically oriented Ancient Oriental cultures toward the alphabetic discrete principle, as in Western Semitic traditions and Ancient Greece, has revealed a parallel development between understanding of the role of the elements of the universe and the elementary units of writing. In alphabetic cultures, elements are usually denoted by nouns, e.g. atoms, molecules, genes, quanta, particles, strings, phonemes in the European scientific traditions. This differs from such languages as Iroquois, the Onondaga dialect, and many other American Indian languages in which verbs are the main linguistic means of description. We have become so accustomed to thinking in terms of discrete elements that without the impetus from this comparison to American Indian languages we might not have been aware of how greatly these two world-views differ. This example may help illustrate why knowledge of American Indian languages is so important. Building on the notion that an understanding of the universe and the formation of language are fundamentally connected, it is possible to articulate the importance of comparing different language systems for understanding other cultures. Because each language represents a separate world-view and a distinct semantic model of the universe, one can only deplore the rapid extinction of languages, and the ignorance of archaic sign systems.

Early written cultures already used mythological images to make clear some basic ideas that we now call humanistic. As a specific example of an image typical of hieroglyphic cultures one may choose a religious rite and myth representing a slave being "liberated from debt-slavery" (Hurrian *kirenzi* "remission, liberation" translated in the first half of the II mil. B.C. by Hittite *para tarnumar*,

Akkadian *anduraru*). The fate of a large city might depend on the realization of this rite. Contradicting the simplified descriptions of these ancient societies as based on slave-ownership, the text describes the necessity to liberate a god if he has been taken debt-prisoner and become a slave.[29] The necessity of liberating a god who had become a debt-slave serves as the introduction to a similar case related to a human being. In the same Hurrian-Hittite text in the discussion in the Council of Ebla an important official refuses to liberate a man. That is considered enough of a reason to destroy the whole city.

Hieroglyphic global mythological and ritual images, like "to liberate," give concrete ritualistic and mythological representations of some aspects or notions, such as freedom/slavery and liberty as a special case connected to the debt-release or slave-release. These may later be reinterpreted in logical or legal terms from the "alphabetic" or rational point of view.[30] This is an example of how an early myth was concerned with the main issues of the social structure. It reveals the early development of ideas that became popular much later, starting with the Old Testament—Hebrew deror with the same meaning of 'liberation' as in the Hurrian, Hittite and Akkadian words cited above.[31]

While there is no return to the archaic systems of many shamanistic societies some continuity is still important for cultural transmission of values.[32] The movement toward a subsequent stage of the noospheric development and the spread of modern technology, science, and informational infrastructure need not presuppose getting rid of the symbols of the archaic types. From this point of view, fundamentalist movements may be viewed as attempts to preserve or restore older systems of beliefs. In societies of a less rigid kind, it is important that a balance of the religious and scientific models of the universe and a peaceful cohabitation of several symbolic systems be found. A diversity of semiotic models presupposes that mutual translation ability and a certain set of notions common to all of them. The language of science and the study of culture need not be seen as mutually threatening to each other, rather they can be combined. One method of preserving these archaic or "traditional" systems is to show how important they are for understanding the development of the human brain. For example, the relationship between the older hieroglyphic sign systems and the later cultures based on an alphabetic principle, if seen in the light of neurosemiotics, might help to relate the values derived from the history of culture and the cognitive sciences.

In this work it is important to point out that the noosphere is more than a collection of disparate isolated systems and beliefs of different times and of different countries, like a kind of historical Internet. The main task of the intellectuals does not consist simply in digging out ancient symbols or reproducing them again. It is also necessary to apply the intensity of the human mind to the present-day problems by using the whole perspective of the noospheric development.

Although not always easy, it is possible to translate some general notions of great religions of the Axial time—in Karl Jaspers' sense—into a language of modern science. Thus, at the end of his book, *What is Life?*, describing biological data from the viewpoint of modern physics, one of the founders of the quantum mechanics, Schroedinger, also used the language of the Indian Buddhist philosophy.

Different kinds of linguistic and semiotic diversity can be partly continued although their future depends on the general worldwide situation that might affect their preservation in a global capitalist world. The end of the 20th century was characterized by attempts to find a general synthesis and to escape from the extreme specialization and isolation of numerous fields of human activity. In physics, theoreticians are trying to fulfill Einstein's dream of Great Unification. In art, synthetic experiments are becoming more and more popular. But, perhaps the most courageous of them was that of Skriabin's "Mysterium."

Keeping in mind Berdiaiev's idea about modern politics as a kind of continuation of avant-garde art, one may ask whether the performance planned by Skriabin was continuously rehearsed after his death by the forces that determine the modern history of the world. The total performance of the "Mysterium" was supposed to impress all the senses. This included music, which had been partly written; words, the poetical text of the "Preliminary Act" by Skriabin published posthumously; light-and-color music, which was based on a combination of sound and color and thus included the line *Luce* 'Light' in the scores; and perfumes. Skriabin had planned to present the performance in India, in 1917. However, he died in 1915.[33] Because Skriabin was thinking about the deepest problems in the religious philosophy of his time, using all the most radical devices of modern avant-garde art, his "Mysterium" might have become a decisive breakthrough in cultural history. It was intended to be the ultimate expression of human creativity. He had studied the problem of final things, long before Fukuyama's work made it fashionable.

In sum, the concept of a noosphere contributes to progress in the field of semiotics by virtue of the way in which its relationship to the biosphere brings science and the study of human culture into closer alliance. Introducing the notion of the noosphere to a wider audience, a lay audience, if you like, would promote the sense that preserving human culture should be conducted with the same urgency as preserving the diversity of the biosphere. The noosphere provides a concrete term and a place for the intangibles of human thought. And the noosphere, because it is built around the capacity for self-conscious life, provides the key to its own survival, a greater awareness of that which it contains. Bringing people's attention to the noosphere is especially crucial at this point in time.

Endnotes

1 - Being not only one of the greatest Russian natural scientists and a founder of modern biogeology, but also an important political figure in the Provisional Government, he had been persecuted by the Bolshevik secret police and arrested before he was allowed to leave the country to which he returned only in 1926 after some years in France.

2 - Reading "Évolution *créatrice*" (*Creative Evolution*) by Bergson arose the initial interest Chardin took in evolution in his formative years, M. Barthelemy-Madaule, *Bergson et Chardin de Chardin* (Paris: Editions du Seuil, 1963). For a critical appraisal and comparison of both Bergson and Chardin from an existentialist positivist point of view. Jacques Monod, *Le hasard et la nécessité: Essai sur la philosophie naturelle de la biologie moderne* (Paris: Editions du Seuil, 1970), 39-40, 44-46, 129-130, the English translation: Jacques Monod, *Chance and Necessity. An Essay on the Natural Philosophy of Modern Biology* (New York: Alfred A. Knopf, 1971), 26-27, 31-33, 115-117.

3 - For the early meaning of the term in Greek, see the discussion in the first part of the study: Karl R. Popper and John C. Eccles, *The Self and its Brain* (Heidelberg: Springer-Verlag 1976), 167, 170, 172; 178.

4 - Pierre Teihard de Chardin, *La Vision du Passé* (Paris: Editions du Seuil, 1925), 92.

5 - Pierre Teilhard de Chardin, Toward the Future (New York: Harcourt Brace Jovanovich, 1975), 213.

6 - See on Chardin's approval of Huxley's formula: Man discovers that he is nothing else than evolution become conscious of itself, Pierre Teilhard de Chardin, *Le Phénomène Humain* (Paris: Editions du Seuil, 1955) 220. English translation: Pierre Teilhard de Chardin, *The Phenomenon of Man* (New York: Harper & Row Publishers, 1961), 122-123. Remarks on Chardin's critical attitude towards Huxley in a dogmatic catholic biography seem exaggerated. Henry de Lubac, *Teilhard de Chardin: The Man and his Meaning* (New York: Mentor Omega, 1967), 90, fn.5; 122-123, fn.21.

7 - Sir Julian Huxley, "Introduction," to Pierre Teilhard de Chardin, *The Phenomenon of Man,* 13-14.

8 - The letter was written three years before Florensky's last arrest leading to Siberian exile, imprisonment in Solovki camp and finally execution. Pavel A. Florensky, Pis'ma V.I. Verandskomu (Letters to V.A. Verandsky) (Paris: Atheneum, 1986), 281.

9 - This ideas can be fond in: Vyacheslav Ivanov, "Florenskii: A Symbolic View—Elementa" *Journal of Slavic Studies and Comparative Cultural Semiotics,* vol 2, no.1 (1995), 13.; K.G. Isupov, Russkaja Estetika Istorii (History of Russian Aesthetics) (Saint Petersburgh: Vysshie Gumanitaarnye kursy, 1992), 136-140.; S.M. Polovinkin, P.A. Florensky, Logos protiv Khaosa (P.A. Florensky: Logos against Chaos); *P.A. Florensky: Pro et contra.* (Saint-Petersburgh: izd. Russkogo khristianskogo gumanitarnogo instituta, 1996), 625-648. A comparison to de Chardin is suggested.

10 - Jurij M. Lotman, *Universe of Mind: a Semiotic Theory of Culture* (London: I.B Tauris & Co., Ltd. 1990) 163-300.

11 - Vladimir I.Vernadsky, "Neskol'ko slov o noosfere" (Some words on Noosphere) *Uspekhi sovremennoj biologii,* t. XVIII, (Moscow: Nauka Publisher's, 1960), 113-120 (reprinted in Vladimir I.Vernadsky, *Khimicheskoe stroenie biosfery Zemli i ee okruzhenija (Chemical Structure of the earth's Biosphere and of its Environment; in Russian),* (Moscow: Nauka Publishers, 1965), 323-330.

12 - Pierre de Chardin, *Le Phénomène Humain* (Paris: Editions du Seuil, 1955), 146. English translation: Pierre de Chardin, *The Phenomenon of Man* (New York: Harper & Row Publishers, 1961), 180.

13 - Vladimir I. Vernadsky, *Khimicheskoe stroenie biosfery Zemli i ee okruzhenija* (Chemical Structure of the earth's Biosphere and of its Environment; in Russian), (Moscow: Nauka Publishers, 1965), 193, 202-fn 9 271-272, 326. For a survey of recent data on the evolution of brain and the theory of encephalization see: JH. Jerison, *Evolution of the Brain and Intelligence* (New York: Academic Press, 1973). and Harry J.Jerison, "The Theory of Encephalization".- In: Masterton, R.B., Bitterman, M.E., Campbell, C.B.G., Hotton, (eds.) *Evolution of Brain and Behavior in Vertebrates.* (Hillsdale, New Jersey: L.Erlbaun Assoc., 1976), 146-160 (with a long bibliographical list starting with Aristotle but not including Dana; as Vernadsky rightly observed he had not been mentioned by most later authors who wrote on the subject); Stahl, Barbara J. "Early and Recent Primitive Brain Forms" in Dimond, Stuart J. and Blizard, David A. (eds.) *Evolution and Lateralization of the Brain.* Annals of the New York Academy of Sciences, vol. 299. (New York: The New York Academy of Sciences, 1977), 90; on the modern description of last period of this evolution cf. also Monod *Le Hasard(...),* 1970, 145ff.; *Chance(...),* 1971, 126ff.. As Vernadsky remarks that he had found this general principle in the early twenties and that later on this conclusion was confirmed in his discussion with paleontologists (Vernadsky *Kimicheskoe stroenie...,*1965, 193, 272) it seems evident that he had in mind his Paris talks to Chardin (whom he described as a paleontologist in his book).

14 - Pierre de Chardin, *Le Phénomène Humain,* 227.

15 - Pierre de Chardin, *Toward the Future,* 278.

16 - Ibid.

17 - Vladmir I. Vernadsky, *Trudy po istorii nauki v Rossii* (Works on the History of Science in Russia) (Moscow: Nauka Publishers, 1988).

18 - The idea was widely discussed in several evolutionary and paleoneurological studies of the last decades, see references in Vyacheslav Ivanov, *"Nechet i chet Asimmetrija mozga i dinamika znakovykh sistem* (Odd and Even, Asymmetry of the Brain and Dynamics of the Sign System) "Izbrannye sochinenija po istorii kul'tury i semiotike" (Selected Writings in the History of Culture and Semiotics) vol 1, (1998); Jacques Monod, *Le Hasard(...).* See also the last comprehensive study (almost completely neglecting an important aspect of the hemispheric specialization maybe as a sort of counterbalancing of a somewhat exaggerated interest in it in the previous literature): Trence W. Deacon, *The Symbolic Species: The Co-evolution of Language and Brain* (New York: W. W. Norton and Co., 1997).

19 - As several scholars suppose that some other important functions of the human brain may be described in terms of quantum mechanical processes R. Penrose, *The Emperor's New Mind: Concerning Computers, Minds and the Laws of Physics* (Oxford: Vintage Press, 1990). R. Penrose *Shadows of the mind: A Search for the Missing Science of Consciousness* (Oxford: Oxford University Press, 1994); John C. Eccles, "Do Mental Events Analogously to the

Probability Fields of Quantum Mechanics?," *Proceedings of* the Royal Society of London, vol 227 (1986): 411-428.) Technological models built on this principle might become important for the development of the engineering side of the noosystem (in Huxley's sense, see above) in the future. On the abilities of the right hemisphere that still are very distant from everything possible for modern supercomputers cf Robert Ornstein, *The Right Mind. Making Sense of the Hemispheres* (New York: Harcourt Brace & Co, 1997); Marcel Kinsbourne, "Unity and Diversity in the Human Brain: Evidence from Injury" *Daedalus.* vol.127 no.2. (1998): 233-256. With further references on the general possibility of building machines that would appear to possess consciousness see: Francis Crick, *The Astonisthing Hypothesis: The Scientific Search for the Soul* (New York: Charles Scriber's Sons, 1994), 257.

20 - One of the most challenging tasks is to build a semantic system of correspondences between meanings of words and/or combinations of words rendering the same concept in different languages. Although its necessity is dictated by technology of simultaneous automatic translation, such a system might become very important to investigate similarities and differences in linguistic patterning of the outer world. Some interesting preliminary results were reached in the historical linguistic investigation of the main notions of European Judeo-Christian culture as seen through different languages: Leo Spitzer "*Essays in Historical Semantics*," (New York: S.F.Vanni,1948); "*Classical and Christian Ideas of the World Harmony. Prolegomena to the Interpretation of the Word "Stimmung*," Ed. A. Granville, (Baltimore, MD: Hatcher, 1963).

21 - Vyacheslav Ivanov, *The Russian Orthodox Church of Alaska and the Aleut Islands and its Relation to Native American Traditions—An Attempt at a Multicultural Society, 1794-1912* (Washington: Library of Congress, 1997).

22 - As for example, prohibition to speak in some monastic orders: E Buyssens "Le langage par gestes chez les moines," *Revue de l'Institut de sociologie* no.4, 1956. Also, obligatory ritual silence in connection with funerary ceremonies among the Aranta tribe in Austrailia. A. Sommerfelt, *La langue et la societé* (Oslo: Universitetsforlaget, Institut for Samlide Kulturforskning, 1938), 36-37; 174.

23 - In a recently published letter of 1880, Cushing wrote that among the Zunis "a most elaborate gesticulation accompanies excited or emphatic oral demonstrations- yet many of the signs thus used being too artificial to have had origin in simple natural conceptions, and from this not only but also from their close affinity to those of other tribes, we must infer that they have been remotely acquired or at least that they are survivals of an ancient intertribal gesture speech". Frank Hamilton Cushing, "Cushing at Zuni", ed. Jesse Green *The Correspondence and Journals 1879-1884* (Albuquerque: University of New Mexico Press, 1990) 98,99. See also: Cushing, Frank Hamilton " Manual Concepts. A Study of the Influence of Hand-Usage on Cultural Growth," *American Anthropologist*, vol. 5, 1892, no.1, 289-317.

24 - G.W. Hews, "Primate Communication and the Gestural Origin of Language," *Current Anthropology*, vol.14, no.1-2 (1973).

25 - Howard Poizner, Edward S. Kilma, and U. Bellugi, *What the Hands Reveal About the Brain* (Cambridge, MA: MIT Press, 1987).

26 - Leroi-Gourhan, André "Le geste et la parole: Technique et langage—La mémoire et les rythmes." *Sciences d'aujourd'hui*, Collection dirigée par A. George. (Paris: Éditions Albin Michel. 1964-1965).

27 - D. Schmandt-Besserat, *Before the Number* (Austin: Texas University Press 1992).

28 - Ignace J. Gelb, *A Study of Writing*, revised edition (Chicago: Chicago University Press, 1963).

29 - Hurrian [a]-a-i hé-en-ni DTe-es-su-ub hé-en-za-a-du ki-i-re-en-za-am-ma [s]a-a-ri-ib hé-en-za-a i-su-uh-na-i DTe-es-su-ub si-ik-la-te-em-ma i-su-uh-ni a-ar-ri-waa-as = Hittite[DI]M-as [si-is-]si-ya-ni-it da-mi-is-ha-an-za [pa-ra-a tar-nu-mar ú]-e-wa-ak-ki ma-a-an DIM-as [si-i]s-si-ya-u-wa-za nu ku-is-sa DIM-un-n i [IGIN KÚ. BABBAR pa-a-(I) "when being opressed by a difficult situation (of debt) the God of the Thunder Tessup is suffering and asks to set him free, when lacking silver and money Tessup is suffering, then everybody would be glad to give him a unit of silver, K Bo XXXII 15 Vs. I-II 4'-6'a; E. Neu "Das hurritische Epos der Freilassung. I Untersuchungen zu einem hurritischethitisches Textensamble aus Hattusa," *Studien zu den Bogazkoy-Texten*, S.288-289 (1996). cf. Hoffner , Harry A., Jr. "Hurrian Civilization from a Hittite Perspective."- In :*Urkesh and the Hurrians: Studies in Honor of Lloyd Cotzen*. Urkesh/ Mozan Studies 3, Bibliotheca Mesopotamica, Vol. 26. Ed. G.Buccellati and M. Kelly-Buccellati, (Malibu: Udena Publications, 1988), 182.

30 - In this light it is interesting to find the law term in Archaic Latin erus "owner, master of slave" (as early as in Plautus' comedies). Its original meaning may be reconstructed by a comparison to the Hittite eshas'ishas"master" (according to Kapantsian's hypothesis the Hittite term was borrowed into Old Armenian as isxan "king, ruler"; im the modern language it can designate, for instance, salmon from the lake Sevan as "the king-fish"; on Hittite and Indo-European words cf. Gamkrelidze, Thomas; Ivanov, Vyacheslav *"Indo-European and Indo-Europeans"*, vol.I, (New York: Mouton de Gruyter; 1995), 240, 244, 252, 758-759: Sumerian logographic EN, Akkadian heterographic BELU (cf. also an equivalent Luwian Hieroglyphic sign N 390 "DOMINUS"); in the prayer of the Hittite king Mursili II to the gods he called them by this term meaning that they are as slave-owners in respect to the human beings. Latin-Hittite correspondence presupposes the common origin of the Hittite and Latin from a Proto-Indo- European reconstructed term *esHo-s "master, god (from the point of view of his slave - a human being)."

31 - Harry A. Hoffner, Jr., "Hurrian Civilization from a Hittite Perspective" *Urkesh and the Hurrians, Studies in Honor of Lloyd Cotsen* (1998), 180-183. This equivalence may be an example of linguistic correspondences between words of different languages expressing one idea, cf. above.

32 - That does not exclude the possibility of a temporary revival both of some of native languages and of those systems of beliefs that were connected to it. Thus after Gorbachev's reforms it became possible to print a Ket Abecedary for elementary schools restoring the teaching of the language (with less than a thousand speakers) in the Western Siberia; at the same time a revival of Ket shamanistic traditions followed.

33 - For Skriabin, India was important not only because of the ancient Indian thinkers with whose ideas he became acquainted through theosophy. Skriabin studied Sanskrit and remarked that one had to go through it but then to come to some other means of communication that should be higher than a natural language.

CHAPTER 11

PROGRESS: A TALE OF GALOSHES OF FORTUNE AND OF A SHOE THAT FITS

Barbara Sundberg Baudot

Hans Christian Andersen's vision of progress captured the advantages of wealth, the thrill of scientific discovery, the miracles of technological innovation and all of these promising greater horizons for the adventure of human life. He held that the rapid advance of science and knowledge should inspire poets, in the way it had moved him to write:

> Thin iron ties were laid over the earth, and along these, the heavily laden carriages flew on wings of steam like the flight of a swallow; mountains were compelled to open themselves to the inquiring spirit of the age; plains were obliged to raise themselves. And human thoughts were borne in words, through metal wires, with the speed of lightning, to distant cities. 'Life! Life!' sounded through the whole of nature. It's our time! Poet you possess it! Sing of it in spirit and in truth![1]

His peer, the philosopher and theologian, Soren Kierkegaard commented: "Lo! Andersen can tell the fairy tale about "Galoshes of Fortune"—I can tell the tale about the shoe that pinches."[2] These two Danish thinkers were among those who stirred the intellectual circles of Western Europe in the early 19th century. Their dialogue and interpretations of the meaning of spirit in their time offer valuable insights on the currently, crucial issues of the content and meaning of "progress" for individuals and society.

Kierkegaard's writings emphasized fundamental choices people confront in realizing their "existence" in society. He discerned three progressive stages in the actualization of the person: the aesthetic, the ethical, and the religious.[3] In advancing from one stage to the next, by deliberate choice and/or act of faith, the individual experiences greater satisfaction and happiness, independent of general physical circumstances. The first or "aesthetic" stage, Kierkegaard [1813-1845] identified as the mental place of worldliness. Essential features of this existence include, on the one hand, the absence of universal moral standards and determinate religious faith and, on the other hand, the presence of strong desire to enjoy the whole range of emotive and sensual experiences circumscribed only by personal discrimination and taste.

Believing humans to be more than psycho-physical organisms with emotional impulses, Kierkegaard senses dissatisfaction, metaphorically "the pinch of the shoe," in circles where lives are dispersed in the pursuit of wealth, status, and pleasure. When dissatisfaction gives way to despair, some choose to move to the ethical stage, where moral standards and obligations govern existence and reason gives form, purpose, and consistency to life.[4] At this stage, misery at the realization of the limited human capacity to fulfill moral law impels a few people to leap by faith to the religious stage where unification with Spirit brings peace and fundamental identity.

Societies, wherein the vast majority of people fail to move beyond materialism and hedonism, suffer from spiritlessness, the most widespread form of despondency experienced by both the economically poor and the well-integrated, even institutionally religious, bourgeoisie.[5] For Kierkegaard, this kind of spiritually dormant life has negative and even pathological consequences. With no basis for true Self-hood "a frustrated self" may be driven to escape into the cult of the aesthetic, religious fanaticism or even madness. More generally there is widespread resignation to a life of mere worldliness.[6]

Unlike Kierkegaard, Andersen [1805-1875] came from the poorest stratum of society and held that by the grace of Providence he was able to achieve a level of education permitting full realization of his literary gifts. He wrote: "My life is a beautiful fairy tale, so rich and full of bliss! (...) The wonderful story of my life will say to the world what it says to me: that there is a loving God who directs all things for the best." These are the opening words of *Mit Livs Eventyr (The Fairy-Tale of My Life)*, Andersen's final autobiography and the recurrent motif of his autobiographical writings.[7] The "galoshes of fortune" convey the awe that wealth and technological progress in the early days of the industrial revolution appear to have inspired in this poet and natural philosopher. His respect for these advances lay in the opportunities they could open for the realization of individual and social aspirations. At the same time, many of his tales deplore the petty-mindedness, the snobbery, and selfishness he experienced in society; they give voice to the children, the under classes, and the oppressed. The beautiful fairy tale of his life is not about a prince in a palace, but about an ordinary man living in simple accommodations, who, despite heartbreak and disappointment, successfully realizes the potential of his genius thanks to Providence and the grace and generosity of others.

Although, Andersen's belief in the beauty and relevance of material advances appears to challenge Kierkegaard's demanding view of progress in terms of spiritual advance and Self-realization, these perspectives are not in opposition. Rather, they represent two fundamental, complimentary dimensions of human advance. Andersen's conception of progress, although trivialized by Kierkegaard as the "galoshes of fortune," was envisioned in the context of a society with significant respect for humanist, aesthetic and transcendent values. He shared, with many thinkers and intellectuals of the 18th and 19th centuries, the vision that linked the discoveries of science and technology to belief in a benevolent God. In reading his autobiography, some of his essays, his poetry, and fairy tales, it is not difficult to perceive Andersen as a realist—unlike Kierkegaard, he always had to seek monetary and other support—with a strong idealist inclination. His high esteem for material progress and its great advantages for society did not detract from his convictions concerning the necessity to meet transcendent needs and to promote values that enable individuals to flourish.

Societies need both "galoshes" and a "shoe that fits." "Galoshes," in a developmental context, symbolize wealth invested in economic expansion and in the arts and sciences offering greater possibilities for a comfortable existence. Deprived of a modicum of such progress, the majority of today's population is hard-pressed to find time and energy for Self-realization, let alone awareness of their spiritual needs. While it is neither prudent nor realistic to expect individuals to travel Kierkegaard's spiritual path in a religious sense, however valid and rewarding, it is absolutely vital for humanity that there be ample nurturing of moral courage, unconditional love, and the quest for wisdom. This means giving much greater emphasis to intangible, but no less real or meaningful values; in other words to emerge out of a state of spiritual dormancy wherever this exists. The aspirations fueling material progress should be consistent with what the heart and spirit have taught humanity about its origins, its essence and, most importantly, its purpose.

Debates on how or whether material progress and spiritual well-being can be reconciled, such as the one between Kierkegaard and Andersen in the middle of the 19th century, already took place in the 18th century, continued in the 20th century, and are occurring today, but with a major difference. Previously, the ideas of most participants in this discourse were rooted in some level of acceptance of the relevance of moral virtues and/or of the existence of a transcendent power. As a minimum, most of the essential players were influenced either by humanism, stoicism, or deism, or by beliefs derived from adherence to specific religious institutions.

These moral and spiritual mindsets buttressed arguments that favored tempering economic forces, providing space, even justification for progress in the fulfillment of non-material aspirations.

Today, these moral and metaphysical perspectives are no longer as influential. Quantum advances in science and technology and the secularization of society have given appreciable weight to a Promethean conception of humankind. Concomitantly, the prevailing conception of global progress is material, focused on improvements in levels of living and centered on the market. Its moral dimension does not extend beyond promoting multicultural tolerance and the universalization of political, social and economic rights.

To resituate progress on wider intellectual and metaphysical premises, it is relevant to revisit perceptions about society and human nature expressed in previous epochs. The challenge is to generate an acceptable and sustainable vision of economic, social, and scientific progress, shepherded by beliefs that may defy rational calculation, but able to generate an inexorable advance toward a higher status of knowledge, culture, and moral estate. We can derive some guidance for meeting this challenge by confronting the economic, political, and technological forces that have worked against such a holistic vision of progress. This becomes necessary because of general failure to keep part of social and cultural life insulated from the demands of technology and the exigencies of the market. We can also attain direction by enriching the discourse with a wider perception of credible sources of knowledge, with idealist perspectives, and with a different approach to human dignity.

Why the Shoe Pinches

There are many reasons why a narrow technological approach to progress can create a great deal of malaise in society. Although economic progress contributes to a comfortable existence and sense of security, it does not usually nurture such non-material resources, as for example, the search for harmony, wisdom, and beauty, which is essential to coping well with life's personal hardships.

The following lines from T.S. Eliot express this limitation and inform society of the costs of a narrow material focus:

> The endless cycle of idea and action
> Endless invention, endless experiment,
> Brings knowledge of motion, but not of stillness;
> Knowledge of speech, but not of silence;
> Knowledge of words, but ignorance of the Word. (...)
> Where is the Life we have lost in living?
> Where is the Wisdom we have lost in knowledge?
> Where is the knowledge we have lost in information? [8]

Without linkages between information, knowledge and wisdom, or between technological change and the flourishing of the individual in nonmaterial ways, modernization might just mean seeing the world abstractly, objectively, and generally quantifiably. Science and economy tend to become their own ends, offering humanity the prospect of life anchored in spiritually dormant societies where the shoe pinches inordinately.

From the beginning of the industrial revolution a number of economic and political thinkers have alluded to the negative effects technological progress could have on the human spirit if society failed to take precautions. It is ironic that among these are the two intellectual giants—Adam Smith [1723-1790] and Karl Marx [1818-1883]—whose writings provided the very foundations for the most materially progressive economic ideologies of the 20th century, *laissez-faire* capitalism and scientific socialism or communism. As implemented, capitalism and communism have tended to promote increasingly sophisticated machinery, mindless material progress with diminishing human effort and input, and enormous concentrations of wealth in mega-corporations or in government enterprises. Both have promised a radiant future on the basis of material output. In practice, they ignored the negative externalities that both Smith and Marx foresaw.

A careful reading of the *The Wealth of Nations* would certainly give pause to consider whether "the invisible hand" of the market was all that Adam Smith considered necessary for the well-being of humanity. Although he railed against an economy under state control and governed according to mercantile beliefs, he suggested there was cause for governments to protect individuals and societies from the negative effects of modern technology. In *The Theory of Moral Sentiments,* Smith elaborated the virtues of a good society. Then in *The Wealth of Nations* he predicted trends that would erode them. Influenced by Stoic philosophy and Christian values, he believed that economic actors should operate according to a conception of self-command and self-interest determined by what contributed most to the general welfare. He considered the marketplace, the dynamics of which were the antithesis of moral sentiments, incapable of overcoming the impoverishment of the human intellect and spirit resulting from uncontrolled technological advance. For Smith, the most serious implications of specialization and the division of labor were the erosion of imagination, invention, courage, and control over one's environment. Thus, he argued that government must protect society from the inevitable decline in the art of living and the widespread degeneration, vacuity, and ignorance to which these advances would lead.[9] He wrote:

> The man whose whole life is spent in performing a few simple operations, (...), has no occasion to exert his understanding, or to exercise his invention in finding out expedients to removing difficulties that never occur. (...) His dexterity at his own particular trade seems (...) to be acquired at the expense of his intellectual, social, and martial virtues. But in every improved and civilized society, this is the state into which (...) the great body of people must necessarily fall, unless government take some pains to prevent it.[10]

A century later, Karl Marx took an even stronger position on the negative social externalities of material progress. Not only were courage, individuality, and creativity eroded by alienation because of the nature of the prevailing "relations of production" and of capitalist proclivities for exploitation, but even more seriously, ever improving machinery threatened virtual enslavement and the stultification of human thinking. In a speech delivered on the Anniversary of the *People's Paper* in London, 14 April 1856, Karl Marx commented on the future of a society following blindly this narrow path to progress. He observed:

In our days, everything seems pregnant with its contrary. Machinery, gifted with the wonderful power of shortening and fructifying human labor, we behold starving and overworking it. (...) Even the pure light of science seems unable to shine but on the dark background of ignorance (...) All our invention and progress seem to result in endowing material forces with intellectual life, and in stultifying human life into a material force.[11]

These remarks of Marx and Smith have certainly not lost their relevance. Documented evidence of the accuracy of their perceptions of deterioration in intellectual and cultural life, marked by passivity and spiritual dormancy, came, for example, with the work of Seebohn Rowntree, a renowned pioneer in research on poverty lines and basic needs. In his 1941 study, he reported that:

The survey we have made of the ways people spend their leisure reminds us how much greater today than in the past is the temptation to seek fullness of life by indulging too largely in forms of recreation which make no demands on physical, mental, or spiritual powers.[12]

Although, aware that intellectual and spiritual factors are not amenable to quantifiable measurement, Rowntree had no doubt that they should figure in a comprehensive assessment of society's progress in its search for higher and more humane living standards. Referring to the implications of this spiritual and intellectual degeneration, Rowntree noted that the well-being of democracy depended on maintaining a high level of mental and spiritual life. In other words, a "spiritually dormant society" is hard pressed to provide a stimulating environment for a viable democracy. In Rowntree's words:

To raise the material standard of those in poverty may prove difficult but to raise the mental and spiritual life to a markedly higher level will be an infinitely harder task, yet on its accomplishment depends the lasting greatness of the state. Everywhere democracy is challenged. A totalitarian state does not demand high intellectual or spiritual standards from its people. A democratic state can only flourish if the level of intelligence of the community is high and its spiritual life is dynamic.[13]

Today, the dominance of unleashed capitalism in the globalization process poses an even greater threat to the nobler ends of life—the Good, the beautiful, and the noble—than in Smith's or even Rowntree's time. It is the relentless pursuit of progress dependent on the upward spiraling of material needs which is spreading to many parts of the world. There are growing misgivings about this form of globalization and the quality of life that it generates. So far, however, few governments and intergovernmental organizations appear in a position to adopt countervailing policies that strongly emphasize the elevation of society's mental and spiritual life. The demonstrations that now regularly greet the meetings of the World Trade Organization, the Bretton Woods institutions, and the Group of Eight, together with evidence of a widespread decline of civic interest in normal political life, are symptomatic of this failure of public policy. The high average number of hours spent by youth and adults on TV programs, the content of which is increasingly determined by commercial interests, is another indicator of the malaise of contemporary societies, a kind of spiritual dormancy. Another symptom is the state of public education, particularly for the poor, in the most advanced market economies. It seems that society does not take seriously the need for measures to prevent the mental impoverishment that could stem from division of labor and specialization and to offset the chilling impersonality that results from the penetration of economic rationality into all spheres of life and society.

It is questionable whether today's democratic governments have the will or capacity to treat the economy as a tool for creating a more humane and an intellectually and affectively spirited society. Some would argue that they can only contribute to making "the shoe squeeze tighter." More than two millenniums ago, Plato observed that institutions were reflective of the values and aims of the people that composed them. He rejected democracy as a political form because he considered the citizens neither noble nor trustworthy. Nevertheless, in the intervening millennia, democracies evolved naturally with the rise of the middle class and the generalization of education. They also evolved as liberal complements to *laissez-faire* economics. But, presently, democracies appear to be threatened by the social impact of the very economic forces that have helped them to evolve.

In contemporary societies, the sapping of the human spirit by the juggernaut of the modern machine is painfully reflected in losses in the variety of social institutions and communities. These establishments traditionally recognized the importance of character, creativity, and the rights of individuals to live with security and to die in dignity. In developing this thesis, Norwegian sociologist Nils Christie noted that global capitalism has prompted institutions embracing production, trade, and money to a virtual combined take over of other major social bodies including governments, religious centers, schools, health care organizations, and the military. The political imposition or contagiousness of market values has rendered these nurturing and protecting institutions either subservient to the market or obsolete as effective independent social structures.[14] The paradigm of the resultant mono-institutionalized society is the "market society" wherein human relations are reified into cold, commercial transactions.

Describing such a time when democratic societies will have no other goal than increased output, Francis Fukuyama wrote: "We might summarize the content of the universal homogenous state as liberal democracy in the political sphere where life is a tedium of economic calculations, an endless solving of technical problems, environmental concerns, the satisfaction of sophisticated consumer demands, (...) and the perpetual care-taking of the museums of human history."[15] One critic, in apparent agreement, added that humankind would be left with the dull duties of tending to its bodily needs and satisfactions: "the ultimate trivialization of humankind and its relegation into a merely animal order."[16]

This perception evokes the epitome of Kierkegaard's spiritless society. From the perspective of Andersen's vision, this diagnosis implies that the marvel of discovery and invention has lost its luster and that the magic attached to many new machines has become as illusory as "the emperor's new clothes." The notions of spirit and society have limited meaning or purpose if all human needs are to be met by a comparatively small oligarchy of impersonal corporate chains of command; if all the questions that are asked can be answered by modern science; and, if there is no place nor time for sympathy, solidarity, and community.

214

Making the Shoe Fit

To restore a noble sense of "spirit" to modern societies without pushing back the clock or holding back the tides of change is a major challenge. "To make the shoe fit" material progress must be balanced by attention to humanity's moral and spiritual condition. This task demands respect for philosphical enquiry, intuition, and revelation as ways of knowing in addition to empiricism and instrumental rationality. It requires humility and an idealistic attitude. It also calls for revisiting the concept of human dignity.

The now, almost forgotten, philosopher, Johan George Hamann [1730-1785], a contemporary of Adam Smith, also writing in the period when literature was expected to mirror demonstrable truth and material reality, deplored the sovereignty of reason's artificial treatment of the unclassifiable. Hamann conceived the universe as a place in which every person lives but cannot fully describe, because the only tools one has are symbols which limit, abstract, and cut reality into arbitrary slices. Reality is multi-dimensional. Nature engages the senses and emotions. Therefore no general proposition, or explanation can convey the variety and concreteness of life.[17] Moreover, since thoughts, ideas, and all psychological events are experiences within the universe, there is no place beyond from which humans would be able to judge, condemn, justify, explain or prove this universe. Importantly and consistently, Hamann characterized universalism, as an idle craving, a futile effort to reduce the rich variety of life to a bleak uniformity, an attempt to imprison the universe in some prefabricated logical envelope, an insult to creation.[18]

Breaking the monopolies of empiricism and scientific and instrumental rationality can well begin with the humble realization that the most advanced and demonstrable scientific theories remain no more than human beliefs. On this subject, Albert Einstein offered that: "The whole of science is nothing more than a refinement of everyday thinking (...) Even the concept of the 'real external world' of everyday thinking rests exclusively on sense impressions (...) The differentiation between sense impressions and images is not possible, or at least it is not possible with absolute certainty."[19] Thus, from a scientific perspective, Einstein gave legitimacy to the philosophical current—inherited from the pre-Socratic thinkers—that challenges the monopoly accorded to scientific rationality to the exclusion of other ways of knowing.

Empiricism is appropriate to such spheres of knowledge and activity as economics, natural sciences and engineering. It is insufficient to formulate and address questions of self-realization, human destiny, and transcendence. It is also ill-suited to comprehend normative needs and values. Addressing spiritual and moral needs requires working with the belief that reality includes ideas, qualities, and relationships not necessarily evident to the physical senses but discernible through philosophical inquiry, intuition, and revelation. To these ends, positive mysticism and pure rationalism based on *a priori* knowledge of universals offer additional references for thought. Such thinking abounds. It is embedded in prose, poetry, philosophy and many other haunts of the creative and receptive spirit, but not in the discourse on economy, modernity, progress and development that is dominated by instrumental reasoning and material values.

An idealist attitude, rare in current public discourse, is also a necessary input in efforts to bring back the sense of the spirit.[20] The writings of Ralph Waldo Emerson eloquently articulated this approach in the 19th century, in a manner particularly poignant today for those alarmed by the seemingly overwhelming domination of materialism. Emerson drew a contrast between idealists and materialists. For him, both are cognizant of the same power and security dilemmas facing humanity, but the idealist devises an outline of human relations built on considerations transcending material facts, appearances, and assumptions about basic instincts for self-interest. In his words:

> (...) the idealist draws on the power of Thought and of Will, on inspiration, on miracle, on individual culture. Idealists concede all that the materialist [the realist] offers, admits the impressions of sense, admits their coherency, their use and beauty (...) but will not see that alone (...) but (...) looks at these things as the reverse side of the tapestry, as the other end, each being a sequel or com-

pletion of a spiritual fact which nearly concerns him. By contrast the materialist, secure in the certainty of sensation, mocks at fine spun theories, at star gazers and dreams and believes his life is solid, (...) knows where he stands and what he does.[21]

Emerson's idealism works to balance empirical objectivity with intuition and imagination. It frees life from what can be described as the drab blur of triteness and endless calculations, or the familiarity that comes with the appropriation of things, such as Fukuyama evoked. Idealists are not subservient to machines or material progress. Things are not their masters, as Marx observed. Introduced into the discourse on problems confronting contemporary society, affluent or destitute, idealistic perceptions extend the horizons of thought and open new avenues for creative action. They encourage awareness of the consequences of over-reliance on empiricism and abstract models and draw attention to matters of the heart and the spirit.

Separating the notion of "human dignity" from material well-being and returning the former to its original connotation would contribute significantly "to making the shoe fit." Currently, to mainstream experts on development, "human dignity" is, as described in Robert Clark's *Power and Politics in the Third World*, an "overarching concept that reflects the specific mixture of values of power, well-being, respect, and enlightenment," that is commonly associated with the outputs of a political system and political modernization.[22] This view suggests that dignity is something that can be given and taken away—something external to the human spirit. Such a conception of dignity, commonly expressed in international development forums, is self-defeating for progress, material or otherwise, and strays far from the term's original meaning.

According to the *Oxford English Dictionary*, "dignity" refers to bearing, conduct, or speech indicative of self-respect; nobility, elevation of character; worthiness; and the degree of excellence, either in estimation or in the order of nature. As such, dignity is inherent to the human spirit. To exercise their dignity, humans ought to live nobly, endure hardships with equanimity, and exercise the moral courage and impetus to seek wisdom. Current development thinking renders the notion of dignity dependent on material circumstances and political and economic rights. It convinces the poor that dignity awaits material development. Indigents are driven to feel deprived of the wherewithal to progress on meaningful paths—in other words, to have the capacity for their own intellectual and spiritual fulfillment. Developing countries, accepting a materially founded and externally granted conception of dignity, easily become willing and passive tools of forces shaping the global economy. Such paths to development can deprive them of their own values and aspirations.

A classic example of acceptance of different ways of knowing, of an idealistic perception, of human dignity treated as an inherent human quality and of progress conceived on spiritual and intellectual bases was already offered in the 19th century by John Stuart Mill [1806-1873]. Mill envisaged the integration of intellectual, spiritual and scientific activities in a society where the pursuit of industrial art would have a greater purpose than material enrichment. He opposed the struggle for material enrichment to the "Art of Living" encompassing the cultivation of the graces of life, stimulation of the intellect, artistic creativity, meditative thought and character building.[23] It was surely this vision that Andersen intended as the outcome of scientific and technological progress. It is also hard to imagine that such progress could lead to Kierkegaard's spiritually dormant societies.

Conclusions

Economic progress has modernized human life, making it infinitely more comfortable, convenient and promising for millions of people. But, its contribution to the higher pursuits of intellectual, spiritual, and artistic self-fulfillment in compassionate societies is dubious. In the global society, a pervasive and insidious insufficiency seems to threaten the quality of life for many millions of people. Indeed, it may be as Smith, Marx, Rowntree, Fukuyama, and many others have variously foreseen, humankind is in danger of becoming subservient to the exigencies of the market economy as a result of a narrow vision that confuses the purpose of material progress with the goals of human life.

Yet, still in the wake of the colossal pressures of the expanding world economy, the generous, compassionate and Providential sensibility anchoring Andersen's vision stubbornly persists in a few countries and communities, albeit in the shadowy wings of the world's stage. And, some citizens in the global society courageously promote them. Likewise, Kierkegaard's vision remains fine repast in intellectual circles. But arguments for a combination of these visions of progress, influenced by compassionate humanism and/or faith in the transcendent nature of human life, are muted partly because they imply public intervention in the course of economic development to render it compatible with and supportive of other public goods. The questions these arguments raise and the challenges they pose are down-played or ignored in the world's power centers where material goals are driven by continually rising expectations and insatiable desires for more. Sadly, public policies will never erase the vacuity of the modern human condition unless the deeper roots of this problem are also treated. Moreover, it is futile to hope for cohesive communities and a peaceful world when unimpeded economic forces reduce humanity to competing individuals seeking gratification and satisfaction of appetites.

In the modern development discourse, whether it takes place in international organizations, in governments, or in academic institutions—ideas that do not support present trends and that argue for values that defy scientific rationality are ignored or summarily rejected. Unconsciously or consciously, their relevance is perceived as attached to some outgrown age in human thought. As one well respected, literary critic has put it: "If [in the 21st century] we have become more tolerant of standards in other contemporary cultures, we have not extended our cultural generosity to the past. (...)The temporal barriers are not only high but repeatedly ivied over with accumulating layers of distrust and habit."[24] The contention here is that such barriers must be broken down. To enrich the discourse on progress and development there is good cause to revisit earlier assumptions about the values and aims of progress, even the accomplishments of humankind in pre-industrial age conditions.

In the struggle to reclaim the capacity and space for cultivating the art of living as opposed to promoting its "proclivities for having," John Kenneth Galbraith reminds contemporary societies that: "We continue to think of the economic solution as the end of effort. We fail in giving children the full enjoyment of education and knowledge (...). We fail fully to achieve the rewards of well-being as we have seen them in the past." And as to the past, he continues:

> The art of the Renaissance, which we view and enjoy, was the product of communities far inferior in wealth to our own. William Shakespeare, as I have elsewhere said, was the product of a society with, by present standards, a very low gross domestic product. The great artistic talent of our time is now employed in advertising goods and services. We must ask ourselves whether our economic success is matched by equivalent achievement in the art of living.[25]

If non-material goals and aspirations are to be met and human beings given the opportunity for fuller intellectual and spiritual self-realization, then society should offer the tools needed to fulfill these goals. No society should overlook the value of an approach to progress that takes into account the mental, affective, philosophical, and artistic qualities of the spirit. In laying out its path, society must bring to bear on the dominant ethos, the wide breadth of possibilities for human satisfaction and appreciation of multiple, currently under-valued intangible facets of life: the notion of beauty and social harmony.

> This earthly life has plenty of sorrows and miseries. So let us help each other as best we can and praise the one who can find new means and ways.
>
> *Soren Kierkegaard* [26]

> Shouldn't we all of us give the best we have to others—offer what we can? It's true, I've only given roses; but you, who are yourself so gifted, what have you given to the world? What will you give?
>
> *Hans Christian Andersen* [27]

Endnotes

1 - H.C. Andersen, *In Sweden*, translated by K.R.K. MacKenzie (London, 1852), as cited in Elias Bredsdorff, *Hans Christian Andersen*, (London: Souvenir Press, 1993) 226-227.

2 - Ove Kreisberg and F.J. Billeskov Jansen, "H.C.Anderson," in *Kierkegaard Literary Miscellany, Bibliotheca Kierkegaardiana vol 9*, ed. Niels Thulstrup, et al. (Copenhagen: C.A. Reitzels Boghandel A/S, 1981): 123

3 - Søren Kierkegaard, *Stages on Life's Way* contained in *Søren Kierkegaards Samlede Værker (The Collected Works of Søren Kierkegaard)*, 1st ed., eds. A.B. Drachman, J.L.Heiberg, and H.O.Lange (Copenhagen: Gyldendahl, 1901), Vol. 6., 499. Hereafter references to these volumes are denoted as SV Vol., with volume numbers following.

4 - The aesthetic and the ethical life views are treated in dialogues contained in Kierkegaard's second major work *Either/Or*, first published in 1843, [SV Vol. 1 and 2] These ideas are updated and further refined in *Stages on Life's Way* appearing in 1845 [SV Vol. 6]. Stages are also mentioned in *Concluding Unscientific Postscript*, published in 1846 [SV Vol. 7].

5 - Søren Kierkegaard, *Sickness Unto Death*, published in 1849 [SV Vol. 11, 111-241. See also Bruce K. Kirmmse, *Kierkegaard in Golden Age Denmark* (Bloomington: Indiana University Press, 1990), 359-378.

6 - Søren Kierkegaard, *Sickness Unto Death* (London: Penguin Books Ltd., 1989) as cited in Alastair Hannay, "Kierkegaard, Søren Aabye," *The Oxford Companion to Philosophy* (Oxford: Oxford University Press, 1995), 443.

7 - H.C. Andersen, *Mit Livs Eventyr*, revised 1951, H. Topsoe Jensen (Copenhagen: Nordisk Bogproduktion A.S., Haslev, 1996), 1.

8 - T.S. Elliot, "Choruses from 'The Rock'," *The Complete Poems and Plays 1909-1950* (New York: Harcourt Brace and Company, 1980), 96.

9 - Adam Smith, *The Wealth of Nations*, (New York: The Modern Library, 1994); Idem, *Theory of Moral Sentiments*, (Indianapolis, IN: Liberty Fund, 1984).

10 - Smith, *The Wealth of Nations*, 839-840.

11 - Karl Marx, Friedrich Engels: *Collected Works*, Vol. 14:1855-56 (London: Laurence & Wishart, 1980), 655. Speech first published in *The People's Paper*, no. 207, 19 April, 1856.

12 - B. Seebohn Rowntree, *Poverty and Progress: A Second Social Survey of York*, (London: Green, Longmans, 1941), 476-477.

13 - Ibid., 477.

14 - Nils Christie, "A Place For All," unpublished manuscript, University of Oslo, 3 March 1998.

15 - Francis Fukuyama, "The End of History," *National Interest* (Summer 1989): 18.

16 - Allan Bloom, "Responses to Fukuyama," *National Interest* (Summer 1989): 19-20.

17 - See J.G. Hamman, *Briefwechsel*, ed. Walter Ziesmer & Arthur Henkel, (Wiesbaden: Insel, volumes published 1955-75), Isaiah Berlin, *Magus of the North: J.G. Hamann and the Origins of Modern Irrationalism*, (London: John Murray Publishers, 1993); James C. O'Flaherty, *Johann Georg Hamann* (Boston: Twayne Publishers, 1979).

18 - As interpreted by Berlin, Magus, 38.

19 - Albert Einstein, "Physics and Reality," *Ideas and Opinions*, based on *Mein Weltbild, Carl Seelig ed.*, (NewYork, Bonanza Books, 1984) 290-292.

20 - As opposed to philosophical idealism derived from the work of Descartes, Berkeley, and Kant, etc.

21 - Ralph Waldo Emerson, "The Transcendentalist," *The Selected Writings of Ralph Waldo Emerson*, edited by Brooks Atkinson (New York: The Modern Library, 1992), 81-82. Similar ideas were expressed by J.R.R. Tolkien, "Tree and Leaf," *The Tolkien Reader*, (New York, Ballantine Books, 1966) 80-81.

22 - Robert P. Clark, *Power and Politics in the Third World*, 4th ed. (New York: Macmillan, 1991), 5.

23 - John Stuart Mill, *Principles of Political Economy* (New York: Oxford University Press, 1994), 129.

24 - J. Paul Hunter, "Sleeping Beauties: Are Historical Aesthetics Worth Recovering?" *Eighteenth-Century Studies*, vol. 34, no. 1, 2000: 2.

25 - John Kenneth Galbraith, An Informal Note prepared for the Triglav Circle and addressed to the Special Session of the UN General Assembly to Review the World Summit for Social Development Five Years Later, Geneva, Switzerland, June 2000.

26 - Søren Kierkegaard, *Journals and Papers*, Vol. 1, A-E, 201; Vol 8, A419, trans. Anne Marie Krassowska.

27 - Hans Christian Andersen, "The Snail and the Rosetree," in *80 Fairytales* (Copenhagen: Hans Reitzels Forlag, 1976), 327-329.

CHAPTER 12

PHILOSOPHICAL REFLECTION ON THE PATH OF ART

Noriko Hashimoto

In Japan, there are two concepts, the "Way" and the "path," which govern the human journey towards understanding life—its meaning and its harmony. Both are essential to transcendence from the level of phenomenal experience to an encounter with the "Value transcending death." There is a third concept linking these two concepts in seeking this encounter. This concept is *Geido* meaning the path of art. Because they are inextricably related, the journey to the "Value transcending death" requires deep understanding of all three concepts.

The Japanese people attach profound symbolic meaning to "Way." A modern Japanese poet and sculptor, Kotaro Takamura, wrote the following highly appreciated passage about the "Way":

> In front of me, no "Way" can be found,
> Behind me a "Way" was created.[1]

Takamura's characterization of the Way refers to the essence of Nature, the essential principle of Life, the dynamism of Being. In this concept there is no human ego or individualism. Life and the ego or the human "me" are one, like a drop of water and the ocean, or a ray of light with the sun.

The Japanese character for "Way" derives from the famous Chinese word *Dao* or *Tao*, referring to the ultimate power and the absolute order in the whole universe. *Dao* is the fundamental principle from which all creation, including human life, is derived and the ultimate existence to which all things return. All things, including human beings, are formed by the self-generation of *Dao*. Dependent on *Dao* and participating in the absolute *Dao*, all things have their own reason for existence. Thus, on the level of phenomenal existence, each and everything in Nature possesses some characteristic of the Absolute reflected to the degree of its participation in It.

Japanese philosophy also explains the "Way" as the subject in the classic grammatical relationship of subject and predicate. Thereby, the "Way" makes its own path. This idea includes the human "me," which does not outline its being nor control its own actions. Thus, it is not the ego, or "i," that acts independently when the human being is in harmony or "in realization" of the "Way," or, in other words, has somehow transcended the phenomenal experience to an encounter with the Good, that is the "Value transcending death."

In Christian thought, the concept of "Way" is similarly understood by the Japanese people. Christ said, "I am the way, the truth, and the life." Christian believers follow him.[2] In 1560, Thomas A. Kempis wrote *De Imitatione Christi* (*The Imitation of Christ*).[3] According to him, the holy life of Christ is the "ideal" for Christian believers. By the 17th century, this book had been translated into Japanese and the people found it easy to understand because to follow or imitate "the Way" of Christ was a familiar idea. They perceived the spiritual meaning of Western Christianity although it was then foreign and new to them.

The second concept is "path." To approach an understanding of being or to participate to some degree in the Absolute, it is essential to embark on the "path." Thereby, one can experience the harmony that comes with encountering a glimpse of the "Way." The word "path" is the English translation of the Japanese word *michi*. This is a keyword in Japanese culture.[4] "Path" used as the English translation of *michi* means "the linear process leading to the end," which is to be understood as the value or goal sought. The divine path, *Kami-no michi* is the path that leads to divine providence. This is a religious path. The human path *hito-no michi* is the moral path that human beings should travel. This path is composed of the elements of ethical behavior. There are other paths that are subordinate to these primary paths. *Uta-no michi*, referring to the path of poetry, is one example of the paths subordinate to the human path.

In distinguishing the two concepts, "Way" (*Dao*), and "path" (*michi*), it is emphasized that *Dao* refers to the dynamic process of Life, and the "Ultimate Perfect Destination," while the "path" is the process beginning on the phenomenal level of human consciousness that leads towards this "Way." Thus the "path" is situated between the individual's personal consciousness and the Essence or Principle of Life, the source from which religion emanates for humanity.

Binding these concepts together in the Japanese cultural tradition, is the third concept, *Geido*, which in English means, "the path of art." It was in the middle ages that this concept was elaborated. The individual who wishes to be purified and perfected through his or her aesthetic experience takes this path. This is achieved not only by artistic creativity but also through appreciation of works of art. Through this process of purification and perfection, *Geido* sculpts an individual into a moral person capable of understanding his/her relationship to things, other persons, and ultimately to the "Value transcending death." Tenshin Okakura, a famous aesthetician, published *The Book of Tea* at the end of the 19th century. In this book he wrote:

> The masterpiece is a symphony played upon our finest feelings (…) At the magic touch of the beautiful, the secret chords of our being awakened, we vibrate and thrill in response to its call. Mind speaks to mind. We listen to the unspoken: we gaze upon the unseen. The master calls forth notes we know not of. Memories long forgotten come back to us with a new significance. The masterpiece is of ourselves, as we are of the masterpiece.[5]

It should be noted here, however, that having established the distinction between *Dao* and *michi* above, the introduction of the term *Geido*, as "path of art," must raise some questions in the mind of the reader. There is a confusion of terminology that begs further explanation in this introduction. The path of art, *Geido*, is the path leading to beauty and *Dao* as its ultimate destination. In this instance, a derivative of *Dao* has been used where *michi* would seem more appropriate. The apparent confusion, which exists between these two concepts, arose when the old word *michi* was identified with the Chinese word *Dao*. During the 3rd century A.D., Chinese culture was being imported into Japan. Logically, however, *Dao*, already understood to mean the absolute Dynamic Whole or Spiritual Infinity, could not be the path to itself.

There are other illustrations of the mixed use of these terms relating to the "path of art." For example, *Shodo* is not the "way" of calligraphy, meaning the principle of the art of calligraphy, but it is the process of calligraphy as a path to gain a glimpse of the spiritual essence of nature or, more concretely expressed, the process by which the beauty of calligraphy is realized. As another example, *Kado*, meaning flower arrangement, is not identification with the principle of the material world, but the process of expressing a spiritually purer idea by using natural living materials such as flowers. In the discussion that follows, the distinction between "Way" as the ultimate value, the dynamic and ever unfolding of life, and "path" as the linear process seeking to find the "Way" is maintained.

The Path of Art—Geido

There are three stages in the process of practicing the "path of art." Each stage brings the practitioner closer to a sense of transcendence beyond the veil of mortality, and thus to an understanding of the essence of Nature and the eternal unfolding of the "Way." On the first stage, the practitioner imitates the ideal technique of the master. This is the technical, phenomenal stage whereon the practitioner strives to imitate the metaphysics of the Master of the Art. On the second stage, the practitioner advances spiritually with a degree of perception. It is through ascetic and ethical training that the practitioner arrives at the point where he/she must wait for this perception. On the third stage, the purified spirit transcends the phenomenal world through metaphysical vision. The passage through these three stages is the process of the "path of art." While each stage on the path is pursued on the level of phenomenal existence, it is through this process that human vision and perception may gradually transcend the veil of mortality to sense the presence of the "Ultimate Value" or "Good."[6] Creative activity along the Path of Art must be ascetic and transcendent in this way. The Ultimate Value is found in the integration of the elements of aesthetics, ethics, and religion along the "path." These stages are developed and illustrated below.

Stage I: Imitation of the Ideal Technique of the Master

After discovering a masterpiece made by an artist from among a lot of other artwork, a person feels a strong longing for it. One feels the desire to possess the same techniques as the artist who made such a wonderful piece. These special artistic techniques, however, go beyond imitation of skill or method. This stage on the path of art cannot be objectified in terms of learning a methodological system, but rather it is a process to be experienced personally. On this subject Tenshin wrote:

> To the sympathetic, a masterpiece becomes a living reality towards which we feel drawn in bonds of comradeship. The masters are immortal, for their loves and fears live in us over and over again. It is the soul rather than the hand, the man than the technique, which appeals to us,—the more human the call the deeper is our response.[7]

So we must absorb technique from the master through living and working together with him. This is the perfection to be attained on the first stage, which is the concretion of the ideal type of technique that moves a person from the technical/phenomenal state of consciousness in the direction of the "Way."

Because Tenshin insists that the masterpiece becomes a living reality in the sense of comradeship or kinship, there is a strong tendency, in this context, to think of sympathy as the communication between souls. Through artwork, creator and appreciator recognize human existence in the other and respond to each other.

From the perspective of *Dao*, the path of art is a passage traveled by human beings. It is independent of the dynamic power of the cosmic One. And, Tenshin's point, "the soul rather than the hand, the man than the technique (...)," is very important.[8] Moreover, "living reality" and the master's "immortality" are expressions that strongly stress the present in relation to eternity. This is one of the characteristics of Japanese thought on art. Therefore, this stage of the path of art bears some relation to both ethics and religion.

Stage II: Path with Way as Nature

Through ascetic training, one may be able to experience the second stage. By training hands, eyes, ears, and so on to be sensitive, one becomes bodily and spiritually integrated and awaits the encounter with profound spiritual concentration. And, in the end, the banishing of the boundary between body and spirit allows new creative activity to emerge. A person is entirely free and creative the instant it appears. This new phase goes beyond all preceding ones towards perception of the Way as the "Value transcending death."

In the oriental tradition, the most important sense of being is the sense of harmony and oneness with Nature; this refers to the realization of "Spirit" meaning *Chi* in Japanese. A fundamental philosophical thought in natural philosophy is that Nature and human beings are not opposed to each other. Human beings are a part of Nature: Nature is within human beings. This is so because human beings and Nature are linked together by *Chi* in the sense of being part of the vital power and essence of the Cosmos.

"Spirit" is Life, the vital, dynamic power that penetrates the entire Cosmos, or all Existence. This traditional thought means that to be conscious of the Truth in all expressions of natural existence, for instance even of a tree and grass, is to be conscious of the universal Truth or the Cosmos. And, to understand the essence of Nature in material things such as in a stone or in the soil is precisely to understand the principle *arche* of the living Nature of human existence. Both these ideas are to be held simultaneously. Emotions toward Life and Life's vital power are experienced by everything—even by a tiny blade of grass in the field and by a stone beside the road: each thing has an intuition of the essence and reality of the Cosmos.

It is, therefore, that the artistic masterpiece must represent the Spirit of Nature even if the pictorial replica falls short in form and color. The identification of a mountain or a natural thing for what it is materially and geographically is not important. Therefore, Japanese artists' oriental landscapes are black-ink paintings composed of white space and vivid black lines and drawings, with no color. But the viewers, when beholding the painting, should normally feel the noises and faint sounds of the movement of the wind in the mountain and the waterfall. The person contemplating the black-ink painting, moreover, should appreciate all the colors in his/her own intensive insight. Sometimes such a contemplator says, "I can feel every color in black." Since the goal of the painting is to express the Spirit of Nature, it is better to contemplate the landscape drawing where the Spirit is expressed more purely than even to go oneself into the natural landscape. In the 8th century, the Chinese painter Wan Wei said: "When a painter draws a mountain, he must grasp and draw the *spiritus* of the mountain, not identify which mountain it is."[9]

In the 6th century, a Chinese aesthetic critic, Tiang-Huen-Jen, speaking about the six norms of painting, said that the highest test of a masterpiece is whether "the vital and dynamic rhythm of natural *spiritus*" is expressed or not. We, Japanese have accepted this point of view, and the person who searches for *Geido* sometimes goes into the mountain and practices asceticism to accept the Spirit of Nature into his/her own "spirit."

The German philosopher, Eugene Herrigel, who came to Japan and studied Japanese archery in order to understand Japanese philosophical and cultural thought, wrote *Die Ritterliche Kunst des Bogenschiessens* in 1936, in which there are many relevant passages including the following:

> We speak of Japanese archery as *kyu-do*, namely the *Dao* of archery (...). His master said, 'You must not sight a target. You must not think about your target and where to aim, or about other things. Pull the arrow, and wait till the arrow leaves you naturally. You should leave everything as it is.' (...) Herrigel must close his eyes so as to see the target vaguely, and then the target seems to be coming near. Then the target will be unified with himself. (...) According to his master, this mystic unification is realized by concentrating on oneself. He said, 'Aim at yourself, not the target.'[10]

Japanese haiku poet, Matsuo Bashō, who decided to dedicate his whole life to perfecting the art of haiku (a seventeen syllable poem), abandoned his social position to enter into Nature to enable himself, namely, his spirit, to be unified with the Spirit of Nature. He said, "Learn of the pine tree about pine tree, and learn of the bamboo about bamboo."[11] For him, the master of haiku is Nature itself.

In summary, the master must be one with the Spirit of Nature and represent It in his/her work of art; the person who appreciates the art thereby learns about the Spirit of Nature. Travelling this path of art, human beings are purified and perfected. They concentrate on nature to be one with Spirit or of the Cosmos, not only through creation but also through the appreciation of works of art and thereby have possibilities to experience a cathartic ecstasy that lifts them from the pains and grief of the real world. On this stage then one finds unification of aesthetics and religion.

Stage III: Spirit and the Value Transcending Death

Beyond the spatial-temporal limitations of the body, by means of the ascetic process, the purified spirit's vision and perception transcends the phenomenal world to enter the metaphysical stage. This can be accomplished instantly by intuition. This form of transcendence has aesthetic, ethical, and religious aspects. While the Cosmos, Nature and human beings are one from the point of view of Nature, they are not entirely the same. Nature is the Cosmos and the Life of Eternity, manifested in endless circulation through individuals. The human being is a defined temporal existence that participates in Nature by having a unique place in it.

The separation between human beings and Nature is not subject to objective calculation. It must be subjectively experienced and learned by the individual. In so doing, he/she can understand the aesthetic concept of *ma,* which in Japanese, refers to a dynamic phenomenon that directs separate identities into patterns of harmonious relationships. *Ma* establishes proper relationships between separate individuals, but individuals must learn to discern them. And, in the same way, human beings must discern their relationship with God, the Deity, Cosmos, or Nature. The Japanese expression *machigai*, meaning an error or a mistake in timing and situation, suggests an inharmonious relationship between individuals as well as between God and human beings. Such a failure to perceive *ma* can, for example, be attributed to a lack of morality. Therefore, development of the understanding of *ma* is an objective of *Geido*. It is perfect understanding of *ma* that generates the intuition necessary for perception of the "Value transcending death."

Flower arrangement is one of the arts associated with *ma*. In English, one may say, "flower arrangement," but in Japanese one says, "path of flower" or "path of flower composition." The art of flower arrangement was born in the 15th century, simultaneously with the tea ceremony. On this beginning, Tenshin said:

> Our legends ascribe the first flower arrangement to those early Buddhist saints who gathered flowers strewn by the storm and, in their infinite solicitude for all living things, placed them in vessels of water.[12]

The master of the "path of flowers" cuts the life of flowers off and composes the work of art to realize temporally limited beauty; this act is the human imitation of the complexity of *ma* in the Cosmos. Tenshin says:

> Anyone acquainted with the ways of our tea and flower masters must have noticed the religious veneration with which they regard flowers. They do not cull at random, but carefully select each branch or spray with an eye to the artistic composition they have in mind. They would be ashamed were they by chance to cut more than were absolutely necessary.[13]

Through flower composition, one learns the dynamic significance of spatial and temporal relationships in Nature; and at the same time, through this work of art resulting in flower compositions, one learns about relationships between two persons. In the process of flower arrangement, one learns attitudes, forms and manners for expressing heartfelt wishes to others with whom there is some meaningful relationship. It is paradoxical that, by depriving or cutting the lives of the flowers, one generates another form of life, albeit artificial—in the dynamics of an interpersonal relationship through the creation of a work of flower art. By practicing this art, people learn about vital, ethical relationships between themselves and others. The process of practicing this art as an expression of appreciation for others, is, in actuality, the exercise of ethical expressions towards other people and other things. From the perspective of flower arrangement, *Geido* is the practice of *ma* shaping proper relationships between people and Nature and among individuals.

This stage of the path of art is also to be experienced in the *No* play. The *No* play embracing moral ideals, religious beliefs and artistic aspirations is a work of art saturated with deep meaning. Zeami, who founded the theory of the *No* play in the 15th century, wrote about his ideas of aesthetics in *Fushikaden*, which was for centuries a very carefully hidden document, entrusted only to one family. The title of the document literally means "Transmission of "wind-figure-flower." "Wind" (*fu*) refers to the atmosphere of the performance, "flower" (*ka*) is the symbol of the *No* player and what he practices, "figure" (*shi*) means the phenomenon of the actor or the play. In this teaching, beauty is presented as reflected in the flower of articulated temporality, the beauty of limited time, *jibun-no-hana*, such as the beauty of youth. Such beauty is contrasted with the true flower, eternal beauty, *makoto-no-hana*.

Following the tradition established by Zeami, the son of the family entrusted with the *Fushikaden* is initiated into the secrets of this document. This is a gradual initiation which takes many years beginning from the time the child is seven-years old and continues through different stages until the child is twenty-five, at which time he begins to read the script and act in the play. From the beginning, in everyday life, this future *No* player must try to express temporary beauty. Although he must also aim for perfection, he can rarely express the true flower, or the eternal one. Because Zeami insists on the expression of the "flower of temporality" by each *No* player, this implies that every player responds to the other, given particular circumstances, by respecting each one's identity and building harmonious relationships among themselves in accordance with *ma*.

According to Tomonobu Imamichi's modern interpretation of the *No* play, the principal paradigm of the ethical virtue of responsibility is sought among the actors in their responses to each other. In the modern *No* play, Nature, itself, appears as a phenomenon, a temporality in the great Eternity. The *No* player must practice asceticism to transcend the phenomenal level in his reach for Eternity. Then he looks for unification with the Cosmos.

An illustration of a *No* play that exemplifies the union of moral ideals, religious meaning, and artistic expression is the *No* play entitled "*Yama-Uba*," presented and interpreted in the book by Daisetz T. Suzuki. *Yama-Uba*, meaning "old women of the mountains," illustrates this combination as the temporal incarnation of the Principle of Love that in reality secretly and endlessly moves in every person. Humans are usually not conscious of, nor perceptive of, Love and disregard Her regularly. On the phenomenal plane, assuming Love to be embodied in what appears as a young and beautiful person, the players on the stage fail to recognize Love's incarnation in the play, which is that of an old white-haired and wizened woman. Her temporal appearance reflects the actuality of Her ceaseless struggle in the world. She suffers many pains gladly as She travels the world around, knowing no rest, respite, and interruption in her work of bringing blessings and resolving problems. *Yama-Uba* incarnates the unknown and invisible agent, in Nature and in humanity, that human beings will gladly imagine in a happy beautiful way but with whom they must come face to face in the full light of reality in their deepest conscience to grasp the actuality of "Nature." Most will either shirk this effort because of its demands or fail to do it because of insensitivity.[14]

Final Word

The present age beginning in the 1970s, according to Tomonobu Imamichi, is to be denoted as "the formless period." It is characterized by the technological world fully occupied by objective calculations. In this technological society, concrete forms do not indicate the functions of the artifacts or objects they incorporate. For instance, a black box conceals many different forms with different functions. Also in this modern era, moving images are more important than forms. In the dimension of art not only images but dynamic figures, that is to say a series of concrete moving forms, are essential. Therefore, interpreting art as a "path" for the purpose of realizing humanity's relationship with Nature as a state of perfection is no longer possible. Without the possibility for such interpretation, art is shorn of its knowledge of *ma*. If one does not know *ma* as the harmonizing agent between human kind and the "Cosmic Spirit," he or she makes mistakes and confuses aesthetics, ethics, and religion.

The essential significance of *Geido* is, as Tenshin said, "Seeking always to be in harmony with the great rhythm of the universe;" and only the Artist "who has lived with the beautiful can die beautifully."[15] Thus *Geido* is the path on which every person learns to experience the "Spirit" of nature in creating or appreciating the work of art. This work of art is the ultimate of spiritual unification of aesthetics, ethics, and religion.

Endnotes

1 - Kotaro Takamura (1883-1956), poet and sculptor, influenced by Rodin, Baudelaire, and Verlaine.

2 - John 14:6 KJV (King James Version).

3 - Thomasa. Kempis, [Thomaas Hammerken (1379 or 1380 – 1472], *De Imitaione Christie, Finitus et Completus Anno Domini 1441*, per manus Thomas Kempis is in Monte Sanctae Aquetis, prope Zwelle. His most important thought was supported by "sursum corda habeamus as Dominum." This book, translated from Latin into Japanese, was read by Japanese Christians in the 1560's.

4 - Michi Koji Fukunaga, *Dao: Chinese Philosophy of Art* (Tokyo: Tokyo University Press, 1984), 213-246.

5 - Okakura Kakuzo, *The Book of Tea* (Tokyo: Charles E. Tuttle Company, 1956), 78. Tenshin is the name commonly associated with Okakura in Japan and is used in this text to refer to his work. Tomonobu Imamichi, *Betrachtungen ueber das Eline* (Tokyo: Tokyo University Press, 1968). Tomonobu Imamichi, *Aesthetics in Orient* (Tokyo: TBS Britanica, 1980), 382.

6 - Soren Kierkegaard also perceived three dimensions of experience or consciousness in his theory of Existence: the aesthetic, the ethical, and the religious. There is a difference, however, between oriental thought and Kierkegaard's perception of these stages. Kierkegaard's stages were sequential planes towards realization of one's self in Spirit. It is despair that moves the individual to make a conscious choice to move from plane to plane until he/she reaches harmony with themselves in spiritual realization. In the Orient, there is not the differentiated escalation as in Kierkegaard's perception. Ultimate Value is found in the unification or the mutual integration of these three elements: aesthetics, ethics, and religion.

7 - Okakura, *Book of Tea*, 79-80.

8 - Ibid.

9 - Tomonobu Imamichi, *Aesthetics in China* (Tokyo: TBS Britanica, 1980). Tomonobu Imamichi and Noriko Hashimoto, *The Modalites and Essence of the Beauty - History and Systematic Thoughts in the Aesthetics* (Tokyo: Universe of Air Press, 1987), 44-45.

10 - Eugene Herrigel, *Die Ritterliche Kunst des Bogenschiessens (Japanese Archery),* (Tokyo: Iwnami-Shoten, 1994), 42. Original publication in German in 1936, and translated into Japanese by Jisaburo Shibata in 1994. Herrigel came to the Institute of Philosophy at Tohoku University and became the Master of Japanese Archery.

11 - Basho Matsuo, *Aesthetics of Japan* (Tokyo: Sanzoshi, 1980).

12 - Okakuro, *The Book of Tea*, 101.

13 - Ibid., 100.

14 - Daisetz T. Suzuki, *Zen and Japanese Culture* (Princeton, NJ: Princeton University Press, 1959), 419-427.

15 - Okakura, *The Book of Tea*, 113.

CHAPTER 13

THE DYNAMIC NOW—A POET'S COUNSEL

Allison W. Phinney

> Sometimes I feel ashamed that I've written so few poems on political themes, on the causes that agitate me. But then I remind myself that to choose to live as a poet in the modern super state is in itself a political action.
>
> *Stanley Kunitz*

This moment, just past the edge of a new millennium, has startling urgency for issues of social progress. Moral outrages continue with tireless re-invention in many parts of the world. Ethnic cleansing and rape, ever subtler modes of racial and class oppression, the withering of human rights justified by supposed economic and national interest, disquiet comfortable assumptions about "progress." But, in the Western world, another specter has arisen that is more unusual and ultimately more threatening to humankind than any natural regime. Deepening doubt and intellectual distrust of the very existence of the human spirit, like some suffocating stratospheric smog, now drifts across the surface of the globe.

World historian, Arnold Toynbee, commented in 1975 on "an increasing number of Westerners living in a spiritual vacuum."[1] To suppose that people can live in a spiritual vacuum is as reasonable as saying they breathe without air. The economic and technological changes producing wealth and leisure in a homogenous world culture by no means have had the promised effect of liberating the human spirit. Moreover, the traditional narrow focus of most leaders in seeking primarily outward economic and social improvements offers little hope of stirring human beings increasingly dispirited by pervasive materialism. And without humanity's morale or will to sustain outward social improvements, they are negated by shifting circumstances and deteriorating attitudes.

On the level of popular polls much is sometimes made in the United States of a resurgence of faith. The issue, of course, is not really how many are affirming belief in divinity, but whether this acculturated belief any longer has effect on the way society is conducted. In *The Wonder of Being Human*, neurobiologist Sir John Eccles, and psychologist Daniel Robinson point to the more elemental ebbing of humanity's faith:

> We think science has gone too far in breaking down man's belief in his spiritual greatness, (...) and has given him the belief that he is merely an insignificant animal that has arisen by chance and necessity. We can have hope as we recognize and appreciate the wonder and mystery of our existence as experiencing selves. Mankind would be cured of its alienation if that message could be expressed with all the authority of scientists and philosophers as well as with the imaginative insights of artists.[2]

A Poet's Passion and the Human Spirit

Poets are not usually assumed to have very much to do with social engineering. But the underlying crisis of the human spirit that has so rapidly weakened idealism may engender a new necessity for looking pragmatically not only to poets, but also to filmmakers, dramatists, artists, musicians and composers, philosophers, and theologians. If humanity is to be fulfilled, rather than enslaved by continuous acquiescence in finitude, we desperately need reminders of who we are. We need whatever articulates the core "humanness" of which we must become sharply conscious in order to make choices that do not oppress.

Poets and playwrights have often supplied the voices for revolution—in Poland, Czechoslovakia, Nigeria, and Russia, for example. The reason may lie in poets' peculiar senses of urgency and immediacy. Theory, logical debate, dogmatics, they believe, can come later; for centuries the greatest issues have been sufficiently clear!

What issues? Issues of the human spirit denigrated, violated, oppressed, starved, unfulfilled, or destroyed. As Primo Levi, the twentieth century Italian poet and author put it in his "Song of Those Who Died in Vain:"

> (...) outside in the cold we will be waiting for you,
> The army of those who died in vain,
> We of the Marne, of Montecassino,
> Treblinka, Dresden and Hiroshima. (...)
> The Disappeared Ones of Buenos Aires,
> Dead Cambodians and dying Ethiopians,
> The Prague negotiators,
> The bled-dry of Calcutta,
> The innocents slaughtered in Bologna. (...)[3]

Nazim Hikmet, a Turkish poet of the 1920's and 1930's, writes of a passion that is willing to die for the sake of more life and freedom for the living:

> Living is no laughing matter:
> you must take it seriously,
> so much so and to such a degree
> that, for example, your hands tied behind your back,
> your back to the wall, . . .
> you can die for people—
> even for people whose faces you've never seen,
> even though you know living
> is the most real, the most beautiful thing.[4]

A poet does not live a daily life of heroic choices any more than anyone else, and in point of fact, the hardest battles are often fought, not with visible opponents, but with inertia, apathy, and dullness that constrict, or deconstruct life and spirit more efficiently than any gulag. Wislawa Szymborska, a Polish Nobel-prize winning poet, acknowledges, in her poem "Reality Demands," that life itself may simply, subtly, and steadily move on, until the bland and personal fades out those very events the human spirit feels instinctively ought to be kept alive in memory forever.[5]

The evidence in Szymborska's choosing to write her poem in the first place, however, is that someone—the poet—does feel compelled to remember, no matter how self-interested and forgetful successive generations might be. Her overlaying of the personal patterns of everyday life on place names associated with tragic events brings a sudden stabbing recognition and poignancy. She writes:

> Reality demands
> that we also mention this:
> Life goes on.
> It continues at Cannae and Borodino,
> at Kosovo, Polje and Guernica. (...)
> Music pours from the yachts moored at Actium
> and couples dance on their sunlit decks. (...)
> Where not a stone still stands
> you see the Ice Cream Man
> besieged by children.
> Where Hiroshima had been
> Hiroshima is again,
> producing many products
> for everyday use.[6]

In their private lives, poets may be no more moral, courageous, or perceptive in regard to family and friends than any other humans, but wittingly or unwittingly poets create a record of the consciousness of being alive. Theirs is often an isolated passionate struggle to find the words to share "what it was like" with unknown others—to find words for scarcely expressible joys and sorrows, for the nuances of yearning, the cosmos that is human consciousness. A poet knows the indefinable must be said, the flesh made Word, as it were.[7] As American poet John Hall Wheelock writes in "To You, Perhaps Yet Unborn:"

> Here is my joy, here is my sorrow, my heart's rage,
> Poured out for you. What tenderness brooding above you
> Hallows these poems! I have made them all for you. I love you.
> What love, what longing, my reader, speaks to you from this
> page! [8]

Pragmatic Effects of the Erosion of Spirit

With the loss of authority of many religious and moral traditions, the erosion of spirit has been unchecked, with concrete negative consequences for social progress. Holes in the ionosphere, pollution of seas and rivers, death of species—they signal not simply encroachment on the human environment but far more seriously the loss of spirit that underlies a heedless "self-interest." While it is difficult to prove that self-interest is greater than ever before, it is not so difficult to see that self-interest is less held in check by idealism than in previous centuries. Opportunities for self-interest to wreak havoc through global interconnectedness and advanced technology are greater than in all the earlier centuries taken together.[9]

Poets, filmmakers, dramatists, as a race are, of course, no more optimists than the rest of humanity. As the American mid-century poet Robinson Jeffers stated it in his poem "Birds and Fishes:"

> Justice and mercy
> Are human dreams, they do not concern the birds nor the fish
> nor eternal God. However—look again before you go
> The wings and the wild hungers, the wave-worn skerries, the
> bright quick minnows
> Living in terror to die in torment—
> Man's fate and their—and the island rocks and immense ocean
> beyond, and Lobos
> Darkening above the bay: they are beautiful?
> That is their quality: not mercy, not mind, not goodness, but the
> beauty of God.[10]

Jeffers was writing at the height of uncritical acceptance of materialism and naive willingness to be intimidated by it. Now humanity is again struggling out from under the overwhelming "evidence" of meaninglessness, imperfection, and entropic decay. In some fields and disciplines, the scientific reductionism of the last century and half, which tended to equate man with machine and process, is being seen as a temporary mind-set that has been extremely harmful to humankind's self-image and hence, to its progress.

It is a long, slow dawning. At the very moment when light is appearing, the darkness has never seemed blacker. Some of the horrors that have been so alarming in this century have been of the old and familiar tribal ilk, magnified by modern tools of warfare. But, in other instances, we have seen a new cold-blooded absence of soul. It is as though we have caught glimpses of a new kind of human being whose imposed mesmeric will can succeed in effacing any memory of the human spirit, not just in a few leaders but, for millions of enthusiastic followers. If this has the sound of science fiction, it is not, and that very fact should make everyone feel the urgency of recognizing the spirit of humanity more widely and, at once, through all the legal and governmental venues of humankind.

Uprising for the Sake of Humanity

Revolutionary change is needed. The ponderous pace of theory and debate is simply too slow to save humanness from being swallowed up in the opportunism of materialism, from being redefined, dispersed, swept away, unremembered. Now we need not so much the historian's late and sober assessment as the poet's, the dramatist's, the human being's passionate outrage and wakened alarm. More primary than each person's self-awareness of national or academic or professional identity—lawyer, economist, educator—must be a readiness to measure one's own consciousness of the human spirit against, not only terrible atrocity, but the equally terrible deadening of morality and spirit that leads to unchecked crimes against humanity and the loss of civilization.

We need to hold such a vivid sense of the practicality and concreteness of the human spirit that we are able to discern and to resist the sophistries and mesmerizing promises of progress by everything from genetics to sociobiology. In hundreds of variations the promise is repeated: if we will only acquiesce in materialism and give up a "naïve and unscientific" trust in individuality and the human spirit, we will be saved by the irresistible progress of civilization (i.e., unrestricted capitalism and scientific discovery).

The Christian text "Man cannot live by bread alone."[11] is paralleled in every great religious teaching. It can be taken not so much as a tenuous ideal as a profoundly valid, pre-scientific perception. In six words it sums up the human condition, and implies another necessity. This necessity for feeding, not just the literal hunger of man, lessening his poverty, increasing his equality and justice, but feeding his spirit, must now at last begin to find a place in the deliberations of world leaders. The sinuous logic of Dostoevski's "Grand Inquisitor," who accused Christ of having failed humankind by refusing to turn stones into bread, must finally be purged.

At a time of immense darkness—the fear of defeat, not just for an alliance of nations, but for civilization itself—Antoine de St. Exupéry wrote in *Flight to Arras*:

> If what I seek is to dig down to the root of the many causes of my defeat, if my ambition is to be born anew, I must begin by recovering the animating power of my civilization which has become lost.

He said:

> There exists a common denomination that integrates all the qualities I demand in the man of my civilization. There exists a keystone that sustains the arch of the particular community which men are called to found. There exists a principle, an animating force, out of which everything once emerged—root, trunk, branches, fruit. That principle was once a radiating seed in the loam of mankind. Only by it can I be made victorious. What is it? [12]

Saint Exupéry prophetically recognized the need to regain the essential of the human being, to get beyond the myopia of self- and national interest, and to act on what is actually a more basic instinct, that which preserves humanity itself. In effect, he saw something of the exigency of restoring the "spirit of humanity." Yet, he also suspected the practical difficulty of doing this in a culture that was apparently losing the notion of God altogether.

Since that loss of faith has accelerated greatly over the last century and a half, how can we reasonably urge the recovery of the "spirit of humanity" as primary and essential for social progress? We can do it for several reasons. First, the increased desire of the human community for sustainable social development and the demands related to attaining it are themselves pointing, more obviously than ever before, to the necessity for spiritual and ethical values to shape discussions of social development.

The question of whether this is likely to happen or can happen is obviated by the fact that it is happening. For the first time in United Nations history, for example, a UN seminar report was produced entitled Ethical and Spiritual Dimensions of Social Progress. It was submitted to the World Summit for Social Development held in Copenhagen in 1995.[13] Second, the Western world is, of course, not the world, and many countries and areas continue to be grounded in religious and moral traditions of great richness and resilience. Third, the evident loss of God in a materialized Western world is not quite what it appears to be. It may well be more the loss of non-sustainable myths and superstitions than some final inability of human beings to find or know.

Often after losing faith in traditional doctrines, and still ineradicably conscious of the cruel absurdities in trying to make sense of a material universe, poets in the last half century have stumbled deep into a world of transcendent meaning. Czeslaw Milosz writing of his wife's cremation in "On Parting from My Wife, Janina," says:

> Do I believe in the Resurrection of the Flesh? Not of this ash.
> I call, I beseech: elements, dissolve yourselves!
> Rise into the other, let it come, kingdom!
> Beyond the earthly fire, compose yourselves anew! [14]

He writes in "Powers":

> Though of weak faith, I believe in forces and powers
> Who crowd every inch of the air.
> They observe us—is it possible that no one sees us?
> Just think: a cosmic spectacle and absolutely no one?
> There is proof, my consciousness. It separates itself,
> Soars above me, above other people, above earth,
> Obviously kindred to those powers,
> Able, as they are, to see with detachment.[15]

As it always has been, for nineteenth-century poet William Wordsworth or for ninth century Chinese poet Po Chü-I, so for twentieth-century American Pulitzer Prize winner, Mary Oliver, the conjunction of nature and consciousness is a source of renewable vision and the affirmation of the soul's self-worth. Unsparingly noting the imperfections of beautiful pond lilies she speaks directly:

> Still, what I want in my life
> is to be willing
> to be dazzled—
> to cast aside the weight of facts
> and maybe even
> to float a little
> above this difficult world.
> I want to believe I am looking
> into the white fire of a great mystery.
> I want to believe that the imperfections are nothing—
> that the light is everything—that it is more than the sum
> of each flawed blossom rising and fading. And I do. [16]

Contemporary poets do not shy from the cruel and unjust, if beautiful, world of a Thomas Hardy or a Robinson Jeffers. [17] But as is evident in Mary Oliver's "The Ponds," some are no longer thinking of either justifying a traditional Creator in terms of material order, design, and beauty, or of displacing one. They are beginning with their own fullest immediacy of being, which is of course inner experience or consciousness, and in this, at times finding an inescapable sense of divine dimension. James Hillman, a psychologist, writes:

> I believe anybody can find a way into the world: some landscape, a particular room, neighborhood street, a building such as a barn with its smells, or a thing privately treasured, for instance a baseball glove or a pair of shoes. 'All things are full of Gods' is an ancient Greek saying; 'In my Father's house are many mansions,' a Christian one. These suggest that there is something divine even in the baseball glove and the neighborhood street.[18]

This text does not imply that God is in the street nor that He caused the street. It simply suggests that there can be such a unity of consciousness with a familiar object or place, and its thousand-and-one memories and associations, that the resulting sense of love, awe, and conviction of meaning can release one from one's self into a feeling of transcendent recognition. Delmore Schwartz, in a poem titled "Seurat's Sunday Afternoon Along the Seine," makes a similar observation, one with which poets from many different cultures, careers, and personal styles would readily identify. Schwartz's close, humane attention to Seurat's painting brings back the immediacy of the very summer afternoon the paint was squeezed from the tube, and he writes:

> If you can look at anything for long enough,
> You will rejoice in the miracle of love,
> You will possess and be blessed by the marvelous
>   blinding radiance
> of love, you will be radiance. [19]

"Something . . . is Being Born"

Czeslaw Milosz, in *The Witness of Poetry*, confronts the possibility that the race between development and disintegration may well end in the victory of disintegration. Yet finally he speaks of hope, and a reason for it that makes it "neither chimerical nor foolish":

> On the contrary, every day one can see signs indicating
> that now, at the present moment, something new, and on
> a scale never witnessed before, is being born: humanity
> as an elemental force conscious of transcending Nature,
> for it lives by memory of itself, that is, in History. [20]

Milosz, writing in 1983, noted reasons for discouragement; and we have had, since that time, additional years of atrocities and oppressions and wars to confirm despair. Yet some part of humanity has changed or is changing for the better—something is being born—and what is being born is a humanity more conscious of itself, not simply of its own misdeeds but of what it means to be human in the most profound and inspiring sense.

A friend of mine, who is a film critic, calls today's cinema the modern equivalent of "tales of the tribe," the stories we tell each other not around the campfire but in the silvery half-light of the darkened theater. If these tales too often feed materialistic appetites, at other times, they express emerging insight in regard to the spirit of man that is astonishingly powerful.[21] Audiences in the billions are finding something far beyond escape and entertainment. For many, the theater is a kind of church in which they are roused much more deeply about moral issues, love for fellow human beings, and spiritual hope and yearning than by religious institutions which they sense to be lacking both in fire and realism about the human condition.

For centuries humankind has looked outward, from behind its eyes, at a universe of incredible beauty and evil, astonishing heroism, invention, and sin. But the observed has seemed far more concrete and significant than the observer. In the past two centuries, the platform of observation, the consciousness that records and knows, has been gaining self-awareness. This revolutionary turmoil has led to opposite extremes, from physicist P.T. Bridgman's humanistic solipsism to Einstein's affirmation of the universe's unity and purpose, from poet T.S. Eliot's nihilism to his Christian conversion, and from poet Wallace Stevens' brilliant amoral relativism to his own glimpses of the concreteness of consciousness and aesthetics.

Stevens could write nearly cynically, on the one hand, in "A High-Toned Old Christian Woman:"

> Poetry is the supreme fiction, Madame
> Take the moral law and make a nave of it
> And from the nave, build haunted heaven.(...)[22]

Yet, it was Stevens who would, on the other hand, struggle with the flux and relativity of the "metaphysical streets of the physical town," and in "Final Soliloquy of the Interior Paramour" write :

> Within its vital boundary, in the mind.
> We say God and the imagination are one. . .
> How high that highest candle lights the dark.
> Out of this same light, out of the central mind,
> We make a dwelling in the evening air,
> In which being there together is enough. [23]

And in "The Well Dressed Man with a Beard":

> After the final no there comes a yes,
> And on that, yes the world depends.(...)
> One thing remaining, infallible, would be
> Enough. Ah, douce campagna of that thing!
> Ah, douce campagna, honey in the heart,
> Green in the body, out of a petty phrase,
> Out of a thing believed, a thing affirmed:
> The form on the pillow humming while one sleeps,
> The aureole above the humming house.(...)
> It can never be satisfied, the mind, never. [24]

"On That, 'Yes' the World Depends"

Something is happening in human consciousness that is different and which must now be taken into account. We seem only at the beginning of grasping it, though insights have been coming for centuries. The idea of the solidity of spirit and the pervasiveness of consciousness still seems elusive or evanescent, but what we are seeing is really no more fragile than a view of mountains seen through mist. Changes of consciousness in history have often seemed audacious and naive at first, not subservient enough to the prevailing culture. Later, the substantiality of the original glimpse is confirmed. Let us hope these social and cultural changes, taken in the aggregate, can be said to involve some recovering of the image of the human spirit—or what was long ago defined by religion and theology as God's image and likeness. If so, they may also point towards humanity's reviving capacities for deepening exploration of the meaning of God here and now in human lives. The more we comprehend of the essence of humankind, as something beyond a material machine that thinks—or that kills its brothers—the more we sense a Creator, or Spirit, or universal divine Principle that is worthy of awe and trust.

In a world that is plainly global, one sphere—economically, environmentally, and culturally—the spiritlessness of one society or the barbarism of another cannot possibly be expected to be without wider effect. The lack of moral strength in the industrialized societies does not go unnoticed among critics or self-interested nationalities. Nor can the hedonistic consumption, the fascination with self-centered sensuality, and the increasing willingness to market a mindless ennui through the faces of mannequins, models, and rock videos fail to seem threatening, instead of freeing, to any remaining outposts of rationality. The barbarism and atrocities of "ethnic cleansing" and "the disappeared," should send a chill up the comfortable consumer's spine. They raise inevitable questions about similar, if sublimated, tendencies in every supposedly civil society.

Ultimately, however, it is not alarm but comprehension and a fresh sense of possibility that move us forward. A growing recognition of the sheer practicality of the "spirit of humanity" can achieve more than all the threats. Human beings are rapidly learning through experience that this spirit is vital to everything from the immune system to recovery rates after surgery, from international conciliation to mental health, from lessening inner city crime to corporate vitality and environmental stability.

Humanity, like the individual human being, does not progress socially so long as it distrusts its own deepest feelings of love, which would otherwise be expressed in sacrifice for the good of others, cooperation for the sake of community, and intuitions of being linked to some transcendent meaning. If humankind believes the spirit of humanity is merely nature's elaborate genetic survival mechanism or an outmoded superstitious reflex, rather than revelatory and opening on to some larger reality; failure becomes the norm, inertia a law, and civilization sinks deeper into darkness. As Yeats phrased it poetically but brutally:

> Things fall apart; the center cannot hold;
> Mere anarchy is loosed upon the world,
> The blood-dimmed tide is loosed, and everywhere;
> The ceremony of innocence is drowned.
> The best lack all conviction, while the worst
> Are full of passionate intensity.[25]

The increase of scientific knowledge is not the problem. Humankind's lust for knowledge and resulting loss of vision of the true nature of humanity is the problem. As in the Garden of Eden mythology, man and woman distrust what has already been given, what is already theirs to fulfil, and so they choose disastrously.

The most immediate task in these times may be to summon living, spirit-centered convictions among those who have leadership roles. Today, their discourse and actions, viewed from a slight remove, seem cool and colorless. It is as though they were responsible for administering and governing humanized objects rather than beings with the full dimension of humanity. They act like furtive, indentured servants of necessity—political and economic—who cannot afford to be caught siding with the spirit of humanity. Yet, it is after all, the human species that is at stake. And, only the spirit of humankind, more consciously recognized, can possibly continue life on this planet in a way that is bearable and nurturing for leaders or the rest of society.

Religious philosopher, Nicholas Berdyaev wrote in his final book, *Truth and Revelation*: "Man as an animal is an object, that is to say something which is different from and opposed to the depth of his existence. But, there is in man a deep-lying stratum which is anterior to objectification."[26] And he concluded: "Sooner or later a revolution in thought must take place which will set it free from the power of the objective world, from the hypnosis of so-called objective realities, (...)." [27]

In drawing a parallel to preface the larger point about having received "not the spirit of the world but the spirit which is of God," St. Paul once asked what must have seemed to him a fairly self-evident question: "What man knoweth the things of a man, save the spirit of man which is in him?"[28] That "small" question assumes huge, new dimensions in the twenty-first century.

Endnotes

1 - Arnold Toynbee, "Life After Death," essay *in The Sunday Times* (London), 25 October 1975.

2 - Sir John Eccles and Daniel N. Robinson, *The Wonder of Being Human: Our Brain and Our Mind* (New York: The Free Press, 1984), 177-178.

3 - Primo Levi, "Song of Those who Died in Vain," in *Voices of Conscience: Poetry from Oppression,* eds. Hume Cronyn, Richard McKane, Stephen Watts (Northumberland, England: Iron Press, 1995), 62. The majority of the poets represented in this anthology were victims of political repression, exile, imprisonment, or torture.

4 - Ibid., 165-166. Hikmet was imprisoned for 35 years in Turkey for inciting revolt. He was eventually exiled.

5 - Wistawa Szymborska, *View with a Grain of Sand: Selected Poems* (New York: Harcourt Brace, & Company, 1995), 184-185.

6 - Ibid.

7 - John Hall Wheelock, *This Blessed Earth: New and Selected Poems, 1927-1977* (New York: Charles Scribner's Sons, 1978), 13.

8 - The intent here is not to reverse or alter the profound theological meaning of a phrase from the Christian Bible that has had import for millions. I am endorsing neither immanentism nor pantheism in the phrase "the flesh being made Word." But in ordinary lives here and now—in the texture of conversation between strangers on a bus or sunlight slanting into a familiar room—we can experience a sudden quality of transcendence and of sacred meaning. Poetry frequently strives to express this meaning, and often with a sense of the near sacred power of the word, or language, to re-create that immediacy.

9 - Other papers in this volume offer ample illustrations of the erosion of language, community, and culture, based on social research.

10 - Robinson Jeffers, *Selected Poems* (New York: Vintage Books, 1963), 108. The theology popularly labeled as "death of God" sought to surmount the problem of doing Christian theology without the main character to write about, in effect the "ology" without the "theos."

11 - Matthew 4: 4 KJV (King James Version).

12 - Antoine de St. Exupery, *Flight to Arras* (New York: Harcourt, Brace and World and World, 1942), 135, 137, 140, 145. The concept of man as used by Saint Exupery was gender neutral. The term as used in the first chapter of Genesis refers to male and female "man."

13 - UN Secretariat, *Ethical and Spiritual Dimensions of Social Progress,* prepared for the World Summit for Social Development 6-12 March 1995 Copenhagen (New York: United Nations Publication, 1995).

14 - Czeslaw Milsoz, *The Collected Poems 1931-1987* (New York: The Ecco Press and Penguin Books, 1988), 459-460.

15 - Ibid., 461-462.

16 - Mary Oliver, *New and Selected Poems* (Boston: Beacon Press, 1992), 92-93.

17 - Hardy's concept of fate produced a bitter caricature of an alien, bemused deity, e.g., in his poem "God's Education": "Said I, we call that cruelty—/ We, your poor mortal kind. / He mused. "The thought is new to me. / Forsooth, though I men's master be, / Theirs is the teaching mind!" *Selected Poems of Thomas Hardy*, ed. John Crowe Ransom (New York: The Macmillan Company, Collier Books, 1960-1961), 38.

18 - Robert Bly, James Hillman, and Michael Meade eds., *The Rag and Bone Shop of the Heart* (New York: HarperCollins Publishers, 1992), 474.

19 - Delmore Schwartz, *Selected Poems: Summer Knowledge* (New York: New Directions, 1967), 191-192.

20 - Czeslaw Milosz, *The Witness of Poetry* (Cambridge: Harvard University Press, 1983), 116.

21 - A thorough listing of examples of films from the last four decades would be out of scale with this paper, but see, e.g., Ingmar Bergman's "Seventh Seal," (Sweden), "The Soldier"(Russia), "Aparajito" (India), "Mask"(U.S.), "The Elephant Man" (U.S.), "Dead Man Walking" (U.S.), Robert Benton's "Places in the Heart (U.S.), "Tender Mercies" (U.S.),Wim Wender's "Wings of Desire" (Germany), "Il Postino"(Italy), Robert Duvall's "The Apostle" (U.S.),"Life is Beautiful" (Italian), "Children of Heaven" (Iran).

22 - *Poems by Wallace Stevens,* selected and with an introduction by Samuel French Morse (New York: Vintage Books, 1959), 26-27.

23 - Ibid., 157-158.

24 - Ibid., 104.

25 - William Butler Yeats, "The Second Coming," *The Rag and Bone Shop of the Heart*, 216.

26 - Nicolas Berdyaev, *Truth and Revelation* (New York: Collier Books, 1962), 17.

27 - Ibid., 79. (Cf., Martin *Buber's I and Thou*).

28 - I Corinthians 2:11-12 KJV (King James Version).

PART IV

VALUES FOR A GLOBAL SOCIETY

Individuals and institutions have the power to promote or to discourage moral and spiritual values. These values do not belong to some abstract realm. They take on very practical meaning in the daily life of people and the regular functioning of institutions, be they private or public, national or international. To be a "true realist" is to recognize this centrality as well as the eminent practicality of what is moral and spiritual. The concluding part of this book suggests how some candles can illumine the work of some central political and economic institutions and shed light on domains of human behavior critical for the building of a viable world community. These contributions touch the United Nations, the practice of development, the preservation of linguistic diversity, the financial industry, the practice of diplomacy, and the making of foreign policy.

> Enhancing the moral power of the United Nations, to give it a leading role in addressing the pressing problems of the time, is not a utopian notion. It corresponds to the vocation of the Organization, and to an obvious need. But there are evidently several conditions to be met and obstacles to be overcome, for the United Nations to play this role effectively.
>
> *Jacques Baudot*

The move towards a viable and reasonably, peaceful global society would be facilitated if the United Nations were endowed with more attributes of a world government. Global problems, global actors in the economic, financial, and even cultural domains point to the need for a global political power acceptable to all nations. But, argues Jacques Baudot, enhancing the United Nation's legislative, judiciary, and military power must be guided and sculpted according to the highest universal moral principles. As demonstrated by its current Secretary General, Kofi Annan, moral power is the essence of an institution ordained to promote the common good of humankind. Three important constitutive elements of this moral power are intellectual rigor, ethical clarity, and selfless political imagination. The latter, in line with the ordered pluralism advocated by Nitin Desai, is particularly necessary to harmonize the different, but equally necessary, roles of local communities, states, regions, and global institutions. Among the conditions for the fulfillment of its mandates,

Baudot mentions the United Nation's need for adequate financial resources, a strong international civil service, an active presence of non-governmental organizations, and the enrichment of the diplomatic culture with an ethic of commitment to the good of humankind.

> Present globalization processes continue to separate the material and political realms from the values that sustain communities. In the past, interfamily political systems demanded that all elements requisite for a satisfying personal environment be distributed to each community member through an inviolable ethical contract. Today, patron-client and corporate-consumer systems distribute those elements through the interplay of market forces and political influence. Those without property or influence are left out or shortchanged.
>
> *Robert Gamer*

The vision of development, presently propagated by the international institutions, and the "developed" nations is flawed, says Robert Gamer. It aims at transposing a perception of individual and collective progress and well-being from the West to other societies in deliberate ignorance and often contempt for the social structures and mentalities of those who have to be "assisted." It ignores the fact that all material and intangible aspects of well-being have to be viewed in the context of the individual cultural values from which they derive their sense. Excessive attention to quantification, "targeting," and others devices of development economics leads to the neglect and destruction of the unique personal environments that define the real lives of people. Individuals, communities, and nations are treated as abstract statistical objects. Gamer shares the views of Peter Marris on meaning and attachments as the central sources of happiness for individuals. He claims that the very notion of development has to be reformulated with a fuller understanding of the needs of the human person seen as part of a specific and always unique community.

> In truth, in this country of few old monuments or relics, the sagas are Iceland's ancient castles—words are the building blocks for these fortresses. Iceland's modern identity rests on pillars of ideas generated and preserved in these literary forms—and part of the reason that this identity remains dynamic is that the heritage is so rich in imagination and eternal in appeal. (...) Thus, language diversity is like a tapestry woven

with thousands of threads in different hues. The vast array of traditions and rituals sustain the body of the tapestry. As a language is lost, one thread fades. As another disappears, the fading spreads. In the end, the details of the tapestry have blurred away and the world is left with a monotonous uniformity.

Vigdis Finnbogadóttir

The essential thread that binds a community, providing identification and cohesion to its members, is its language. A language, as explained by Vigdis Finnbogadóttir and Birna Arnbjörnsdóttir, is the voice of a nation's thought, the vehicle of its history, the expression of a collective identity and a distinct way of perceiving and describing reality. They note that a community that loses its language loses a sacred part of its identity because this language is the treasure chest of experience passed from one generation to another. Languages are rapidly disappearing. A reliable estimate is that of the world's approximately 6000 remaining languages, 50 to 95 per cent are in danger of disappearance in the course of the 21st century. And yet this impoverishment of humankind is not a necessary price to pay for a more open and smaller world. Vigdis and Birna give the example of their own country, Iceland, which has managed to reconcile economic prosperity and participation in the emerging global market with the protection of its unique ancient language. Similarly, in the other Nordic countries, the use of English as the language for communication with the rest of the world has not been detrimental to their own languages. This wonderful resilience of the Nordic cultures shows that it is possible to reconcile globalization and diversity and protect the unique spirit of a people and a nation for the good of the whole.

> The leaders of tomorrow's major financial service organizations will not be just producers. The leaders will of necessity be a lot like old-fashioned general managers, familiar with the basic business of banking and securities, of course, but also technology, law, regulation, and controls, capable of inspiring others to outstanding efforts and achievement. (...) The highest value a firm can have is the long-term, risk-adjusted value of its business franchise. A company can only achieve this through sound principles, sound standards, and their repeated communication. And everyone has to pitch in.
>
> *Ingo Walter and Roy Smith*

It is possible, indeed imperative, to introduce high ethical standards into the functioning of financial institutions, which are a major force in the current process of globalization and an indispensable element of a future global society. Roy C. Smith and Ingo Walter describe the advent of what is commonly called financial liberalization in the 1980s and 1990s. They show how, under the influence of increased competition, increased uncertainty, increased risks, and dramatically increased profits, the financial firms with a global reach developed a culture of aggressiveness, amorality, and ultimately fraud and deception. These firms gave a distorted and highly negative image of global capitalism with quick hiring and layoff of people, with tolerance and sometimes encouragement of the leadership for fraudulent and unethical behavior on the part of their employees. They promoted the common sentiment that rules and regulations are made to be respected only by "mediocre" and "little" people, with the making of enormous profits disconnected from any service to the community and the real economy. Some spectacular collapses and lawsuits acted as useful correctives to the excesses of this industry, and Smith and Walter do indeed believe that morality and respect for the law are in the long run better ingredients for success than recklessness and arrogance.

> Held as a captive and peering into the eyes of the masked inter-locutors somewhere in Lebanon, I realized that neither theory, nor mathematical formula, nor rationality could serve to guarantee either my safety or, even less, the success of this mission. These were now abandoned to the grace of human ingenuity and irrationality; my own, I presumed, and that of the abductors. (…) Art in the task of making choices was also required in the Middle East negotiations. The situation required choosing a right course of action according to the principles of the UN Charter and consistent with universally respected personal ethical standards. Making choices also entailed taking responsibility for the consequences of the decision and living with them for the rest of one's life.
>
> *Giandomenico Picco*

The last two contributions to this book offer insights on ethics and diplomacy. Giandomenico Picco draws lessons from his experience in highly sensitive and sometimes dangerous diplomatic missions with the United Nations which show that individuals, their principles, courage, imagination, judgment and empathy without concession to the "enemy," matter much more for the success of such missions than abstract rules of conduct. He shows that the capacity to make choices and to take responsibility for one's own actions are essential virtues in the practice of diplomacy. Giving concrete content to the ethic of commitment that Jacques Baudot sees as a necessary enrichment to the diplomatic culture, Picco reintroduces the human factor in international and global relations. He believes in commitment, in credibility through personal engagement, in human subjectivity oriented and shaped by strong moral principles. Reforms, including those necessary for the building of global institutions cannot be effective without such changes in individual mindsets.

> Humankind is witnessing in many parts of the world moral outrages and threats to stability that seem beyond its control. Its very senses are sometimes wearied by the incessant messages of tragedy and conflict from the news media. Where in this environment is the moral footing? How much are we our brother's keeper? And in those cases of great conflict, what is the responsibility of a great democratic power to its own people and to others in the use of its tremendous, but in the end still limited, military power? These will be the moral and practical dilemmas of the world in the early years of the millennium.
>
> *Princeton Lyman*

Princeton Lyman draws also from his personal experience in the making and conduct of the foreign policy of the United States to analyze ways to overcome basic contradictions between a code of universal ethics and the defense by almost any means of the nation-state. He asked two basic questions: in serving national interests should diplomacy be bound by ethics beyond those that relate to the interests of the state? And, should diplomats pursue any means to achieve objectives of the state, whether legal or illegal, or injurious to others or not? Democracies have not always provided morally satisfactory answers to these questions, sometimes precisely because the belief that one's nation is the paradigm of democracy blurs good judgment. Lyman recalls that Hans Morgenthau, whose influence on US thinking on foreign policy has been considerable, was a realist—suspicious of idealistic schemes disconnected from a clear perception of national interest—and at the same time a deeply ethical and moral philosopher. Impractical and hypocritical moralism is as pernicious as the unprincipled pursuit of the national interest. Having written his essay for this book before the events of 11 September 2001, Lyman stated that his government had to find, and will find sufficient means to express its basic ethical principles to its citizenry and to the world. The still small voice of conscience, of morality, perhaps of God, says Princeton Lyman, cannot be ignored.

CHAPTER 14

THE MORAL POWER OF THE UNITED NATIONS

Jacques Baudot

The world needs a more powerful United Nations. First and foremost, peace and security, more than any other time in history, require the organized cooperation of national governments under a legitimate global authority. A great number of increasingly deadly weapons are available to States, organizations, and individuals with aggressive aims. Determined terrorists have horrendous capacity to inflict death and destruction, as tragically experienced by the United States, on the 11ᵗʰ of September 2001. Threats to the integrity of the planet and the pressing need for collective measures provide the second reason for a strengthened United Nations with capacity to promote and enforce international treaties for disarmament, and the environment. And, the globalization of the world economy, made possible by technological innovations and currently shaped by a few public and private actors, also calls for a United Nations with some attributes of a world government. The vast power of the private international economic and financial actors leading the process of economic and cultural globalization must be balanced, regulated, and directed towards the common good of humanity by universal democratic institutions, such as the United Nations.

261

The United Nations has the general mandate and the potential to effectively address the global problems of the 21st century. It has a quasi-universal membership. Its Charter, with some adjustments in the composition and functioning of its principal organs, remains an inspiring document.[1] It has a dedicated and competent international civil service, and many idealistic, young people dream of giving their enthusiasm and energy to such a benevolent and potentially effective international organization. To play an effective role in meeting the international and global issues of the day, the United Nations needs some of the same legislative and executive capacities that are currently exercised by nation states and by some regional organizations. It also needs a judicial branch. The laborious establishment of the International Criminal Court is an important step in this direction. It may even need a permanent police force and a permanent military force to prevent violence and stem conflicts, domestic and international, and to act rapidly when necessary.

But "power," for a universal institution built on high principles and intended to serve humanity with reason and wisdom, cannot be reduced to elementary components. Judicial and military "arms" will not insure the effectiveness of an organization whose essential mandate is the betterment of the human condition. They are, as yet, inadequate instruments to address the symptoms of the diseases of an imperfect world. If these instruments were granted to the United Nations and used in a manner not fundamentally different from that of a nation-state, this institution would lose its *raison d'etre* and its soul. The United Nations is not and should not be a super-state—to be looked upon with awe and fear. It derives its legitimacy from its moral power. It will enhance its ability to bring some harmony into this chaotic world if it deepens its message of peace and solidarity, if it cultivates its ethos of equality and cooperation, and if it conveys to the people the image of an organization dedicated to the pursuit of the common good.

Such moral power of the United Nations has three elements of critical importance: intellectual rigor, ethical clarity, and political imagination.

Intellectual Rigor

In all aspects of its work—peace and security, international law, development, human rights, humanitarian relief—the United Nations needs scrupulous respect for facts. It needs the perspectives of a variety of disciplines to capture the diverse facets of the issues on its agenda, and its needs careful attention to the language it uses. These qualities—objectivity, versatility, and attention to language—define the intellectual rigor that should be one of the sources of the moral power of the United Nations.

Early in its existence, the United Nations acquired a remarkable capacity for assessing issues and objectively measuring demographic, social, and economic trends. Its demographic and statistical publications and its global and regional economic and social surveys rapidly gained a reputation for excellence and objectivity. Likewise, its legal work and publications. Later, efforts were made to develop similar capacities in political affairs and security matters. These efforts were less successful because of the complexities involved in quantifying and measuring such matters and because of the paucity of financial resources and personnel.

Since the end of the 1970s, although maintaining the quality and objectivity of its reports, the United Nation's demographic, social, and economic statistics and publications have increasingly come under the pressure of competition from the publications of other international organizations. The World Bank, notably, was given considerably more resources to devote to this type of activity.[2]

Today, the United Nations still benefits from its reputation for objectivity, but its statistics and analyses reach a limited audience and have less influence than in the past. This situation needs correction. The world should be informed of its current conditions by an organization, which, because of its universality and mode of financing, is in the best position to pursue objectivity as its highest priority.

In addition to a lack of resources and relatively low interest in statistical and research activities currently within the United Nations membership, blurred distinctions between advocacy for a cause and respect for facts are other obstacles to overcome. Less emphasis now needs to be placed on international comparisons including the ranking of countries according to their perform-ance—in whichever domain—and more needs to be placed on glob-al and atypical phenomena. With these changes, the precious repu-tation for objectivity and the capital of trust that the United Nations continues to have would be furthered.

From its beginnings, the United Nations attracted persons from different disciplines. International lawyers, diplomats, econo-mists, statisticians, political scientists, together with some sociolo-gists, anthropologists, and philosophers brought their varied knowl-edge and different perspectives to the work of the Organization. This has not fundamentally changed, but difficulties from the past remain, growing perhaps more prevalent given the wider scope of activities of the United Nations.

The first difficulty is that each domain of activity tends to be overly dominated by a particular discipline: peace and security by diplomacy and law, human rights and humanitarian affairs by inter-national law, development by economics, population studies by demography, and the production of yearbooks and national accounts by statistics and econometrics. The administration and management of the institution itself is dominated by public administration. A cer-tain level of specialization is, of course, desirable to avoid ama-teurism and laxity, but the monopoly of a discipline is rarely advan-tageous. Over the years, departments and offices have tended to acquire a culture of their own, with specific methods of work and specific approaches to the problems under their responsibility. The lack of debate and confrontation between proponents of different dis-ciplines can be a source of conservatism and sclerosis. Economists have something to contribute to the prevention of conflicts, philoso-phers to the understanding and control of the process of globaliza-tion, and anthropologists to the protection of human rights.

The second difficulty with the multidisciplinary work of the United Nations is the integration of its various elements into a coher-ent and readily intelligible whole, intellectually and politically.

For economists to benefit from the views of international lawyers, for diplomats to be aware of the insights of philosophers, and for these exchanges among others to be reflected faithfully and coherently in the main documents, pronouncements, and policies of the Organization, constant and extremely demanding efforts are needed. Overall policy guidance and inspiration is provided to the staff by the annual *Report of the Secretary General on the Work of the Organization*—requested for presentation to the General Assembly by Article 98 of the Charter. This report is both a record of current activities and a program. But, in addition, detailed and time-consuming procedures for cooperation have to be set in place and kept alive. Some of these are already in place and effective. Others tend to generate confusion between the synthesis of different perspectives and the reduction of these to their least common denominator.

The Organization is trying to use several disciplines more effectively and harmoniously to deal with the central questions of development and the process of economic and financial globalization. There, economics, and often economics alone, gives the conceptual framework, the integrating logic, and the operational objectives. Social questions are mainly treated as consequences or as obstacles to economic change and progress.[3] Politics is largely put in parenthesis. Similarly, the human rights discourse is essentially independent of the development discourse.[4] By relying on a more diversified and more integrated set of disciplines, the United Nations can, in these domains, increase its capacity to analyze, in depth, the questions on its agenda. It would also increase its ability to expand its agenda and to deal with issues currently deprived of political visibility or considered too complex to be usefully addressed.

The growing evidence of the multiple dangers that confront humankind and of the problems and limitations of the current process of globalization should encourage the United Nations to develop and propagate a new vision of the world—one where cooperation and altruism would replace egoism and hate, and where material progress would not be an end but a means for moral and spiritual advancement. The 21st century could be the age of a new enlightenment, reestablishing a balance between instrumental reason and normative thinking. It is useful to recall that Adam Smith wrote not only *The Wealth of Nations* but also *The Theory of Moral Sentiments.*[5] He considered economics a critical part of life in society but not an autonomous sphere under which all other institutions and human aspirations should be subordinated. A renaissance of the spirit is a necessary and enormously difficult task, but the United Nations has the capacity to take the lead. Then, a new form of moral and political philosophy, of which many elements at present are under consideration here and there in the world, will become progressively a unifying and integrating discipline in the work of the United Nations.[6] With this ambition, intellectual rigor cannot be separated from moral rigor. But for this, a prerequisite is that the Organization must give considerable attention to the language it uses.

The vehicle for intellectual rigor is a language without ambiguity.[7] And the best and most relevant conclusions, recommendations, and exhortations risk being discarded if not expressed in a sober and clear language. Paraphrasing the famous aphorism of Heidegger one could say that the United Nations is the language that it uses.[8] When its language is soft, vague, flat and excessively prudent, this Organization, as any other, is ineffective. If terms belonging to the current language of market economics were to invade the overall discourse, and therefore, the thinking of the United Nations, this institution would be in the process of losing its soul and vocation. Examples of words with such intrusive power beyond their original sphere of application abound. To mention a few: "shareholders," "stockholders," "consumers," "labor market," "competition," "satisfaction of needs," and the ubiquitous "human resources." These expressions are best kept in the domains of economics and finance.

Ethical Clarity

A moral philosophy, inspiring to the various activities of the United Nations and to the world at large, requires ethical clarity in a context of openness and participation.

The capacity to formulate the question as to whether a particular action is ethical and to provide the answer rests on distinctions between the morally right, the morally wrong, and the morally indifferent. Evident in many cultures and periods of history, this indispensable moral foundation of ethical standards is somewhat shaky in the dominant conception of modernity that shapes the economically advanced societies and the process of globalization.

Excessive moral relativism leads to amorality. The prevalent utilitarian vulgate has severed any relation with two foundations of morality—religion and natural law—and tends to ignore the third, secular humanism. It does not offer much guidance to people, beyond a simplistic and primitive form of hedonism. The result is that both radical moral relativism and various forms of fundamentalism mark the current moral landscape of the world, pressing people into obedience to moral codes imposed by an external authority. And these extremes feed each other. The hedonistic and amoral popular culture of the Western world gives an excuse to those who are maintaining oppressive moral codes. The desires of fundamentalists of all persuasions to put human beings in straitjackets, notably their efforts to hold women captive in situations of subordination, provides an alibi to the ultra-liberals for not reassessing their conception of freedom and responsibility.

The United Nations conferences in the 1990s, and most recently the Millennium Summit, elaborated many principles on which the Organization can draw to orient its policies and make judgments on contemporary problems and issues.[9] Its universality, prestige, traditions of diplomatic restraint, capacity to attract persons of quality from various cultures, and openness to organizations and movements from the non-governmental world make the United Nations the ideal place for debating and deepening the moral and ethical questions that permeate international and global relations. For, if all persons of good will share a common core of moral values that define human decency and human dignity, there is nevertheless considerable room for discussion on the application of these values and on the ethical standards derived from them. Democratic and participatory efforts and debates are crucial in determining these standards and the scope of their domains of implementation. This is not only because all civilizations, traditions, religions, and professions have something to contribute, but, more fundamentally, because codes of morality and ethics become ossified or oppressive, or both, if not constantly immersed in the cauldron of controversies and challenges.

This point on the legitimacy and usefulness of debates and research on moral and ethical questions in the framework of the United Nations deserves further elaboration. It is true that the moral values, which are fully internalized and, therefore, quasi-automatically and unconsciously acted upon by individuals and societies are not normally subject to debate. This is so not necessarily because of fear of doing harm to them, but mostly because there is no felt need for discussion. Moreover, it is generally considered wise not to open Pandora's box. It is also true that pressing ethical issues, as well as seemingly intractable political problems, are sometimes better addressed by the passage of time than by open confrontation.

These arguments, however, have validity for stable and generally consensual societies. They lose much of their relevance in a world of constant change, mobility, insecurity, and violence. And it is to this world that the United Nations must carry its universal message of peace, freedom, solidarity, and justice. This message has a chance to prevail if there is an effective judiciary to prevent and punish international and global criminal acts. The establishment of the International Criminal Court is a step in the right direction. This endeavor, however, must be accompanied by the strengthening or creation of a number of institutions, procedures, and processes through which the people of the world can reflect on the moral values and norms of behavior that are or should be universal.

Would the creation of a commission or committee on moral values and ethics be of assistance to the United Nations in the discharge of this most important function? There are several possible formulas. This body might be permanent or ad-hoc, meeting at the request of the Secretary General. It can be what is called a functional commission, as, for example, the Commission on Population and

Development, or a committee of the General Assembly or the Economic and Social Council. Its members can be representatives of governments, of the civil society—in its various components—and of the private business sector. An alternative to this structure might be a commission made up of individuals selected for their excellence in their disciplines or activities, and for their familiarity with the diverse cultures, traditions, and religions of the world. It can be a body studying and debating general moral principles and their ethical implications, or, using an inductive method of inquiry, a body taking concrete issues of international or global politics and reflecting on their moral dimensions. Or it can do both.

Work on general principles can include the elaboration of a declaration or statement on global ethics, on a core of values to which nobody objects. Lately, there were several attempts of this type at the periphery of the United Nations. Another much more controversial example of the same approach is to revisit the Universal Declaration for Human Rights and its two Covenants on Civil and Political Rights and Economic, Social, and Cultural Rights from the perspective of the moral principles and ethical standards embodied in these legal instruments. The rationale for such reviews would be to strengthen these instruments that were undermined by the Cold War atmosphere that surrounded their adoption.

Examples of projects requiring a more inductive method of work that a United Nations committee or commission, responsible for moral and ethical questions, could adopt are obviously numerous. One example is the study of underlying moral values of the great world conferences of the last decade of the 20th century, their consistency and the conditions for their application. Others include consideration of the moral rationale for official development assistance to developing countries and, more generally, for a redistribution of resources at the world level. Similar examples include: harmonization of an ethic of competition with an ethic of solidarity in a global world economy; harmonization of moral reasons for the search for sustainable patterns of production and consumption; and harmonization between ethics and the role of money in modern economies and societies.

269

This sort of focused work on the moral dimensions of contemporary trends and issues can bridge the current gaps, or even abysses between politics and ethics, economics and morality, and international relations and moral principles. Should the establishment of a "specialized" commission be impossible, or premature, the United Nations has the possibility to continue what it initiated some years ago—the progressive incorporation of an explicit moral and ethical perspective in its deliberations and documents. The Rio Conference on Environment and Development, the Copenhagen World Summit on Social Development and the Millennium Summit are examples of these efforts at constructing a morally viable global economy and community.

Political Imagination

Political imagination is an indispensable ingredient of the moral power of the United Nations.[10] To have it means to treat political constraints as obstacles to be overcome rather than unconquerable boundaries, to offer unexpected solutions to seemingly intractable problems, and to design strategies to address long term issues. It is to decipher the political landscape of the time and to detect opportunities for innovative action. It requires intellectual courage and moral determination, the capacity to read accurately the signs of the time as well as the capacity to stand against the current.

The political imagination of the "ancestors" of the United Nations was remarkable. For example, at the beginning of the 18th century l'Abbé de Saint Pierre proposed, in his "Plan for Perpetual Peace," international agencies to promote cooperation in such domains as commercial law and monetary systems. In his famous "Perpetual Peace," published in 1795, Immanuel Kant imagined a federation of republican states with a congress to settle disputes and a cosmopolitanism based on the right to hospitality for any stranger in any member country.[11] The creation of the United Nations was itself a display of political imagination.[12]

The Charter is a precise treaty and an inspired document. Along its relatively short history the Organization took a number of initiatives, which were not always consistent with the political mainstream. It led the decolonization process. It spearheaded the international struggle against apartheid. It adopted treaties or declarations on the law of the sea, on the use of outer space, on various aspects of the protection of the environment, on racism and discrimination, on equality between women and men, on social justice and the eradication of poverty, and on many facets of the situation of the economically underdeveloped countries.

Success was not always there, even in terms of the recognition of the legitimacy of the concerns expressed by the Organization. For example, the United Nations tried in the 1970s to exert some control on the activities of transnational corporations via the negotiation of a code of conduct. It also tried to orient the development of scientific discoveries and technological innovations towards the common good of humankind.[13] It failed in both cases, because the vested interests in keeping a liberal regime in these domains and the ideological opposition to an enhanced role of the United Nations in the regulation of the world economy were too strong. All the same, the issues remain, and the process of globalization is giving renewed urgency to the democratic control of world private economic and financial powers.

Globalization is, indeed, a prominent example of today's world issues requiring political imagination from the United Nations, on a basis of intellectual rigor and ethical clarity. The United Nations must be instrumental in sorting out the elements of the process that are morally good, such as the growing openness of societies, from those which are wrong, notably the monetization of social relations and the dissemination of a culture of competition and greed. It must also play a leading role in controlling and orienting the various facets of globalization towards the common good of humanity. In turn, this common good has to be democratically debated and defined within a framework of shared moral values. New institutions, new political processes have to be invented to allow for such debates.[14] New articulations and complementarities have to be found between different levels of citizenship and loyalty, from the local and the national to the international and global, and between different institutions having sovereignty, authority, and responsibility in different domains.

An international and global system adapted to the circumstances, opportunities and threats of the 21st century, does not have, however, to be a "rigorous architecture" or a "rigid order."[15] Only totalitarian designs do not leave room for imperfection, imprecision, improvisation, dissent, and change. In leading and guiding the efforts, initiatives, and debates necessary for the building of a democratic, just, and harmonious world community, the United Nations will have to display rigorous and fair political imagination to reconcile peace and pluralism, solidarity and creativity.

Political imagination sometimes means the capacity to revisit the past and the courage to react against powerful trends. Particularly in troubled and rapidly changing times, an institution with its own culture has the right, even the duty to look at its historically honored principles, methods of work, and institutional arrangements that were abandoned or undercut for reasons unrelated to its well-being and efficiency. Often, the opposite of political imagination is a mediocre pragmatism that is nothing more than a thinly disguised cynicism. And, it requires courage to remain unmoved by intellectual fashions and ideological pressures. But the handmaid of courage is humility, without which determined and imaginative political initiatives must bear the mark of arrogance.

Enhancing the moral power of the United Nations, to give it a leading role in addressing the pressing problems of the time, is not a utopian notion. It corresponds to the vocation of the Organization, and to an obvious need. But there are evidently several conditions to be met and obstacles to be overcome, for the United Nations to play this role effectively. Within the limits of this chapter, and focusing on conditions/obstacles which are more or less under the control of the Organization, let us briefly cite four of them: sufficient financial resources, maintenance of a strong international civil service, the presence of non-governmental organizations, and enrichment of the diplomatic culture.

A sound financial basis is a *sine qua non* for the United Nations to function effectively. There are currently three main problems. First, the Organization is forced to operate within the severe constraints of a precarious, uncertain and fragile financial situation.

It is not authorized to borrow money. It is often short of cash and does not have the financial security necessary for innovative policies and long-term programmes. Second, since the launch, at the turn of the 1980s, of what has been called the "reform" of the United Nations, the dominant ideology surrounding this institution is that its work and expenditures should be curbed and reduced.

This objective of a reduced or stable level of expenditure, rather than the assessment of the activities that the Organization needs to perform, determines the beginning and the end of the budgetary process. Solutions to the financial difficulties and constraints of the United Nations are increasingly sought from voluntary contributions, especially from the private business sector. This is not appropriate for a public institution entrusted with the defense of the general interest. However generous and disinterested private donors may be, the United Nations loses moral authority and political credibility if it opens itself to suspicion of collusion with the profit-making sector. The United Nations is the type of institution that ought only to be financed from contributions of its Member States and from international or global taxes.

In Chapter XV of the Charter of the United Nations, devoted to the Secretariat, Article 101 states: "[T]he paramount consideration in the employment of the staff and in the determination of the conditions of service shall be the necessity of securing the highest standards of efficiency; competence, and integrity. Due regard shall be paid to the importance of recruiting the staff on as wide a geographical basis as possible." During the first decades of its existence, the Organization built a strong international civil service, multicultural, multilingual, and yet cohesive and united by a common ideal. It is still alive, but in serious danger. The neo-liberal ideological wave that swept the world at the turn of the 1980s targeted the international civil service for several "reforms." Independence of the staff of the United Nations was put in question when high-level personnel were increasingly seconded from their governments. Security, hence independence, and also "esprit de corps," were damaged when long-term contracts ceased to be granted. These "reforms," plus diminished control of the General Assembly over the resources of the United Nations led to a reduction of the staff financed by the regular budget. These conditions were aggravated by an increase of the number of staff financed from extra-budgetary sources or directly seconded by governments or private organizations. In addition, elements of a corporate culture, ill-suited to the traditions and mandates of the Organization, began to develop. In many respects, a deliberate attempt was made to "privatize" the Secretariat of the United Nations. Reversal of this trend is of the utmost importance for the future role of the Organization.

Pressure from competent and dedicated non-governmental organizations (NGOs), is necessary for the United Nations to develop its moral influence. It would be wrong, however, to assume that only the NGOs can bring fresh and generous ideas into the United Nations' forums. The Secretariat and representatives of Member States also play innovative roles. But it would be even more erroneous to consider the NGO community merely as an adjunct to the intergovernmental bodies that structure the United Nations. Many of the persons who devote their time and energy to influence the policies of the world body are citizens of the world seeking neither power nor recognition, but only the advancement of causes that are in the general interest of humanity. Their role is critical in the building of that global democracy whose contours and processes are still vague, but whose necessity is beyond doubt. Ideas such as the convening of a World Peoples Assembly should be explored. Also, the relationships between the United Nations and the intellectual, artistic, and scientific communities should be greatly enhanced. Beyond recruiting occasional consultants, the Organization would greatly benefit from the knowledge and views of individuals striving for excellence in various domains.

The diplomatic culture has many instrumental and "procedural" virtues. These include civility, tolerance, and desire to search for compromises. This culture implies a minimum of respect for the other, either colleague or nation. Its formalism is a good protection against excesses of all types. Peaceful international relations would be severely jeopardized if, with the current preeminence of the corporate culture, the diplomatic culture were to be abandoned as a vestige of the past. At the same time, while perfectly suited to relations among states within an institution in charge of maintaining peace and security, the diplomatic culture is much less able to address global issues requiring innovative ideas and forceful actions in favor of the common good. Development of poor countries, promotion of human rights, protection of the environment, regulation of the activities of transnational corporations, and, *a fortiori,* the struggle against international corruption, crime, and terrorism, all require much more than diplomatic suavity. An ethic of conviction is also needed to guide action according to moral principles and sacrifice short terms gains to the attainment of long term objectives. Applied to the culture of the United Nations, this ethic places the traditional attributes of power at the service of the common good of humankind. It is the antidote to opportunism and expediency.

Such are the main dimensions of the moral power of the United Nations and some of the conditions for its enhancement. The state of the world, today, is reason for renewed determination to strengthen this institution, which has the vocation and mandate to promote the common good of humanity.

Endnotes

1 - The Charter of the United Nations was signed in San Francisco on 26 June 1945 and came into force on 24 October 1945. It is a treaty, obligating the members of the U.N. to respect its provisions. Its preamble and its first chapter, on Purposes and Principles, outline the main elements of a philosophy of international cooperation for "the promotion of the economic and social advancement of all peoples". With the Charter, the International Declaration of Human Rights, can be considered the major founding text of the United Nations. Its Article I reads: "All human beings are born free and equal in dignity and rights. They are endowed with reason and conscience and should act towards one another in a spirit of brotherhood." And, Article 29 starts as follows: "Everyone has duties to the community, in which alone, the free and full development of his personality is possible."

2 - The main regular surveys produced by the United Nations are the World Economic Survey, the Report on the World Social Situation, both from the Department of Economic and Social Affairs, and the Trade and Development Report, issued by the United Nations Conference for Trade and Development (UNCTAD). The United Nations Development Programme (UNDP), financed by voluntary contributions of the industrialized countries, produces the Human Development Report, and the World Bank produces, also annually, the World Development Report.

3 - The World Summit for Social Development, a United Nations Conference held in Copenhagen, Denmark, in March 1995, and attended by 117 heads of State or Government, produced the Copenhagen Declaration on Social Development which stems from a different logic. "Social" is taken in a comprehensive sense, meaning the well-being of individuals and the functioning of societies, and treating the economic as a means to achieve social goals. The implementation of this approach in the work of the United Nations would have far-reaching consequences and can only be progressive. The Copenhagen Declaration is also the first reference in a United Nations text to the responsibility of societies to "respond more effectively to the material and spiritual needs of individuals, their families and the communities in which they live." See World Summit for Social Development (New York: United Nations, 1995), 3.

4 - Human Rights instruments include the Covenant on Economic, Social and Cultural Rights, which is a treaty, and the Right to Development, which is still essentially a declaration. But there is very little relation between the monitoring of the implementation of this Covenant by the Center for Human Rights and the work of the Department for Economic and Social Affairs. And the Right to Development has yet to be fully recognized by the main powers of the United Nations membership.

5 - *The Theory of Moral Sentiments* was first published in 1759 and *The Wealth of Nations* in 1776. For a convincing explanation that there is no contradiction between the ethical message of the two books, and no fundamental changes in the thinking of Adam Smith who was a moral philosopher strongly influenced by the Stoics, see Adam Smith, *The Theory of Moral Sentiments,* ed. by D.D. Raphael and A.L. Macfie (Indianapolis: Liberty Fund, 1984).

6 - An example of this search for a renewed intellectual and moral framework for global relations can be found in *Building a World Community, Globalisation and the Common Good*, ed. by Jacques Baudot (with the Royal Danish Ministry of Foreign Affairs, Copenhagen), (Seattle: University of Washington Press, 2001).

7 - The second Secretary General of the United Nations, Dag Hammarskjold, wrote: "Respect for the word—to employ it with scrupulous care and incorruptible heartfelt love of truth—is essential if there is to be any growth in a society or in the human race. To misuse the word is to show contempt for man. It undermines the bridges and poisons the wells. It causes Man to regress down the long path of his evolution." See *Markings*, (New York, Alfred A. Knopf, 1965), 112.

8 - Heidegger wrote that "we do not so much have a language as it has us." He is quoted by Terence Ball, "Imagining Marketopia," in *Dissent*, Summer 2001.

9 - The United Millennium Declaration, adopted by the General Assembly on 8 September 2000, had Heads of State and Government of most countries of the world reaffirm their faith "in the Organization and its Charter as indispensable foundations of a more peaceful, prosperous and just world" and recognize their "collective responsibility to uphold the principles of human dignity, equality and equity at the global level." In this same declaration, freedom, equality, solidarity, tolerance, respect for nature, and shared responsibility are seen as values "essential to international relations in the 21st century." See *United Nations Millennium Declaration*, General Assembly, Fifty-fifth session, Resolution 55/2.

10 - The notion of "political imagination" is borrowed from Richard Falk. He referred to the need for such quality during his participation in the Copenhagen Seminars for Social Development organized by the Danish Government in the context of the follow-up to the World Summit for Social Development. Richard Falk developed the same idea in *Predatory Globalization: A Critique* (Cambridge, U.K.: Polity, 1999), 58-63 and 182-184.

11 - A recent French edition of Kant's *Vers la Paix Perpetuelle*, together with other texts of the same author, contains a very useful introduction by Francoise Proust, notably on Kant's cosmopolitism as a political principle linking citizens of each State through the experience of freedom; see Immanuel Kant, *Vers la Paix Perpetuelle* (Paris: Flammarion, 1991).

12 - For a summary of the origins of international organizations, see in particular A. LeRoy Bennet, *International Organizations, Principles and Issues*, (New York: Prentice Hall International, 1995), 1-23.

13 - The Center on Transnational Corporations and the Center on Science and Technology for Development were created at the beginning of the 1970s within the Secretariat of the United Nations, in New York. They were de-facto suppressed in the context of the "reform" of the UN at the beginning of the

1980s. In the same vein, but more ambitiously and more ideologically, the Declaration on a New International economic Order (NIEO) and the Charter on Economic Rights and Duties of States, were adopted by the General Assembly in 1974-1975, at the initiative of developing countries, with the concurrence of the European countries, and against the strong opposition of the United States. The aim of these texts was a redistribution of economic power in the world. Keys provisions were the right of every state to manage and own its natural resources, and to regulate foreign investment and the activities of transnational corporations. The protection of the environment was seen as a common responsibility. Such vision of an egalitarian world order was swept away in the United Nations and in the world by the neo-liberal revolution of the beginning of the 1980s, made possible in particular by the collapse of the Soviet Union.

14 - For several seminal ideas on new institutional arrangements for the United Nations, see our *Global Neighborhood: The Report of the Commission on Global Governance* (New York: Oxford University Press, 1995). This report contains, in particular, the proposal to create an Economic and Social Security Council. This idea was taken again in June 2001, in the Report of the High Level Panel on Financing for Development, by a group of 11 high level international experts convened by the Secretary General of the United Nations and presided by former Mexican President Ernesto Zedillo.

15 - For an excellent outline of a pluralistic and democratic world system, see Michael Walzer, "Governing the Globe," in *Dissent,* Fall 2000.

CHAPTER 15

DEVELOPMENT REFLECTING HUMAN VALUES

Robert E. Gamer

A moral action is an action in which we actualize ourselves within person-to-person encounters. Its principles are the love whose backbone is justice; the love which, though unconditional itself, listens to the concrete situation and its changes, and is guided by the wisdom of the past.[1]

Paul Tillich

Development inherently disrupts the material conditions and human interactions through which specific cultures and values are maintained. In the most favorable circumstances, and especially when development is endogenous and progressive, a new culture and new or modified values emerge to maintain a community. In many countries of the South, values have already been severely disrupted by Western colonialism and imperialism. Modern development efforts bring further disruptions, because development policies, strategies, advice and assistance do not pay enough attention to the concrete structures; customs; habits of the hand, of the mind, and of the heart; and, therefore, human values of the peoples who are supposed to be helped. Development is a legitimate universal project and aspiration, which has only concrete, specific, essentially local manifestations.

Theologian Paul Tillich plumbs the depths of a Christian paradox. Christians believe in human progress and adherence to principles. They also believe in doing unto others as they would have others do unto them. What happens when notions of progress and principles leave decision makers inattentive to, and indeed place them in conflict with the human needs and desires of those they serve? In an ideal world, these leaders would follow the Golden Rule when making choices to promote progress for everyone. This is what Tillich suggests in order to resolve this paradox—that those in charge listen to those people whom progress is designed to serve.

While, trying new things involves risk, there is risk also in adhering slavishly to past wisdom. "No moral law fits any concrete situation totally."[2] But in order for decision-makers to practice the Golden Rule, they must be aware of how their actions impact the values of others.

Development meets some people's needs. At the same time, it harms others' interests. In the Western world, urban planners consider how their schemes affect such values. Because every member of a household has different needs, planners use extensive surveys, interviews, focus groups, and community meetings to develop a strategy. That accords with Tillich's moral imperative to listen to concrete situations on a person-to-person basis; there is no substitute for asking those concerned.

When Western social scientists prescribed political development for the South, their principles for action were based on western liberal ideology and experience—terms that now seem ignorant of both the historical experiences of targeted countries and individuals' values and needs. Their remedies worked in the North, so why not in countries at other, albeit very different, stages of social and economic development? They consulted with countries' leaders, but not with ordinary citizens who were seldom in a position to share their leaders' visions. These planners failed to observe Tillich's moral imperative.

One American theorist saw development in the new nation-states as a passage through five crises: creating national identity, legitimacy for national leaders, broad citizen participation, fair distribution of goods and services, and penetration of national institutions into all regions.[3] Tradition must give way to modernity, led by the middle class, industrial labor, the intelligentsia, and modern bureaucracy. Conceding that this progression might cause unspecified pain to individuals, he did not examine—as Tillich would have—how it could improve lives or accord with values. Are cultural nationalism, delegitimization of traditional elites, participation by powerful radicals, penetration of police surveillance, and the supply of all kinds of goods: goals individuals do or should cherish? Why must tradition give way?

Other scholars defined development in terms equally insulated from considerations of their impact on individuals in the South. They viewed it as balance between a process of social mobilization (increases in income, literacy, and availability of media) and a process of assimilation into modern social groupings,[4] coercion and information,[5] mass mobilization and institutionalization,[6] or inputs into and outputs from government.[7] One theory[8] saw the need for an intelligentsia[9] and bureaucracy with will and ability to transform imbalances in the direction of intrinsic capacity to generate and absorb continuing transformation. None of these scholars explored how balances might relate to human values in concrete situations, or improve individual well-being. They pursued Western principles as if it were moral law, without Tillich's personal encounter.

Dependency theorists, viewing development as reducing imperialist exploitation, also avoided examining individual values. They proposed self-sustained industrialization,[10] emphasizing language and culture as unifying themes, and strengthening elements of the army, bureaucracy, religious leadership, and land ownership.[11] One theorist suggested people need new consumer goods, education, and lifestyles to adapt to industrialization; no one discussed how industrialization and cultural nationalism harm individuals.[12] They gave little attention to how even nationalized industry might improve consumption, reduce dependency, or otherwise improve lives.

Addressing Individual Needs

The primary concern of many people in the South is getting adequate food, housing, and community support. While working in South and Eastern Asia, I saw factories built amid squatter colonies, and the Green Revolution pushing villagers from their land. In traditional Western economic terms, these developments are beneficial, but I wondered how they squared with the values of these people. Rather than macro balances among social, political, and economic institutions and forces, individuals need personal balances such as whether they have a job that allows them to support their children, or both a house and a neighborhood that is pleasing to them. How do we achieve those balances?

I defined people with satisfying personal environments as those with enough food; adequate health care; affordable, satisfying housing; agreeable neighbors and cultural surroundings; a stable, gratifying job offering above-subsistence income; and appropriate multi-generational education.[13] Every individual differs in what is satisfying, and changes such a notion as he or she grows older. To apply the Golden Rule in development policy, the decision-maker must assess the impact of the intended project on individual needs and desires in each of these realms.

This assessment is difficult because some individuals focus primarily on material comfort or even ostentation as they approach these aspects of their personal environment, while others concentrate more on relationships, solitude, aesthetics, or spiritual achievement. Sometimes people who are dissatisfied with their personal environment produce great art and show deep compassion. This does not provide sufficient reason, however, to ignore people's desires. If development experts ignore the wishes of those they are trying to assist, they will end up treating them more as passive objects than human beings with spirit. Therefore the task requires listening to people's desires, or at least modifying their values by socialization and persuasion, rather than imposing one's own values on them.

In Canada, the United States, and Western Europe, high employment and government services help assure that large portions of the population are satisfied with the balances among the various aspects of their personal environment. But in many developing countries close-knit communities that formerly guaranteed these balances are gone. Those few individuals with ties to landowners or bureaucrats may achieve satisfying personal environments. The rest are barely employed. Those are the people—the least of these my brethren—but the vast majority of the populace, who must be recipients of the unconditional love referred to by Tillich in the quote above. To make them such, we must listen to their needs.

That requires more than increasing the Gross National Product (GNP), or even distributing houses, schools, hospitals, roads, jobs, free speech, and participation in government. These projects can actually exacerbate imbalances between values and environment. People outside "safety nets" may spend money needed for food, clothing, and shelter on unnecessary luxury items. Media images can breed discontent. A nice new house may be unaffordable and far from work. Greater freedom can tempt people to destroy families, spread hatred, harm other groups, or disrupt order. Those monopolizing land, education, and commerce might find it easier to retain control. None of this accords with the Golden Rule, which calls for concrete solutions when development initiatives disrupt lives.

Wisdom in Accessing Personal Environments

The wisdom of the past implores us to examine another factor in assessing personal environments. This is the role export economies play in concentrating power and control of resources. Personal environments were more in balance before international trade started the process now called globalization.[14] Those villages had communal land tenure, and councils of elders determined distribution and use of land and food, and settled disputes. James C. Scott argues that their "moral economy" guaranteed everyone subsistence needs.[15] Samuel Popkin shows this did not shield villagers from arguments, jealousies, and attempts to better one family at the expense of another.[16] But the communities, themselves, controlled most aspects of inhabitants' personal environments and this is why they should be called "interfamily political systems." For Plato, the dual political role of the polis was to assure the community a good life and the individual an eternal destiny. The common norms and rituals through which interfamily villagers defined their ideal personal environments entwined those two goals and blended religion with politics and economics. Personal fulfillment and civic responsibility required fulfilling economic obligations to fellow villagers.

Three millennia ago in China, two millennia ago in Japan and in medieval Europe, interfamily systems evolved into manorial rule; noble families took the land and turned villagers into dependent clients. When European and the Middle Eastern traders started plying world seas in the fifteenth century they extended that patron-client relation by prompting breakdown in communal land tenure and self-sufficient inter—family villages. Then some villagers no longer needed to obey community norms; they could support themselves as patrons and clients helping these foreign patrons export local commodities. Then the patrons used guns and cadastral surveys to commandeer village land and drive out the majority of villagers not needed as clients. The villagers could find few jobs in the new cities—formed as a result of these movements. Interfamily systems, sharing power among all community families, gave way to patron-client systems with power shared by a few patrons with their few clients, leaving the rest powerless.

Today, this process has become a globalized phenomenon. The numbers of powerless, "the rest"—deprived of community and land, and unable to assimilate into cities or modern economies—has burgeoned. The resources whose exchange provided material sustenance and spiritual bonds of interfamily interdependence belong to a few families who use them as commodities for export. They employ only small percentages of the existing population, whom they can attract with low wages. The others, the unemployed who are not needed by this new system, have little voice in government and receive scant assistance from political leaders. Such has been the result of globalization, which radically shrank the portion of the Third World populace experiencing satisfying personal environments; this condition persists.

Globalization, however, has largely expanded satisfying personal environments in places where the Industrial Revolution began. New European cities brought decline to patron-client relations in surrounding villages. Its leaders put people to work creating low-cost goods and services. Businesses sought to sell products at home, paying workers enough to become customers. These nations became corporate-consumer systems. Their governments encouraged full employment and internal consumption to keep the economy strong, and also fostered world trade. Third World patrons bought these cities' manufactured products and sold them cheap raw materials.

The same dynamics and interdependencies that created the two systems of the North and the South stay in place as modernization through globalization progresses. Patron-client systems do not transform Third World societies into corporate-consumer systems because the patrons are against such change. While the patrons' wealth and influence grows, satisfying personal environments are prevented from proliferating.

Present globalization processes continue to separate the material and political realms from the values that sustain communities. In the past, interfamily political systems demanded that all elements requisite for a satisfying personal environment be distributed to each community member through an inviolable ethical contract. Today, patron-client and corporate-consumer systems distribute those elements through interplay of market forces and political influence. Those without property or influence are left out or short-changed. Meanwhile, citizens have been persuaded by moderniza-tion forces that material conditions and contractual obligations are unrelated to the fulfillment of the human spirit. The nature and des-tiny of individuals and of the community are explored as separate realms, and politics examined apart from both. The sacred fruits of the earth that enable humans to bond into communities and guaran-tee their members satisfying personal environments have been reduced to property. The state guarantees personal property rights, but not the right to a satisfying personal environment. Individuals owe allegiance to the state, but not the community. Technological change renders obsolete the very norms that limit its influence. It replaces shared experience and empathy with unlimited self-aggran-dizement, consumerism, social intercourse based on market ration-ality, and impersonal altruism. Such contemplation of the "self" opposes and inhibits both moral and spiritual experience.

Approaches to Personal Environments

Emphasis on personal environments is compatible with and adds new dimensions to two theoretical approaches: rational choice and neo-institutionalism. Rational choice theory has wide populari-ty in social sciences. Anthony Downs saw voters motivated by self-interest, and governments responding with programs.[17] Current development programming operates on such a premise. People want and need clean water, sewers, houses, and schools; agencies respond to those choices. If people want satisfying personal environments, rational choice becomes more complex. In the Third World that means persuading those controlling most of the land and resources to help internal markets and unemployed people. So long as they can make the rational choice to stay wealthy by selling largely to foreign markets they can ignore most of their own people. How does one provide them with rational reasons to spread food, jobs, gov-ernment subsidies and other resources among "their" people? If they pocket most of the money earmarked for clean village water, or build dams or ports diverting jobs and money away from the home market, they harm personal environments.

Neo-institutionalists analyze political behavior limited by cultural and institutional constraints. Joel Migdal sees triangles of accommodation among middle level bureaucrats, their supervisors, and local strongmen controlling resources in Third World countries.[18] This concurs with Fred W. Riggs' concept of dependency syndromes where entrepreneurs consume a large portion of the national product, sharing with public officials in exchange for protection.[19] Peasants, plantation workers, craftsmen, and assembly line workers—the producers—give back nearly everything they earn to pay their obligations to entrepreneurs and bureaucrats. The elite then passes profits around to one another as bribes, taxes, banquets, public works, and sinecures.

This negative development harms personal environments of those left out of the exchanges, draining capital investment and resources from those who originally had and need them. The challenge is to spread resources beyond these few. This cannot be done piecemeal. Individual programs to introduce rational approaches in business-government relations, change recruitment, eliminate government intrusion into business, or aid the materially impoverished, become entangled in these reciprocities. Elites subvert reforms to perpetuate the dependency syndrome.

Globalism feeds into this negative situation by continuing to provide external markets to those in control of Third World resources, giving them steady profits to further entrench their power; thus avoiding reform, popular participation, and a switch to production for internal consumption. It also gives them access to vast capital resources from international agencies.

Rethinking Development Projects

For all the above reasons, one needs to seriously rethink some development activities, noting their effect on personal environments:

• Development loans and grants
International agencies often bring bits-and-pieces modernization, disregarding impacts on cultures, values, and recipients' overall personal environments. The World Bank, Asia Development

Bank, and many other funding organizations give little attention to projects (especially in the informal sector) that promote internal commerce without enhancing international trade.[20] These agencies and local elites often favor projects exploiting labor, forests, agriculture, and minerals for export. They ought to think about the local populace and markets as well, providing housing, schools, medical facilities, guidance counseling, jobs, and strategies to assure workers continuing employment and assimilation into modern communities that can generate additional jobs. They ought to ask themselves two questions: Are the overall personal environments of those displaced and unemployed improved by the projects?[21] Will these projects generate future jobs?

- Keynesian economics
  Since the founding of the International Monetary Fund in 1944, aid agencies have focused on regulating monetary exchange, raising interest rates, lowering government expenses, and raising or lowering tariffs and taxes when giving loans or guaranteeing investments. They should also examine profitability, transparency, and turnover in capital investment. Is profit likely amid leveraging and distributions to relatives and political supporters? Is there public accounting of bank collateral, corporate earnings, and disbursement of funds? How many goods produced will be consumed there? Will workers earn enough to buy them and generate more internal investment? If fired during a downturn, will they be as well off as before they took the jobs? Will the businesses create ecological problems that degrade personal environments and cost government money?

- Bank bailouts
  Government defaults on repaying loans present opportunities. Instead of restructuring and providing guarantees, international agencies might consider forgiving them in exchange for shutting off future letters of credit and a moratorium on loans for outside trade. Loans or grants encouraging production for local consumption could continue—NGO small loans to women, loans to help develop local agriculture markets and small business and village water projects, and World Bank infrastructure projects. Farsighted

private foreign investors and export-deprived local patrons could set up plants selling to local markets and drawing more people into the formal economy. Such a radical approach has never been tried. The biggest obstacle is the idea—revered as economic law—that development requires free trade; therefore, loans and guarantees should encourage international trade. In a country where this is tried but government cannot repay, one might favor a policy based on generating investment in internal, rather than foreign markets.[22] No general law fits any situation totally.

- Education
Radical increases in high school and university admissions without commensurate job opportunities for graduates helped recruit Peru's Sendero Luminoso revolutionary armies. Countries undergoing change must help their populace adapt through education extending beyond school, but not beyond job horizons. Proper education helps individuals achieve their true-selves. Education must be universal, but also compatible with the culture, life experiences, and future employment of those it trains. Otherwise it can actually harm personal environments, fostering dissonances between knowledge and experience, and goals and potential.

- The organizational culture of international agencies
To approach personal environments holistically, agencies must address their own organizational cultures. They have three constituencies: those providing funding, those acting as national hosts, and those directly affected by projects. The first two directly elect these agencies to serve them, have numerous channels to communicate their views, and cannot be kept from the bargaining table. The third, often the economically poor in villages or urban areas, do not elect these agencies and cannot demand a place at the table. Because their perceived needs may be hard to reconcile with plans, it is easiest to "represent" them through surrogates. Anthropologists, sociologists, and social workers who interact closely and regularly with affected groups are cautious about recommending changes to their way of life, and may not interface easily with host governments or international agencies. Yet they are better positioned to articulate needs and views of those individuals

than experts flown from abroad or associates of host governments. It is important to recognize that their presence in project assessment is inherently adversarial (like any advocacy) but vital to achieve compatibility with values of affected people, whose concrete situations are far removed from the concrete situations of hosts and donors, but lay right in the path of the projects themselves.[23] Therefore, it is essential that these people have a place at the table, even when individuals in host and donor organizations do not want them and procedures only allow them to be represented obliquely. Moreover, the representatives of government and international agencies must be individuals the local people trust, with whom they have regular person-to-person encounters, who understand their concrete situation and its changes.

In general, because satisfying personal environments require balance among several aspects of life, agencies that affect those aspects must coordinate. Together, they must think of the overall personal environments of their funders, hosts, and those affected as they generate and implement projects. If serious about those missions, agencies will constantly adapt comfortable routines, assess qualitatively as well as quantitatively, and work with individuals and ideas unpopular among hosts and other agencies. They must also be prepared to cancel projects whose implementation veers from initial objectives and to pay for cleanup after them. Politically, that is seldom easy. Abandoned dams, roads, houses, piers, and air strips, accompanied by tales about individuals who took money and ran, are archeological monuments to the disconnect between lending agencies and personal environments of their Third World constituents.

Conclusion

The great majority of the peoples of the Third World have failed to achieve satisfying personal environments because the few enjoying such environments control the resources others need to achieve them. Control of those resources must be more widely distributed. That will not happen through some friendly osmosis. Those with the resources will try to keep them. Individuals in national and international bureaucracies with temporary responsibility for resources can help spread them if they develop the will and capacity to channel the assets into projects beyond the grasp of this elite. To do that, these officials must learn to empower a different constituency. In Paul Tillich's thoughts, such justice is achieved by meeting potential persons and acknowledging them as real persons, by listening to their concrete situations and uniting with them through love—through the Golden Rule. Development must move out of the grip of a few, away from mass politics based on race and communal appeals, via a politics based on a broader spectrum of citizens with economic and political influence.

An emphasis on home markets could trigger a political and moral renaissance. The inviolable norms that bonded interfamily communities are unlikely to return. But those in informal economies cooperate to find and cook food, operate street markets, guard households, repay NGO loans, resist authorities, march in rallies, hold and expand squatting territory, fight aggressors, and otherwise survive. They live in close proximity and group together to obtain water, fuel, vaccinations, and other necessities. They treat goods less as property than as material needs to exchange. They repair old vehicles and radios, work in teams with simple tools, walk, keep animals, forage, live on marginal lands exposed to the elements, and revere sacred lands, giving them praxis with nature. They respect blood and communal ties. Some still practice communal land ownership. Many obey religious leaders calling for adherence to community norms, including bans on usury. These are people with deep moral and spiritual resources. They might be more prone than we can imagine, in the most change-driven regions of the globalized world, to use expanded market and political opportunity for community sharing rather than simply individual accumulation, reuniting instead of separating the material and the moral. They might think of marketing to satisfy needs rather than to multiply wants. They may use recycling and appropriate technology, seek fulfillment in labor and transcendent values in education, freeing time for meditation, and deriving meaning from ordinary life rather than growth for the sake of growth. That alternate vision of economic progress and human potential, with well-being measured not by increased consumption but by a spread of satisfying personal environments, is at least worth exploring.

Unconditional love requires person-to-person encounters with the recipients of the love. Such encounters can both broaden the economic and political influence of those who require such grace and help the donors to actualize themselves as caring moral beings.

John C. Bennett declared that:

> It is hard to keep self-interest enlightened (...) It is necessary to have those in public office who really care for the welfare of other peoples. To seek to do the will of God in our concrete situation is to seek the good of all his children.[24]

In a book dedicated to Bennett, Reinhold Niebuhr remarks: "Every experience proves that the real problem of our existence lies in the fact that we ought to love one another, but do not." He suggests that this cannot be remedied by "some simple moral word, which will resolve by love the tragic conflict in the world community." Niebuhr asks us "to set all propositions of justice under the law of love," thus creating "the freedom and maneuverability necessary to achieve a tolerable accord between men and nations in ever more complex human relations."[25] This realism does not allow us to ignore what is right; it reminds us that doing what is right is a difficult imperative, moving beyond principles and procedures into the creative tension of struggling to understand unfamiliar settings. Those settings must include those we purport to help.

Endnotes

1 - Paul J. Tillich, "Ethical Principles of Moral Action" in Wayne G. Boulton, Thomas D. Kennedy, and Allen Verhey, eds., *From Christ To the World* (Grand Rapids, MI: William D. Eerdmans Publishing Company, 1994), 251.

2 - Idem, 250.

3 - Leonard Binder, "The Crises of Political Development," in Leonard Binder et al., eds., *Crises and Sequences in Political Development* (Princeton: Princeton University Press, 1971), 3-72. For summaries of theories in this paragraph and next, and others, see Robert E. Gamer, *The Developing Nations: A Comparative Perspective,* 2nd. ed. (Boston: Allyn and Bacon, 1982), 226-287.

4 - Karl W. Deutsch, *The Nerves of Government* (New York: The Free Press, 1966); *Nationalism and Social Communication* (Cambridge, MIT, 1966).

5 - David E. Apter, *The Politics of Modernization* (Chicago: University of Chicago Press, 1965); "A Comparative Method of the Study of Politics," *American Journal of Sociology* 64 (November 1958): 221-237.

6 - Samuel P. Huntington, "Political Development and Political Decay," *World Politics* 17 (April 1965): 386-430; *Political Order in Changing Societies* (New Haven: Yale University Press, 1968).

7 - Gabriel A. Almond, Taylor Cole, and Roy C. Macridis, "A Suggested Research Strategy in Western European Government and Politics," *American Political Science Review* 49 (December 1955): 1042-1049; Gabriel A. Almond and G. Bingham Powell, Jr., *Comparative Politics: A Developmental Approach* (Boston: Little Brown, 1966); Gabriel A. Almond, Scott C. Flanagan, and Robert J. Mundt (eds.), *Crisis, Choice, and Change: Historical Studies of Political Development* (Boston: Little Brown, 1974).

8 - Manfred Halpern, *The Politics of Social Change in the Middle East and North Africa* (Princeton: Rand, 1963); "The Revolution of Modernization in National and International Society," in Carl J. Friedrich, *Revolution-Nomos* VIII (New York: Atherton, 1966); "The Rate and Costs of Political Development," *The Annals* 358 (March 1965): 20-28; "A Redefinition of the Revolutionary Situation," *Journal of International Affairs* 22 (1969): 54-74; "Egypt and the New Middle Class: Reaffirmations and New Explorations," *Comparative Studies in Society and History* 11, no. 1. (January 1969): 97-108.

9 - John H. Kautsky, *The Political Consequences of Modernization* (New York: John Wiley, 1972). Kautsky called these individuals "modernizers."

10 - James D. Cockcroft, Andre Gunder Frank, and Dale L. Johnson, *Dependence and Underdevelopment: Latin America's Political Economy* (Garden City, NY: Doubleday, 1972).

11 - Immanuel Wallerstein, *The Modern World System: Capitalist Agriculture and the Origins of the European World-Economy in the Sixteenth Century* (New York: Academic Press, 1974).

12 - Irving Louis Horowitz, *Three Worlds of Development: The Theory and Practice of International Stratification* (New York: Oxford University Press, 1966).

13 - Gamer, *The Developing Nations,* 8-9; Robert E. Gamer, *Governments and Politics in A Changing World* (Madison, WI: Brown and Benchmark, 1994), 480-481.

14 - Gamer, *The Developing Nations,* 12-16; Gamer, *Governments and Politics,* 479-491.

15 - James C. Scott, *The Moral Economy of the Peasant: Rebellion and Subsistence in Southeast Asia* (New Haven: Yale University Press, 1976); *Seeing Like A State: How Certain Schemes to Improve the Human Condition Have Failed* (New Haven: Yale University Press, 1998).

16 - Samuel L. Popkin, *The Rational Peasant: The Political Economy of Rural Society in Vietnam* (Berkeley: University of California Press, 1979).

17 - Anthony Downs, *An Economic Theory of Democracy* (New York: Harper and Row, 1957).

18 - Joel S. Migdal, *Strong Societies and Weak States: State-Society Relations and State Capabilities in the Third World* (Princeton: Princeton University Press, 1988); Joel S. Migdal, Atul Kohli, and Vivienne Shue, *State Power and Social Forces* (Cambridge: Cambridge University Press, 1994).

19 - Fred W. Riggs, *Administration in Developing Countries: The Theory of Prismatic Society* (Boston: Houghton Mifflin, 1964).

20 - See Robert E. Gamer, *The Politics of Urban Development in Singapore* (Ithaca: Cornell University Press, 1972), 114-127; Hernando de Soto, *The Other Path: The Invisible Revolution in the Third World* (New York: Harper and Row, 1989).

21 - Gilbert Rist, *The History of Development: From Western Origins to Global Faith* (London: Zed Books, 1997), 207-210, 243-245.

22 - Gamer, *The Developing Nations,* 385-395.

23 - See David Price, *Before the Bulldozer: The Nambiquara Indians and the World Bank* (Cabin John, MD: Seven Locks Press, 1989).

24 - John C. Bennett, *Christian Ethics and Social Policy* (New York: Charles Scribner, 1950), 60, 64.

25 - Reinhold Niebuhr, *Christian Realism and Political Problems* (New York: Charles Scribner, 1953), 109-110.

CHAPTER 16

LANGUAGE AND THE HUMAN SPIRIT

Vigdis Finnbogadóttir and Birna Arnbjörnsdóttir

Every nation should treasure its language, just as it should treasure its natural surroundings, its heritage, and its means of sustenance. More than the eloquence of its sounds and structure, language is the voice of a nation's thought, the vehicle of its history, and the seat of its learning and experience.

Language provides the most systematic mirror of the human mind. Language is the thread that binds a culture and community in a common heritage of memory, poetry, and song. The *Universal Declaration of Linguistic Rights*, adopted by numerous institutions and non-governmental organizations participating in the World Conference on Linguistic Rights, in Barcelona, 8 June 1996, describes languages as "the expression of a collective identity and of a distinct way of perceiving and describing reality."[1] Being collectively constituted, languages are available within the "community for individual use as tools of cohesion, identification, communication, and creative expression."[2] A community that loses its language loses a sacred part of its identity because this is the treasure chest of experience passed from one generation to another.

The vital importance of languages and the necessity to protect linguistic diversity have largely been overlooked in the tumultuous rush towards economic globalization. In a global market society, language diversity would seem to be unnecessary. Certainly this would be the case if the essence of human activity is to be centered exclusively on production, commerce, and consumption, which we see encouraged by the global network of transnational corporations communicating in what is fast becoming a single dominant tongue.

Language diversity is like a tapestry woven with thousands of threads in different hues. The vast array of traditions and rituals sustain the body of the tapestry. As a language is lost, one thread fades. As another disappears, the fading spreads. In the end, the details of the tapestry have blurred away and the world is left with a monotonous uniformity.

The immediate question is what can be done about the loss of languages and cultural diversity linked to processes of globalization? Any solution is extremely problematic—and yet efforts are being made all over the world by governments and international institutions to protect and encourage the use of minor and/or endangered languages. This essay examines these problems and questions, beginning with thoughts on what language can mean to a particular people. The processes by which languages can be lost and the measures that have been taken to protect language diversity are also addressed. In this discussion the example of Iceland is most frequently used, not just because Iceland is the country from which we, the authors, come, but because its experience in maintaining a distinct culture and linguistic identity is particularly instructive.

The Value of Linguistic and Cultural Diversity

In the Nordic countries, there are languages that have aged well to this day. They have managed to withstand the challenges presented by much stronger ones. While maintaining the integrity of their own languages, these countries have adapted themselves to modern life and the process of globalization by clearly distinguishing their mother tongue, which prevails in literature, memory, and creative usage, from the international business language which they conveniently use to communicate with the world. This capacity requires relatively good mastery of a second language and a strong sense of the worth of preserving linguistic and cultural diversity.

Danish, Swedish, and one of the two types of Norwegian have changed considerably from the Old Norse that was spoken in the Middle Ages, with successive influences from Low German, French, and most recently English. But these remain at once distinct languages and more or less mutually comprehensible. Icelandic and Faroese remain virtually unchanged from the ancient tongue brought to these countries by the first Viking settlers more than a thousand years ago, and the second language spoken in Norway is a restored older form.

Homogenous as Scandinavian culture may appear on the outside, it actually represents a unique linguistic mix. The national language of Finland is one of the few in Europe that is not of Indo-Germanic origin. Another non-Indo-European language, spoken by the Saami people living in the northernmost territories of Scandinavia, is the most threatened in the Nordic countries because this traditional way of life is gradually disappearing. Last but not least, the Inuits of Greenland also have their own language, which is widely used for official purposes these days and is closely related to that spoken by Inuits in the north of Canada, Alaska, and eastern Russia.

A nation's memories and cultural traditions are chronicled in its language. It is through language that nations and peoples preserve their histories, be they oral or written. It is the tie that binds generations together into a common value system within which they operate and co-exist. The experience of Iceland is illustrative and has gained wide respect. Iceland is a fine example of a small nation that has become industrialized and advanced in a very short time, but has managed to protect its identity and old language. Despite economic prosperity and participation in the global market, Iceland has largely kept at bay the influences of the dominant language of international commerce and refused to relegate the treasure houses of its poetry and literature to the archives of dead languages.

Throughout centuries of colonial rule and poverty, language was the thread that gave the Icelandic people a sense of belonging, a sense of national unity—an extra dimension to their lives, beyond the scant material one. The realm of language was where their need for expression and fulfillment had free rein. Language was their wealth in poverty; its resources were unlimited. What makes the Icelanders unique among the people of Europe is that they are the only ones to have detailed records of their origin as a nation, preserved in the vernacular in the renowned medieval sagas. In the 9th and 10th centuries, the forefathers of modern day Icelanders left the Scandinavian mainland and the Northern Isles of Britain to settle in their new home. They used their language to tell stories of these origins and the birth of nationhood, passing them down to successive generations orally at first and later, in the 13t[h] and 14th centuries, writing them down on vellum manuscripts. The result is that the Icelanders have been able to preserve their language, the ancient Viking tongue, virtually intact.

In truth, in this country of few old monuments or relics, the sagas are Iceland's ancient castles, and words are the building blocks for these fortresses. Iceland's modern identity rests on pillars of ideas generated and preserved in these literary forms—and part of the reason that this identity remains dynamic is that the heritage is so rich in imagination and eternal in appeal.

Besides the masterful character portraits and human dramas of the sagas, we have detailed descriptions in Icelandic of the ancient cosmogony and mythology that were once believed across a great part of Europe but have now been almost completely lost elsewhere. We can read about the mightiest of the gods, Odin (known in English as Woden, but hardly part of the heritage any more aside from a few place names and the day dedicated to him, "Wednesday"). A wealth of myths have been recorded in the old Icelandic Edda poems and also in lively prose retellings by Snorri Sturluson (died in 1241), who was also a great historian and wrote, among other things, sagas about the lives of the kings of Norway. In Snorri's *Edda*, for example, modern Icelanders can read without difficulty how Odin had two ravens called Huginn and Muninn—"thought and memory"—who sat on his shoulders. These ravens flew out into the world every day in quest of news. Upon their return, the ravens whispered to him the tidings of the day from all around. In this way, Odin had constant knowledge, conveyed by vision and by the word, of everything that was happening at any time. From his throne on Hlidskjalf situated on the top of the world, Odin had what one would call today a "world-view."[3]

In Snorri's work we also find a playful and puzzling modern realization that language can be used not just to convey information, but also to state the impossible. He describes the magic fetter used to bind the wolf Fenrir, which will ultimately take part in the destruction of the gods. This fetter, says Snorri, "was made from six things: the noise a cat makes when it moves, the beard of a woman, the roots of a mountain, the sinews of a bear, the breath of a fish, the spittle of a bird." We could go so far to say that cultural identity is just such an intangible phenomenon. And identity, as Snorri says of the fetter, "is smooth and soft as a ribbon of silk, but trusty and strong."[4]

Sometimes this cosmogony is profoundly lyrical and emotive, as in the account of the noblest and fairest of all the gods, Baldur. He is the white innocence that evil forces would kill and who would rise again, or in another story life, symbolized by an ash tree, nourished and well protected by three norns or fates called Past, Present, and Future. Other stories are less reverent, such as when the mighty god of thunder, Thor, is forced to dress up in drag. The myths span a spectrum of vision that the modern world has lost—except in these sources. Together with the historical accounts of nationhood, such visions kept the Icelanders' hearts and minds fertile and replete during the long centuries of hardship when they struggled to eke out a physical living. They continued to inspire poetry throughout the centuries, and shaped the independence of mind that eventually manifested itself in national independence. And what is more, this strange and different world is written about in a language that the Icelanders still can, and do, read and understand.

Although their tongue is ancient and their society was for centuries geographically remote, the Icelandic culture has never been static. It has always been open to multiple influences from abroad, molding the latest "isms" into the Icelander's world-view. The sagas reveal that the Icelanders knew the medieval romance as well as classical authors. In successive later periods, Icelandic literature would reflect all the fashions of mainstream European culture—everything from baroque styles to the Western Enlightenment, and from romanticism and realism to modernism and post modernism—while remaining distinctly "national" in character, language, and thought-pattern.

There are many other essentially pragmatic reasons for protecting language diversity. Living languages provide data vital to the understanding of linguistic development. When one dies, an opportunity is lost to better understand the nature of a language and its acquisition, human cognition, and the human brain.[5] If a goal of linguistic study is to uncover universal aspects of language, a single loss means less information to shed light on principles common to all. This is particularly serious since current understanding of linguistic systems comes from studies of a handful of languages. Linguistic inquiry encompasses more than just the study of grammar. It includes the sounds and sound systems, their morphology, semantics, and also the social behaviors that children learn along with their native tongue. Thus, the loss of languages means loss of the intricate patterns of social behavior enabling individuals to survive and thrive in complex social systems.

An illustrative pattern of such social behavior is the practice, when people in Iceland meet for the first time, of spending what may strike outsiders as an unusual amount of time establishing a common acquaintance, friend, or place where their roots lie. This may be, in part, because "great practical importance is attached to maintaining strongly established kin and friendship networks over long distances and through many generations."[6] This almost ritual speech act seems to be a remnant of that system, even though the need to rely on the support of family, or friends, or chiefs is no longer there. But this is precisely what the sagas gave people centuries ago—a sense of belonging, a shared identity, common roots. Individuals could flourish in the security of being part of a whole.

An individual's language is her or his voice and since culture is primarily transmitted through language it gives the language community, whatever its size, a voice. Preserving a language and a culture is an integral part of the meaning of preserving freedom of expression and thus has been considered a human right. To protect this human right implies protecting linguistic and cultural diversity. The nexus between protecting cultures, including language diversity, and fundamental human rights has been implicitly or even explicitly recognized in a number of international covenants, declarations, and resolutions. These are all cited in the Preliminaries of the *Universal Declaration of Linguistic Rights*.[7] This declaration and its subsequent implementation is supported morally and technically by the United Nations Educational, Scientific, and Cultural Organization (UNESCO).

The idea of invoking "human rights" in the discussion on language and cultural diversity is particularly significant because the majority of the world's endangered languages belong to communities of non-sovereign peoples. The principal factors that prevent the development of these languages and that accelerate their disappearance include the lack of self-government and the existence of policies that impose official languages. These factors are rooted in the colonial legacy, which still affects easily half the world's population. According to the *Universal Declaration of Linguistic Rights*:

> *Considering* that invasion, colonization, occupation and other instances of political, economic or social subordination often involve, the direct imposition of a foreign language or, at the very least, distort perceptions of the value of languages and give rise to hierarchical linguistic attitudes, which undermine the language loyalty of speakers; and *considering* that the language of some people, which have attained sovereignty are consequently immersed in a process of language substitution as a result of a policy which favors the language of former colonial or imperial powers.[8]

In light of these considerata, a global democratic community of cultures should assure that each voice has a right to be heard.

Languages Under Threat

It is difficult to determine exactly how many living languages there are in the world and even more difficult to determine how many of them are in danger of becoming extinct. One reason is that there is no agreement on the definition of a dialect, or whether the numbers should include all the varieties of a particular language. Also, there are languages about which it is difficult to determine the number of speakers and its robustness. Nevertheless Michael Krauss, a linguist and authority on language attrition, suggested in 1992, that of the world's approximately 6000 languages, 50-90% were at risk of dying out in the next century.[9] By 1998, Krauss had revised that number to 95%. Already, half of the so called "living" languages included in the statistics are what Krauss terms as "moribund," i.e. languages that are no longer spoken nor learned by children, and which are doomed unless drastic measures are taken. There are moribund languages on all continents, with the bulk being found in the Pacific region, Africa and Asia. Ninety percent of the indigenous languages of Australia, and 80% of native North American languages, and a quarter of the native languages of Central and South America are on the endangered list. According to the *UNESCO Red Book on Endangered Languages*, more than two-thirds of languages in Europe, or ninety-two languages, are potentially endangered or worse. Only 40 European languages are not considered threatened.[10]

To preserve linguistic diversity, people must understand why languages die out. In reviewing the research on language attrition, three main factors emerge. The first is the small size of the speech community; the fewer the speakers, the more likely the tongue is to become extinct.[11] Of the world's approximately 6,000 languages, 52% are spoken by fewer than 10,000 people, 28% have fewer than 1,000 speakers and 10% have fewer than 100 speakers, with the median number of speakers being between 5,000-6,000.[12]

A generally negative attitude towards a minority language by its own speakers, as well as by the dominant culture, is the second significant reason for language attrition.[13] A universal misconception holds that minority languages and minority dialects are somehow linguistically inferior to official languages and standard varieties. It is a social and political judgment projected by the majority (or minority) in power. It is only effective if the speakers themselves buy into the stigma. Half a century ago, a regional dialect characteristic of Icelandic—the apparent collapse of the vowels [I] and [Y]—became stigmatized to the point of becoming officially targeted for eradication. A campaign was mounted in Iceland's public schools that was so effective that today, 50 years later, only a few older speakers still have the feature, and it is no longer found in the speech of the younger generation. Although not as devastating as official campaigns against native and indigenous languages worldwide, it illustrates how social stigma can lead to the demise of a dialect feature.[14]

The third reason for the decline of the number of languages "[is] the immense economic and political pressures on minority communities which weaken the new generation's motivation for holding to their traditional language."[15] To confirm this, one need only look to the demise of Irish, Scottish, and Manx Gaelic, Frisian, Breton, Macedonian, many of the Sami languages, and the other 92 European languages listed in the *UNESCO Red Book on Endangered Languages*. This publication includes detailed lists of languages in various degrees of attrition (not to mention the thousands in other parts of the world).[16] Most of these languages are abandoned because the economic survival of a community is dependent on knowing the majority's language. There is very little economic value attached to retaining the old language.

Moreover, maintaining linguistic diversity is expensive and the phenomenon of diversity forms an obstacle to valued aspects of participating in the globalized market of information, communications, and culture. At the same time, the advance toward global homogenization disrupts spheres of interrelationships and interactions that might favor the internal cohesion of language communities. The prevailing political economic paradigm of development that identifies process with de-regulation and competition with freedom generates growing economic and cultural inequalities. It is the extensive marginalization of peoples that threatens language communities, at least the thousand that do not have the wherewithal to protect their cultures, lacking as they do effective governments and weakened by small populations, communal cultures, and fragile economies.

The Death Process of a Language

Three phenomena are particularly important in accelerating the process of language attrition. First, is the grammatical and lexical influence from a dominant, encroaching language as transitional bilingual communities gradually become monolingual. Second, is the narrowing of the functional range of a language as it moves from being the speakers' only tongue to becoming an intra-home and family language, while the dominant language is used in the broader spectrum of the speakers' lives.[17] Third, is the deliberate political effort to suppress a minority language.

The grammar of a language changes from within as children opt for simplified structures or seek to regularize an inflectional paradigm. A number of scholars have dealt with this question in studies on attrition. Wolfgang Dressler found "fluctuations and uncertainties" in the speech of informants in immigrant groups.[18] He observed that uncertainty results in free variation of rules, which in turn renders perception rather difficult. Dressler claims that: "if a rule is optional with the older generation (...) it is lost in the disintegrating language of the younger generation."[19] When an adult speaker is no longer certain about a specific rule of grammar then the next generation of language learners are exposed to grammatical inconsistencies, which in turn lead to further attrition and in some cases the loss of that particular rule.

Variability in the speech of adult bilinguals is social as well as linguistic. When the functional range of the language is reduced, its verbal repertoire and stylistic range are also diminished.[20] There are fewer occasions to speak, fewer occasions to write the language, and the range of likely topics of discussion narrows. When a child is exposed to a language at home that no longer meets the needs of individuals to function in all aspects of life, outside the home, he/she will use the majority language. Gradually, as more children opt for the majority language it also takes over in the most intimate speech acts.

Languages are all too often repressed for purely political purposes. The story of the Kalmyks is illustrative. Like other Mongolians, the Kalmyks are Tibetan Buddhists, but their Buddhism has a strong admixture of indigenous beliefs and shamamistic practices. Kalmykia is the only Buddhist republic in Europe. Exiled for a period of 13 years by the Soviet regime to Siberia [1943-1956] on the false pretext that they were German spies, the Kalmyks were deprived of their linguistic environment and spoke only Russian. The oldest generation died off during exile. And when the Kalmyks returned home they realized that they had lost many of their native words to describe their own cultural reality. The education system in Kalmykia was partly destroyed and Kalmyk was no longer taught in schools. Also important during that time was the flow of Russians who settled down in Kalmykia. Today, as the Kalmyks speak Russian and rarely use their mother tongue in everyday life, the Kalmyk language is in great danger of extinction. More than 40 years had passed before anything was done. The intervening generations had broken the vital link with the Kalmyk heritage—young people regarded their forebears' language as old-fashioned, difficult, irrelevant or simply boring.

Language Preservation

One of the major challenges for modern society is to understand that linguistic diversity is not an obstacle to globalization nor is it a barrier to identification with other countries. Harmonization and unity among the Nordic countries exemplify this. With present tendencies toward global homogenization, deliberate steps are needed to protect language diversity and to stanch the loss of language communities. Ideally, a political framework is needed that allows for linguistic diversity, placing value on intercultural respect, harmonious co-existence, and the recognition of mutual benefits from a vast variety of world-views.

In this respect, the notion of the smallness of a language community being an argument against attention to its language needs to be revisited. Here the experience and vision of the Nordic countries may be instructive. Together the several language communities of the Nordic countries have a population of 20 million people. Iceland contributes only 270,000 to that number. And the Nordic countries are considered to lie on the periphery of Europe. Do these facts imply that the Nordic peoples are a small and insignificant people and that their language and cultures have only incidental relevance for the world as a whole?

This is certainly not the Scandinavian perspective. After all, the world is round, so that every place on its surface is its center: wherever a single person thinks, talks, and acts is the center. The Nordic countries have never felt a sense of marginalization. They have been quick to adapt what they want from the rest of the world to their local conditions. They have contributed greatly to the artistic processes of the world through their prestigious presence in literature, music, film, theatre, painting, dance and design. And yet they remain content in their own soul—in their own language communities. They are part of the world *and* maintain their linguistic and cultural identity as the source of their strength and credibility.

Just as every nation should realize its centeredness on the planet, so it should ignore the negative connotation of smallness. All Nordic peoples have always thought of themselves as possessing the same right to live on earth and to make their voices heard, as loudly as any other group. Moreover, to be but relatively few is considered by Nordic peoples a great strength, for these small societies allow people to matter to each other. At the global level, the Nordic countries have a reputation and influence far in excess of what mere population statistics would seem to merit. Democracy and its promotion are central to their societies, and they are widely seen as a model for democracy and progressive social justice for the rest of the world.

Language policy-making is highly political. There are political and economic advantages inherent in decision-making processes when a nation determines its official language(s). The chosen language(s) receive national and institutional support and their speakers have better access to power and the decision-making that affects minorities. Speakers of non-official languages are often marginalized or even obliged to abandon their linguistic heritage in favor of the language that is more socially and economically viable. Politics is also involved in language preservation because someone pays for the maintenance effort.[21] Language politics in Iceland have always been favorable to supporting the preservation of the ancient tongue against threats—last century from Danish, and this century from English. Maintaining political ties and allegiances across long distances discouraged dialectical divergence.

Today, worldwide efforts are being mounted to increase understanding of the value of linguistic and cultural diversity. These efforts include documenting languages that cannot be saved as well as those that are endangered, strengthening languages at risk through policy and international collaboration, and encouraging bilingualism and biculturalism among the world's youth. In order to preserve the diversity of the world, and thus guard people's linguistic human rights, international organizations, governments, and policy-makers are asked to make language preservation a priority. A major effort in this connection has been the *Universal Declaration of Linguistic Rights* previously mentioned. It is also encouraging that numerous institutions are actively engaged in the language preservation effort. These include universities and foundations all over the world that have created web sites and Internet list serves to facilitate the exchange of ideas and resources among those interested in linguistic diversity. International organizations and governments have already responded to these needs. For example, UNESCO published the *Red Book of Endangered Languages* mentioned above and increased its funding of research projects on endangered languages.[22] The Japanese government, at the request of UNESCO, set up the International Clearing House for Endangered Languages in 1994 at Tokyo University. The Clearing House compiles data on endangered languages, and serves as liaison between linguists working on language attrition. Many private organizations, such as the Summer Institute in Linguistics, in the US, have documented endangered languages.

Several countries have adopted policies pertaining to the maintenance of minority languages. The government of Nicaragua plays an active role in maintaining its indigenous languages. The Nicaraguan Constitution includes the "Autonomy Statute," which declares that one of the functions of government is "to promote national culture, as well as the study, preservation, promotion, development, and dissemination of the different cultures and traditions [of its] indigenous populations (...) including their historical, artistic, linguistic and cultural heritage."[23] As a result the Rama language that had only 2,000 speakers in 1980 is being resuscitated. Through the collaboration of the Rama people, the Nicaraguan government, and professional linguists, Rama is taught to children and hopefully will be saved from extinction.[24] In 1990, the US adopted The Native American Languages Act. This law seeks to promote and preserve Native American Languages and Culture with a focus on education.[25] As for the Kalmykia, it should be noted that the Ministry for Minorities of the Russian Federation requested UNESCO to provide their authorities with technical assistance for re-establishing Kalmyk as a first language in the primary and secondary school curriculum. Today, they are using pilot materials to make children realize that Kalmyk is their mother tongue. Kalmykia could serve as a platform for a pilot project, which, if successful, would subsequently be extended to surrounding regions.[26]

Additional governmental support for rights of linguistic minorities is indispensable. Funding for scholarly institutions to enable the study and documentation of endangered languages needs to be strengthened. This will not happen if there is little respect for diversity. Tolerance has often been identified as one of the key issues for ensuring social stability in the coming millennium, and is central to affording equal opportunities for all peoples irrespective of race, gender, ethnic, or linguistic background. To go beyond tolerance and to engender attitudes of respect for multilingualism, public awareness efforts, as well as, education and promotion of cultural diversity and multiculturism are requisite.

Most important is the requirement to educate the younger generations about the importance of linguistic and cultural diversity.

A linguistic community is viable as long as its language is practiced. Thus, young people must be encouraged to learn, use, and articulate ideas artistically in their native languages. Bilingualism is also essential because their future economic survival may depend on it. Resources and educational materials are necessary for children to achieve this capacity. This includes, but is not limited to, increased funding for the education of individuals in endangered linguistic communities to become native language teachers. Heritage language education should become part of each country's national curriculum.

Final Word

Facing the impending loss of half of the world's languages, one must ask: At what cost? Preserving creative expression is a far greater social responsibility than many politicians, policy-makers and business people realize. Language represents "in a coded way all the concepts a culture uses to define itself and its society." Language is "a very overt symbolization of ourselves and our universe (...). These symbols are the means by which we define ourselves and others."[27] Because language as a system provides access to how the human mind works and to human behavior, language loss could seriously impede knowledge of the architecture of the brain, and limit "the reconstruction of linguistic prehistory around the world, a key component in the unraveling of global human prehistory."[28]

The loss of a language means a loss to the interpretation of the universe, the varied symbolism expressed by individuals through literature and oral histories. The Icelandic Nobel Laureate, Halldór Laxness said, upon his return to Iceland, after having accepted the Nobel Prize in Literature in 1956:

> [When] we are swept into some superpower's ocean of nationhood, when the last old woman who can recite an Icelandic verse is dead, then the world has become poorer. And the superpower who might have swallowed us would not be left any the richer for it.[29]

Everyone loses if even one language is lost, because along with it goes a unique interpretation of life. We lose the unique view of the next Laxness, of future potential Nobel Laureates, of the set of symbols expressed in literary and scholarly masterpieces yet to be written, but which will further enrich, deepen and expand everyone's understanding of the world and the people who inhabit it.

Laxness knew, too, how profound a meaning any mother tongue carries and how far it reaches into the cosmos:

> His mother taught him to sing. And when he was a grown man and had listened to the song of the world he felt that nothing was more precious to him than to be able to return to her song. In her singing dwelt the most heartfelt and indefinable dreams of human kind, when the moors would grow and become one with the skies and the birds of the air would listen in wonder to that song of life.[30]

Endnotes

1 - *Universal Declaration of Linguistic Rights*, Title I: Article 7, Sec. 1, General Principles Diposit legal B44116-1996, (Barcelona: RomanyaValls, S.A., 1996); http:/www.troc.es/mercator/dill.htm.

2 - Ibid., Title I: Article 7 Sec. 2, General Principles.

3 - Snorri Sturluson, *Edda*, trans. Anthony Faulkes, (London: Everyman, 1995).

4 - Idem, "Gylfaginning," *Edda*.

5 - Andrew Woodfield, *The Conservation of Endangered Languages* [database online]; available from www.bris.ac.uk/Depts/Philosophy/CTLL/ (April 22,1999). Anthony Woodbury, *Endangered Languages* (Linguistic Society of America Committee on Endangered Languages and their Preservation, 1995) [database online]; available from www.Isadc.org/woodbury.html (1 May 1999).

6 - James Milroy and Lesley Milroy, "Linguistic Change, Social Network and Speaker Innovation," *The Journal of Linguistics* 21, part 2 (1985): 339-84.

7 - *Universal Declaration of Linguistic Rights.* Preliminaries cite the International Covenants on Civil and Political Rights (Art 27), and on Economic, Social and Cultural Rights; UNGA resolution 47/135, 18 Dec. 1992; various conventions of the Council of Europe dealing with the protection of regional and minority languages; International Labor Organization Convention 169 on Indigenous and Tribal Peoples in Independent Countries; the Final Declaration adopted by the International Federation of Modern Language Teachers, Pecs, Hungary, 16 August, 1991.

8 - *Universal Declaration of Linguistic Rights.*

9 - Michael Krauss, "The World's Languages in Crisis," *Language* 68, no.1 (March 1992): 4-10.

10 - Ibid.

11 - "The Scope of Language Endangerment and Recent Responses to It," presented at the International Symposium on Endangered Languages by Michael Kraus (University of Tokyo, 1995).

12 - Joseph Grimes, *Ethnologue: Languages of the World 13th edition* (Dallas: Summer Institute of Linguistics, 1995) [database online]; available from SIL http://www.sil.org/ethnologue.

13 - Colette Craig, "A Constitutional Response to Language Endangerment," *Language* 68, no.1 (March 1992): 17-24.

14 - Birna Arnbjörnsdóttir, "The Polarization of Sound Change in Different Social Contexts: The Development of Icelandic in North America and Iceland", *Scandinavian-Canadian Studies 4* (1991): 27-41.

15 - Andrew Woodfield, *The Conservation of Endangered Languages* [database online]; available from www.bris.ac.uk/Depts/Philosophy/CTLL/ (22 April 1999). Susan Gal, "Variation and Change in Patterns of Speaking: Language Shift in Austria," in *Linguistic Variation: Models and Methods*, ed. David Sankoff (New York: New York Academic Press, 1978): 345-367.

16 - *The UNESCO Red Book on Endangered Languages,* 1993-1999 compiled by Tapani Salminen (tasalmin@cc.helsinki.fi). Last updated 29 February 1996. Internet.online.24 April 1999.

17 - Jane H. Hill, "Language Death, Language Contract and Language Evolution," in *Approaches to Language*, eds. W.C. Cornmack and S.H. Wurm (The Hague: Mouton, 1978). Birna Arnbjörnsdóttir, "The Polarization of Sound Change in Different Social Contexts: The Development of Icelandic in North America and Iceland" *Scandinavian-Canadian Studies*, 4 (1991): 27-41. Birna Arnbjörnsdóttir, "Language Contact and Language Attrition: The Effect of Categorical Shift in Loss of Case in North American Icelandic," unpublished paper presented at the 1992 Conference of the Society for the Advancement of Scandinavian Studies at the University of Minnesota, April 1992. Birna Arnbjörnsdóttir, "The Life Cycle of a Language," *Canadian Ethnic Studies* 29, no.3 (1997): 31-43.

18 - Wolfgang Dressler, "On the Phonology of Language Death," papers from the 8th Regional Meeting (Chicago: Chicago Linguistic Society): 48-457.

19 - Ibid., 452.

20 - Jane H. Hill, "Language Death, Language Contract and Language Evolution," in *Approaches to Language*.

21 - Nora C. Engand, "Doing Mayan Linguistics in Guatemala," *Language* 68, no. 1 (1992): 29.

22 - *The UNESCO Red Book on Endangered Languages.*

23 - Colette Craig, "A Constitutional Response to Language Endangerment," *Language;* 68, no. 1 (1992): 18.

24 - Ibid., 18.

25 - Lucille J.Watahomigie and Akira Y.Yamamoto, "Local Reaction to Perceived Language Decline," *Language* 68, no.1 (1992): 10-17.

26 - UNESCO, Summary of briefing for Director General for the visit of the First Vice-Chairmen of the Government of Kalmykia, 23 June 1999.

27 - R.B. LePage and Andree Tabouret-Keller, *Acts of Identity* (Cambridge: Cambridge University Press, 1985), 248.

28 - Anthony Woodbury, *Endangered Languages* (Linguistic Society of America Committee on Endangered Languages and their Preservation, 1995) [database online]; available from www.Isadc.org/woodbury.html (1 May 1999).

29 - Halldor Laxness, Speech on His Homecoming, published in *Gjorningabok*, Helgafell, February 1959. See also Halldor Laxness, *Independent People*, 2nd ed. (New York: Vintage International, 1997).

30 - Ibid.

CHAPTER 17

VALUES AND LEADERSHIP IN MANAGING HIGH PERFORMANCE FINANCIAL FIRMS

Roy C. Smith and Ingo Walter

The cab hit another pothole as it lurched its way towards the firm's offices in lower Manhattan in the late autumn of 1998. Its sole passenger was a distressed John Gardner, 47, the chief executive of Carter-Winter, a major New York investment bank. He had just got through an unusually unpleasant lunch seated at a table with the chief investment officers of two of his major institutional clients. Both had severely criticized the business practices in the investment banking industry:

"This Bankers Trust thing is just too much, even by Wall Street standards," one of them said. "Purposely misrepresenting products they were selling to their clients and lying to them about their value, even as they were supposed to be serving as an adviser." He was referring to a *Business Week* article that quoted excerpts from tapes of a Bankers Trust trader talking with a colleague about how he positioned himself between two clients of the bank in order to extract an exorbitant profit. "And do not tell me that sort of thing could never happen at your firm. All of you people are just trying to kill each other, and in doing so you run right over your clients. Look at Salomon Brothers and the Treasury auctions, Merrill Lynch and

Orange County, and Prudential Securities and those limited partnerships!" In the first instance, Salomon Brothers had admitted that it had falsified bids on a government bond auction, the aftermath of which nearly destroyed the firm. Merrill Lynch acted as an advisor to Orange County, California, which went bankrupt after trading extensively in risky securities with Merrill and cost the firm almost $1 billion in settlements. Prudential Securities aggressively sold poor-quality real estate, and oil and gas partnerships to unsuspecting and inappropriate individual investors, and many of the partnerships fell apart. Together with insurance mis-selling, Prudential had to pay over $2 billion in restitution, penalties, and legal costs.

"What's it been, John, five or six major ethical disasters in your industry in recent years?" said the man from the larger of the two clients. "And maybe a dozen or so altogether over the past two decades?"[1] Each one of these events reveals unbelievable lapses in business and ethical standards, not to mention breaking the laws, and each in the end imposes an enormous cost on you and your partners, one sufficient to ruin your firms. The penalties you guys face in criminal and civil litigation and the loss of confidence that clients and customers have in the firm has got to be way out of proportion to whatever you might gain from bending the rules and exploiting people just a little too much.

Increasingly, what folks in our positions see in all this is an industry out of control. Too many securities firms have been involved in abuses of clients or customers, or have been unable to control their own people. I've been involved in this business for nearly thirty years, John, and the frequency of violations of ethical conduct by broker-dealers has never been this high during all that time. You people had better start realizing that if we can not trust you, we're not going to trade with you. We'll set up our own broker-dealers, or electronic trading networks to deal with each other directly. The only money you guys will be making will have to come from trading with each other, and that's not much of a future, is it?"

John Gardner, now a veteran of two decades at the firm, became the CEO of Carter-Winter a few years before many of the events his clients were discussing. It was considerably more difficult being the head of a major securities firm than he ever imagined. Things moved so fast, competition was so sharp, and there were no prizes for coming in second. The institutions, like those who had just been dumping on him, were part of the problem. They wanted everything: the "first call" on a new idea, the lowest commissions, and aggressive use of the firm's capital to support their trading activities. It was also complicated, John remembered, and disorienting to lurch from slashing costs in 1990, to runaway expansion in 1992 and 1993, and then back to cost-slashing again the next year. Layoffs and the fear of layoffs followed by frenzied talent hunts contributed immensely to the industry-wide anxieties. Volatility in take-home pay and uncertainty about the industry's future also extracted a heavy toll in the firm's relationships with its employees and senior producers. Too many of its important, income-producing employees had been hired away from other firms (for a lot more money) and never had been trained in the firm's business practices and standards. The industry's erratic personnel decisions in the past few years certainly did not encourage employee loyalty.

Without doubt, they were all now mainly concerned with themselves and what they felt they had to do to "get ahead" or even to stay employed. And that was to produce revenues and produce profits. That was certainly what we needed them to do, John thought, and encouraged them strongly to do. Well, John thought, many of these people must be figuring that as long as we pay them incredible amounts for producing, they will take whatever chances they have to in order to be one of the producers. After all, if bad stuff happens, well, the prospective producer's money was not at stake— the capital being risked and about to be sued belongs to the firm's shareholders, not to the errant employee.

John returned to his office. Still concerned with the discussion at lunch, he wondered what he ought to do about it. Those investment officers were pretty hot, but they were realists too. They knew that they needed firms like his to help them compete with each other. Everyone was competing, and competitive results were all anyone appeared to care about. Many of the biggest financial institutions, for example, could be just as bad as those criticized at lunch;

Prudential Securities, for example, which was part of a large insurance company. Some thought it did not matter anymore how revenues and profits were produced, as long as they were produced. Others would add that if one practice or another seemed a little shady, well, others were already doing it.

Determined to understand better why these things were happening, and what his firm could do about them, John decided to confront the issues systematically. He thought he might break them down into some basic elements: (a) the types of frauds and deceptions attached to the industry, (b) reasons for the questionable behavior, (c) management's role in aiding or abetting this conduct, (d) the adequacy of laws and regulations, and (e) steps that might be taken to help the financial institutions serve rather than cheat society. He began to write down some of his thoughts.

Ethics and Professional Standards in the Securities Industry

We use this case at the beginning of an MBA course on "Professional Responsibilities in Financial Services," the required half-term "ethics" course for finance majors at the Stern School of Business of New York University. Each student has to say something about each of the categories John has identified in the case. Each has to try to come to grips with John's real problem—he is running a business that has to operate in the world as it is, although he has a fair amount of latitude in which to set his firm's policies. He must be cognizant of the forces imposed on him and his employees by sharp market competition. Equally, he must be aware of the dangers to the firm, mainly to its principal shareholders, including himself, from criminal prosecution, civil litigation, and the loss of customer support and other forms of economic value as a result of misconduct. In this context, he must also remember that few industries anywhere are so extensively and intricately regulated as the securities industry, and what regulatory penalties do not exact, a horde of civil class-action litigants can be expected to.

If John ever hopes to be able to persuade any of his colleagues that policy actions are necessary to improve the conduct of the firm in the market, he *must* be able to persuade them that the proposals are essential and unquestionably necessary to preserve the firm's economic values. This, he knows, is a very tall order. His colleagues are competent and experienced men and women who believe that they know the risks of the business and how to manage them. They also know where the rewards are and what has to be done to get them. They see their business as being in a state of equilibrium in which the risks and rewards are balanced. They do not want someone like John to upset the balance by urging policies on them that would impede their ability either to compete or to survive. And John's contemporaries, CEOs all over the Street, face the same dilemma: having recognized that changes are necessary, how can they get them made, accepted and put into practice without themselves being set aside?

Financial marketplaces have a very long history. There are two basic types, those that are regulated by national authorities, and those that are not. There were no banks in Roman times (the government did not allow them) but there were abundant financial transactions in insurance, land and real estate, and shipping, none of which appeared to be much regulated. It was the Romans who guided us with the lasting principle of *caveat emptor* (let the buyer beware). This principle was thought to be sufficient for public purposes because the only ones transacting in these items were wealthy merchants or landowners who had the means and ability to look after themselves. In the middle-ages, Italian banks made loans to foreign heads of state, to secure their positions in the wool business, or in some other trade. Periodically these statesmen defaulted on their loans, leading some to amend the ancient principle to *caveat vendor* (let the seller beware).

In the early 1600s, the first European financial exchanges were established, to bring order and regulation to the rapidly expanding markets for commodities and monies of all types, A new principle was set—the market will perform better if all members treat each other alike. This was perhaps the first appearance in modern financial history of Aristotle's "golden mean" (or *golden rule*), and the idea later evolved into the "motto" of the London financial exchange (one supposedly practiced throughout Europe): "My word is my bond." This motto was never intended to mean that traders did not try to outsmart, or wrong-foot, a trading counter party. It simply meant that "if I say I will trade at this price, I will deliver, on time, at that price, and you can count on it!"

But the market was still populated only by rich people able to look after themselves. This did not change until the early part of the twentieth century, especially during the 1920s, when thousands of ordinary people became active in the stock market in New York. They had savings, and sought to invest them in the new, high-tech stocks of the day (like RCA) and especially in a new series of mutual funds, many of which were leveraged and used their assets to buy into other leveraged mutual funds. The market was heady in the 1920s, and traders saw opportunities to take advantage of the new money coming in by manipulating the markets through bull-and-bear pools and other devices. In the early 1930s, the bubble burst and the stock market crashed, causing many individual investors to lose almost all they had entrusted to the market. In the 1930s, there was also a massive banking crisis that resulted in the closing of thousands of banks, wiping out the savings of a great many Americans, and having a more severe effect on the financial system than the stock market decline.

In the years that followed, the new government passed landmark legislation that drastically changed the way US financial markets have operated ever since. The *Securities Acts of 1933 and 1934* made investment bankers liable for untruths in marketing new issues, required them to refrain from market manipulation of any kind, and created the Securities and Exchange Commission to be sure they behaved properly. The *Banking Act of 1933* separated banking and investment banking (until 1999), provided for deposit insurance, and imposed strict banking regulation. The *Investment Act of 1940* established standards for investment managers. Subsequently, the courts became involved in establishing penalties for insider trading. The exchanges also became more active as regulators of their own businesses. There were penalties (which increased in severity over the years, now including prison sentences) for violating any or all of these new rules, and these penalties could be greatly increased by payment of damages from civil lawsuits following an adverse judgement in a regulatory matter.

By 1990, the US securities market had become an extremely regulated environment, with court actions occasionally resetting the rules (to clarify what could be considered an infraction) after the fact. Such an environment was dangerous. The essential principles that had emerged were that markets should be *open and reliably transparent*, and *no one could take advantage of others through the use or withholding of information* with impunity. Gradually these principles became part of the national financial regulatory framework in other European countries and in Japan, although in each case the rules were a bit different and great attention to detail was necessary to remain compliant in all markets in which a firm operated during the 1990s.

By contrast, the world's largest financial marketplaces (foreign exchange, commodities trading, syndicated bank lending) were completely unregulated. These markets operated outside of any single national control, involved only wholesale market players where the principle of *caveat emptor* still applied. And as marketplaces globalized by admitting banks and traders from Asia, the Middle East, Latin America and other parts of the world not accustomed to these market environments, standards eroded. One *did* have to be careful. One did *not* do business with certain people who were out there. Market self-regulation of this sort was slow and weak but the market had low regulatory costs, and the market was open and innovative, and has proven (after nearly forty years) to be robust, healthy and growing. To operate simultaneously in both market environments (the regulated and the unregulated) meant that financial firms had to have dual operating systems.

Or did they? The system used in the regulated environment could surely be used in the unregulated one as well. If firms followed the main principles of the financial marketplace, those that had emerged over thousands of years, would it not be on a sound foundation? Buyers must protect themselves. Market participants should treat each other as they themselves want to be treated. Sellers must be wary of rogue clients. Tell the truth to clients when selling

319

securities. Allow competitors in the market as long as they reveal the truth about themselves. Do not deliberately mislead clients or trade on inside information. Those are not such difficult principles to adopt, especially if most of the rest of the market has to adopt them too. They are reasonable, and indeed, essential, if one's business depends on customers and client support. They become the firm's *values*.

If the values are reasonable, what does it take to have a system for internal compliance to insure these values are adopted by everyone in the firm? What does it take to inculcate understanding and defense of the firm's own policies aimed at meeting these objectives? What management methods are necessary to deal with the many requirements for a compliant firm. These are the key contributions that John can make to his firm. Installing such management methods is a matter of *leadership*, in this case leadership in support of values. This is where we want our MBA students to take John as they try to answer the questions for him. What key leadership contributions are necessary? We want to see real world professional conduct problems fixed. Let's review John's list of troubling areas.

Frauds and Deceptions

In the 1980s, flagrant violations of the securities laws began to surface. Generally they were related to insider trading and market manipulation. These involved some of the industry's most important merger specialists, arbitrage traders and junk bond specialists, several of whom were closely associated with each other.

In the 1990s, the most serious violations of the governing principles concerned trading and risk management. A number of important securities firms failed, were forced into mergers, or otherwise suffered substantial losses and embarrassments due to increasingly flagrant actions of employees and ineffective or complicit management. Some of these involved rogue traders working for firms and cheating internal control systems, some involved rogue brokers cheating their clients, and some involved the rogue clients and failure on the part of firms to insulate themselves from their unethical or even criminal behavior. These individuals are called "rogues" to set them apart from the other employees of the firms that allowed them to operate, illegally and in their own interests. Before being identified as rogues, however, these employees were normal or even exceptional and well regarded employees.

Firms commit enormous amounts of capital to their various trading activities, and increase their exposure to large trading losses caused by sudden market movements or human error. Rogue operators can, therefore, be extremely dangerous, having the potential to destroy entire firms (for example, Barings, Kidder Peabody, and Daiwa Bank).

Baring Brothers, the most distinguished British bank, found itself suddenly overexposed and unhedged in the Japanese equities market when the 233-year-old firm lost control of a trader in its small Singapore office. Nicholas Leeson had built up a large open (unhedged) position on the Nikkei 225 index, which resulted in massive losses after the market plunged following the 1995 Kobe earthquake. He had been fiddling accounts for at least a year before the market plunge. He was able to disguise transactions and misreport them to the head office, making his unauthorized trading more difficult to detect—even though Barings' positions had become enormous and were widely known to dominate the futures market on the Nikkei index.

Similarly, a highly respected American investment bank with roots going back to 1865, Kidder Peabody was embarrassed by having to restate earnings for 1993 to remove $130 million of trading profits that were never earned. Joseph Japp, Kidder's head government securities trader, who had received a $9 million bonus the year before, was fired. Subsequently the firm sued him for misrepresenting billions of dollars of government bond trades. Unaccountably, due to computer mis-programming, Kidder counted as profit trades that were in fact only "wash" transactions. Larger problems in the mortgage-backed securities market, which the firm had attempted to dominate through aggressive trading under declining market conditions, emerged. Large losses then followed, the result perhaps of a business plan that aimed at ambitious market-share building by offering generous incentives for success, but risking all of the firm's capital in the process.

In 1995, Toshihide Iguchi, head of Daiwa Bank's Treasury bond trading department in New York sent a "letter of confession" to Akira Fujita, President of Daiwa Bank Ltd. in Japan.[2] In his letter, Iguchi outlined how over the previous 11 years, he had accumulated and concealed U.S. Treasury bond trading losses of the astonishing amount of $1.1 billion: "For the last 10 years, I have been alone in the darkness, shivering with fear," he wrote. In 1984, Iguchi was responsible for setting up Daiwa's U.S. Treasury trading operation. He became active in the markets, regularly trading up to $250 million at a time (later even topping a billion a day)—several times the volume of typical government trades. When his trades were not profitable, he engaged in larger, riskier ones to cover previous losses. On September 23, 1995, Iguchi was arrested at his home in New Jersey. Pleading guilty to charges of fraud, money laundering, falsifying bank documents, embezzlement of $500,000., and misappropriating $1.1 billion of bank funds, he also implicated senior managers in a cover-up. Daiwa's president and two top executives resigned as the scandal unfolded to include Japanese government officials. Shortly thereafter, Japanese investors sued Daiwa, accusing the bank of inadequate risk management. Daiwa's license to conduct banking operations in the United States was withdrawn by the Federal Reserve. He also was assessed a record fine of $1 billion. The Federal Reserve Bank and various state banking agencies cited false record keeping and reporting, failure to notify regulatory officials as required by law, and deceptions by senior officers.

Broker rogues, like their dealer cousins, were on the rampage as well in the early nineties, misrepresenting investments they were selling to customers and acting on behalf of unscrupulous characters engaged in all sorts of improper transactions. There are now (and always have been) many complaints of improper conduct by brokers. For example, the Prudential scandal involved the sale of approximately $8 billion of limited partnerships in the 1980s and 1990s. Investors lost more than $1 billion in these partnerships, including real estate and oil and gas properties that were sold to more than 340,000 retail investors—often with no concern for whether the investment was suitable for the customers involved. In 1994, Prudential paid millions to settle lawsuits related to fraudulent valuations of real estate holdings of PRISA, Prudential's prestigious real estate investment fund for pension funds. And, in February 1996, its insurance group announced that it was prepared to pay as much as $1 billion to settle allegations of abusive sales practices by its insurance agents.

The Prudential Securities case motivated the Security Exchange Commision to look into the activities of other retail brokers selling limited partnership investments in the 1980s. The result of such scrutiny at Paine Webber, for example, resulted in an agreement to pay $300 million to settle charges of fraud arising from sales of limited partnerships over a six-year period.[3] Similarly, Banker's Trust was involved in a highly visible lawsuit that involved the sale of derivative securities to supposedly unsuspecting customers, including Procter & Gamble, whom the bank allegedly had misled and subsequently fleeced by misvaluing the complex, custom-designed structured derivative products it sold to them. The total of losses allegedly caused by such fraudulent trading practices by the bank amounted to about $500 million, a precipitous drop in its reputation to the bottom rank among large American banks—and its eventual sale in 1999 to Deutsche Bank.[4]

Sometimes it is the customer, not the firm, who is the rogue. But this hardly immunizes brokers against contamination and responsibility for their losses. After all, when losses are large, it is almost certain that injured parties will sue any others involved in the transactions who continue to have money. For example, in the 1995 Orange County, California case, the client lost $1.2 billion as a result of trading losses in the county's co-mingled investment account operated for the benefit of various municipalities and agencies. For several years, the county's Treasurer, Robert Citron, invested the county's funds successfully, always achieving impressive above-market returns. In 1994, however, Citron misjudged the market and lost heavily. This forced a cash flow crisis, and the county was forced to declare bankruptcy.

In virtually all of these cases, the losses were the result of highly valued, lavishly compensated revenue-producers going overboard, with only the lowly "back-office guys" to stop them, which in all of these cases they were unable to do. Management was either impotent or complicit. By the time the damage was done, the shareholders had lost fortunes. The institutions were either totally destroyed or severely damaged. Rogue trading occurred, but should have been detected by independent internal controls and corrected by responsible superiors. It was not. In time, a variety of signals and revelations made top management aware of serious irregularities that they did not correct and did not disclose until it was too late.

Kidder's management, knowing of the huge volume of bond deals involved, was neither able to explain why it had not investigated the underlying economics behind such a major commitment of the firm's capital and risk-taking capacity, nor did it discover the irregularity. When the Dutch group ultimately stepped in to take over Barings' business, it immediately fired the firm's top 23 officers. The new owners believed the officers either knew about the situation and did nothing to correct it, or were in positions where they should have known about it, but did not. Reports to and by the Bank of England and the British Treasury were extremely critical of management's poor grip on the bank's operations, having ignored or otherwise failed to act despite numerous warnings of potential trouble as early as six months before the firm's failure.[5] And after receiving Iguchi's letter of confession, Daiwa officials informed Yoshimasa Nishimura, director of Japan's Ministry of Finance, of the situation. However, U.S. officials were not notified until over a month after Daiwa informed Nishimura. Daiwa admitted to telling Iguchi in order to continue hiding his losses after his confession to give bank officials time to investigate the matter internally. Ministry of Finance officials claimed that the delay in informing U.S. regulators was merely an attempt to give the bank time to complete its internal investigation.

Reasons for Unethical Conduct

In the 1980s, most members of the financial community believed that the aggressive roles played by the various competing financial players, investment bankers, commercial lenders, takeover lawyers, arbitrageurs, and junk bond experts were appropriate and indeed healthy. In a competitive environment, which subjected all of its participants to the discipline of market forces, and where the control of corporations itself should be contestable, the ability to challenge for control of corporations in the market was considered a good thing. Being aggressive meant challenging the ambiguities and imperfections of the system whenever one could and being willing to take risks and occasionally get into trouble with the regulators.

Firms took calculated risks, based on a popular perception in the industry that such illegalities were hard to define, detect, or prove in court. And, when proven, the offenses did not involve jail time. No one from a prominent Wall Street firm had been to jail for crimes committed on the street since Richard Whitney—head of Richard Whitney & Co., and president of the New York Stock Exchange—had gone to Sing-Sing Prison for embezzlement in 1938. The economic incentives to cheat and abuse the system in the 1980s were heavily weighted, it would seem, in favor of the cheaters and abusers.

Moreover, there was the confident perception that no one from the regulatory world would discover the abusive activities. The regulators were understaffed, underpaid, and nowhere near as sophisticated about financial market activities as the offenders. Regulators observed countless cases where stock prices of target companies rose before bids were actually made. And, while some well-known court cases were brought against small traders, financial analysts, journalists, and printers (many of which did not survive appeal), regulators were not successful at tracking down those thought to be big-time insider traders.

Today's market remains exceptionally competitive, after a generation of deregulation that has encouraged new players, ideas and capital to come into the markets. Price has become the most important determinant in trading (not relationships, but reliability and value contribute in other ways). Firms find themselves exposed to lower fees and the requirements for greater trading risks than ever before. Revenue producers find that they get the trade because their price quotation is the most aggressive and therefore the riskiest. All things being equal, the profitability of traditional client business has been in decline for many years despite a huge increase in the volume of transactions.

To counter this trend, firms active in the capital markets have been forced to seek new revenue opportunities. When they can, they invent new products and services for which higher spreads can be charged, at least for a while. They move into new markets, such as foreign exchange, or junk bonds. Or, they enter into transactions where firms take more trading risks on their own books. This is usually called "proprietary" trading when it involves special strategies or arbitrages devised by the firm—though often the trading strategy is no more complex than deciding that a particular investment opportunity will rise in value. Firms can also engage in "merchant banking," when its own capital is allocated to bridge loans or minority interests in private placements of debt or equity in small or mid-sized companies. All of these efforts to ferret out new business opportunities, especially proprietary trading, involve taking on increased risks. And, the firm often has to make a substantial investment to be able to take them on.

The process works this way: The revenue producers create the risks that the firm funds with its own capital, which is owned by its shareholders or partners. Usually, the risk-creator is compensated on a performance basis, in which a bonus is paid according to the profits that the risk-takers' activities generate. If no risk is taken, profit generation can be expected to be negligible. If an individual is going to be successful as a trader, he or she will have to take as much risk as possible—risk, that is, with shareholders' capital. This creates what economists call "moral hazard," when a risk-creator has great incentive to maximize the risks to be taken, but minimal exposure to the losses because they affect the account of the shareholders. The risk-taker is given an incentive to take risks with the owner's capital, which if successful, will justify a large bonus. But if not, the owner takes the loss, not the employee.

At the same time, serious lessons concerning trading and risk management have had to be learned. Acutely aware that profits come from taking risks, not avoiding them, a new cadre of employees skilled in sophisticated trading methods emerged. With these groups, however, also emerged the need for expensive control systems, management methods for containing firm-wide risk exposures and controlling the human-risk element in the business. When moral hazards exist the firm has to look out for itself. Often the commitment and the expensive techniques of risk control have lagged behind the trading techniques, or have been poorly enforced. In many of such cases disaster has not been far behind.

Adequacy of Laws and Regulations

James Stewart's best-selling book *Den of Thieves*, published in 1991, examines more than a dozen cases of criminal activity on the part of financial professionals. These demonstrated the need for securities laws. Stewart, however, also points to failures to enforce the rules. These failures were reflected in the perceptions of the ·Wall Street abusers who felt so uninhibited by the law that they took the risk of violating the rules, or at least not determining whether they were in violation of them. In this graphic and sweeping book, Stewart concludes that financial markets have shown remarkable resilience and an ability to curb their own excesses. Yet he found these markets to be surprisingly vulnerable to corruption from within. If nothing else, the scandals underscore the importance of the securities laws and their vigorous enforcement. The Wall Street criminals are consummate evaluators of risk and the equation as they see it suggest little likelihood of getting caught.

This equation was seemingly rewritten, however, after Drexel Burnham pleaded guilty to several criminal violations and was fined $630 million, triggering the firm's subsequent bankruptcy and liquidation in 1990. Sentences were also handed down to the rest of those found guilty. In this case, the major players were not caught until a string of informers stepped in.

The information revolution may be having a salutary effect on the issue of professional conduct and ethics in financial markets. It is said that "sunshine is the best disinfectant," and the omnipresence of equity analysts and the rapid communication of their findings to investors worldwide make it increasingly difficult to prevent bad news from affecting share prices. People are increasingly aware of that, and take it into account when thinking through the consequences of their behavior.

Revisiting Ethical and Professional Values

John Gardner looked out over the lower Hudson River. He considered his role as the leader of a high-performance financial organization against the backdrop of the unsettling events in his industry during the 1980s and 1990s. Several principles seemed compelling in managing an organization such as his—an organization with extraordinary power and one that stood at the center of the global economic and financial structure. Yet his was an industry that traditionally had plenty of trouble maintaining a reputation for decent ethical and professional values. John looked over a set of guidelines that a task force on business ethics had prepared. These "Basic Rules for Appropriate Conduct in Finance" included five simple questions to be addressed by all employees when complicated situations arose:

- Basic Responsibilities: Would my actions violate any one of several responsibilities anchored in law, social and ethical norms, professional codes, and company policies?

- Infringement of the Rights of Others: Could my actions, or those of my firm, appear to be judged by a well-informed and impartial observer as "unfair"? That is, would they impair the rights of others, rights that have been defined by a consensus of society as a whole, and known to everyone?

- Franchise Value: Would my actions, or those of my firm, compromise our reputation for fair and honest dealing, even in tough business situations, and thereby cause lasting damage to shareholder value?

- Reputation: Would I be comfortable seeing a fair report of my own actions, or those of my firm, prominently and widely disseminated in the media?

- What if it were done to us? If this action were undertaken by one of our competitors, would we grudgingly admire their savvy, or would we cry "foul"?

Asking oneself these questions before taking action made a good deal of sense to John. But could John rely on the responses of all the individuals, without somehow doing more to train them in business principles. How many of them would say, "Look! the deal's waiting to be done, why ask all these questions? What if someone else comes along right now and takes it away? My boss will kill me, and I doubt he wants me wasting time on these big picture questions? I gotta do the trade." Would these Basic Rules really matter. Could they be put into place in such a way as to actually change the firm's behavior? He was doubtful. But the thought made him reach into his pocket for some notes of his own than he had recorded since his lunch a few weeks ago with the angry clients.

Having strong ethical values as a chief executive of a firm is not enough, John had noted, they must be taken seriously by all the employees. And for this to happen they must be communicated, frequently and repetitively, so as to influence the new employees and to remind the old-timers of the most important guidelines for the firm's future. Ambitious new hires should be encouraged to study and apply the principles as a blueprint for the firm's whole culture, and for some insight into what it takes to get ahead.

But no principle will be believed unless everyone from the CEO on down, believe and practice it. Credibility at the top is critical for creating a strong culture that reinforces both professional standards and performance. That doesn't spring forth all by itself. Employees know everything there is to know about their leaders. They are fascinated by them and want to be like them, or figure out how to get around them. They pay close attention to everything the leader does. They pay much less attention to what he says. The key is how he handles crises, emergencies, and general difficulties. How effective are his business ideas and principles? How effective is his basic business strategy? How often does he cave in to or get rolled over by others? How often does he take the initiative and pave the way for something different? These issues determine the difference between strong and effective leadership that has the power to set the directions for the future and the expectation that others will follow. They also determine who does not.

Few characteristics are more useful for top managers than being predictable, especially being predictable with respect to particular business policies and practices. True, employees always have to feel they can come in and talk to the boss. But they should not be encouraged to believe that the boss is prepared to meet every issue with an open mind. Bosses stand for something. When they stand for high standards, they should not have an open mind about discussing deviations from those standards. That also goes for being known as a tough defender of the standards. When a high producer makes serious mistakes, he is out of the firm, not invited to "work things out." Exceptions are not made for top producers. Firing a couple of uncooperative "star" producers or "prima donnas" who are numerous in the industry, may be the best thing a firm can do for society. There should be clear expectations, that when certain offenses occur, the ax will fall.

There should also be predictability and transparency with regard to other things. After something goes wrong (in one's own firm or in another's) there has to be a debriefing revealing all relevant facts. When litigation considerations permit, the facts should be discussed openly with senior managers. More generally, when a disaster occurs, everyone in the industry should be well informed about the issues involved. A close look at some of the major disasters befalling securities firms and banks indicates that the trouble almost never began with an individual's explicit intention to commit a violation. In most cases, something happened inadvertently, and then got worse. Subsequent efforts to either cover the problem up or "trade out" of the situation failed. In some cases, supervisors were involved and they went along with the effort to repair the damage rather than report it to regulators or to a higher authority in the firm. Perhaps they also felt a need to conceal their own involvement. In the end, it all fell apart.

Would the situation have occurred if the employees knew how to avoid the "inadvertent event," or realized the seriousness of a cover up, or had a good understanding of what they were supposed to do when such conditions arose? Would it all have gotten out of hand if a watchful colleague had noticed something amiss and reported it? Control infractions are often portrayed after the fact, in technical detail. But in reality they are almost always failures of human judgment and management systems.

There is also no substitute for strong controls and alert watch keeping. But good controls are often lacking because they are so expensive. No firm can afford to monitor the action of every trader and salesperson. Too often employers cut corners by relying on trusted employees to do the right thing. As the recent scandals pointed out, this doesn't always work.

In the end, of course, someone must be held accountable. That "someone" must be a senior official, to be sure. Accountability should not be lost as responsibility trickles down to operating levels. And accountability, like leadership development, should be tied to compensation and promotion. Accountable people are watchful, and watchful people are the ones who ring the alarms when they are needed. A basic objective should be to turn all of the firm's employees into accountable ones—that is, to minimize the need for controls by improving the quality of the people being controlled and reduce the probability of an accident that may grow into something toxic later on.

Operating a sound control system and developing good people cannot be dependent upon a company's profits. Controls and training cannot be turned on and off based on how the markets are doing, although many firms have reputations for doing just that.

For the best results, there has to be a system of checks and balances. The highest value a firm can have is the long-term, risk-adjusted value of its business franchise. A company can only achieve this through sound principles, sound standards, and their repeated communication. And everyone has to pitch in. Employees must be educated as to what these values and standards are, and what policies and practices are acceptable to achieve them. An employer must seek out and reward the best performers while recycling the weakest ones through leadership training and development.

"The leaders of tomorrow's major financial service organizations will not be just 'producers,'" John Gardner thought. Indeed, as difficult as being a good producer may be, there are thousands of them. The leaders will of necessity be a lot like old-fashioned general managers, familiar with the basic business of banking and securities, of course, but also technology, law, regulation, and controls, capable of inspiring others to outstanding efforts and achievement. Organizations lacking such leaders may be lucky to be in business at all, given the escalating risk of destruction by regulatory or litigious land-mines that seem ever more prevalent. The more difficult the business: the more important the leaders.

Endnotes

1 - Anita Raghavan and Stephen Lipin, "Restructuring Angers Clients of Goldman," *The Wall Street Journal,* 1 February 1995.

2 - Daiwa Bank Ltd. was the tenth largest commercial bank in Japan and the 19th largest bank in the world at the end of 1995, with 243 branches worldwide and assets of over $211 billion. Its principal activities included pension trust management and small business loans. It opened its New York office in 1956 and in 1986 was one of the first foreign firms designated as a primary dealer in U.S. Treasury securities.

3 - *USA Today,* 16 January 1996.

4 - "What CFOs Really Think About Investment Bankers," *Investment Dealer's Digest,* 6 February 1995.

5 - Nicholas Bray, "Barings Failed to React to Warnings Preceding Collapse, Evidence Suggests," *The Wall Street Journal,"* 19 July 1995.

CHAPTER 18

PRINCIPLES IN THE PRACTICE OF DIPLOMACY: A PERSONAL EXPERIENCE IN INTERNATIONAL AFFAIRS

Giandomenico Picco

In 1513, Niccolo Machiavelli, wrote to Lorenzo Di Medici:

> With the utmost diligence I have long pondered and scrutinized the actions of the great, and now I offer the results to Your Highness(…) and although I deem this work unworthy of Your Highness's acceptance, yet my confidence in your humanity assures me that you will receive it with favor, knowing that it is not in my power to offer you a greater gift than that of enabling you to understand in a very short time all those things which I have learnt at the cost of privation and danger in the course of many years. I have not sought to adorn my work with long phrases or high-sounding words or any of those superficial attractions and ornaments with which many writers seek, as I desire no honor for my work but such as the novelty and gravity of its subject may deserve. Nor will it, I trust, be deemed presumptuous on the part of a man of humble and obscure position to attempt to discuss and direct the government of princes: for in the same way that landscape painters station themselves in the valleys to draw mountains or high ground, and ascend an eminence in order to get a good view of plains, so it is necessary to be a prince to know thoroughly the nature of the people, and one of the populace to know the nature of princes.[1]

In some respects the intentions of this essay may be expressed in words similar to those chosen by Machiavelli in his introductory note to Lorenzo Di Medici. It is my desire to share with you my experience in international affairs. The paths I have taken in the process have also exposed me to danger and deprivation. You will find my approach simple and unadorned as it seeks no honors for my work "but such as the novelty of its subject may deserve." Furthermore, it should not be deemed presumptuous for an ordinary diplomat, in the service of the United Nations, to discuss the conduct of international relations, seeing that he was a witness and a participant.

But here the parallel ends. Machiavelli's observations and experiences led him to the conviction that the exercise of political power should be independent of moral constraints, and that in matters of politics, the ends of power justify any means necessary to achieve them. Nearly 500 years later, my experience has led me to very different conclusions. It was in the line of political duty that I came to understand the value of moral principles, intuition, and the human spirit. I also learned the limits of theory and rationality.

Rationality's Limits

One night, during the operation that led to the liberation of the western hostages from Lebanon in 1991, I was seized on the streets of Beirut, thrown into a car and transported to a hideout of my abductors, members of the Islamic Jihad. Hooded and ignorant of the when and the where of my ultimate destination, I had time to reflect. I could do nothing else in that predicament. A voice within reminded me of the strong advice I was given when I entered the professional world: "Never mix your professional life with your private life," I had been told. While my face was being squashed on the rear floor of the car accelerating in the narrow, murky streets of Shia Beirut, I thought about this rule of institutional behavior. I smiled ironically to myself as I thought: "Now Picco, try to keep your professional and personal lives completely separate!" Such advice and the practice of rational theory in real life confrontations do not always constitute wisdom.

Modern society has taken the literal teachings of Voltaire's rationalism to a ridiculous extreme.[2] Mathematical models, computer programs, and the Internet all derive from a mindset tending to marginalize the human factor in society. Is this marginalization a mere by-product of progress for its own sake? Or a form of deliberate policy based on the assumption that human subjectivism is the root of society's problems, crises, and errors and, therefore, must be excluded in any consideration of conclusions leaving the field to rational methodology?

To free societies from the "whims" of the king, institutions developed. It was a natural occurrence, because power and knowledge had become widely accessible to great numbers of people and a large middle class had emerged. The very structure of nation-states is based on such institutions, perhaps the greatest achievement of the Voltaire revolution. On the positive side, institutions, including bureaucracies, ensure that the irrationality of the individual is kept in check; but on the darker side, institution building and expansion also dampens the genius of the individual.

Held as a captive and peering into the eyes of the masked interlocutors somewhere in Lebanon, I realized that neither theory, nor mathematical formula, nor rationality could serve to guarantee either my safety or, even less, the success of this mission. These were now abandoned to the grace of human ingenuity and irrationality; my own, I presumed, and that of the abductors. The theoretically-devised techniques of negotiation taught to me in university classrooms had little if any relevance to my present experience. Nor, for that matter, did they apply at other times, in war-ravaged Afghanistan, in Baghdad, or in Tehran where I was also to be assigned. Nor in any of these situations was I in a position to apply such good counsel as I could derive from intellectual exchanges at diplomatic soirées. Even Voltaire was irrelevant in such causes, not because people were irrational, but because the citizens involved in the affairs of state and war in the Middle East were "fully committed to their causes."

What I learned from my arduous work and experiences as a UN peacemaker in the Middle East has little to do with diplomatic tactics and strategies. Nor does it involve game theories, power plays, bargaining advantages, and other devices and schemes elaborated in universities and bureaucracies sheltered from the fray and shielding individuals from political realities. I learned about the importance of the individual, of humaneness, of principles, and of law. These things necessitate commitment, credibility, making choices, and taking responsibility for the consequences of one's own actions. They are about understanding and appreciating the humaneness of the "enemy." They are about respect for the worth and dignity of every individual.

Commitment

In the downtrodden quarters of the Jihad and in war-torn sectors of Afghanistan, I learned the full meaning of commitment.[3] It is far more difficult, although possible, to find a similar type of commitment in the corridors of the European palaces where learned diplomats and functionaries often converge. Commitment to one's objectives is directly linked to one's beliefs. Terrorists are so committed to the achievement of their goals that they are willing to sacrifice their lives for them. To this extent professional and private lives are one and the same. Concomitantly, total commitment to "the cause" disregards all principles and the rights and lives of others. For the Jihad terrorists, total commitment was the equivalent of total war.

My commitment to the mission of seeking the release of the hostages in Lebanon was not total in the same sense of commitment conceived by the members of the Jihad. I was not prepared to sacrifice any universal principles or to violate international law to attain the mission's objective. Therefore, "less than total commitment on my part" was the difference between my masked interlocutors and me. I was prepared to put my life on the line but not the lives of others. Systematically, I refused any deal that would have included the liberation of the hostages in exchange for the freedom of legally convicted terrorists then sitting in Western jails. I was willing, however, to secure the freedom of others detained "without due process" in Israel. Nevertheless, I was resolute in my determination to succeed—much more than professional duty required.

Straightforward principles are easy to abide by. Refusing to enter into any discussion that meant liberating individuals who had been duly tried and sentenced to prison terms in Western or in Israeli jails was not difficult. Human beings should always hold to the basic principles that are universal way-marks in the human journey. Holding to these principles enables one to sleep well at night, to be able to look frankly into the eyes of one's children while being honestly proud, and possibly, even convinced, that one has made some modest contribution to the betterment of this world.

Failing "total commitment," was the success of my mission in Lebanon, nevertheless, more important to me that my own life? Was the cause bigger than the actor? Of course! No actor can be so arrogant as to believe that he or she is more important than the cause to which he or she is dedicated. In this respect, the terrorists and I understood each other very well. Both of us in a strange way accepted that we as individuals were expendable, if that was to be required. Indeed, one of the many permutations of the deal was my capture and imprisonment in Lebanon. My captivity, which was hopefully for only some limited period of time, six months to a year, was a swap for the freedom of the unfortunate hostages. To use less dramatic terminology, I defined myself as "UN bail" posted for the release of the hostages.[4] In this instance, one can say that holding to principles and the success of this mission were more important to me than my own life.

Credibility and Impartiality

Thankfully, I survived. And, by putting my life on the line, I achieved two important objectives: establishment of the sincerity of my commitment and credibility in the view of the terrorists. By allowing myself to be taken, without protection, into the den of the Jihad, I offered myself, de facto, as a pawn in the negotiations. Of the sincerity of my commitment there could then be no doubt. Concomitantly, I established credibility, the most important key to success in negotiations. Perhaps their problem was the posture of impartiality, which is not helpful if credibility is needed.

Impartiality is a misconception. It is a cloak often used in Western European parlance to conceal one's inability to come to a decision and, accordingly, to assume responsibility. To be impartial is not an operational concept, even though it is very fashionable to profess such in United Nations and other diplomatic circles. Current usage of the term is a vestige of Cold War thinking, when being impartial meant to be considered neither with Moscow nor with Washington. Although the concept was elevated to nobler heights through instruments such as peacekeeping, in actual negotiations it is never useful. Each side will regard the person in the middle as being partial to the opponent, even if the mediator takes a position that is equidistant between the two sides. An accusation of impartiality by either of the parties is usually a pressure tactic imposed on the arbitrator. If the mediator gives into the pressure, he or she is lost as a credible go-between. Was I expected or even asked to be impartial when negotiating the fate of innocent hostages with the Jihad? What could possibly have been the meaning of impartiality in this case? It was never a question.

A key requirement for a mediator is to be able to deliver what has been promised or what the parties expect to be delivered. This implies credibility. Values and principles accompany credibility, which is both an institutional and personal quality. It is enhanced by a sense of commitment, which can only be personal and thus measured in actions and deeds of individuals.

Choice and Responsibility

Art in the task of making choices was also required in the Middle East negotiations. The situation required choosing a right course of action according to the principles of the UN Charter and consistent with universally respected personal ethical standards. Making choices also entailed taking responsibility for the consequences of the decision and living with them for the rest of one's life.

When in, March 1992, the UN Secretary General and his political advisers proceeded as a team to remove Afghanistan's President Najibullah from power, the country entered a period of chaos and human torment more devastating than that suffered under all the ten years of Soviet troop occupation in the country.[5] At the time I thought that stripping authority from the only relatively powerful person in the country, thus, leaving a vacuum of power in this politically unstable country was foolish to say the least. I failed, however, to convince the other two members of this team that this was an unwise decision.

This ill-advised action cost the life of Najibullah and the lives of thousands of Afghans, swept away in the years of civil war that followed. In conscience, the responsibility for this great loss of life will always be with the three of us. There is no way of denying it. Accompanying the power to make choices is personal responsibility. All too often individuals try to hide their responsibility behind the veil of the institution. Individuals can try to do this but the truth of the situation is always there in one's conscience. When making choices that affect the lives of people, in the most literal sense of the word, an individual must rely on ethical principles if there is to be any comfort when the situation does not work out for the best. What else is there to guide the negotiator, when put in the position of having to play God with people's lives?

Judgment Call

Unfortunately, neither questions of life nor matters of diplomacy are always very clear. Making a choice may require one to decide which people are to be helped when it is impossible to save everyone. This is certainly not an enviable choice to have to make. In the hostage negotiations, this was the position in which I was placed. In the triangulation that involved Western hostages, Israelis—Missing in Action (MIA's), and Lebanese detained "without due process" in Israel and south Lebanon, the ideal objective was to free everybody as part of a complete package.[6]

The package deal broke down and difficult choices had to be made. My options were to either try to rescue the package intact and to take the risk that nobody would be freed; or to choose to free those who could be liberated immediately, thereby sacrificing the bargaining chips that could be useful to free others later. As usual, when decisions have to be taken, the luxuries of theory and academic council were not available. In the Lebanese situation, not only was time short, but I was almost alone in making the required decisions. I had the comfort of knowing, however, that Perez de Cuellar, the Secretary General of the United Nations, would support whatever choice I felt compelled to make.[7]

To complicate matters I was also aware that whatever decision I would make would engender criticism. It might be asked: What right did Picco have to decide whether to risk further imprisonment for some or to diminish the chance for somebody else to be freed? Why was Picco in that position? Why did Picco have to make that choice? The answers were brutally simple. I had chosen to undertake that mission and had requested to be assigned this opportunity to help fellow human beings in difficulty. It was my fate that the UN Secretary General acquiesced to my request. Assuredly, I could not now retreat when confronted with a difficult decision to make, one much more excruciating than I could have foreseen.

Beyond the criticism, I will never be able to efface from my memory the sad countenances of the family members of those who had to remain imprisoned. At the beginning of the process, the task was easy. I had been asked to choose which hostages should go free first. I simply refused to do so. It is not difficult to refuse to exclude anyone from a comprehensive deal. But, later on, when there was no more time, nor means at my disposal to save everybody, how could I possibly decide whether to keep the complete package together at very high risk of failure, or try to secure freedom for some at the risk others? Could I really evaluate the odds against one or the other of the choices? Could I weigh in balance the sufferings of each prisoner and his family and try to secure freedom for those whose sufferings were the greatest? Could I resort to a mathematical model to determine the best course of action? At the decisive moment, could I have all the elements relevant to the decision that I would surely have with hindsight? The answer to all those questions was, indeed, a resounding "no." But failure to make a choice, which meant failure to play my role in the scheme of things, would mean loss of credibility and, accordingly, the collapse of any possible deal for anyone.

As institutional images go, however, I was neither the model diplomat nor the model bureaucrat: I made decisions on my own, even when I found no precedents to refer to. I could not procrastinate, because each day meant extra suffering for the unjustly incarcerated individuals. And, indeed, procrastination could have meant that no one would go free. In the end, the eleven Western hostages came home. But some Israelis, missing in action, and many Lebanese detained without due process of law did not. I was comforted only by the thought that sometime in the future I might be able to develop new bargaining chips to help the remaining few.

There was little consolation, after my mission was finished, that no further advancement was possible in any of the remaining cases. More than seven years have now passed. Perhaps, I made the right decision, perhaps not. By day I have been satisfied for having helped some people regain their freedom, at night I still think of those remaining undeservedly in prison.

Accountability

Large institutions offer refuge from personal accountability. Attempts to improve institutions by way of "reform" accomplish little if reform is not accompanied by change in the mindsets of the individuals working in them. Personal accountability applies in international affairs just as it does for everybody else in life. Over

341

the last decade, people have repeatedly heard political leaders and even scholars explain the tragedy of internal conflicts and war as the unavoidable consequences of history, religion, culture, or the breakdown of institutions.

What a mistaken notion! Religion does not kill, culture does not rape, history does not generate refugees, and institutions do not destroy human lives. How convenient it is to justify decisions that can only be made in human minds as the consequences of great mysteries of history, the exigencies of religion, and the power, or lack of it, in institutions. When a human life is lost or damaged, it is always the consequence of some action taken by one or more individuals: only people perform those acts.

It is time to bring to the fore with courage and dignity, personal accountability in international affairs. The United Nations did not fail in Afghanistan; those who did are individuals with first and last names. They are the ones responsible, and should be held accountable. It is inconceivable that those who worked and still work for the United Nations accuse this organization of their own failures! Should not the organization be shielded and individuals take on the responsibility for their mistakes for the sake of the larger community represented by the institution? There will be no improvement in the running of world affairs until and unless individuals take onto their shoulders what belongs to them: accountability for their decisions, for better or worse.

Should a Secretary General of the United Nations be allowed to use the expression, "It is not my fault."? And even if it is not his or her fault, what does it matter? Is the goal to shield such a person from the judgment of others whether right or wrong? Should not the role of such a person be likened to that of any other politician or is it to tread ethically and morally where ordinary politicians do not dare to go? To raise the level of the office so as to appeal to new generations of people across borders, of different cultures, and beyond political differences should be the objective of such a unique position.

What, for instance, might have happened in 1992 and 1993, if the UN Secretary General, instead of claiming that the Bosnian tragedy was not his fault, had simply moved his office physically to Sarajevo? Would the killing have continued to the same degree? Would not his moral standing have risen in prestige? And what if he had been killed? Do not junior UN officials risk their lives every day? Indeed, in Bosnia, quite a few had already been killed.

The Human Factor

Not only do institutions shield individuals from personal accountability but a mindset seems to prevail in some societies where people insist that historic, economic, and social trends are unaffected by individual behavior. Thus, a common belief is: "There is nothing anyone can do to change those trends." This perception is quite convenient because it further absolves individuals from any personal responsibility in society.

To illustrate: it has been said that the crisis in the Balkans was the unavoidable consequence of the atavistic hatred between Croats and Serbs. A careful reading of history would emphatically prove that Croats and Serbs never before fought each other as distinct ethnic groups. Prior conflicts took place for the causes of the different political entities to which they each belonged. Even in 1941, when the Croat Ustashia fought along-side Adolf Hitler and the Nazis, they had the backing of the monarchist Serbs and their enemies were not the Serbs, per se, but the Communists. Among the latter was Marshal Tito, a Croat.[8]

The great religious divide, which was played up as one of the causes of the Bosnian conflict, could hardly be used as an explanation if it were generally known that 40% of the marriages in Bosnia until the early 90s, were mixed marriages. Moreover, the Muslims in Bosnia are Serbs who converted to Islam in the 1600's, some for tax reasons. Thus, the ethnic divide in real terms is hard to find.

A more accurate explanation for the conflict in the former Yugoslavia, which can now be reported, is that it was the result of a deliberate decision taken by five individuals—Presidents Milosevich and Tudjman, together with one Croat, and two Serb generals—when they met in Austria in late 1989. At that time, both

Milosevich and Tudjman had presidential ambitions but they shared only one country. To satisfy their mutual aspirations they established two countries, one for each.[9] Over the course of negotiations they even selected the three villages in which they should ignite "the ethnic spark." Bosnia was supposed to be carved up between them and there was no intention that it should ever become independent.

Real Politik

Emerson once wrote, "There is properly no history, only biographies." In international politics, an individual can make a difference. Therefore to believe in biographies rather than history, means to ignore the supremacy of the dictates of political realism. If political reality is explained by balances of power and the consequences of sweeping trends, beyond the control of any human being, then biographies would have insignificant meaning; indeed, no single person could ever have dented the course of history. My experience is not that. In fact, my experience is that *real politik* can be and is being challenged all the time.

By mid 1988, the war between Iran and Iraq had been going on for 8 years; Iraq had gained the upper hand now for practically the first time since the beginning of the conflict. And, of course, the powers that were in the East and the West were lending support to Saddam Hussein against the Ayatollah. Because the outside world cheered for Iraq, the war, in Hussein's view, was a battle fought on behalf of the entire world against the "obscurantist" forces of fundamentalism.

The military advantage Hussein enjoyed during that summer of 1988, was intoxicating and Iraq was strongly tempted to conquer part of the Iranian territory. Conquering the oil-producing land of Iran became a real option. That this invasion and occupation would probably produce tens of thousands of civilian casualties and unleash a worldwide wave of terrorism concerned few people.

The UN Secretary General's small team conducted the negotiations to end this war. Pressure mounted very critically and specifically on me and the Secretary General, to allow the negotiations to flounder so as to give more time to the Iraqi army to enter and occupy part of Iran. The weight of political power favoring this outcome was definitely against the UN negotiators. On the 8 August 1988, however, despite this strong governmental pressure, the bloody eight-year war came to an end simply through the negotiations persuasively conducted by a team of UN officials. We did not give into *real politik.*

Individuals do matter; they can alter the course of human events. Yet, political realism, as opposed to idealism, and even common sense is the prevailing diplomatic wisdom. To me such confidence in *real politik* signifies submission to fatalism. Indeed, if impersonal power prevails in matters of humankind why even bother waking up in the morning. If individuals cannot make a difference why even enter the game of life? Political realism is also a good excuse to avoid personal responsibility. Submission to *real politik* is to abdicate personal responsibility. If everything happens because of forces superior to and unmanageable by the individual, then the individual cannot be held accountable for whatever may happen. This concept helps, on one hand, to reduce the resistance to might: it makes one believe that such resistance is useless. This form of fatalism weakens determination to do anything at variance with sheer might—whether it be morally right or wrong.

Experience in the valleys of Afghanistan and in the dens of Lebanon's Jihadland, and in many places geographically in between, has impressed on me the relevance and necessity for personal responsibility. Individual knowledge, courage, and determination can at times, though not always, defy many odds and prevail. History is the complex, compounded results of the actions of many. I may only be able to better the world by an infinitesimal amount, but I will never abdicate my right to do so.

An Unbearable Presence: the Enemy

The concept of the "enemy" has accompanied me in my journey from Pakistan westward to the shores of the Mediterranean, and in this journey, through four conflict situations and three actual wars.

During the epoch of the Soviet Union, political meetings in Moscow were scenes with casts of thousands. I still remember the long table and equally long list of Soviet officials that might sit beside Foreign Minister Gromyko during those official meetings. Suspicion was the order of the day when a Western diplomat would travel alone to Communist countries during the cold war and vice versa. Neither side trusted the individual. The individual was the weak link in systems of institutions, competing ideologies and power balances.

I did my best in my UN career to learn about the family lives of my interlocutors. I spoke with Abdullah, my masked Jihad militant counterpart in Lebanon, about his children. I learned about the children of my Iranian contacts. With this approach I searched for some common denominator between a Western educated UN official, a young Lebanese man involved in terrorist activity, and an Israeli defense official, more knowledgeable about intelligence than I could even imagine, and a Soviet bureaucrat continuously under scrutiny by his "minder."[10]

Common denominators always exist between human beings. All of us, in different ways, want the same thing. When ideology is stripped away, when religious barriers are overcome, when cultural biases are accepted as such, what unites us all is the desire that our children have a better life than we have had. It is that simple. We are all ready if necessary to sacrifice our own lives for our children. Offspring are a great human motivator for the vast majority of individuals.

If this is the case, we can meet on this common ground if only we are allowed to do so. In a discussion about children, we can understand each other and "really" communicate. But to do this we must be willing to go where institutions do not dare to tread. And that is why, perhaps, many state structures do not permit such common sharing to occur. They do not wish that understanding to develop because it would underscore the fact that we are alike in our basic human instinct of loving our children. Even the "enemy" is like me. But, so far in human history, the enemy has always been an important tool of nation building and management. There has yet to be a leader who could lead without an enemy.

But, if the enemy is like me, then part of his enmity has vanished. Being an enemy justifies so much. Indeed it justifies unfriendly behavior, unethical behavior, and worse. Most of all, the concept of the enemy has to be supported; nothing is better than ignorance to support enmity. Accordingly, allowing individuals in opposite camps to get to know each other on a one to one basis is to be avoided, if ignorance is to be fostered. Ignorance, in turn, will feed more enmity and enmity will make it easier to manage power.

I asked Abdullah if he had ever sat down with an Israeli to talk about hopes for the lives of their sons and daughters, rather than to discuss the faults and problems of their ancestors, or even their own. How many close encounters, one on one, have happened in the conduct of international affairs? How much room is still left to the genius of the individual and his untapped resources, which are part of his soul, mind, and heart? How come these words never appear in the rules and regulations of institutions? Are they not part of the experience of the human beings that those institutions are supposed to manage, help, and assist?

Voltaire was right and his legacy of rationalism has given us a better world. But have we taken it too far? Have we become what John Ralston Saul called Voltaire's bastards? [11]

Have we gone from the dictatorship of a monarch to that of cold reason? I entered the UN, in the early 70s, with idealism. I left twenty years later with my idealism untouched; in fact it was strengthened because I had succeeded in realizing some of my aspirations, even my dreams to help end wars and to save human lives; in other words, to make a bit of a difference. I had an even greater opportunity to test the wisdom of adherence to moral principles than I thought was possible. When asked to carry out an assignment in violation of these principles, I resigned. I have no regrets.

Endnotes

1 - Niccolo Machiavelli, *The Prince,* trans. Luigi Ricco, in *The Prince and The Discourses* (New York: The Modern Library, 1950), 3-4.

2 - The age of reason and of enlightenment of the mid 1700s challenged the world of monarchs and tyranny by way of knowledge and logical thinking. Diderot, Voltaire, Rousseau, among others, introduced the logic of reason there where faith, dogma and unquestioned authority prevailed.

3 - Islamic Jihad became the standard name to indicate the groups of Islamic militants who had claimed responsibility for the kidnapping of the Western hostages in Lebanon.

4 - A complete account of the operations which led to the liberation of the Western hostages from Lebanon is contained in the author's book *Man Without a Gun* (New York: Times Books, Random House, 1999).

5 - Najibullah had become President of Afghanistan in 1986 during the presence of the Soviet troops in the country. He remained in power until April 1992, well after the Red Army had withdrawn in 1989. He was convinced to relinquish power and seek asylum in India by the UN Secretariat. The entire plan failed.

6 - Detainees without due process were called the Lebanese militants taken prisoner by Israel in South Lebanon. They were incarcerated in Israeli controlled South Lebanon or in Israel, but were never charged nor legally tried.

7 - Javier Perez De Cuellar was UN Secretary General from 1982 to 1991.

8 - Ustashia were the pro-Nazi Croatian nationalist who fought alongside Hitler's army during Germany's occupation of the Balkans.

9 - Both succeeded in becoming Presidents of Serbia and Croatia, respectively.

10 - "Minder" defines, in intelligence, a controller or supervisor of agents, officials or individuals, not trusted by the political system to act without control.

11 - John Ralston Saul, *Voltaire's Bastards* (New York: Vintage Books, 1993).

CHAPTER 19

ETHICS IN DIPLOMACY: CRISES OF CONSCIENCE AND SELF-INTEREST[1]

Princeton N. Lyman

For many years, I have been taken by a phrase in the *Unsahneh Tokef*, a prayer about God's judgment that Jews recite on the High Holidays of Rosh Hashanah and Yom Kippur. The phrase says, "The great Shofar is sounded, and a still small voice is heard." What, I have long asked myself, is the meaning of that "still small voice?" The Hebrew words suggest a smallness that is infinitesimal, a stillness that is almost silent.

Fortunately, I can now turn with such questions to my son-in-law, the Rabbi. Like any good Talmudic scholar, however, he does not answer quickly. He pondered my question for some moments, then the moments stretched into weeks. Finally, he sent me a letter, saying that there are few references to this phrase in the literature, but it could refer to the angels, cited in the next sentence of the prayer; or it could be one's conscience; or it could even be the voice of God. He closed by saying there would be more. A few weeks after that, I received a notice that my son-in-law had enrolled me in a correspondence course by a group ironically called, "A still small voice." One lesson in this course went to the heart of the subject of this essay: ethics in diplomacy. That lesson, to which I will return at the end, is about a paradox. There are some who would suggest that ethics in diplomacy is a contradiction in terms. I am constantly reminded of the saying: a diplomat is someone who is prepared to lie for his country. More seriously, there is an inherent contradiction between a code of universal ethics, which is propounded by most religions, and the defense, by almost any means, of the nation-state, which is, as yet, the highest political form humanity has created to protect its lives and institutions.

The place of ethical values in the conduct of state affairs has been at issue for centuries, debated in the Greek city states, in the Middle Ages by political theorists like Machiavelli and Hegel, by philosophers like Spinoza and Kant, and by religious thinkers such as Milton and St. Augustine. The key questions are: In serving national interests, should diplomacy be bound by ethics beyond those that relate to the interests of the state itself? Should diplomats pursue any means to achieve objectives of the state, whether legal or illegal, or injurious to others or not?

For the most part, political thinkers, including Locke, Spinoza, Kant, and Montesquieu, concluded that the nature of the political system supplied part of the answer. Constitutional systems that provided carefully structured means for defining both the national interest and threats to it were seen to protect against the moral abuse of the supremacy of the state.[2] History has confirmed that judgment to some extent. It has been frequently noted, in recent years, that democracies rarely go to war with each other, suggesting an inherent check on unreasonable ambition. But, in many democracies, certainly in the United States, these systems have not fully absolved humankind of the problem. Indeed, the extra justification provided by being a democracy may tempt some leaders to take greater leeway. Under the guise of security, and sometimes by misguided interpretations of the national interest, democracies have been involved in actions of questionable, if not fully objectionable, morality.

The "Iran-Contra Scandal" that rocked the United States and the presidency of Ronald Reagan is one example. In this case, high officials engaged in an arms-for-hostage deal contrary to stated policy, and then used the proceeds of the deal as an illegal means to support anti-government "contras" in Nicaragua. The issue, argued out in dramatic Congressional testimony, was whether those who violated the law, or the will of Congress, were acting on the basis of a higher imperative. The defendants saw their actions as serving the interests of the country and believed themselves to be patriotic. Many in the United States agreed and believed that exoneration rather than punishment was appropriate. Those who disagreed raised questions as to whether the defendants were compromising the very principles that made the country worth defending and, if there is no respect for law, what kind of society does one have? I know several of the individuals caught up in this controversy. They are persons who believe deeply in their country and the righteousness of what they did. They personify the dilemma of ethics in diplomacy.

I will address this dilemma by referring to United States history and by drawing on my experiences as a scholar and practitioner of international diplomacy. The analysis that follows is divided into three time frames. The first frame treats the subject by reviewing the history and practice of United States diplomacy from the early years until World War II. The second frame is the Cold War period. This analysis includes a more profound examination of the scholarly writings that had an influence on the dilemma during this period. This time frame coincides with the years that I was a student of international relations and just beginning my work as a diplomat. The third time frame offers contemporary examples of actual dilemmas I experienced in work as a senior level diplomat. Taken together, these frames lead to consideration of the paradox and to the place for conscience.

The Historical Sweep

From its origins, the United States has always considered itself the embodiment of the democratic ideal. The founding fathers were not timid in espousing this ideal as one of universal significance and therefore giving the United States a special, moral role in the world. That role was not to be played by active intervention in the affairs of other nations. Both by inclination and by the smallness of its power, the United States preferred to keep foreign policy a minor aspect of its early years. An active foreign policy, it was argued, would lead to actions, such as war and alliances with non-democratic regimes that would undermine the democratic principles of its polity.[3]

These attitudes were challenged and they changed as the country's power increased and as the temptations of an empire beckoned. In the Spanish-American War at the turn of the century, the United States acquired the beginnings of an overseas empire. These steps were justified by the President on moral grounds, even as the United States suppressed a rebellion in the Philippines that represented, at least ostensibly, the very principles of liberty and independence that this country so proudly proclaimed to the world in 1776. The principle of non-intervention in Latin America was breached many times. In some instances, the policy was broken to restore order and to promote democracy; in one case, it was to make it possible to build the Panama Canal, a clear commercial and military imperative. These actions were spurred not only by the hubris of power, but also by influential writers such as Admiral Alfred Thayer Mahan. The Admiral who argued that the balance of power depended on sea power and that the country's future security depended on developing that power and all the overseas stations and support facilities that power required.[4]

Thus, this country was squarely facing the moral and political dilemmas that other nations have faced for centuries. The issues became more pronounced when the United States emerged as a world power. Questions of moral obligation and power were drawn sharply in the debate over the League of Nations. Although the United States entered World War I initially to deter the challenge to sea power posed by Germany's submarine warfare, Woodrow Wilson transformed that objective into something far grander—a war to end all wars—and to establish a system of world order that would protect and defend democracy.

If the United States appeared to be responding to the voice of conscience, there was still the question of what price was the country willing to pay.

In the debate over the League, Wilson was challenged at home by those who questioned, not the moral value of democracy, but the country's proper role in promoting it. Wilson felt a world league could do so without recourse to force, or if force proved necessary, at least not on a major scale. His opponents questioned that and therefore questioned whether America's interest—defined in terms of its own security—demanded making a commitment so broad that the country might be called upon to defend it by war itself. In the end, the United States retreated from this precipice and withdrew from the League. However, it had to reenter Europe and face similar issues in the wake of World War II.[5]

The Cold War and Superpower Status

During this era, the historic debate over raison d'etat, power politics, and morality was renewed and restated in contemporary terms. I grew up in this era. I was drawn to diplomatic service because I studied international relations and the place of the United States in the world. The writers and thinkers of this period shaped much of my own thinking until, later, I was in a position to judge these matters from the different perspective of a participant in the formulation and execution of policy itself.

The Cold War and the assumption of super-power status focused the dilemma in a different way. The United States saw the Cold War in both strategic and moral terms. The country was fighting for survival against what it saw as an aggressive and imperialist power. It also saw it as a fight for democracy, cloaking all its allies in the term "free world." The ethical questions took on new aspects during this long and turbulent period. The government supported some allies who were anything but democratic; it sufficed that they were not communist. It built significant security structures, ones that, at times, impinged upon domestic freedoms as much as upon its principles abroad. The United States engaged in wars in the Third World, most notably Korea and Vietnam, but also indirectly in Central America, Angola, and Afghanistan, that tore at its ethical values and occasioned some of the deepest torment in the country's history. The collapse of the communist empire may suggest that these compromises were the right and necessary ones, but not all would agree, and certainly not in every case.

One of the most influential writers of this period was Hans Morgenthau. In his path-breaking work, *Politics Among Nations*, he sharply criticized the overly moralistic tone of traditional American foreign policy as epitomized by Wilson and some of the later advocates of world order. He emphasized that national security depended historically on a balance of power between key nations, and that the United States' own security depended, therefore, upon understanding that balance and maintaining it. Pursuing universal idealism independent of, or contrary to, such considerations, he considered both dangerous and foolish.[6] Morgenthau became the guru of a school of *real politik* that dominated much of U.S. foreign policy thinking for many years. Writers that drew upon his work focused on the factors of power balance and the narrower definitions of national interest. Leading policy analysts and practitioners, who followed in his wake were coolly calculating professionals, who were committed, but were neither overly idealistic nor emotionally "Cold Warriors."[7]

The nuclear balance reinforced that approach. One could be a committed anti-communist, but one did not want to risk nuclear war over the marginal gains of one communist thrust or another. Schools of nuclear balance produced the most extraordinarily cool calculators of balance, leading to such bizarre but effective concepts as Mutually Assured Destruction (appropriately "MAD"). Both the Soviet Union and the United States assured each other that nuclear war would obliterate them both, and established sophisticated schemes of mutual satellite spying that were designed not so much to hide, but to display mutual capacity so as to prevent miscalculation and thus preemptive attack.[8]

All of this was heady stuff. And it suggested that cold rationality, rather than morality and ethics guided truly sound foreign policy. But, then I had the great good fortune of spending a summer as teaching assistant to the formidable, Professor Hans Morgenthau, himself. And, I found out something that his disciples had missed, or chose to miss. A refugee of Nazi Germany, Hans Morgenthau was a deeply ethical and moral philosopher. He understood better than his disciples that, what made a nation is not only its power and physical survival, but also its ethical sense of itself. I listened as he lectured passionately in favor of a nuclear test ban, and against some of the cruder forms of Cold War activity that sometimes characterized U.S. policy during those years. Morgenthau argued against impractical and hypocritical moralism. He did not argue for abdicating the fundamental morality that should help define the nation itself.[9]

Another influential scholar and writer was Zbigniew Brzezinski. Brzezinski was firmly entrenched in the *real politik* school. But writing about the then Soviet Bloc, he laid out a principle applicable to all modern nations. When a country follows, over time, a foreign policy that runs counter to its own domestic values, either the policy eventually collapses or the domestic values begin to be compromised. Brzezinski was writing about the Soviet Union's hold over the countries of Eastern Europe, explaining why it was critical for the regime to keep those countries locked within a communist system. Prophetically, he saw that if Eastern Europe were allowed to liberalize, the tenets of Communist control within the Soviet Union could no longer hold.[10]

The same principle affected U.S. policy in Vietnam. The United States was pursuing a war policy which, whatever legitimate aims might have been involved, led to actions that ran counter to values held at home. So great was this conflict of values that it began to tear the country apart, and indeed the scars remain today. The anti-war movement took on, not only mass, but also potentially violent forms. Eventually, the policy in Vietnam collapsed; it could only have been sustained by further eroding the principles cherished at home. It was a formidable lesson.

But it is a lesson often misread. One of the reasons is that there is a popular tendency, both within government and outside of it, to make a distinction between "humanitarian" and "foreign policy" concerns. It is, as if they are on completely separate planes, with the former comprising acts of charity carried out without any foreign policy gain and the latter, a scheme of base motives. This tendency is, ironically, fostered often by humanitarians wishing to be clear and clean of what they consider to be crass and materialistic objectives. But practitioners of "realism" make the same mistake. However, that is not how the system works. United States foreign policy contains, and must contain, if it is to be sustainable, a strong humanitarian and moralistic element. That is not the only element, but it must be part of it. When the country violates that principle, its mistake is soon realized.

On several occasions, I have seen policy makers leaning toward decisions, too narrowly based to be supportable by the general public. In the drought that gripped Ethiopia in 1984-85, some persons flirted, if only momentarily, with the idea that the country should not respond with humanitarian aid lest support be given to its then communist-leaning dictator, Colonel Mengistu. But with the first television images of the starvation occurring in Ethiopia, public opinion washed over such concerns. And, as the tragedy in Somalia was first developing, some argued that the United States had too little direct interest in Somalia to undertake the cost and commitment that it demanded. But there too, the clear humanitarian reality of the situation overwhelmed such considerations.[11]

The other side of the coin is also true. Although it may sound cynical, history has shown that a country's security interests can be pursued with greater support, if they also carry a moral aspect. That is why Lincoln was led to add the emancipation of slavery to the cause of the Civil War, and why Wilson caught the imagination of Americans in his widened purpose for World War I. This is a dangerous truth, however, for morality can thus be used to mask rather than enhance other motives, to the detriment of both morality and policy. At best, it can confuse a country's citizens as to its government's real purposes. Did the U.S. fight the Gulf War to stop aggression and establish the parameters of a new world order, or was it simply defending access to Middle East oil? The answer is a combination of both, with the latter reinforcing its will to do the former. This leads us to another truth.

Although Americans are not saints, they are soon disillusioned if United States official policy lacks moral grounding, and they will not long support one that has none of it. But, they are also concerned with the outer limits of the commitment of their country's power and resources. This is the same dilemma faced after World War I and which, now looms even greater in the wake of the Cold War. During the Cold War, the danger was hubris and the overuse of power. The high ideals of democracy and the global nature of the conflict with the Soviet Union contained the dangers of excessive use of power, the justifying of inordinate means by idealistic ends, and, at the same time, the pursuit of unrealistic goals on behalf of democratic principles.

Three Challenges in Contemporary Diplomacy

Today, the danger is of a different kind, that the U.S. can find neither sufficient will nor adequate means to express its basic ethical principles, leaving its citizenry in a moral and ethical vacuum. Three examples come immediately to mind. The first example involves military power, another basically economic and social, and the third a balance of the ethical and the pragmatic.

1. FORMER YUGOSLAVIA: DEFINING THE LIMITS OF INTERVENTION

The horror that confronted the world every day in former Yugoslavia for three years, and then again in 1998 in Kosovo, was most painful. It seemed inconceivable to many Americans, in the years when atrocities were being committed against Muslims, Croats, and Serbs alike, that something could not be done to bring this atrocity to an end. But Americans, as they approached the brink of military action, found themselves in a quandary. How much were they responsible for ending this tragedy? And, was the moral issue enough? Where moral and other vital interests are at stake, Americans might pledge themselves to a conflict of long duration, as they did in World War II. But today, with the human costs of war made ever more immediate through television and modern communications of all kinds, and the direct threats to national security less evident, the weighing of those costs becomes more troublesome.

There was also the factor of practicality, the other lesson from Morgenthau. Would intervention in the Balkans, where World War I was ignited, serve to rekindle the Cold War just as the United

States had emerged from that dreadful period? Moreover, could this country bring about an end to the horror, even with military intervention or would it be embarking on a moralistic crusade that would only drain resources and commitment? One of the legacies from Vietnam has been the fear, among policy-makers, that Americans would not tolerate a long war of almost any kind, certainly not one with an indefinite outcome. This may be a superficial understanding of the American psyche, but it has influenced the entire debate over what is now being called humanitarian intervention. The revulsion and ultimate retreat from involvement in Somalia, after the loss of eighteen servicemen reinforced the lesson that America was less willing to tolerate casualties, even relatively few, if the stakes for it were not extraordinary.

In Yugoslavia, and again later in Kosovo, the United States eventually moved to provide the military force, necessary even to enforce basic humanitarian objectives, not to mention the political ones. But, this force was introduced only after strengthened Muslim and Croat forces had reversed the military balance and were beginning to retake much of the territory they had lost to the Serbs in the previous three years. This deployment occurred when air strikes alone, would be sufficient to turn the tide, and when the massacre at Srebrenica had raised moral outrage to a peak.

During the agonizing period before the decision to intervene was taken, colleagues in the State Department faced an ethical challenge. After all the sound and fury of practicality—the position papers, communiqués, speeches, dutifully and loyally prepared—there was that still small voice. Several resigned in the face of what they felt was a morally indefensible refusal to intervene. Later, in the case of Kosovo, the long struggle, first to agree on the dimensions of any intervention, and then, to obtain allied support for it, left many deeply upset over the human tragedy played out, once again, before such action was agreed upon.

Note, too, that in both cases, the decision to use or threaten force, once taken, was limited to air strikes, a form of military intervention which minimizes risk of casualties. The introduction of ground troops after the Dayton Accords, even when fighting had stopped, was much more controversial and, to this day, has only grudging Congressional support.[12]

The drawn-out Balkan experience, following upon the calamitous one in Somalia, led the Clinton Administration, in 1994, to enunciate principles of future military intervention, much stricter than propounded in the presidential campaign, two years earlier. They placed an upper limit on the proverbial, "price to be paid," especially for a largely humanitarian effort. In respect to the use of U.S. forces, the Administration proposed:

- Any deployment of U.S. forces abroad should be vital to U.S. interests.
- The United States should not intervene militarily unless it is clear that it will win.
- There must be clearly defined political and military objectives.
- Any deployment must be continually monitored.
- Any deployment must have the support of the American people and the Congress.
- Any use of force must be a "last resort."

Similar, but less sweeping, restrictions were placed on future support for UN peacekeeping operations. These operations should henceforth have some strong U.S. national interest at stake, a clearly defined set of goals and objectives, and an exit strategy. These principles were formalized in a Presidential determination, PDD-25.[13]

These may be politically and pragmatically sound principles. One could even argue that, in raising the stakes for the risk of human lives, they serve an important ethical principle. As heralded by Locke and Kant, they represent democracy's restraint on a leadership's readiness to go to war. But, these are strict principles that can undermine response to situations where, as in Yugoslavia, the use or threat of force would be essential to achieving humanitarian objectives. They would thus influence the limited U.S. response to the situation in Rwanda in 1994, the Congo in 1996, and Burundi that same year. In sum, they posed upper limits on the country's readiness to intervene, which continues to create moral dilemmas.

2. Haiti: The Limits of Domestic Tolerance

The second example is from a more domestic point of view. It involves the Haitians, who fled their poverty-stricken and dictatorially governed island for the United States, following the overthrow of elected President Aristide, in 1991. During the debate that followed, the issue was often framed in humanitarian terms, but it was more complex, posing far greater issues of commitment and sacrifice than some advocates would admit.

The dilemmas were great. There is no question that life on Haiti was miserable, and made all the more so, by the overthrow of democracy and the imposition of economic sanctions that followed. No one can fault those who tried to leave. At the same time, traditionally, U.S. policy on refugees has been one of the most generous and forthcoming in the world. This country takes in more than 100,000 refugees from all over the world each year. The United States is the largest single contributor to the UN High Commission for Refugees. Moreover, the United States has lobbied other countries to honor the principle of asylum for peoples fleeing similar situations elsewhere. All things considered, this level of commitment is far more responsive to the country's basic ethical principles than to any other foreign policy objective. But, in this particular instance, both Presidents Bush and Clinton, in turn, found it necessary to block the wholesale entry of Haitian boat people into the U.S.

Critics argued that the decision was racist, contrary to international law, and inhumane. Haitians, along with Jamaicans, however, have constituted the largest group of legal immigrants in the United States, in recent years. There are more than one million legal immigrants in the United States from Haiti. Race, if not entirely absent, was hardly a factor. What was driving U.S. policy in this regard was the sheer practicality arising out of Haiti's proximity to this country's borders. When Bill Clinton suggested, in the 1992 campaign that, if elected, he might lift the restriction put on by President Bush, preparations began on the beaches of Haiti for as many as 200,000 Haitians to set sail the day of Clinton's inauguration.[14] This crisis was more than a refugee movement; it was wholesale migration.

I participated in the debate over Haitian refugee policy throughout 1992, and it was one of the most painful I have experienced. There were simply no ready answers. Haiti was gripped by poverty and dictatorship. Turning back all those fleeing deprivation and oppression violated the basic principles, if not the legal technicalities, of the very refugee policy the United States had advocated around the world. But, wholesale migration of Haitians to the United States was politically and practically impossible. Communities, in the United States, normally generous to refugees, resisted so great an influx, especially at a time when the country was facing economic recession. The significant prevalence of HIV infection among the Haitian refugees added to the emotion of the issue.

Unless there was a middle ground option, and, I confess, we failed to find one, we were confronting an impossible dilemma. Haitians piled up on U.S. Coast Guard ships, collected in Guantanamo, then in large numbers, were returned to Haiti against their will. American human rights groups filed lawsuits, and the Congressional Black Caucus expressed outrage. I remember particularly one meeting in the Capital, receiving from Congressional members I admire, a torrent of abuse heaped upon our policy. And I wondered where was the moral footing here. In a strange, ironic way, however, the crisis itself—with its irreconcilable pressures—was moving the United States to a new plan of moral, if practical, activism. Only a major change within Haiti could resolve this dilemma.

This conclusion led to the decision, by the Clinton Administration, to restore Aristide to power, indeed, to use American troops to do so a difficult decision especially in light of the new policy on military intervention cited earlier.[15] In doing so, the government helped to bring about a shift in international thinking on refugee policy. Increasingly, and often for the same practical reasons—with Kurds pressing against the Turkish border, Rwandans migrating into and destabilizing the former Zaire, and Croats moving into Germany—emphasis shifted from asylum to addressing the root causes of the refugee problem in their home countries.

There is moral gain here: greater international readiness to bypass traditional arguments of sovereignty to intervene on human rights and humanitarian grounds against oppressive regimes. Some refugee experts perceive a loss of that generosity of spirit that welcomed those fleeing persecution and saved them from lingering, often for years, in political limbo, until and if, the political will and/or military will was mobilized to enable their safe return home.

3. SOUTH AFRICA: FINDING THE CORRECT BALANCE

South Africa occasioned much and, often passionate, debate in the United States during the apartheid era. During the 1980s, the debate over sanctions was one of the most tearing in the country. If ever there was an issue of ethics in foreign policy, apartheid has been it.

The debate over sanctions, however much as it seemed one of ethical considerations, was at least equally over the practical nature of the policy. Supporters of sanctions charged that the opponents were driven by Cold War considerations, interest in the mineral wealth of South Africa, and commercial profit. There were even suggestions that policy-makers wanted to help sustain the apartheid system.

I sat in on six years of debate within the State Department on South African policy, before becoming Ambassador there in 1992. Contrary to what some have charged, that debate was quite different from what they have thought. Not once, in six years, did I hear a policy-maker express concern over minerals as relevant to policy about apartheid. Not once did I ever hear anyone even suggest that apartheid should be sustained, even for a moment. The debate was over what would work and over what time period. It was a debate over means, not ends.

The issue became one of ethical clarity versus practicality—a debate over whether, by adopting sanctions, the U.S. would be engaging in an idealistic crusade rather than a clear "thought through" policy. Frustrated by what he thought was moral posturing, then Assistant Secretary of State, Chester Crocker once described sanctions as the "moral equivalent of a free lunch." He saw apartheid being undermined, precisely by the momentum of economic modernization and by the outside influences that sanctions would weaken. In the view of those favoring sanctions, however, their opponents seemed to lack any sense of moral outrage over the crimes of apartheid. How ethical could be an approach of cool, practical, gradualism in confronting an evil system? In the end, the opponents of sanctions lost the battle.[16]

It is not the place here to debate whether sanctions were right or wrong. But, it is relevant that the opponents lost on the issue of ethics, as much as on anything else—a clear signal of how much this factor can play in foreign policy, and how it did so in South Africa.

Subsequently, with the sanctions debate out of the way, and later, the collapse of communism and the proxy threat it presented in Angola, the U.S. had few dilemmas or internal disagreements over policy in South Africa. Its ethical and practical concerns converged. Its political, commercial, or strategic (such as may exist) interests in South Africa were not attainable unless the apartheid system was dismantled and democracy instituted. Its objectives were not attainable, unless South Africa could be restored to a path of growth and equity; while, under apartheid, there was a steadily downward path of stagnation. And because those objectives were attainable, and—thanks to the farsighted leadership that prevailed there at that moment of history, they could be achieved without civil war or great chaos—the United States was ready to mobilize all the positive instruments at its disposal in support of those goals. America's support for change became unequivocal, its urging of haste even sometimes irritating to those in South Africa, who feared the consequences of too rapid change.[17]

For the diplomat, one concerned with ethics, this made South Africa a good assignment, indeed. The ethical dilemmas that I have described in this essay, which bedevil foreign policy in so many parts of the world, and, which have bedeviled the United States throughout history, were remarkably absent in that final period of dramatic transformation—that dismantling of one of the most morally repugnant systems in the modern world.

Facing the Paradox

What do these examples demonstrate? They should be a warning to humanitarians as well as to practitioners of *real politik*. In democratic governments, facing cases of major commitment, a policy must stand on ultimate support from its citizens. That support will not come for a policy, so narrowly based on military, material, or other such objectives that it lacks or contradicts the moral base on which the country was founded. But equally, no policy will be supported, if it seems to contain a commitment of unending duration or to appear as unduly idealistic without regard to its costs to the citizens. When the United States was immersed in the debate over Haitian refugees, I was reminded of a survey, in Canada, that showed communities are more sympathetic to refugees and immigrants when the policy seems to be under control than when it seems out of control—by a flood of illegal or ineligible immigrants. Tolerance has its limits as does patience. Happily, there are times, as in South Africa, where all the political and ethical interests come together. But in reality, that will be the exception more than the rule. The reality is that, in this world, lacking an overarching construct, humankind will be faced repeatedly by dilemmas of the kinds described here—by more crises of conscience and self-interest.

Humankind is witnessing, in many parts of the world, moral outrages and threats to stability that seem beyond its control. Its very senses are sometimes wearied by the incessant messages of tragedy and conflict from the news media. Where in this environment is the moral footing? How much are we our brother's keeper? And in those cases of great conflict, what is the responsibility of a great democratic power to its own people and to others, in the use of its tremendous, but in the end, still limited, military power? These will be the moral and practical dilemmas of the world in the early years of the millennium.

No simple resolution of this paradox is at hand. Thus, I take comfort from the instruction in one of the lessons provided by my son-in-law. It says that paradox is an essential element in Judaism, whereby we must often embrace as true, two contradictory and mutually exclusive realities. Indeed, it says that in Judaism, the "hero" is the one who can formulate the perfect question. And the perfect question, by definition, has no simple answer. I take my hat off therefore to the heroes who have framed this question of ethics in diplomacy over the centuries. But, my task is not over. For paradox, as this lesson goes on to state, follows us home, makes the sidewalk tremble beneath our feet, fills our bed with quicksand. We cannot leave it alone. No one in diplomatic service can thus be satisfied with the paradox alone, but he/she must try to grasp the answer on a higher plane.

The German writer, Friedrich Meinecke, suggested that the answer lies in the individual. He concluded that he who makes himself the instrument of the necessities of political survival must nevertheless accept the odium that attaches to violating the moral code.[18]

There is, perhaps, another way to put this for the individual diplomat and for the nation as a whole. Once the issues of political necessity and national interest have been propounded, in all their fullness and importance, the still small voice must still be heeded. That is the voice of conscience, of morality, perhaps of God. And, that voice cannot be ignored.

Endnotes

1 - An earlier version of this paper was published in *Jewish Affairs* 48, no. 4 (Summer 1993): 5-13.

2 - C.J. Friedrich, *Constitutional Reason of State: The Survival of Constitutional Order* (Providence: Brown University Press, 1957). See also Carl Joachim Friedrich, *Inevitable Peace*, (Cambridge, MA: Harvard University Press, 1948), especially Chapter 8.

3 - Henry Kissinger, *Diplomacy* (New York: Simon and Shuster, 1994), 33. An exception, of course, was the expansion across the continent, which became an almost messianic faith in our own destiny. See Paul Johnson, *The Birth of the Modern* (New York: Harper Collins, 1991), 165-224.

4 - Alfred Thayer Mahan, *The Influence of Sea Power Upon History, 1660-1783*, 12th edition, (Boston: Little Brown, 1918 [1890]).

5 - Kissinger, *Diplomacy*, 50-55, 218-245.

6 - Hans Morgenthau, *Politics Among Nations* (New York: Alfred A. Knopf, 1960). See also Morgenthau, *Scientific Man vs. Power Politics* (Chicago: The University of Chicago Press, 1946), 196, where he writes: "That political action and doing evil are inevitably linked becomes fully clear only when we recognize not only that ethical standards are empirically violated on the polit- ical scene, and this to a particular degree, but that it is unattainable for an action at the same time to conform to the rules of the political art (i.e. to achieve political success) and to conform to the rules of ethics (i.e. to be good in itself)."

7 - Dean Acheson, *Power and Diplomacy* (Cambridge, MA: Harvard University Press, 1958). Kenneth Waltz, *Theory of International Politics* (Reading, MA: Addison-Wesley Publications, 1979). John Vasquez, *The Power of Power Politics: A Critique* (New Brunswick, N.J.: Rutgers University Press, 1983). One who addressed these issues from a deep philosophical as well as policy point of view was Walter Lippmann, *The Public Philosophy* (New York: Mentor Books, 1956).

8 - See for example, Thomas C. Schelling, *The Strategy of Conflict* (Cambridge, MA: Harvard University Press, 1960). Also Henry Kissinger, *Nuclear Weapons and Foreign Policy* (New York: Harper Brothers, 1957). For an overview, see John Baylis and John Garnett, eds., *Makers of Nuclear Strategy* (New York: St. Martin's Press, 1992).

9 - Disciples perhaps overlooked Morgenthau's warning in his *Dilemmas of Politics* (Chicago: University of Chicago Press, 1958), 357, to wit, "It is a dan- gerous thing to be a Machiavelli. It is a disastrous thing to be a Machiavelli without *virtu*."

10 - Zbigniew K. Brzezinski, *The Soviet Bloc: Unity and Conflict* (Cambridge, MA: Harvard University Press, 1960), chapters 4 and 16.

11 - John L. Hirsch and Robert B. Oakley, *Somalia and Operation Restore Hope*, (Washington, DC: U.S. Institute of Peace, 1995), chapter 3.

12 - Laura Silber and Allan Little, *Yugoslavia: Death of a Nation* (New York: TV Books, Inc., 1996), 319 ff. See also, Leo Tindemans, et al., *Unfinished Peace*, Report of the *International Commission on the Balkans* (Washington DC: Carnegie Endowment for International Peace, 1996). Two of the Commission's conclusions (p. 74) were, "The primary cause of the failure of negotiations over Bosnia-Herzegovina, until summer 1995, was the refusal of the leading international powers to exert a credible threat of force much earlier in order to impose a settlement(...) The gap between the rhetoric and the actual willingness of the leading international powers to back their words with actions had devastating and shameful consequences."

13 - Selig Harrison and Masashi Nishihara, *UN Peacekeeping: Japanese and American Perspectives* (Washington DC: Carnegie Endowment for International Peace, 1995), 85-86. See also remarks by National Security Advisor, Anthony Lake in *The New York Times*, 6 February 1994, 1. These principles were, in fact, foreshadowed in the previous administration. See Colin Powell, "U.S. Forces: Challenges Ahead," *Foreign Affairs*, (Winter 1992/93): 32-45.

14 - Morris Morley and Chris McGillion, "The Clinton Administration and Haiti," *Political Science Quarterly* (Fall 1997): 367.

15 - Ann Devroy and R. Jeffrey Smith, "Debate Over Risks Splits Administration," *Washington Post*, 25 September, 1994.

16 - Chester Crocker, *High Noon in Southern Africa* (New York: W.W. Norton, 1992), 304-330.

17 - Pat Schroeder, *24 Years of House Work: My Life in Politics* (Kansas City: Andrews McMeel Publishing, 1998), 86-92.

18 - Friedrich, *Constitutional Reason of State*, 126.

EPILOGUE

THE NEW SPIRIT AND THE "GOOD PLACE"

Candles in the Dark challenges contemporary societies with ideas to awaken thought to brighter horizons and a sense of a better, realizable state of the world. In critically exploring and offering inspiration for desirable and practical modifications in the prevalent conception of development and progress, this book is *eutopian* as it seeks the "Good Place." The ethos of the "Good Place," like a candle in the dark, sheds light on a new spirit for this plural world.

WHEREBY IS THE "GOOD PLACE" TO BE FOUND?

Getting to this place requires a radical but straightforward change in thinking about the nature of the world. It means looking up and beyond the material surface of life to the realization that the world is, in essence, a rich, intricate fabric of unbounded thought forces. Thoughts and ideas are the atoms and the molecules of society. Concomitantly, the world and the spirit of the time are the sum totals of human expressions, feelings, aspirations, and ideas. These are, in turn, informed by reason and its interpretations of sense impressions, intuitions, and revelations. It is these forces that determine cultures, build institutions, fuel actions and reactions, and, in the end, write history. A prerequisite for getting to the "Good Place" is ensuring the quality and richness of these elements.

The "noosphere" is an attempt to conceptualize the thinking realm composing the universe—the sphere of reflection, of conscious invention, of the union of souls. If this orb exists and consciousness is the foundation of it all, then it is certainly in assuring the highest quality of those intangibles of human existence that one can move towards that "Place." To keep this noosphere alive and expanding is humankind's present challenge. It requires, among many things, protecting the multiplicity of human languages, gestural systems, and other modes and symbols of communication expressed, for example, through music, philosophy, poetry, art, and myth.

The most powerful thought force is the sentiment that humankind is subordinate to a greater Consciousness. That Superior Mind or Power, which is somewhere beyond the human consciousness or within the human spirit, enjoins the individual to act in accord with nature and love and to link with past and future generations. It stimulates philosophers, drives scientists with the high ambition to serve humankind, and inspires its listeners to pursue meaningful relationships. It is found in great philosophical and religious teaching. It has enlightened the wise scholars and holy people of the East, the great sages and healers of Africa, and prophets and thinkers in Christian, Islamic, and Jewish traditions, to note but a few. It is in the roots of classic ideas of goodness, perfection, and beauty—the meaning of pure truth in an Eastern tradition. It breathes love into human relations shared through hospitality, charity, and compassion. This acceptance of some transcendent power, even if it cannot be known or identified, except to consider it "good," defines, with mystery and awe, that humility indispensable to reaching the "Good Place."

With such humility, philosophers and religious teachers illumine paths to the "Good Place." Their meditations reflect centuries of study of what makes humanity peaceful, harmonious, and wise. Wherever and whenever this realization has emerged from the heart and spirit of humanity there is to be found love for the other and for nature, human dignity in self-sacrifice and service, the need for contemplation, and the flourishing of each individual according to his or her particular gift of the spirit.

With such humility, art, literature, and poetry may lead to the "Good Place." Art, by imitation of the master and immersion in the spirit of the work, brings both practioner and observer closer to the realization of his or her relationship to Nature and Love—the Value transcending death. Poetry conveys the cry of the soul that seeks meaning, understanding, and harmony with the self and the universe. Sometimes those cries are answered and the answer is in the poem.

WHEN WILL SOCIETY GET TO THE "GOOD PLACE"?

Individuals must take the lead. If they are enlightened and inspired by grace within, transported by great works of art, music and nature, and governed by inner dignity, individuals will build institutions that protect and nourish inclusively, all lives in a plural world. These institutions, whether local, national, international, or universal will then be governed by the same ethic that centers and informs the individual, who sees his or her purpose in relationships to others. These institutions will reflect and, in turn, foster the rich variety of gifts brought to them by the diverse talents and skills of all their components, revealing that "Good Place" in a plural world.

Society will know when it begins to arrive. There will be many practical signs. Diplomats will be talking and negotiating with compassion and respect for each other, and for each other's country. Love, moral courage, and high principles will be at the helm of political and economic negotiations, relativising utilitarian concerns and technical calculations. International organizations will exercise moral power. Businesses will operate according to principles of honor, universal ethical standards, and service to humanity. Every country will make efforts to esteem the other as the center of the world, respect its language, and learn from its unique perspective. International developers will help nations realize their unique aspirations according to their worldviews, traditions, and sense of spirit and dignity.

WHAT IS THE NATURE OF THE "GOOD PLACE"?

Fair play, mutual respect, and harmony in the outward relations between, and among individuals, and all kinds of combinations thereof, are indigenous to this Place. Basic material needs are met and human wants are subordinated to the consideration of the necessities of all creation. Social harmony stems from the instinctive and genuine sense of caring, respect, and responsibility that lies deep in the dignity, courage and unselfishness of the spirit of humanity. For, as Plato has inferred to the world: to exist, a "Good Place" requires good human beings. And, finally there is a purpose for living, which is profoundly satisfying, worth achieving for the genuine peace and security it brings. This purpose begins in the forming, nurturing, and flourishing of harmonious and mutually respectful relationships between individuals, and between individuals and institutions at all levels—be they families, communities, nations, or the planet. In this Place, freedoms are tempered by responsibility to the other, the universe, and to Nature.

Living in the "Good Place" is akin to experiencing a great symphony. The music soars, swells, and bursts in thousands of harmonies. The millions of instruments are each tuned to their greatest perfection. The score has been written somewhere "in the heavens that stretch above us all." The Conductor, from within or without, moves each musician to this glorious unison of creative expression.

Does this Place exist? Yes, it is only a mindset away. But, finding it will be a gradual and an arduous adventure. The reward maybe human survival.

Barbara Sundberg Baudot